*Additional Praise for*
# Everyday Leadership

"After decades of extraordinary experience and very hard thinking, Daniel Mulhern provides a uniquely insightful, practical, and inspiring guide to leadership. Among a handful of truly fine books on the arts of practice, *Everyday Leadership* tackles the full range: from the politics of change that creates progress into the future while honoring the wisdom, virtues and competence of the past, to the personal anchors that enable authentic living and professional endeavor. I love this book."

—RONALD A. HEIFETZ, HARVARD UNIVERSITY

"Finally, a book that's about the true essence of leadership: service. By shifting the paradigm, Dan Mulhern helps us understand that leaders don't suddenly emerge from the boardroom or the battlefront. They emerge slowly, from the soul."

—DESIREE COOPER, *Detroit Free Press*

"*Everyday Leadership* is a wonderful road map for all of us that want to become better leaders. Dan Mulhern explains how we can all become great leaders when we understand the basics of true leadership. It helps us lead and serve our organizations, our fellow men and our families better. It will help you bring out the best in others and more importantly the best in yourself. You will *love* this book. Buy it, read it, and then live it!"

—CHESTER ELTON, COAUTHOR OF THE
CARROT BUSINESS BOOKS ON EMPLOYEE ENGAGEMENT

"Isn't it funny how we like to think we are leading only when we think we are leading. In *Everyday Leadership*, Daniel Mulhern reminds us that leadership truly is an everyday thing, an every moment thing, and an every role thing. Whether I am in the boardroom or in the family room, my grasp of my humanness and my responsibility to others is critical to my success as a leader. Kudos to Mr. Mulhern for bringing these lessons closer to home with a special and accessible book for all of us."

—CHRISTINE O. WILLIG, PRESIDENT, THINKRONIZE, INC.

*Daniel Granholm Mulhern*

# Everyday Leadership

## Getting Results in Business, Politics, and Life

*Aug. 4, 2009*

To Magic —
Lead with your best self!

Dan Mulhern

THE UNIVERSITY OF MICHIGAN PRESS

*Ann Arbor*

2011   2010   2009   2008      8   7   6

A CIP catalog record for this book is available from the British Library.

Library of Congress Cataloging-in-Publication Data

Mulhern, Daniel Granholm.
    Everyday leadership : getting results in business, politics, and
life / Daniel Granholm Mulhern.
        p.     cm.
    Includes bibliographical references.
    ISBN-13: 978-0-472-09972-6 (cloth : alk. paper)
    ISBN-10: 0-472-09972-8 (cloth : alk. paper)
    ISBN-13: 978-0-472-06972-9 (pbk. : alk. paper)
    ISBN-10: 0-472-06972-1 (pbk. : alk. paper)
    1. Leadership.   I. Title.

HD57.7.M852     2007
658.4'092—dc22                                          2006028208

*To my beloved Jennifer*

*hero, mentor, editor, and*
*best friend*

## ACKNOWLEDGMENTS

I learned the most about leadership—in my bones—from my dad, who spoke it as a father and a city councilman, and from my mom, who listened it out of seven children with patient love. Great Jesuits taught me about the mind of a leader and wonderful Dominican nuns taught me about leadership of the hands and heart and voice.

My friend and mentor Ron Heifetz opened hidden doors to inner passageways of leadership that led down many of the paths explored in this book. And Jim Kouzes has always been generous with his time, counsel, and considerable wisdom; his moniker "love 'em and lead 'em," is not just talk. My business partner M. A. Hastings is nothing short of brilliant, and her intellectual courage marks much of what I have written in these pages. Chris Willig gave me confidence, good advice, and an occasional well-deserved kick in the pants. My coach and friend Cathy Raines believed in this project from day one. Cindy Eggleton saw the possibility in this book and designed the cover for it. Tom Boyle offered editorial insight with heart and humor.

In this effort, I have been led—inspired, encouraged, and very often challenged—by members of the wonderful team I work with in the governor's office: Mary Zatina, Oralya Garza, Cindy Janecke, and Joan Bowman. They are the everyday leaders without whom I could not have offered you this book.

# CONTENTS

## 3. Motivation  56

## 4. Get Yourself Together  78

## 5. Do the Right Thing  96

## 6. Authority  121

## 7. Inclusion      145

## 8. Ego and Team      172

## Notes   197

# Introduction

THIS BOOK HAS ONE CORE PURPOSE: to help you to lead better, *everywhere* you lead, whether as a supervisor, chief executive officer (CEO), parent, principal, or pastor. It offers you an opportunity to reflect on what's working for you and what could work better. Nearly every sentence in this book has been written to be relevant for you, whether you run a business, sit on a board, raise children, or do all of the above. It prompts you to examine and evaluate how you lead by offering ideas, stories, and strategies that will help you lead better. All of these ideas and stories are about the human dynamics of the extraordinary social animals that we call people. Consider a personal example.

In August of 1998 I had a fun-house experience of leadership. It was as if I were standing in front of one of those curvy mirrors so that I was seeing myself all out of proportion. It was disorienting and funny at the same time. Let me explain.

I was one of the crafters of my wife's first truly big speech, her acceptance of our party's nomination for the position of attorney general of Michigan. It was an extraordinary moment for this political newcomer in relationship to her supporters. Many delegates came in supporting her, but many, many more left that day committed to her. She roared the refrain of that speech: "I'll take your case." They heard in her voice, and she heard in her voice, her commitment to serve them, to put them before her own needs or interests.

Now an extraordinary power source comes online when a person is clear with himself and others that he is there to serve. That power flows as long as the leader and those led share clarity of purpose. A servant leader repeatedly orients himself toward the needs of others and taps the power that comes from having a big purpose. This clarity of purpose is what causes the parent of an angry adolescent to take a deep breath and let it pass or to clean up behind the toddlers at 11:00 p.m. for the tenth time that day. It is the clarity about service that causes the doctor to answer every single page. This clarity causes a shop owner to anguish for weeks before laying off workers. And clarity about service gives a school principal the energy to return frustrated parents' calls well after dinnertime. I am convinced that on that day at the Lansing Center, attorney Jennifer Granholm's pronouncement, "I'll take your case," cemented her sense of service as her guiding purpose and source of strength.

In the months leading up to the convention, I, too, had a sense of purposeful and powerful service, for I was helping Jennifer achieve something great. During this lead-up, I had also found myself wrestling with my jealous ego as I watched Jennifer cast in the limelight. But now I was flushed with pride and joy as she delivered a great speech. And this great speech delivered her well down the path to victory. I walked her offstage, exulting, smiling, swollen happily in the moment.

The lesson of service was about to become more graphic. Our girls, Kate, eight years old, and Cece, who was seven, beamed at Jennifer. The crowd was howling, hooting, and loving this little family, and it swept us up. Jack, a couple months shy of one year old, was not impressed. Neither was he impressed when the main actor, Geoffrey Fieger, the nominee for governor, strode to the stage to the labor-packed crowd's wild applause. In fact, Jack was crying, and, let me put it plainly, he stunk. Like any self-respecting parent, I could predict the hideous color and utter liquidity of what was inside this poor baby's diaper. And with him in this condition it just didn't seem right to foist him on my mom and younger sister, who were helping out. Much as I wanted to hear Fieger's speech, Jack was not about to wait, so we ducked out through the heavy black curtains behind the stage.

After what seemed like a quarter-mile walk, I found a bathroom, pulled out the plastic mat, got down on the tiled floor, and took care of the ugly green business. In that little hall of mirrors, I could see this odd reflection of myself and didn't know what to think. I was proud of Jennifer and my work in support of her; on the other hand, I was frustrated and—I'm not proud to say this—a little bitter over the way I was experiencing this historic moment in our family's life. I figured I had missed Fieger's speech by now. And there was Jack, oblivious and wonderful, as babies are. I started laughing at the absurdity of it all, felt myself lighten up, and watched a smile spread across Jack's face. Or is memory tricking me: was *Jack* the one who lightened up and I followed *his* lead?

In the eight years since that day, I have often reflected on the gift of that moment. It was as if life, or God if you please, was saying, "I am trying to help you see that you can serve and lead in a really different way than *you* might think you want to, think you should, or even think you can. Be present. Right here. Pay attention, right now, in the middle of the little stuff." This was by no means a once and for all lesson. Instead, especially in my supportive role with my governor-wife, I have had to learn that lesson over and over again. But that time with Jack offered a singular moment and taught me about the unusual three-way intersection where leading, serving, and being human meet.

This book is about that intersection in the lives of human leaders. Many leaders think they can have the leading without the serving and the being human. When they think of leadership, they think of being in charge, of having it under control, and of being seen as such; in some respects, they expect to be served more than to serve. They pretend to others (and probably to themselves) that they can put on the blue suit of leadership and make it happen. They think they need to keep their human side safely hidden away and can protect themselves by doing so. They pretend there are clear answers and that they have them. They hide from others (and, again, often from themselves) their human sides: doubt, jealousy, fear, big emotions such as sadness, and even small ones such as silliness or momentary embarrassment. They think a good agenda is the same as a good meeting. A clean desk is the same as an efficient business. They still *tell* more than they *listen*. Consequently, their people do listen and promptly head back to their offices, where they say of the boss, "He still doesn't get it." Such leaders think people can be directed, told, and moved like chess pieces. And they don't see that as a result they get lip service, not customer service; compliance, not commitment; what they *want* to hear instead of what they *need* to hear.

On their bad days, these leaders—I'll call them that, for they really do *want* to lead—make people's lives miserable. At some level in their thinking it seems they want everyone to think, speak, and act like them, and because this is impossible they can be neglectful and even abusive of those who differ. Because people spend so much of their lives at work, such managers can cause them great anxiety and even illness, and the people who report to them go home with negative energy that *will* find some outlet. Many of us have lived in homes where we "breathed the secondhand smoke" from a parent's or spouse's toxic boss. These are the extreme cases. I don't believe most such managers have any idea how hurtful they can be.

I say "they" do this, but this book is about how "we" lead humans in such inhuman ways. We can change, and we must.

In the fiercely competitive world in which we work, leaders need whole human effort. Yes, we need people's time and their hands on the keyboard or the product. But if we're going to produce, sell, and thrive, we also desperately need their creativity, their fearlessness, their spirit, their patience to work with other fallible and sometimes annoying humans, and their sweat. That's all *human* stuff. We can't *tell* people to give that level of effort, that much of themselves. We can't bribe them to do that. We can't for very long trick them or scare them into it.

The only enduring way to get humans' best stuff is to *be* fully human ourselves. And being human means sometimes dealing with a stinky diaper. It means facing some of our stinky behaviors, thoughts, and feelings—such as feeling ignored or forgotten or wrong. And it also means we get to face the splendid possibility that we could be much better and happier leaders if we quit doing what we think we should do, what we've always done, what we're comfortable doing, and instead do what our people need us to do.

I am inviting you to consider a more human leadership. It's good for them and good for us. It is a leadership that in its essence lets us be the same person at work that we are at home or in church. It is a leadership that lets us just be us—the person with bumps and rough edges but also the person who can always improve a little more, the person who *isn't* entirely sure but takes action. We get to be the person whose kid drives us nuts but who cries tears of joy at that kid's graduation. We get to be the guy who is driven bonkers by a salesman who never seems to listen, but we also get to be the person who "high-fives" him when he gets better results than we could have imagined. This kind of human leadership lets us be the person who can get what our hearts most desire: a connection with other people in which we make each other better and do something together that we could not have done alone, a person not perfect but perfectly alive.

Leadership is often made out to be a BIG THING; leaders are superhuman, grand figures who make dramatic moves that they know are right! But really leadership for any of us is lived out in seemingly small, always human, little things. For instance, you could not watch Colin Powell's public statements before and after President Bush's decision to lead us into war with Iraq and not see that there were deeply human and personal struggles at play. Some of the struggles were clearly internal—a general turned secretary of state balancing his most cherished value of loyalty against his values of openness, candor, and conscience. And of course much of Secretary Powell's struggle was external, bound up in the ideological battle within the White House. It was an ideological struggle but completely played out by people, and therefore these were personal struggles. Although the *audience* is huge when it comes to players such as Secretary Powell, General Electric's Jack Welch, or Michigan's Jennifer Granholm, the *stage* is very similar to any leadership drama that involves a group of human beings.

So, because the basic nature of human beings does not change, the little, personal stuff of leadership matters. Mahatma Gandhi, Mother Teresa, Buddha, and Jesus did some of their most amazing work in the little moves in the midst of it all. So do you! Little human moves matter. A small, serious conversation with an employee can turn him or her around. Or some clear thinking about your vision of success can get you back on track. Changing a baby's diaper might be the small human moment that will change the way you lead and follow. This book attempts to bring leadership back down to earth. It offers everyday stories that illuminate some of the best ideas—modern and ancient—about *real* human leadership.

The ideas flow from a number of sources. Many come from my direct experiences practicing leadership *of* teams and *on* teams in many different settings. Some of the lessons come from managing in the public sector, others from running a small business, and many from a practice of executive coaching and consulting to large and small businesses and nonprofits. For the past eight years I have also had the opportunity to watch my wife lead in the highly public roles of attorney general and governor of the state of Michigan. And let me hasten to add that since this is a book about *human* leadership many of the most useful lessons come from my *core* human experiences: growing up in a family of seven, raising three children, helping raise three mentees, and coaching many children (and sometimes their parents) in basketball. As you will soon see, some of the dilemmas faced by governors or CEOs distinctly mirror the choices faced by parents with regard to their adolescents.

The book is divided into eight chapters, each dedicated to an important facet of leadership activity. Although leadership takes place in the middle of the muddle of a day spent at work, at home, or at the school board, and though leadership is practiced in small things, anyone who leads must have a sense of direction or destination—a vision. So we begin by looking at vision, quite literally: effective leaders are continually developing and sharing a *picture* of where they want us to go together. We'll see the power of vision at the human level—not something grandiose and esoteric but vision as a practical and engaging everyday strategy. Vision is useless without a strategy to communicate it, so chapter 2 turns to issues of communication.

One of the reasons the old-fashioned, "boss knows best" style of leadership is dead is that people in authority simply can't control information flow anymore. Corporate executives compete with Wall Street analysts and bloggers, who appear inside and outside their companies. Parents have to grapple with kids getting their information from a hundred TV channels and a thousand Web sites. Even pastors compete for mobile followers who can turn to online Bibles or the life interpretations of Oprah, Rush, or a hundred other meaning makers. Competitors know what you're paying your people, and your people can find out exactly what the competition is paying.

The need for quality communication *from* you and quality communication *with* others has never been greater. In this world you can hardly "tell" them anything that they will accept just because *you* are saying it. Furthermore, the world is telling them that their opinion matters. So shareholders, citizens, customers, employees, and even kids increasingly expect to be consulted, not told. Never have the skills of communication been more essential for good leadership.

Of course, leadership is less about what you say than about whether it gets them to move. Leadership is fundamentally about motivating them, or "motor-vating" them, getting their engines running strong. So chapter 3 offers some critical dos and don'ts of great motivation, and it also lays bare some of the things we all do that deflate our teams, our organizations, and even our families.

The fourth and fifth chapters speak to the very heart of a great leader. The leaders we most want to follow seem, as we say in the vernacular, to "have it all together." By this we mean that they are themselves no matter the context; they communicate their values and ideas and intentions clearly. And their actions track their words. Because they have grown comfortable with themselves and don't seem to be acting or hiding, they also seem more at ease with others, neither having to please them nor having to judge them. They engage others in a straightforward way. While we tend to think of this kind of "together" character as something people simply are or aren't, this chapter offers questions to ask and practices to pursue in achieving that kind of wholeness.

No account of human leadership could be complete without looking at our stubborn tendency to mess up! So chapter 5 offers insight into "doing the right thing." It invites us to step back from our own situations to honestly examine what happens when authorities do unethical things. And because "to err is human," it offers workable human strategies to personally rebound and help our teams advance, even when we feel like we are in shameful retreat. This chapter offers a number of ways to build personal capacity to do the right thing and thus develop the credibility to lead and the opportunity to really enjoy a good life.

Most of us have heard ourselves say, "If I were the boss . . ." or "If I was governor . . ." or "When I become a parent, believe me, I'll never . . ." Such statements flow from our *greatest* misconception about leadership, namely, that having authority makes leadership simple. Anyone who has been a parent, a principal, or a CEO knows that for every tool of control that authority brings there also comes a constraint. Once we become the boss, we are observed and heard and followed in a different way. So, whether we are leading *as* the authority figure, or *with,* or perhaps even *against* that figure of authority, we do best to understand the dynamics at play. Chapter 6 offers insight into the nature of authority—ways we can gain it, use it, and avoid some of its pitfalls.

One of the most important dimensions of authority is managing the boundaries of organizations. Parents, coaches, and bosses spend time and energy resolving internal disputes and managing the borders with those outside. We are social animals—from beginning to end. So we're drawing lines: he's in, she's out, okay, he's out, she's back in. When we don't pay attention to who is getting pushed to the edges—and it's darned easy not to pay attention—our organization loses energy and ideas. We turn potentially productive partners into indifferent or even negative actors. Inclusion thus becomes a critical leadership task if we are to advance the health of a group. Why is it that we have such a hard time keeping everyone in the game? Chapter 7 offers some ideas about how exclusion works and some constructive strategies for building more powerful and inclusive teams.

The final chapter brings us face-to-face with our most wonderful, mysterious, vexing, and ever-present friend: the ego. Can you possibly understand the leadership of Phil Jackson, Ted Turner, Eva Perón, or any CEO or mayor or congressperson without factoring in a great quantity of ego? Ego drives performance. It's fuel in the tank. But then we also know about "big egos" too. We all have seen our share of egoists, egotists, and egomaniacs. Of course, the ego most leaders seem to think and talk about the least is their own. So this chapter offers ways to think about the (not so) little character inside each of us that says, "What about me?" It's the voice that says, "I am" or "I can" or "This is me. I did this." Chapter 8 offers ways to tap the ego's wonderful power without being trapped by its wily ways.

Were it not for ego, I wouldn't have opened with the story about Jack at the convention because I would merely have been changing a little baby's diaper. But ego is ubiquitous. And so ego at that moment raised questions about my significance, my role and importance. I have never been able to get far from ego. If conscience has always been hovering over one shoulder, ego has been pretty squarely riding on the other. Life offers us a wonderful chance as humans to play with these kinds of dynamics—working with our ego over one shoulder and our vision and values over the other. A life of leadership invites us both to work in our minds and to work with those we hope to lead. There is nothing like leadership to heighten the importance of our inner and outer journeys. For how we manage ourselves and how we choose to intervene do not just impact our own feelings and fates but allow us to make a great difference to our kids, our staffs, and the organizations we care about.

So this book offers itself as a kind of guide to the two journeys: the adventure of trying to move *others* to accomplish great things; and the companion journey *within* through which you can become the most together, genuine, human, and effective leader you can be.

# 1

## Start with a Vision

IN THE LEADERSHIP FIELD, much has been written about vision. Few have declared the essential role of vision more emphatically than John Kotter in a much quoted article in the *Harvard Business Review.* Kotter writes about why "change efforts" at companies fail, and he says one of the big reasons is a failure to stick to the vision. Vision is so important, and reality so often clouds our vision, that Kotter recommends that we "over-communicate the vision by a factor of ten."[1] Vision is that important.

Vision serves two powerful purposes: it points in a direction so that we can all work toward the same end, and it generates intrinsic energy. The more desirable the vision, the harder people will work and sacrifice to achieve it. A powerful vision is grand, is often far off, and taps deep longing and ideals. We'll explore examples. And we'll also see that vision's power comes in more common everyday forms: aims, destinations, and goals all belong to vision's family. Like the grand vision, these everyday forms give groups future points toward which each member can work, and when such goals or destinations have intrinsic value they too release the group's energy to carry the work forward.

Without giving away the secrets of vision to come, I must clue you in to one thing: vision *ain't* no BIG THING reserved for visionaries or luminaries. It's a really usable tool, available for practical daily use—at work or at home. The following readings are all about the way clear vision brings power to leadership.

## Your Vision Is Your Picture of Success

In many respects leadership is extraordinarily simple. Leading quite literally means you are heading toward some destination; you're going somewhere. You're out in front. When that destination is clear, when it looks like a place that people want to go to, then they will move. Think Moses. Think Exodus. Imagine: the Israelites were in harsh captivity, had the opportunity for . . . well, a dangerous escape, into . . . well, a desert. A desert! What a gamble. So what drew them? It was the destination, "a land flowing with milk and honey." They would have been crazy to go unless they had a *vision*, a picture of a destination better than where they were. Moses held tightly to that vision and expressed it with utter conviction.

Of course, leadership takes much more than just a lofty vision. It takes work, detail, and action. It takes slogging through the desert when it seems that everyone (including you sometimes) wonders whether you'll ever reach the Promised Land.[2] Effective leaders advance (or sometimes just abide) through meetings, strategies, practices, procedures, memos, conversations, politics, disputes, stuff, a whole lot of process—but the great ones don't long lose sight of what they are really after. They keep putting the vision in front for people to see.

Dr. Martin Luther King used images to paint a grand vision. He rightly called his vision a "dream." With his compelling images, no one doubted what that vision was. Everyone could picture the dream he saw; for example, "the sons of former slaves and the sons of former slave owners will be able to sit down together at the table of brotherhood."[3] That vision *moved people* of all races and religions and ages, moved them in their hearts and moved them to action.

If you want to lead, you have to have a vision. But, maybe *vision* is too lofty a word for it. Certainly few of us would consider ourselves visionaries. But all of us can—though it requires greater discipline than most would think—describe a worthy *destination*. So think about those whom you lead—whether you're leading from the top, middle, or below—and strive for clarity about your picture of success. If you're a visual person you might think of painting pictures of what could be. Or, if you like words, you might think about yourself holding a simple sign—the kind a coach might put up in the locker room or an inspiring teacher might emblazon above the chalkboard. How might you simply but clearly describe the destination that matters to you and that you believe can and should matter to them? Here are some signs that people might line up behind enthusiastically:

We make government work for our citizens, treating each as if he or she were a member of our own family.

Each person who meets us feels his or her dignity is honored.

We do legal work that protects our clients so they can be free to live well and work prosperously.

We change the arcs of students' lives by giving them hope and developing expertise.

Our children have great self-respect and are growing and giving people.

Our church makes every member and guest feel like a child of God.

Our business is a place where we never stop learning how to do things better.

Our marriage gives each of us support and encouragement to live our lives fully and happily.

There is nothing stunning about the content of these statements. If anything about them is stunning, it is that one might actually consider *having and articulating* a vision for such normal stuff as marriage, family, or the "little team" at work. Most of us rarely point out vocally the destination we hope to reach. Instead, we're usually on autopilot. Oh, a tragedy or shock to the system may cause us to step back from time to time and ask the big questions about purpose, vision, or ultimate aim. But most of us, often for very long stretches, shift into autopilot. The problem with autopilot, though, is that we're not planes. Each of us wanders off course routinely. And those we wish to lead are piloting their own courses and wandering from those. If we don't clearly, persuasively, and repetitively share a common vision, then we will instead have sweeping vapor trails crisscrossing our skies. (Much more will be said later about the full meaning of "sharing a common vision," but at a minimum, and at the start, I mean that you have to share your vision with others. Get it out in front of people.)

So set your destination. Get clear about where you're going. Get the end in mind. And start talking about where it is and what it looks like. In a wonderful book on the creative life, Julia Cameron catches the magic at the heart of such purposeful leadership: "In my experience, the universe falls in with worthy plans and most especially with festive and expansive ones. I have seldom conceived a delicious plan without being given the means to accomplish it. Understand that the what must come before the how. First, choose what you would do. The how usually falls into place of itself."[4]

## A Great Vision Moves People

Leaders can provide mental images of where we could go together and through those images completely transform the way people see their worlds. Yet, for all kinds of reasons, leaders often miss the chance to offer a compelling image of what could be—even when their people are at a critical crossroads. One weekend I saw an example of vision, and one of its absence, juxtaposed; the contrast was stark.

Every spring, the Detroit Regional Chamber of Commerce sponsors a policy conference held on Michigan's gorgeous Mackinac Island, an autoless refuge, a respite for those who lead companies, nonprofits, and governmental units around the Motor City. One of the conference highlights is the traditional panel discussion among the Big Four: the mayor of Detroit and the chief executives of the three large counties that comprise greater Detroit. The four sit around a table hardly bigger than a card table with a thousand-plus people in the audience and tens of thousands listening on WJR radio, "the voice of the Great Lakes." "The Big Four session" caps the four-day conference. The formal conference agenda sometimes predicts and shapes big ideas. But more often the most salient issues and ideas emerge from the collective conscious and unconscious exchanges among real leaders meeting on the island with its nineteenth-century pace and gentility. It's unplanned. Spontaneous. Unpredictable. And the panel with the Big Four is often where something big comes together . . . or doesn't. On one such occasion, in 2000, it happened . . . and it didn't.

Dennis Archer had decided not to run for a third term as mayor of Detroit. L. Brooks Patterson, the Republican leader of Oakland County, was well known for his lightning wit and played the role of agitator, provocateur, and adversary with regard to nearly everything Democratic. On this day, however, the Republican lauded Archer, a Democrat, for uniting the region beginning with his first day as mayor. As the crowd applauded, I had the feeling I used to get as a kid on a ball diamond when the heavy shadow of a cloud suddenly departed and sun blanketed the field. There would be a sense of awe as the shadow slid beneath our feet and the sun was set free. We bathed in the light of summer, sun, and baseball. It felt like that in the room. People's polite clapping was enlivened and then surged upon a deeply shared realization of how truly this praise was deserved. In a community long in shadow, we could all see the light that Archer had brought. And we were collectively realizing the remarkable fact that white Republican Brooks was giving heartfelt and well-deserved praise to black Democrat Dennis.

The mood in the room mirrored the mood in the broader community. Our region had lived in damp darkness for many years. Coleman Young, during his five-term reign as mayor, had exploited a we-they, city-suburb, black-white mentality to consolidate his political advantage in the largely African American city. And elected officials in suburban Oakland County (Brooks Patterson chief among them) and Macomb County exploited the division, too, widening it even more. Many people accepted this divide as though it were a physical reality, and therefore it became so! Archer stood courageously for lifting the clouds, saying over and over in words and actions that we are one community and the divisions are more mental than real. *His vision fundamentally altered our experience.* Many in the Detroit region live in a very different psychological reality today as a result of the vision he painted of a single community rather than two divided worlds of city and suburbs. The truth began to dawn that city and suburban destinies are profoundly linked in practice and in a potentially great community. Archer's personal articulation of that vision had turned people and moved them in the same direction. It was vision at its best.

Another part of the same session was as cloudy and visionless as the celebration of Archer's efforts was bright and full of vision. The four executives spoke about their apparent agreement to finally do something about regional transit. The Detroit region has lagged when it comes to regional transit. Journalists and urban planners, academics, and many business leaders have passionately argued the necessity of such transit for Detroit's renaissance and the future of the entire region. One could hardly miss the fact that a regional transit policy would—pardon the pun—go miles toward creating the unified, visionary community for which Archer had just been feted.

15

Yet *this* conversation quickly clouded over with comments that were zero-sum, I win you lose, short term, offensive, defensive, divided, and defeatist. The Big Four began by telling the audience they had reached an agreement to create a new regional transit authority. But major details, such as funding, they said, remained to be worked out, and not one of them expressed a clear and powerful VISION that might move that work forward. Not one stood up for anything that would make you want to sacrifice, to give up a little self-interest for something more important to the broader community. Nobody painted a vision of employers accessing wider pools of workers, of poor people gaining economic as well as physical mobility, of students being able to get to colleges, of hordes heading downtown to the just-landed Super Bowl or All Star Game, or visitors marveling at how innovative we had become in moving people around our metropolis. What a missed opportunity. Would that one of the four had spoken with clarity or passion about physically creating the links that Dennis Archer had begun to forge in our relationships. As I write this, six years later, regional transportation efforts have moved no faster than a car at rush hour approaching an accident. I have often wondered what might have happened if the sun had shot through the clouds of self-interest that day, if one or more of those leaders had painted a vision we could share.

Too often we live trapped within reality when as leaders we should reach for what's possible. We live within departments when we need to think for the entire company. We think within the limited view of our class, race, union, or political jurisdiction. We obsess with what is right in front of us and don't look up to see what is possible. Great leaders look beyond the dark moment and point to a brighter future. They wave a banner and they point to a destination, even—no, especially—when others seem unwilling or incapable of looking beyond the reality of what is.

## Visions Are All around Us

Clarity about a vision allows people to orient themselves toward it. Defining success helps people to achieve it. And being direct and clear allows people to move without a lot of hesitation. When a group deeply shares a vision, the vision will work in each of them to create energy and alignment. But a spoken vision of your team's success is just one of the pictures that we can use to move people when we lead.

Another use of pictures is to expose people to a stream of what I call Good Stuff. My dad, Jack Mulhern, was famous for this. When we were in elementary school, he taught Sunday school to high school students and he was on our city council. Dad was a talker, and he loved to talk about kids and adults who impressed him. He in turn impressed their stories on my young mind, so that forty years later I still remember by name people I never met: Glenn Johnson, the state championship debater at our very average high school; Ralph DeSantis, the talented city manager my dad helped recruit; or John LaCroix, the ex-priest turned Ford Motor Company manager, whom Dad lauded for his sincerity and kindness. Dad admired them, so I wanted to be like them. There were others: kids who won academic scholarships and the pioneering women he encouraged and admired at Ford in the 1960s and 1970s.

If you want greatness from your kids or your team members, give them a steady stream of examples of excellence. Overflow with stories, articles, pictures, and—maybe best of all—real, live opportunities for the individuals and the team(s) you lead to see greatness up close. You might consider one of your roles to be a supplier, sharing stuff that constantly takes your people out of their boxes and silos and routines to hear, read, or see pictures of excellence. Here are a few powerful pictures of excellence:

- I was a senior in high school, was learning to love literature, and thought myself a pretty good writer. Then one day Father Polakowski asked us to listen as he read a couple pages from our classmate Bill Kerwin's essay on Dostoevsky's *Brothers Karamazov*. I was blown away. Bill had traveled through a novel with the same title as the one I had read, but he had seen a hundred metaphors, images, and parallels that I completely missed. After hearing that essay, I wanted to read and write like Bill.
- Great high school sports coaches always take their kids to see the pros and college players, and sometimes it's best to just have them see kids playing up a level or two because the

greatness just ahead looks out of reach, but *barely* out of reach, nearly achievable.

- At the beginning of a long-overdue capital campaign for our weary, smoke-blackened, seventy-year-old high school, the school's president put our board of directors on a bus to visit Saint Ignatius High School in Cleveland. When we saw a spectacular, restored, urban high school we knew ours could be transformed, too. And we did it.
- Detroit's mayor, Kwame Kilpatrick, took a delegation to Denver to see the city's new convention center both to learn and to inspire his team about the future back home.
- When my wife was first elected governor (Michigan's first female), many smart moms, dads, and grandmas took advantage of her inaugural visits around the state. Of the fifteen thousand individuals Jennifer greeted, it was the children, and especially the girls, who stood out in the crowd. You could read the looks that came across their faces as they shook her hand: "Wow! This is the governor. *I* could be governor just like her."
- Movies can have the same effect. Whether it is Gandhi or Mr. Holland, George Bailey or Atticus Finch, pictures inspire us.

When we lead, sometimes people develop immunities to us. They have heard our messages, our stories, our language. This is true of staff sometimes, and it's certainly the case with kids. When some of my siblings and I were in our irreverent late teens and early twenties, we would subtly hold up fingers to each other at the dinner table to signify how many times Dad had preached word for word the message we were hearing. We had built up considerable resistance. At such times leaders are advised to choose indirectness: exposure to a book, a movie, or someone "cool" who can convey a vital message. So, for instance, after I have been teaching Detroit's promising leaders about leadership practices for about nine months, they start to develop immunities to me. It's then I love to show an HBO video of Bruce Springsteen in concert. For when they see how Springsteen celebrates his band and how sweat pours off him as he tells the crowd how hard his band members work "night after night after night," they see leadership excellence in a whole new way.

So when was the last time you exposed your team—as individuals or as a whole—to such pictures of greatness? In the state of Michigan we are working to create a "great place to do great work." We try to make that motto come alive by looking for great stories to inspire us, for instance, elevating stories about standout employees or the practices of Michigan companies on *Fortune*

> If you want greatness from your team, give them a steady stream of examples of excellence.

magazine's list of the "100 best companies to work for."[5] If a great speaker is coming to town, we beg that speaker to do a brown bag lunch with us. Inspiration on the cheap.

It's often said that "if you see it, you can achieve it." So make it part of your job as a leader to give your team a hundred opportunities to see it. You can use this technique when you are "leading up" (i.e., without authority), as well as when you are the boss. Think about the behaviors you'd love to see in your team and about where in the world of books, movies, or biographies you might find depictions of such exemplary behavior. Consider a field trip to see a restaurant that has mastered customer service or a group visit to the Web sites of the organizations that are the best in your field. And, for even more fun with and receptivity on the part of your team, send *them* on a search for clear pictures of what you could become.

Supply them with Good Stuff. Let them see what they can be.

### Vision on a Matchbook

Exposing your team members to a steady stream of diverse visions of excellence can make possibilities come alive. In the expansiveness of this exposure to excellence, something will surely hit and fire their engines and their sense of possibility. At the other extreme, simple pictures can help you to *focus* in. Fixing your own gaze on simple pictures of desired outcomes of excellence can make you more purposeful than any other single practice of leadership. And here's a simple picture of how to do that.

At a governor's cabinet meeting, I passed out matchbooks—plain, blank, white matchbooks. We passed them around the long, diamond-shaped table to illustrate a point from one of the twentieth century's greatest communicators. Winston Churchill declared: "If people can't say in one sentence what the speech is about, it's a speech not worth delivering." One of Eisenhower's speechwriters echoed Churchill's wisdom when he said, "You have to be able to write your theme on the back of a matchbook."[6]

Churchill's prescription: Aim to communicate a single message. Put a matchbook (or in our day a sticky note) in front of you and ask yourself what you want your team members to think, say, or do differently. For example, "I want them to walk out the door and . . . " See it. Hear it. And write it on that matchbook.

The matchbook test holds for more than just speeches. You can use it before nearly any leadership action.

- A staff meeting
- A negotiation
- A conference with an underperforming employee
- A layoff announcement
- A back-to-school parent meeting
- A mom or dad sit-down with a teenager who is acting up

Going in with a clear and simple sense of what you want your "followers" to understand, and a simple picture of the action you hope they will take, gives everything a greater focus.

Try the matchbook test on the next activity you commence as a leader. Can you write down what you want your team members to get, and do, on something the size of a matchbook or small sticky note? Don't restrict yourself to words, for again a picture, a vision, an image of what you want them to get may be more powerful than any phrase you might squeeze onto a matchbook and into their minds.

Grab a matchbook. Light a fire.

## Vision? There's Hardly Enough Energy for Reality

Okay, so you feed your people all this vision stuff, and you write your matchbook sayings to focus yourself for specific successes. But then, face it, reality gets in the way, doesn't it? How can you talk about vision when reality is so tough? I hear this often. When people sign up for my "Reading for Leading" weekly e-mail message that goes out to

12,000 readers, I ask them to tell me what their leadership challenges are.[7] One theme comes back to me over and over again: "How do you keep people motivated?" Frontline managers, as well as higher-ups, write about their struggles with unmotivated or difficult employees, stressed-out teams, shorthanded staffs, and even their own weariness. Can you talk about vision when people are so stressed?

Answer: You absolutely *must* talk about vision, *especially* when people are stretched thin and stressed out. Without a destination, people don't move far, fast, or long. And a worthy vision generates a reason for movement and effort when things seem tough. Vision gives a fresh start—whether it's your team, a problematic employee, or you who needs the jolt.

Robert Fritz makes a brilliant connection between the two fields of "leadership" and "creativity." Fritz realizes that leading, like painting or acting, is a creative act. The leader is trying to *create* a new way. He is sculpting a new business; he is writing the story of a winning season; she is the mother as conductor, leading her jazz ensemble; she is the CEO blending two companies together; he is the architect building a new business structure. And so Fritz, in his book *The Path of Least Resistance*, helps break open the mysteries of how artistic creativity works. And, behold, guess what's at the outset: a vision. But Fritz quickly factors in reality, too.

What Fritz saw was that personal vision is vital for the leader's creativity and shared vision is essential to the creative act of leadership in a group. He saw that all leadership can be seen as using the "structural tension" that exists between any vision of what we want and the current reality.[8] Fritz shows that if you can hold tenaciously to both—the vision of what you want and an honest picture of current reality—the natural tension between the two will start to cause reality to move toward vision. If you see a great vision from where you stand, you'll naturally move toward it. For example, if our vision is to be "a shop where we continually learn," and part of our current reality is that we are burned out, then our job is to hold those two entities together: we continually learn—and we are burned out. Where will this lead? Inevitably it leads toward understanding: what's burning us out, how we can work around it, what experiments we can try to reduce it, and so on. Reality is just the context for moving toward our vision.

So I'm suggesting that the threshold question to answer when motivation is lagging for your team, your family, or a tough employee is this: "What do you really want _____ to look like?" You must be able to suspend reality and your natural skepticism.[9] You have to crush the word *but*, as in "We want to make everyone welcome in our community, *but* that's not really possible, so . . ." or "We exceed every customer's expectations, *but* we know that at least 20 percent of our customers . . . " Those artist-leaders—whether they are moms, managers, coaches, directors, teachers, ministers, or CEOs—who accomplish something great are not afraid to dream. And they dream not even when, but *especially* when, the dream's fulfillment seems unlikely. It is precisely when your poetry feels dead, your kids are hopelessly rebellious, your team is totally discouraged, or your boss appears to have given up that you must ask: "How do I want it to turn out?" "What am I after?" *Vision creates an energy all its own.* Hold fast to it, speak it, ask about it, apply it, journal it, tease it out. Just don't lose it.

## Vision to Help You See Reality More Clearly

I envision you using the spectacular power of vision. Yet I sense your current reality may be that you're still not convinced it can work, especially when reality looks about as fluid as that last clod of ink stuck inside an old Bic ballpoint pen. I suggested that especially when times are tough you ask the million-dollar question: "What do I really want _____ to look like?" Perhaps the "_____" for you is a difficult worker, challenging kid, bleeding company, tense marriage, demoralized team, or demoralized . . . self. Nevertheless, I say, dare to envision success and observe what having a clear and compelling vision does to your perspective on reality. You'll be surprised what you see.

First, a counterintuitive law holds sway: when we get a vision in mind, we cannot help but look to see what our reality is. For instance, if your vision is to run a marathon three months from today, your most natural question will be: "Well, how far can I run today?" The reality is just what it is; let's say that today you could barely finish a 5-mile run. Or your vision is to have your creative team win the Imagination Award of your state's Public Relations Association. This vision causes you to see where you stand: you realize you are swamped with a hundred projects that leave no time for that kind of creativity. Or your vision is to have your news team win a Pulitzer and the current reality is that your features editor just quit out of frustration with "writers who can't write." Or your vision is to raise your sixteen-year-old son to become a mature, happy, and successful adult and you look at the reality this morning: he's admitted that his friends were drinking beer in your car, which he was driving last night.

Clear vision causes us to determine where we stand right now. But then the work gets harder. It takes real discipline to continue looking *distinctly* at vision and reality. I must clearly separate vision—finishing a marathon—from reality—a body that's used to 3 to 5 miles at a crack. I don't want to let the two blur, for then I run dangerous risks. One risk is that I may become discouraged by the current reality and give up on the vision. "I could never run 26 miles," I say. "I can't even run 6!" The discipline of creative tension says, "No. You can't run 6 *currently*, you can only run 4, AND still your dream is to run 26. Discipline, man! Hang in there, woman! Hold the vision—as a vision." And, it takes discipline to hold the reality—as just reality. Using the example of the marathon dream, if all I see is the vision—me crossing the finish line at 26.2 miles—hooray!—I may drive myself to injuries by not seeing the current reality accurately and trying to run 10 miles without adequate preparation. I have to respect reality for what it is.

Take a business example in which the vision is: "We are the top-selling sales unit in the entire corporation." I may be tempted to give up this vision when I look at last year's report and find that we were number 27 out of 50 and had fallen 10 places from the year before. No! Hold the vision. On the other hand, if I only see the vision of our team as the company's top sales unit, and don't look long and hard at the reality of why we're number 27, then I invite the equivalent of those marathon training injuries, for example, misleading our customers, overpromising product, burning out staff, or just plain wishful thinking. It will take discipline to see both the vision and the full dimensions of the current reality in order to generate healthy yet ambitious outcomes.

Take one more example from the realm of family. Imagine that I'm exploding inside because my sixteen-year-old son, whom I envision as accomplished, self-respecting, and giving, brought home his worst grades, is hanging out with kids with bad habits, and seems

23

incapable of thinking of anyone in the family other than himself. Again, a tough reality may tempt me to give up on the vision. "Why beat my head against the wall?" I might ask myself and respond to my son with resentment or withdrawal. But, if I can hold the vision and see that reality "is what it is," then I have a fighting chance to learn about it, understand it, and take some steps to intervene. When I don't expect the reality—who he is at this moment—to be equal to the vision—the young man I hope he will become—then I have a fighting chance to be helpful (to someone who consciously wants none of my help).

Disciplined leaders give vision and reality their separate domains. The clearer you are that they are not the same, the more patience, clarity, and determination you can bring to resolving the natural tension between the two.

Here's a really practical way to use vision and the structural tension model to advance your leadership work. (This exercise is similar to one Fritz suggests.) Take any leadership situation in which you're involved. Why not take one that's giving you headaches? Make two columns on a page; on the left, write down the vision you have for those you lead, and on the right describe the current reality. Fairly, dispassionately, and fully describe the current reality. It just is what it is. I'll bet you'll see it in a new light. When you place the vision and current reality side by side, your most natural instinct will be to outline some of the steps that will seem to lead from reality to the vision.

When you keep an eye on the vision, it will renew your sense of purpose, especially in times when you are discouraged by tough realities. And when you are clear about the vision, you'll find it much easier to see the current reality for what it is. Seeing both clearly, you will naturally see the steps you need to take to move reality toward vision.

## They Couldn't Care Less about Your Vision

Almost everything written about the power of vision assumes that it's the *leader's* vision. Some, like Robert Fritz, point the way to giving vision more power, as they argue for a vision that is created and shared by the *group.* Anyone who has been involved in the latter—a serious exercise in which the group generates a truly *shared* vision— knows the power that comes from such an effort. Participants in such a process come away with a stronger sense of ownership of the organization and a more passionate commitment to what it can become. But you can't always do such fully inclusive work;[10] new people come aboard after the shared vision has been created; or the leadership team changes its focus in some way. And under these circumstances, as well as during normal times, you face some frightening questions. What if they don't share our glorious vision? What if they don't care about being the top sales team? What if our son doesn't want to be well adjusted, successful, and giving?

Once when I managed a small team—and had grand visions of the legacy of our work for the institution and the magnificence of our teamwork—I began to take the time to ask my colleagues about *their* visions. A couple of them did not relate noble and grand visions. Instead, they said they sought "economic security" and "career advancement." Initially, I felt disappointed with these articulations, but disappointment gave way to curiosity, and I started to wonder, okay, how do I deal with these honestly expressed visions of success? They're not *my* visions of success, but they're darned important to them. Another time I was talking to our state employees about vision and values, and as I sampled people's visions one fellow said, "I've been working here for thirty-two years, and my picture of success right now is that the governor offer an early-retirement option so I can retire and start playing golf. That's my vision of success!" Yeesh! I'm wondering how *that* is going to help us create a culture that lives up to our motto, "a great place to do great work." It sounds instead like a prescription for mediocrity in effort and morale.

There is, of course, no pat answer to the question of what to do when people's visions are inconsistent with yours. But there are some good strategic responses. First, remember that Moses had to *sell* his vision—over and over again. There were times when the Israelites' current reality was such that it was darned near impossible for them to accept reality and the vision at the same time. So they found idols to worship or suggested to Moses that they should turn back; Egypt wasn't so bad. Moses had to keep his vision alive, prove his (and God's) commitment, and be relentless.

As groups and individuals are continually tempted to lose sight of the vision, leadership becomes an intensely personal challenge to you, the leader. You have to see a great workplace, even while a worker is saying he or she can't wait to retire from it. You have to see a well-adjusted young adult, even when reality is a teen defiantly telling you he's not going to college and wants to spend the next year "chilling" with his friends. Even while they're worshipping what seem to be idols, you must continue talking up the land flowing with milk and honey.

Such times require a leap of faith. Despite their visions of success—my pay, my advancement, my retirement, my chilling out—you can still envision them feeling part of something larger, acting with others for something great, sacrificing to become a successful member of a community. Your vision now must be very personal toward them: you must see them seeing the vision, even as you hear the reality of their lack of interest in it.[11] In other words, you have to *believe* that this rebellious teenager can begin to see himself as much more. You have to believe that this fifty-nine-year-old employee—whose idea of a compelling vision is a bureaucratic memo offering details of an early retirement package—can see the value of accomplishment, or leaving a legacy, or setting an example of perseverance. It takes a leap of faith to become a bridge for others, helping them cross from a very limited view of themselves to a more expanded sense of what they can accomplish.

So, when their vision doesn't match yours, step one is a big step. No, not just a step but a leap of faith to maintain your belief in the vision and to believe that they, too, can see it. A second step follows. . . .

## Taking Their Visions Seriously

You take a second major step toward genuine shared vision as you ensure that your vision of success is broad enough for people to find their own path in it. And you can best achieve that breadth by engaging people around the central question of vision rather than declaring it from on high. The foundation is this: take others seriously. See them not as means to the business's success, or as children who should live out *your* vision and make you happy, but fundamentally as ends in themselves.

Let me illustrate with a story. I was working with a health insurance provider, a business with well over a thousand people. The company was mired in the red, morale was poor, and these two facts were beginning to reinforce each other. I was brought in to work with the executive team, and I convinced them that our first job was to clarify our vision of success. Part of this would involve articulating a clear vision statement that showed where we were going. What would our world look like when we were wildly successful? And I also engaged them around the question of shared values, answering the question: *How* do we all want to work together? After we had drafts of our vision and values, I convinced them that these were just that—drafts—and if we hoped to adopt them, and bring them to life in the company, we would need to let the employees react to them and even shape them. Many on the executive team were nervous about this step. They asked two main questions, and through some honest dialogue between them and the CEO, the questions were asked and answered in this way.

- Did we have the time to do this "vision stuff," given the intense business pressures? They concluded that if we got everyone pulling in the same direction we'd *save* tons of time in the long run.
- What if the employees didn't like the work we had done? Well, their objections might actually improve on our work, but at a minimum—if we did our job right—they would feel listened to and we would know what we were up against. The alternative to hearing these objections was not that they would fail to arise but that people would be muttering their objections and complaints in places where we wouldn't hear them, let alone learn from the employees or perhaps even persuade them of the power and usefulness of the vision and values.

The decision was made. We would "roll out" the drafts in meetings with every employee in the company—about ten meetings with 150 people at a time.

In the meetings, the CEO presented the values and vision, and employees then had a chance to explore their personal values, talk about the proposed vision and values in small groups, and then share their highlights in the larger room. The vision depicted such things as a loyal and committed staff, quality health care, and peace of mind for their many stakeholders: patients, doctors, businesses, and so on. In one of the early sessions, an employee was giving feedback from her table, and she was very passionate about how great customer service could only be delivered by people who felt great about their work, their company, and themselves. But let me share how she made the point, for it is a picture in itself, a vision, if you will.

The point was almost absurdly obvious. Here was an organization, in the stress-filled field of health care, with a grand vision of helping its clients achieve peace of mind. How could the company's splendid vision of promoting peace of mind be fulfilled without taking into consideration the visions of people like this brave woman? She read from a flip chart: "If mama ain't happy, ain't nobody happy." She clearly depicted a vision and everyone was enriched by that vision: happy workers produce happy clients.

We discovered the importance of listening to a vision and *sharing* our vision and values in another way during those meetings. We asked individuals to identify their personal values and share them at their tables. In each roll-out session, we would total all of the values that the employees had identified as important to them. We would add these to those identified at prior sessions—and give that feedback, right on the spot. A curious thing began to be reported out, right from the outset. The employees at nearly every table, when asked to share the values that *they* treasured, talked about family. Indeed, family became the runaway lead value in the data we were gathering from and sharing with them. This had not been one of the key shared values in the draft work of the executive team.

At the first couple of sessions, the CEO responded to these data with candor and empathy, saying something like "None of us lives to work. We all work to live . . . with and for our families." He mentioned that a healthy company would promote the value of family indirectly by offering its employees job security and income and benefits. But he added something like, "Of course, keeping your families happy could never be a central part of our business; our business is satisfying our customers."

After the third or fourth of ten sessions, he began to realize something huge: maybe taking care of the employees' value of family *was* part of the business. The executives began to look for ways to support that value in their business. They have created more flex time, internships for employees' kids, and employee picnics—all to make family a more transparent value.

That CEO was finally grasping the concept that Max De Pree wrote about so eloquently in his book *Leadership Is an Art:* "For many of us who work, there is an exasperating discontinuity between how we see ourselves as persons and how we see ourselves as workers. We need to eliminate that sense of discontinuity and to restore a sense of coherence to our lives."[12] This CEO was seeing the power that could be tapped if he was able to help "restore a sense of coherence" and in reasonable ways within his control to *"make mama happy."*

De Pree's insight applies not only on a corporate level, as in the example of the health care company engaging people around visions and values. His insight also connects in our smaller circles of leadership action, where by listening we can help individuals connect the meaning of *our* work to what matters in *their* lives. For example, those employees who told me that they weren't so interested in my ideas about the legacy of the institution or about great teamwork, but were interested in such things as career advancement, provided me with a great challenge. If I wanted them to take our daily work and our huge goals and vision seriously, then why shouldn't I be taking their goals just as seriously? After all, I didn't want just forty hours of work for forty hours of pay. I wanted them to really care about our work, to give it their best, to continually improve—to live *my*—and hopefully *our*—values of organizational growth. So, I had to commit to *their* vision—both out of respect for them and to achieve success.

The state employee whose vision was an early retirement and the teen who just wanted to hang out provide similar challenges. That employee wants to have a great retirement. Well, what can we do to help that be so? Perhaps by helping him make his last years his very best. We can look for ways to have him leave feeling proud, valued, and a real contributor. And that teen sees success as just "chilling out." How do we engage him around that vision or value? (We may not think of it as a value, but it certainly is something that he values.) We can look for ways to help him think about leisure—in the long run—and the sacrifices required to achieve it. Or perhaps we can look for ways to barter around leisure, giving him access to a car or money for a trip in exchange for something that we value, but do it in a way that doesn't devalue, disrespect, or denigrate the young person's value of slowing down. His value, after all, is probably one that our broader type-A society could learn from.

In all of these examples, vision no longer is a one-way dialogue. It is not something we leaders create and those followers accept. We don't just share ours with them, but we truly share visions together, listening as much as we talk. Articulating vision is not an end point—"here it is, let's slap it on the wall"—but a continuing dialogue about our pictures of success. Like the Israelites in the desert, we all periodically lose sight of why we came here, so we must continually rediscover what we really want out of our lives.

Leaders thus share their visions and values and then listen hard so that their teams can share theirs in return. When each buys into the others' vision and values, commitment rises all the way around.

## Vision Unleashes the Greatness of the Team

If leadership is about anything, it is about going somewhere, about a destination, a purpose worthy of living, having a vision. Although leadership can occur on a one-to-one basis, more frequently it's about a group effort—family, neighborhood, community, division, company, country. Vision helps meld this collective enterprise. With a great vision in sight, people make individual sacrifices, they cooperate, and they work as a whole. Vision elevates people.

Anyone who has grown up with siblings, raised children, coached a team, or been on a team or staff knows that rivalry and pettiness sprout as surely as weeds in a garden. You pull them out, and they're back the next day. Every person I have ever known—and most stubbornly the person I am—houses an ego. By ego, I don't mean a swelled head. I mean a fundamental sense of "I." And this "I" stands apart from any "we." It is the default position to which all of us continually return. Leaders work to create a magnificent collective garden. Meanwhile, egos are pesky seeds in the fertile soil, continually pushing up the weeds of self-interest, pettiness, and destructive competition.

The practice of articulating and building a shared vision is the work of the leader. When we evoke in individuals and build in our groups a shared vision, we touch a deeper "I" than ego. Although we default to the defense of "I," we long to belong. And we also know that great things are not built by individuals. It's not just sports teams but teams of researchers, teams of explorers, design teams, or news teams that do collectively more than they could ever do as separate individuals. It's the leader's job to embody and speak that shared vision—that possibility of group accomplishment. As teams work toward shared visions, they transcend the limits of ego.

George Bernard Shaw once described this transcendence, this rising above the "I" of ego, as he described the way he wanted to live: "This is the true joy in life, the being used for a purpose recognized by yourself as a mighty one; the being thoroughly worn out before you are thrown on the scrap heap; the being a force of nature instead of a feverish selfish little clod of ailments and grievances complaining that the world will not devote itself to making you happy."[13]

Ego—prone to pettiness—is that "feverish selfish little clod." Shaw's words can guide leaders to help others find instead a mighty purpose. Again, leading others toward finding purpose in the group's vision is less about a vision statement than about enlisting, evoking, educing, involving, engaging, probing, and drawing out shared, though not identical, visions. And in that process commitment arises. Through the activity of the continued search for "mighty purpose," community or team is born. If I am your boss, or your boss's boss, and I care about your purpose, dreams, and vision, I give you a reason to care about mine. This vital process creates the connection. And this connection forms the basis for strength in community, company, or family.

Thus, the greatest leadership in some way or another evokes the passion that can only come as people ignite each other's torches. Each individual relates to the vision in their own unique way. For some it is redemption. For others, triumph. For still others, the accomplishment embodied in the vision is about community. For each it varies, but in sharing the vision all feel a collective sense. Individual torches together create a powerful light. Offer people a mighty purpose and see the light and strength that you may spark.

In the end, leaders light torches.

# 2

## Communication, Communication, Communication

LEADERSHIP NECESSITATES THE INTERPRETATION OF REALITY. It is not enough to speak a vision, not when reality is often complex and confusing. Our employees, supervisors, or children face lots of facts, pushes, and pulls, and the complexity creates confusion. When we ask people to change, work harder, and work together under circumstances that already seem complicated, the stress can mount.

Vision sets a direction for the future. But much energy goes into understanding what's going on *now.* And so those who lead well, must interpret. They must provide some context, a *story line* if you will, for what is happening. The good leaders show how the threats and difficulties fit into patterns—predictable patterns—and so the team need not be overwhelmed or overly concerned. The great ones weave their people into ancient stories of heroism and endurance and connect people to a broader sense of their heritage and identity.

The following readings show how a leader's stories are one of his or her most powerful tool sets. And these readings suggest the care required to wield tools of both power and some danger.

## Stories That Connect People to Possibilities

In January, one day is set apart as national "Thank Your Mentor Day."
A couple of years ago, Jennifer and I decided to celebrate by inviting
both our mentors and our mentees to join us for lunch at the Capitol.
The closeness of our relationships made it feel like a family gathering,
but we had a heightened level of purpose about it, and there was a
sense of mystery because the four we invited knew us but none knew
each other.

The six of us at lunch shared an intergenerational connection like
I had never experienced. We were all "in the moment," yet you could
feel a sense of time: Jennifer and I were perched at a fulcrum between
the hard-won wisdom of our elders and the rising hopes of the two
young kids we had been mentoring. Elders have stories. They're lean-
ing back gleaning rich memories from their past. And kids think in
stories. They're happy for guideposts, for interpretations, as they lean
into new territory. The young and old are made for each other.

When we decided on the lunch, I knew exactly whom to call, and
so did Jennifer. Judge Damon J. Keith had been serving as a federal
judge for over a decade when he offered Jennifer a judicial clerkship
in 1987. From the moment she met him, she found the judge to be a
storyteller supreme. His large chambers held five offices and five hundred pictures—the judge with Muhammad Ali, the Temptations,
Jimmy Carter, and Thurgood Marshall and pictures of *all* the clerks
who had worked their way into his heart and his *family* of clerks. One
of the most powerful themes in the stories of leaders is the way they
tell stories that *connect* the current crew with those who went before.
Because Judge Keith's alumni clerks had become district court judges,
circuit court judges, professors, and now even governor, every new
clerk was gifted by the judge's stories with the notion that he or she
could follow in that trail of footsteps. The judge repeatedly reminded
them of these brother and sister clerks and how well they had done.

At our lunch Judge Keith showed almost no interest in the governor other than posing an occasional, "Isn't that right, Jennifer?"
Instead, he was totally tuned in to Chrissean and Brittney, our young
mentees. He talked about how his dad had died when Damon was a
teenager and how badly he had wanted him to go to college and reap

the rewards of hard work in America. This powerful judge, who had walked boldly at the front of the civil rights movement and showed no weakness, welled up and had to stop. The kids were riveted as he talked about how much his dad wanted for him, how much he wanted to honor his memory, and how determined it made him to finish school and do well. When the judge told the kids that they could be whatever they wanted, they knew it was coming from the tips of his toes and the bottom of his heart.

It was an extraordinary moment to watch. Why is it that the judge is always ready to tell a story and teach? And why did our two mentees listen so intently? For the kids were enchanted by what they might have just dismissed as an old man reminiscing. Perhaps he *had* to tell the stories because these were just his stories. And because they were so obviously *his* stories they came alive in that moment—powerful enough to bring puppy dog tears to his eyes and powerful enough to bind the kids to him.

The kids were rapt, despite their having no prior relationship with Judge Keith and no conception of his stature on the bench and in the community. But the power of his storytelling grabbed me for another reason. There was an extraordinary resonance in the themes that repeatedly came from the judge's stories. And the resonance or echoing was with the voice of my wife, *his* mentee. His passion about civil rights had fueled her passion. And his positive messages to young people—"You can be anything you want to be and never let anyone tell you that's not so"—had become her public mantra, a story line she had spun out hundreds of times. His stories and themes had become her stories and themes. The way they both interpreted complex and challenging realities—including racism and sexism in America—strengthened the resolve and fired the hope of first-time listeners, as well as those who frequently heard their stories.

As we seek the attention of those we lead, and as they face complex realities, we do well to remember our stories. What are the stories that explain our passion about where we have come from, about how things should be done around here? Who is the Judge Keith in your world, and how can you flatter him or her and impact others by tapping the stories that reverberate deeply for you? Leaders tell their stories.

My mentor at our lunch shed a different light on stories. That light will provide a sunset to this chapter on the power of stories.

## You Aren't the Only One Telling Stories around Here

We hand down practices from generation to generation. I mimic Dad, as he imitated his father before him. And I taught tenth graders, much like the Jesuits and lay teachers taught me in tenth grade. Oh, I make conscious changes, but more often than observing those departures I find myself thinking, "Oh my gosh, I'm doing just what my dad did" (often something I said I never would). Seldom do we stop and realize that, though our messages are very similar to those of our ancestors, the world around those we lead has changed dramatically. You may be a manager or a supervisor, a priest or a teacher, a parent or a mentor. Whatever your role, you are trying to communicate messages to those you lead and probably doing it much like your predecessor and their predecessors and their predecessors. . . . But consider for a moment how greatly the world has changed!

Imagine you are in the role you occupy now but it's one hundred years ago. Now think about this: where else would your followers be getting messages about meaning? Whose ideas would your ideas be competing with in the minds of those who follow you? The sources of ideas would be something like this:

- Church, synagogue, or mosque
- Family
- Neighbors
- Coworkers or fellow students

And maybe from:

- Books from the library (if there is one and if they read)
- Clubs
- Newspapers (most likely a weekly, perhaps a daily)
- Magazines
- Letters from friends or family

That's about it. Consider, then, what followed over the next five generations.

- A tremendous increase in the sources of information: daily newspapers, the telephone, social and business clubs (e.g.,

Rotary and Kiwanis, both formed in the early 1900s), radio, newsreels, popular magazines, television, cable, the Web, and so on.

- A profound heightening of the vividness of images: from newspapers to radio, silent movies to talk, black and white TV to color, to big screen, to high definition—and from the puritanical and patriotic and polite to "war as it happens" and X-rated sex and violence available 24-7 to anyone with cable.
- A saturation of the clock: from the once-a-week encounters of a hundred years ago to daily newspapers, twelve hours of TV/radio, and finally round-the-clock coverage.
- A multiplication of voices: from network news that had everyone talking about the same things to what Bruce Springsteen called "57 channels and nothin's on." Today, through the Internet, literally *millions* of pieces of information are available at every instant.
- From single images on TV to the bombardment of hundreds of frames rapidly changing in a thirty-second spot, channels surfed, pictures with text scrolling, Web pages with twenty-five hyperlinks, and movies and sound all at once. And people are listening to their iPods while watching TV and handling their e-mail, as if all the sound they hear is layered with multiple tracks all the time.

Increasingly, images are powerful, pervasive, and personal. People choose. They don't have to listen to family, friends, westerns, mainstream national news, and a predictable pastor. Instead, they can listen to techno music, watch the BET network or Univision (in Spanish), get all their "news" from Rush Limbaugh or Bill Maher or the *New York Times* or Al-Jazeera, pick their favorites on AOL, and increasingly choose *their* preferred stream of information.

If your leadership is about moving people to a better place, in part by offering a powerful vision or destination, consider your competition. You are up against Oprah and Rush, Dr. Laura and Dr. Phil, Karl Rove and James Carville, Springsteen and Madonna, Osama and the Dalai Lama, Jack Welch and Jane Fonda, Homer Simpson, Dilbert, and Pat Buchanan. Most of these folks are very consciously generating ideas; they are working every day at snaring and holding the attention of the people you want to be engaged with you. On top of that, the people you are trying to lead are hearing more about their abs and glutes than they're hearing about your vision for your organization and the work you hope they will be excited about doing. When it comes to communicating messages, like it or not, we're all competing with the big boys!

This extraordinary press of information in our age is part of the reason why Jeanie Daniel Duck, in a wonderful article in the *Harvard Business Review*, said this about leading and especially about generating change: "If there is a single rule of communications for leaders, it is this: when you are so sick of talking about something that you can hardly stand it, your message is finally starting to get through."[1]

So, my friends, how often and how vividly are you telling your stories and making your points? None of us has any business thinking we can communicate the way our parents, teachers, or bosses did and expect to get our messages through today. It's a little silly to frame our messages as "it's my way or the highway" in a world of information *superhighways*, where people can go wherever they want. That's the challenge. That's why our messages, like Judge Keith's, have to really grab people. The good news that follows is that meeting this challenge can be both fun and deeply enriching.

## Creating a Positive Sense of Our Identity

Perhaps you wish I hadn't posed the challenge of competing with the likes of Rush Limbaugh, Oprah Winfrey, Madison Avenue advertisers, and Hollywood screenwriters. But you have something they don't. You *really* know your people. Let me emphasize this more accurately: you really know *your* people. And those who lead well craft messages and story lines in which people feel like they are "your" people and "we" are all in it together. In other words, these leaders know they must interpret reality, and in doing so they craft stories of identity—it's about us! My hometown helped me see that this is almost certainly true.

When our son Jack was about five I took him for a ride on the People Mover, an elevated train that circles downtown Detroit. A woman and her niece and nephew got on at the second stop, and soon we were joined in conversation. "It's such a shame what's happened to our great downtown," she said, pointing to one of the grand old hotels with its broken windows and hollowed-out interior.

I agreed, but I pointed out to her the cranes I saw erecting Ford Field, the new home of the Detroit Lions. Jack and I counted ten gigantic cranes there. He pointed out more cranes and construction equipment all around the train's loop—at the Compuware world headquarters, a nearby downtown garage, renovations adjacent to Ford Auditorium, another garage next to One Detroit Center, and new loft apartments on Woodward Avenue. For the first time in the many years I had been in Detroit, there were varied and significant projects going on. So, who was right—the nostalgic woman or me?

What was our identity? Were we people whose past alone was great or people living on the cusp of a renaissance?

One of the arts of leadership is finding vibrancy and goodness in the identities we share. The very same eye can see details that point to Detroit's resurgence or its stagnation, Ford Motor Company's progress or the challenges that might overwhelm it. People love a winner. Organizations of all kinds thrive on the positive and on momentum. And the stories of identity that get told generate—or kill—such momentum.

The interpretations by leaders (especially at the top) are vital in part because they are *not* the only stories that will be told. Leaders' stories must have enough accuracy and richness to compete credibly with alternate interpretations and become the stories that others believe and repeat. The hundreds of individual decisions that determine the welfare of a city—such as business investment, cultural support, or decisions on where to reside—will turn on the stories people find believable, compelling, and worth repeating. Your stories about your city or business will compete with other stories told from without and within. The mayor of Detroit has a story, but so do people in the suburbs and Detroit's neighborhoods. Ford has one story about its financial future, but the financial analysts and newspaper columnists have others. Even within a family stories compete. You tell your kids about their great Irish heritage, but they also hear that the Irish are all drinkers and storytellers. Identity, pride, and momentum are almost always at stake.

As humans we want to fit into a story of "a proud people." Whether it is a story about our national heritage—in which we talk about the founding fathers—or our city, team, or company, we long to belong. For decades now, workers in Detroit have said they work for

Fords (the family) not for Ford. Similarly, my high school gave us all a sense that we were somebody because we were part of a hundred-year tradition—and a tradition of Jesuit education that connected us through centuries and literally across the globe.

Jennifer and I marvel at how powerfully one state has used a story to connect its people's desire for identity and pride; in Houston, San Antonio, Austin, or anywhere you meet Texans, those folks seem to find a reason to remind you: "Don't mess with Texas." Being Texan generates pride. In *Built to Last,* authors Jim Collins and Jerry Porras analyzed why some companies had succeeded not only in "lasting" but in thriving for their shareholders, satisfying their employees, and impressing others in their industries. One of the critical variables they isolated was how these visionary companies had kept alive their founders' stories, values, and legacies for over a century. They found that people felt great about belonging to companies such as Ford, Johnson & Johnson, Proctor & Gamble, and Hewlett Packard.

Communicating messages of identity and belonging can generate a lot of fun, as well as a lot of energy. For example, when the New England Patriots defeated the Philadelphia Eagles in the Super Bowl in 2005, proud Bostonians were delighted when Pennsylvania's governor Ed Rendell made good on a bet and sang the national anthem at a Celtics-Sixers game. And what delight we Michiganians experienced when Governor Arnold Schwarzenegger of California made good on a wager after our Pistons beat his Lakers and sent a photo of himself in a Detroit Pistons jersey, eating Michigan's Better Made Potato Chips and drinking a bottle of Vernor's Ginger Ale. Identity matters. So tell the stories that touch it and generate it.

Perhaps it is even more effective when you can get *your people* to tell stories that interpret in a meaningful way who we are. I remember going to visit two juvenile detention facilities when I was director of youth services in Wayne County. I had heard a lot about the Glen Mills School in Pennsylvania. On the Glen Mills campus, which resembled that of a boarding school, I was escorted by students whose delinquent behavior had landed them there. I asked them a hundred questions. "How do they handle discipline?" "Why don't kids run?" "Why did they think the program worked?" And I pushed to make sure the answers really held up. I was stunned by the degree to which those students understood how the place was being run and why.

Beyond that, they actually showed pride in the institution and their progress within it.

A month later I visited a tough, state-run institution. I asked similar questions of kids and even of staff. Instead of the free-flowing answers I had received from the kids at Glen Mills, this time when I opened the spigot the water never ran. They didn't know why the rules were there, they shrugged a lot, they seemed to be evading some questions, and the answers frequently contradicted each other. Why was the first group so articulate and consistently telling the same story while the other group was so awkward and inconsistent? Two reasons.

First, the director at the first school was *always* telling stories and explaining the school's mission and philosophy. You could not be around him without hearing proud stories of successes and stories of how the administrators were distinct in their approach. Second, the authorized leaders were smart enough to make *others* tell the stories. Goodness, if the *delinquent* kids were explaining how fair and beneficial the discipline was, what more did we visiting policymakers need to hear? And, of course, the kids were reinforcing the messages of the camp leaders as they were speaking out loud. "It's all about choices and consequences," they would say. "If I make stupid choices, there will probably be bad consequences, so whose fault is that? Mine." On the other hand, the tough state training school lacked a storytelling director, nor did it invite kids to be leaders and ambassadors. The facility was so infrequently visited that even the senior staff members answered our questions as though they had never thought of them before. The first group had a strong sense of identity; the other had almost none.

Here was a brilliant idea. When, in the spring of 2005, Ford was facing shrinking market share and the supercompetitive pricing of its rival, General Motors (GM), it offered sales commissions to its employees who persuaded family members or friends to buy Ford cars and trucks; the more an employee sold the more he or she got as a commission. I don't mean *salespeople* but any employee who got someone to buy a Ford (and these employees could sweeten the deal by sharing their employee discounts). Ford realized that it had thousands of salespeople; it just needed to get them to *tell the story.*

One of the benefits of living in the limelight in a governor's family is that by necessity we must tell our children about the Granholm (Mulhern) story—about our "brand" or identity. They need to defend themselves in school, and we need them to speak and act in a manner that is consistent with our shared values. At times, they resent it; who wouldn't? But how fortunate children are who learn that "We Smiths always try to . . ." or "In the Verderbar family we pride ourselves on . . . " I was always a little jealous of my friend John Staige Davis V, for his family had felt good enough about that name to pass it on for five generations! Now there's a story. Now there's identity; John's name is identical with his four forebears'. Of course, the truth is that any family or organization can interpret what's happening with stories that depict its strengths, values, and commitments. And if we are to have stories told by our staffs, our interns, and our former employees, then we have to tell those stories ourselves and create opportunities for our people to tell them as well.

At work we can invite outsiders in to tour our place, so our team can tell its story. We can encourage our people to network and ask them to practice with a thirty-second "elevator pitch" on "who we are and what we're like." We can mine in them the stories that make them proud to be "one of us." Likewise, we can ask our kids or grandkids, "If someone asked what our family is like, what would you say?" When we educate them about our heritage and history, our elders and our model family members, they will have a sense of identity and pride in who we are. We can give our kids or our employees roles—such as greeting guests, giving tours, thanking people for coming—that turn them into owners instead of bystanders, full members instead of potential members.

## The Power of Simple Sayings

Simple sayings support strong stories.

It was the fall of 2002, and Jennifer was running for governor. We were on our way home from my sister's house in Ann Arbor after a pleasant Labor Day picnic. The conversation was all about the things that might change depending on the result of the election. Would we see our family as much if she won? Would the kids find new friends in new schools? How hard would it be if she lost? How would we all deal with that? Jen was explaining that you can't be sure about things; you just have to do your best through it all.

Jack, who had just turned five, was trying to show that he knew what was going on, that he, too, was aware of these big questions. He was regularly trying to prove himself to his big sisters. The conversation must have hit a nerve for him, as he said, from his booster seat behind me, "You know what Dad says. 'There's two kinds of people in the world.'" Parental eyebrows rose, and our eyes met quickly, as if to say, "He can't possibly know this. Does he really know this? Will he remember it?" Kate, oldest and most demanding sister, who had heard this lesson from me about a hundred times, piped up from the far back, "And what are they, Jack?" Her voice seemed surprisingly encouraging, without even a glimmer of teenage sarcasm. I wondered, "Does she actually want him to get it right?"

A long pause. I started to think: too bad he can't finish. But then, like one of those trick birthday candles, he restarted: "Those who say they can do it. . . ." And Kate gave him a second to breathe and prompted, "Right, Jack, and who are the other kind?"

He picked up without missing a beat, "Those who say they can't. And they're both right!" The little guy was trying to look nonchalant about it, but he was beaming in spite of himself, and so was the successful thirteen-year-old teacher behind him. He had the point nailed. Just as Jennifer was telling them that they only had to do their best, he was saying that whether they were successful or not would depend on their attitude. If they thought they could do it, they would. That simple, simple message had soaked deeply into his young mind.

Stories and such simple sayings run like a spiderweb in many directions and far into our ancestries. A couple days after hearing Jack tell us all about "the two kinds of people in the world," I heard Wayne Dyer on the radio, repeating it and attributing the quote to Henry Ford. Ford likely had heard it from someone else, and he, in turn, wrote it down and repeated it to countless others. Someone in the past couple of years had mentioned it to me. How many times and to how many people had they repeated it? From my lips to the ears of my daughter Kate—a "typical adolescent" who understandably bristles when I use it to tell her to beware of a negative attitude. And then the amazing part: as much as she *dislikes* hearing it, it went from her lips to the ears of her five-year-old brother. And now, full circle, he reminds Kate and Cece and Mom and Dad.

Stories about children offer templates for all stories about leaders and followers. And the implication of this one is clear: people listen to, assimilate, and even repeat simple, central messages expounded by credible authority figures. Sometimes they don't even like the saying, yet they repeat it. So, don't underestimate the value of sharing simple sayings, particularly those that are timeless. The basics matter. Look at the popularity of simple stuff in our culture. Witness the interest in best-selling books that offer the simple human "chicken soup" stories or package "all you learned in kindergarten" as all you "really need to know."[2] Think of the endurance of the saying, "Do unto others as you would have them do unto you," which remains as challenging and powerful as when Jesus first uttered it. Look at the great success of Stephen Covey's book *The 7 Habits of Highly Effective People;* it comes in part from the incredibly simple and repeatable lessons that he (re)popularized in it, including "Seek first to understand" and "Begin with the end in mind." The book's extraordinary success—not only in sales but especially in infiltrating the thoughts and speech of business managers—flows in good part from the simplicity of these sayings. In a complex world, don't doubt that simple lines matter; they do, and they can shape an entire culture.

If the people *you* lead were asked to write down your central teachings, could they? Are there sayings they associate with you? Focus on the key messages that matter to you. Write them down. Say them. Repeat them (even when listeners—like my daughter Kate—express annoyance or feign indifference). Can you do

> **People listen to, assimilate, and even repeat simple, central messages expounded by credible authority figures.**

this? If you are thinking, "Come on, I don't have the time to do that," then let me remind you of the words of a young philosopher: "There's two kinds of people in the world. Those who say they can and those who say they can't. And they're both right." I think you can.

## Magic Stories in Difficult Times

Sayings stick with kids and adults. And when it comes to stories, kids of all ages love stories about magic. When we lead sometimes we tell stories that *work* like magic so that people later say, "Hey, how did she *do* that? I can't believe that worked!"

When you are at the front, sometimes you need some magic because there's no *rational* explanation for how things can possibly work. For instance, campaigns are often like this: political campaigns, fund-raising campaigns, or grassroots efforts to get an institution to change its long-established ways. Campaigns test leadership because they require mobilizing people, getting them to jump on board, to demonstrate publicly, or to sacrifice their time or money for a cause.

The first thing I'd say to anyone about to start a campaign is this: Get your story straight! I might as well say practice the magic of storytelling because people just aren't going to believe you. People need a compelling story if they're going to write you a check, make phone calls in your non-air-conditioned storefront headquarters, or give up a Saturday a week to join your campaign to mentor kids. You've got to get them to believe you can win. They have to know they are joining folks who know what they're doing, folks who are part of a great team, folks with whom they'll be proud to associate.

Sometimes that's a hard sell right from the start! Ask an underdog candidate, who does a poll and finds out that only 12 percent of the voters even know who he or she is. Ask a board chair who is trying to raise a million dollars for an organization that's never raised a hundred thousand. Or imagine the kind of story you need when the school you're supporting has lost enrollment in six of the last seven years or your candidate faces a former newscaster who is worth a hundred million dollars. It had better be good!

Inevitably and necessarily we borrow heavily from the land of mythology. We do the verbal sleight of hand that turns our real life circumstances into grander stories from history and the deep communal well of myth. You've seen everyday political candidates who weave a story: they speak of their father as a heroic mine worker or they have a story about cutting down a cherry tree or they wave the magic wand to turn a weakness into a strength. My wife chose the last, as she declared from a thousand podiums on her first run for office, "Isn't America great?! Here I am asking for your vote, and who am I but a no-name, nobody, from nowhere, never-before-elected, with no money." She hitched her story to one of America's greatest myths—the Horatio Alger, rags-to-riches tale.

Leaders invite people to join them in a greater drama. Maybe it's David and Goliath or Cinderella. Maybe it's a comeback like that of the Amazing Mets of 1969. Maybe it's Sir Thomas More and a noble stand for truth. Perhaps it's a story of reclamation, like those told by a candidate, CEO, or pastor who promises to take us back to our true heritage—to the founding fathers, the company's original mission, or the true teachings of Christ.

A fund-raising campaign at our 125-year-old high school rode on the nonsensical slogan "Reclaiming Our Future"; it was a classic story that played on people's pride in the school's storied past. It was pure magic for us to say that we would move *forward* and simultaneously roll *back* the clocks. That was what we said we were going to do, and people quite literally bought into that story. They contributed money to a future that would celebrate the past that they had known at the school.

When times are stressful and require sacrifice, leaders are well advised to find a great story that can be attached credibly to the facts at hand. And it should be a story that gives the group an important and noble role. Thus, President Reagan called for our courage to defeat "the evil empire." President Clinton borrowed from a strong theme in popular culture to say that "change is hard" but sometimes we are better for it. And Jesse Jackson asked people not just to vote for him but to join in a much grander effort to "keep hope alive." President George W. Bush has almost unceasingly relied on simple stories, for example, repeatedly and consistently calling on us to be strong when there are "people out there who hate freedom." Each drew us into the midst of a larger drama that made our struggles seem smaller but well worth the battle.

Storytelling leadership demands that you imagine. The splendid film *Life Is Beautiful* offers an extraordinary picture of storytelling, as a father convinces his five-year-old son that the Nazi concentration camp where they are imprisoned is actually a big theatrical game, with intricate rules, and that the winner receives a real tank. Under extraordinary circumstances the unbelievable story buoys the son through the impossible. This is not unlike a dad who calls forth hope and determination by telling his fifteen-year-old son, "Michael Jordan didn't make the varsity as a sophomore, either. Don't give up." With stories like these, leaders abandon all proportionality and stretch reality wildly to connect it to a moving story during a desperate time. Especially in start-ups and crises, when a leader believes that the impossible truly *can* be accomplished, a little fiction may be required to invent a story that gives hope and inspires action. These stories hang on the fact that we can never know the future with certainty, that the past is filled with improbable heroes, turnarounds, and miracles. And sometimes these stories work like magic to produce the most unlikely results.

How strong is your hope when things are difficult? How creative are you in seeing the possible links to great stories? Do you reach for stories that might unleash magic?

## Magic or Dark Magic

Most of us don't tell enough stories. Our imaginations were largely left behind with our Play-doh, Crayolas, GI Joes, and Barbies, and now our imaginations only peek from their hiding places when we're ensnared by novels, films, or someone's teasing look or tempting dress. We find it enough to just get through the week or the quarter. We are happy to get our kids through their first tryout, driver's test, fender bender, and then prom night. It's hard to find the energy to make up stories of our past and future that we think can shape the current worlds of our staffs or families or neighbors.

Sometimes you have to, especially in times of crisis. When a team is grappling with major downsizing; when resistance to your planned information technology (IT) system is ready to turn into rebellion; when a kid is learning to hit a baseball, you're teaching a parent to walk with a walker, or you're asking someone to do two people's jobs, then, darn it, you *spin*. You spin tales of the huge efficiencies to be had once the IT system is in place; you talk about how even Hank Aaron would strike out, how stroke victims have recovered, and how belt tightening is a temporary solution that will lead to long-term growth and security. You find the tiniest, dying sparks of hope and describe them like they're embers that need a small draft to enkindle a great blaze: "Sure, we lost money this quarter (again), but there are all these indications that we're turning the corner. We're on the same trajectory as Apple was when it came back." You spin. And spin can produce magic—or dark magic.

As we learn over and over at the Hogwarts School in the wonderful tales of Harry Potter, magic must be used carefully. It can be dangerous. And so it is with leaders' stories. In children's stories people live "happily ever after," but we know life does not work this way. People die. Great bosses get great offers and orphan their teams. Enrons end. Global Crossings cross into oblivion. Jobs go to China. Good companies are eclipsed by change or better companies. The humble are passed over. Bad guys do win. Sometimes children die before their parents. And people get hurt.

Sometimes the stories that worked like magic later look like dark magic. The simple and compelling analogy, it turns out, doesn't fit the reality. Southeast Asia was not a gigantic set of dominos in the 1960s. There wasn't a Red under every bed. Saddam Hussein was not Hitler with a dirty bomb, and the people of Iraq did not greet our troops as liberators. Microsoft *was* "the next IBM," but a thousand companies touted as the next Microsoft were *not*. The new sales strategy that was "just like Dell's" has been a dud and a bad deal, and layoffs are coming. The labor concessions that were to be the "last ones we ask of you" have been followed by two more rounds of concessions. Central State was not the perfect place for your daughter, as it had been for you. Tales of purpose, prosperity, and potential—built on convincing analogies and seductive stories—turn out to be castles built on sand. And the tide comes in.

So what are the lessons in the responsible use of the magic of storytelling?

First, you have to have an undying, unrelenting commitment to keep seeing reality. When you get too enamored with your spin, you may start to miss seeing the reality, and trouble will brew for you and those you lead. You can get so set in the story that your team of nurses *will* deliver record levels of customer service that you don't see the reality of their fatigue, lapses in patient care, or departures. When you are too fixed on the Cinderella story of getting elected as mayor, you may start to ignore—or just not see—the real problems that must be addressed if you are to win. Or when you are completely committed to your story that your daughter is going to get a college scholarship to play basketball you may not see things that don't fit that picture—her injuries, rebellion against your controlling behavior, or larger "growing-up" concerns. You may not only miss the chance to help her through the challenges but also miss the splendid chance to reconcile yourself to your own past and its athletic shortcomings (which may be what's driving you in the first place). Worse, you may find that your daughter not only quits basketball but quits trusting you.

When stories are good and necessary, then you must hold on to them. For instance, you tenaciously hold on to the story and belief that your team can lead the company with the new service you are designing. The trick is that you can't allow this *tenacity*—literally "holding on tightly"—to prevent you from letting go of it long enough to hear the problems your team is presenting. And if you can't let go long enough to hear what's really happening you'll ensure their failure. For instance, if you are a boss who is constantly telling everyone how fabulous everything is, what a great team they are, and how they can do anything, they will, without ever telling you, start to see you as irrelevant when it comes to grasping the real business. They know that not *everything* is fabulous, that people don't always live happily ever after, and that they are entitled to a boss who is not ignorant of the difficult realities they face.

Let me address this tendency of magic to go awry in light of the storytelling magician I have observed most closely. My wife's first three years as governor were served in the context of an unceasing onslaught of bad news: a huge budget deficit, an economy that was underperforming and continually blowing bigger holes in the budget, the highest unemployment rate in the country, and a thick column of jobs steadily moving out of the state and offshore. Morale was as low as job production. Jennifer *had* to point to positive signs and tell stories of how the state was transforming and could continue to transform itself. She talked about Michigan's great tradition of entrepreneurism and innovation, of its bold French settlers, of Henry Ford and the automotive geniuses of the twentieth century. She talked about our "cool cities" and pointed to signs of revival despite in some cases greater signs of decay and shrinking populations.

In some cases the stories appeared magical. Her cool cities initiative called attention to research on how cities that embraced young, immigrant, and gay and lesbian populations and the arts and technology were surging, and she offered very modest incentives to communities that committed to becoming cool. This story of cool captured imaginations in city halls, chambers of commerce, and planning groups, and it spawned literally hundreds of proposals, projects, and initiatives to revitalize Michigan's cities. In other cases of storytelling the results were probably mixed at best. For instance, one story she told was that the Michigan government was and would increasingly become a "great place to do great work," a wonderful place for employees to produce. But this initiative was launched at the same time that her chief negotiator was securing economic concessions from state workers. The magic of her story of a great workplace was seen by some as a kind of deception or trickery or at least a bitter irony. In some quarters at least, it generated more resentment than energy.

Given Michigan's challenging realities, Jennifer *had* to tell stories. Through stories she allayed anxieties and stimulated hope and effort. She was constantly spinning threads of hope and possibility. Her critics in politics and the media called her the "cheerleader in chief," as if offering hope is not a vital aspect of seeing troops through battle, helping the wounded through recovery, or rescuing a losing team from the jaws of defeat. But were her stories, on balance, productive, distracting, or irrelevant? When is a story magic and when is it dark magic, deceiving people and taking them away from the tough problems they need to fix?

Spotting the difference between magical storytelling and dark magic is easy in the extremes but tough to assess in the vast gray zone. So, I offer two guideposts. First, in Jennifer's case, I know that she never shielded *herself* from the full reality. She *wanted* to know the unemployment numbers every month—no matter how bad. She welcomed the "revenue-estimating conferences" that would predictably project that the state's revenues were again lagging behind projections, even though this result meant she had to lead another grueling round of budget-cutting negotiations. She wanted to know whether her cool cities grants were stimulating *new* projects or were just an expensive public ribbon on a project that was already wrapped and ready to go. She wanted to know so she could keep midstream correcting. She did not want to hope blindly that her stories would magically come to pass and bail her out. As leaders, we have to test our own gut all the time and ask whether our spin is causing us to ignore difficult realities.

As a manager, you sometimes create—or are flat-out given—big goals. You devise a plan and a story for how you'll reach them. You tell that story to your boss and your team, and people like the story and feel that it's quite doable. And then a little later your manager will ask, "How are you doing on that goal?" And you'll say in response, "Great" or "Fine." After all, you have a story and hope in the story. And when you ask your team members how *they're* doing, they say "Great" or "Fine." But you're at a crossroads. You want to believe in your story, your people, and the way you hope the world works, so much so that you may cheat yourself out of an honest view of reality. You may not let yourself pay attention to the doubt in their voices when they say "Great." Or you may ignore little signs that things aren't "Fine." You don't pay attention to the initial deadlines that weren't met or the things everyone assumed would work out to support the plan—things that aren't happening. In this kind of case—in which the leader lets the story blur his or her view of the facts—the popular line "That's my story and I'm sticking to it," is a prescription for disaster. The story works dark magic when it blurs the leader's vision of reality. So the threshold question for storytellers is: "Am I being honest with myself about the full reality or am I using my story to shield myself from it"?

Our experience with families is very similar. As parents we can feel pretty good about how we're raising our kids. We tell them *magical stories* about great young role models, we see all the good signs in their grades, and we approve of the nice kids they're hanging out with. We tell our friends that the kids in our neighborhood, our church, our school, are all doing great. But sometimes, amidst the stories we tell ourselves and them, we (consciously or unconsciously) ignore little things: new clothes we never gave them money for, visits to the house of a "friend" we don't know, last-minute sleepovers at somebody's house, little inconsistencies in the stories they tell, and so on. We choose stories over realities at great peril.

The second guidepost to look for is whether the full reality is being shared with those you lead. In Jennifer's case, *challenging her lis-*

*teners* was almost always part of the stories she told about our reviving economy, cool cities, or great workplace. During these tough economic times, with a re-election campaign under way, I heard her on the radio program with the largest listening audience in Michigan; she said, "It's shameful that we have the highest unemployment rate in the country." My first instinct was: "Ouch, why is she saying this, when plenty of people don't even know it and some will surely blame her?" But I, and other listeners I assume, heard this in her tone: "We're going to fight this bad boy!"

She wasn't afraid of the truth,[3] wasn't afraid to share it openly, and could convey that her audience didn't have to be either. She both talked about the bad news and challenged people to do *their* part to turn things around. For instance, nearly every talk about the economy would include challenges to workers to get retrained and challenges to young people and our schools to double the number of college graduates. Although she told hopeful stories, she wasn't sheltering people from hard realities. She was putting the work squarely before them.

Sometimes we hide behind our stories because we don't like bad news. Some of us don't like the conflict involved in confronting our employees or managers or teens with troubling facts that don't fit the prevailing story. For instance, we ignore performance gaps that don't fit the story we agreed on. We keep telling our stories—to ourselves, as well as others—as if they are *magic,* as if telling them will make them so. The kids or employees let us have our stories—they humor us with feigned attention, they nod. *They* sure don't want the conflict involved in facing gaps in performance. Our well-intentioned and once useful stories have become irrelevant in a new and problematic world.

In sum, storytelling leaders instinctively or consciously ask two questions: "Am I telling *myself* the whole truth and am I sheltering *others* from the hard work needed for success?" Leaders tell stories. But they never stop listening to reality.

## The Magic of Hearing Stories

This chapter began by introducing you to Judge Damon Keith, a splendid storyteller whose stories gave people a sense of identity and pride and motivated them to excel. There was another great mentor at the lunch that Jennifer and I hosted for our mentors and mentees. Fr. Frank Canfield, SJ, counsels students at Toledo's Saint John's Jesuit High School, just as he counseled me in school thirty years ago. I called him up and asked him how he was. "Hangin' in there," he replied. "Tough day?" I asked. He launched into a story about an eleventh grader who half an hour earlier had grabbed his books and left the school in a flurry of expletives and exasperation. "He's a really bright kid, and he's finally started working, and can't believe the results aren't instantaneous. He got his grades, and said 'I'm outta here.'" I asked if he had talked to him. He sighed and told me, "Not yet." I found out later that within hours he had. For forty years he's been catching falling kids . . . as though they were his own children.

Like most great professionals, Father Canfield makes it look simple. At lunch, he worked his magic on my mentee, Chrissean, just as he had on me. He said, "Chrissean, you've got a great look in your eye." And he turned to me and said—no, asked—"He's quite a kid, this Chrissean, isn't he?" "He's great," I agreed.

Then he was back to my young friend, asking, "Do you have brothers and sisters? What do you like doing with Dan?" And he added the all important question (he's a Jesuit, after all), asked with the spectacular kindness that could only elicit an honest reply: "How ya doin' in school?" Father Canfield's gentle but intense interest opened Chrissean up like the sun opens the petals of a flower.

Where the judge *told* powerful stories, the priest *listened* powerful stories. For instance, one time my dad went to talk to Father Canfield about one of my brothers, who was having a hard time in school. Now Dad was a true man of the mid–twentieth century, which is to say a solid and dependable rock who would rather talk about *anything* other than himself. Yet he spent two and a half hours with Father Canfield, and only the first half hour had anything to do with my brother. For two hours, Fr. Canfield gently peeled him like an orange, and Dad talked about the challenges of raising seven kids and feeling like his career at Ford had stopped arcing upward. Only a magician could have persuaded my dad to tell such stories—not of his kids or coworkers but of himself.

Think again about the unceasing barrage of information that comes at us, often in ways seductive and slick. And I ask you, could anybody possibly be thinking to themselves, "You know what I need; I need *more* information, more ideas, more people talking to (or at) me"? If there is one thing people crave—whether they know it or not—it's an opportunity to have a little time and help to learn what *they* think and feel, to tell their own stories. Whether they are your clients or staff, your mentors or your mentees, the world is often coming at them in fast motion, and they have all kinds of things to say about how we lead, what they need to be successful, and what is driving them nuts. Who is listening, listening it out of them?

On a simple quantitative level, you might estimate the ratio of your talk-to-listen time with those you lead. How much is spent on the former and how much on the latter? It takes discipline to generate some balance. After all, most of us feel a certain sense of urgency about getting *our* message across. Whether it's a manager's need to explain his or her perspective, a salesman's need to demonstrate a new product, or a parent's urgency to tell his or her kids how to stay on the right track, it's hard to believe that talking less could get us more. But if we don't give people—in groups and as individuals—time to catch up, to catch their breath, to push back a little, to share their alternate view of reality, we're foolish to think they are with us.

Father Canfield is an exceptional professional, and exceptional professionals have a way of making their craft look easy. But it's not. Ask any parent who's asked a six year old, twelve year old, fifteen year old, or even their spouse, "How was school or work today?" And 99 percent will report that there wasn't much to listen to. The answer to that genuine question is nearly always "okay" or "fine" or "good." Most of us move on, or turn away, or sometimes subtly attack the person for giving such a hollow answer. Or we spring into the breach with questions that feel more like an assault—like we *deserve* a good answer, darn it—than genuine, patient curiosity. The same is true of the question "How's it going?" addressed to someone at work; it generally elicits a generic, noncommittal reply. Kids, spouses, and fellow workers aren't used to people really *wanting* to know, being willing to spend the time, being willing to listen without judgment; therefore, they hold back.

A great listener can listen through that. Great listeners are working—especially early in their careers—*inside* their own minds, as others are working outside in their talking and arguing. These listeners are noticing their thoughts, as when they find themselves thinking, "How can I believe this employee every time he answers my question about a project by telling me, 'It's going fine'? I'm so frustrated I could throttle this guy. I know it's not all fine!" This manager-listener will counsel himself inside: "It's obviously not a good idea to express this frustration with her, but I've got to ask better questions to see how things are *really* going." Great listeners realize that if they want to hear the truth they have to be ready to hear whatever it is that others think. They have to create a safe context in which to look at tough realities so that those realities don't remain hidden. Great listeners also know there's power in silence, and they have the discipline to ride the treacherous waves of stillness.

In Father Canfield's career, he has heard more confusion, anger, fear, despair, defensiveness, and evasion than ten thousand average bosses hear in their professional lives. And he's had thousands more successes than those frustrated managers. By listening to their stories, he has been able to get many kids back in the game. For a small number, the stories were such that it became clear to the kid and the counselor that the student wasn't going to thrive at this school, and he helped them find a better place. In these cases, the two stories—the kid's story and the school's story—were not consistent. One wanted excellence, the other ease. Or one insisted on discipline, whereas the other had to have wide open space. Neither story was wrong, but they could see together that the story lines would generate continued conflict and weren't going to play out well on the same stage.

Great managers are not afraid to have this type of candid conversation, which reveals the stories both parties want to tell. When a manager creates an open environment to hear the story of a low-achieving and/or unhappy worker, both will often find the basis for the problems—where the two story lines are in conflict—and begin to align them. Or, they—usually the worker and the great listener together—may realize, when the stories are told, that this team or this company is just not right for them. And they can move on together— often without rancor, lawsuits, and all the costs in time, money, and heartache.

So how is it that great listeners generate such candor and clarity? Father Canfield typifies the two driving forces behind great listening: He takes people at their word, and he believes that they can and will make good decisions. He knows that most people deeply want to tell their stories, and if he makes it safe for them (i.e., does not sit in judgment) then they will. He knows that acting out at school is almost always symptomatic of something other than evil or mean-spiritedness, and that the something else is usually causing the student more pain than it's causing anyone else. When *most* people are given a little protected space in which to think things through, they will see ways in which they can improve on where they are and how they fit in. The vast majority of people want to contribute and be reasonably happy.

Some will have to choose between the two stories—the ones they are telling about what *they* want and the conflicting performance expectations contained in the stories of their managers. And so, for some, this company will not be the right place; the two stories are too different, and compromising their own is out of the question. By listening well, a manager can move the situation from one of avoidance and tension to one of clarity and choice. The wonderful work for the listening leader is to create the safe space where trust is born, the stories can be told, and sensible choices can be made.

Stories can lead to a parting of the ways. More often leaders can use stories to motivate, to release energy and enthusiasm. As a leader you stand in a thousands-year-old tradition of helping people find their place in the world they have inhabited and creating a positive place for those who follow. Know your tale and tell it well.

# 3

## Motivation

In over seven years of writing my weekly e-column, "Reading for Leading," I have welcomed people to the subscriber list with a question about what is challenging them as they lead. Hundreds have written back, and one topic is far and away most frequently on their minds: motivation. So they write and ask me, "How do I motivate my staff when they face . . ." and they finish that sentence with things like more work and less pay, staff cutbacks, a tough economy, the pressures in their industry, constant change, the demands of their families, less upward mobility, and so on.

As my business partner M. A. Hastings used to tell clients, "When you're in the leadership business, you're in the *energy* business." You need fuel to motor-vate. I have always thought it would be wonderful if you could buy a set of gauges that measured the key dimensions of leadership. The first gauge I would buy would be the one that gave me a reading of the energy level of the group. Good leaders develop an intuitive mental gauge. This chapter is all about attending to it.

Great leaders know that if the needle's showing that the group is not firing on all cylinders the leader had better change what he or she is doing. They ask themselves the question the conductor-turned-writer Benjamin Zander asks himself when his musicians are not performing with excellence: "Who am I being that they are not shining?"[1]

This chapter offers ways to look at who you are being and what you are doing, and it provides strategies to move the needle on that gauge so that it's up in the optimal range for group performance.

## It's Emotional—Intelligence of a Different Kind

There is no way to greatness that does not demand the expenditure of energy. You don't *fall* into greatness, carried by gravity's pull. You climb. And you don't move like Isaac Newton's first law, which holds that an object undisturbed will continue in a straight line. You move here, then there, try this, then that, fail, fall, get up, practice the same chorus or chords or course a hundred times to get it right. And because leaders achieve greatness through others, they must get *them* to move. They must motivate. The word gurus of the *American Heritage Dictionary* tell us that *motivation* derives from the Latin, *movere,* "to move," and five thousand or so years earlier from the ancient Indo-European root *meu,* meaning "to push away." Motivation is about pushing away from safety, moving into action. Easily defined, tougher to do.

My teenage girls have great goals when it comes to basketball. But sometimes it's hard to "push away" from a summer bed with the breeze blowing or to "move" to the gym when their shoulders are sunburned or they can't find their shoes. What's a leader to do?

Moving other people takes a different skill set than the cognitive tools we were taught. Law school, dental school, engineering, business, and even education (at least when I went through it) fix themselves on ideas and facts, but I can talk facts till I'm blue in the face and I'll never get my daughters to the gym. I can explain the importance of conditioning, the importance of repetition, the importance of developing moves, or even the clearest syllogism of all: "Today is a day. *You* said you wanted to work out every day. Therefore, you should work out today." Hah! Facts and logic are of little use, just as when you as manager sit with the same lawyer you sat with the week, month, or year before, or as school principal you sit with the same social studies teacher, and you say, "So show me what you've done to change your practice the way we agreed you would." Your objective question hangs in the air, and after the echoing silence you can feel what anthropologists and psychologists describe as the "fight or flight" impulse. You want to holler: "Scotty, beam me outta here."

At this precise point of frustration, which every parent, teacher, or manager has known, we should all be ready to accept that if we want to motivate we must sidestep the front door of logic, content, and cognition and instead enter through the side, the door marked "emotional intelligence" (EI). (Notice the same root in the words *motiv*ational and *emotio*nal.) Daniel Goleman, who popularized the term *emotional intelligence,* says this amazing thing about leadership and motivation: "The fundamental task of leaders . . . is to prime good feeling in those they lead. That occurs when a leader creates resonance— a reservoir of positivity that frees the best in people." Goleman then makes this stunning claim: "At its root, *the primal job of leadership is emotional.*"[2]

Wow! Doesn't this turn our work on its head? We see we cannot succeed if we separate this critical emotional energy dimension from the rational dimension of the expectations that we have for the behavior of our kids, our associates, or our citizens. If you don't tend to the energy, they won't tend to the work. Try this exercise. In the next couple of days, come into every leadership relationship with your energy gauge in mind and through the side door of emotional intelligence. As you enter through that door, ask of each leadership relationship, especially the tough ones: "What would be different if I thought the fundamental task I have is to create a reservoir of positivity that frees the best in this person or these people?"

Sometimes it works. I had a lucky dad moment with one of my summer-lazy teenagers. I "primed good feeling" in her by noting how great she is at taking on challenges and by stimulating the energy around her vision of

> If you don't tend to the energy, they won't tend to the work.

being a varsity athlete. Now, she didn't launch herself out of bed; indeed, these types of interventions with kids or staff often fool us, for they produce *delayed* reactions. I may have lit a fuse, but it would have to burn for a while. So, knowing I'd done my best to light it, I had to use a little emotional intelligence on myself: to choose not to do what I could so easily have done—leave with sarcasm or a last, guilt-inducing shot. Instead I just left. I was not surprised, but I was gratified, when she found her shoes and her motivation and showed up at the gym fifteen minutes later.

When we lead well, we often have to enter the side door of our own emotional intelligence and then tap the energy of the emotions of those we are leading.

## Running on a Fuel Called Praise

Imagine running this experiment, which I do with my girls' basketball teams. Get a volunteer and then tell the other kids to watch carefully because they may go next. Tell the volunteer that she'll play a very simple game: she has one minute to score as many times as she can. Ready. Set. Go. At the end, tell her "good job" and announce how many shots she made. Then say to the group: "We're going to do it again, but this time I want you to cheer her on the best you possibly can. You can't touch the ball or her, but let her know how much you're behind her." You can guess what happens, right? Every time I've run the experiment, she scores more the second time.[3] Daniel Goleman would say that her mind (and body!) has been "lubricated" by the positive feeling in the room. You might imagine yourself on the shop floor or at staff meetings with one of those old oil cans. Your job: walk around the place, let the energy flow, and decrease people's internal friction (or the friction between them).

I had a great experience of how vocal (and accurate!) praise can serve as a lubricant. I was running the Capital City River Run, a 10-mile race along a scenic river trail in Lansing, Michigan. The race went out about 5.5 miles and then turned back. What a huge lift and surprise to hear (even before I saw) my boisterous wife shouting, "You can do it! Yeahh! Go! You look great! You can do it!" If you have ever run a race, you know the truth in the expression "She really picked me up." It's as if I felt lighter or stronger, lubricated. Near the end, Alice, a sixtyish woman, was telling the runners, "You're almost there," from a point you could call the "Will the end ever appear?" spot. And then came the cheering throng that lined the last hundred yards. The cheering causes your brain to release chemicals that literally improve your muscles' performance.

Here's the "and accurate" part about vocal praise. One of the most deflating aspects of feedback you can ever get is when you know it's untrue—no matter how well-intended the praise is. After the race I asked my now hoarse wife if she had stayed on the course cheering. She said yes. I told her how helpful it was to me and how helpful I was sure it was for others. "Not everyone," she said. "I was yelling, 'go for it! You're halfway there,' when this guy corrected me, "It's PAST halfway." She went on, "So then I started yelling, 'You're way past the halfway point,' and somebody else corrected me, 'No, we're not WAY past the halfway point.'" Although she said they were polite about it, often such correctives are meted out in exasperated or angry tones.

If you've run, played an instrument, put up a fence, or done any other sustained, challenging task, you know that the most kind and well-meaning encouragement is actually deflating if you know it's not true. It makes you feel disoriented, as if someone is moving the ground under you. This is brutally true when someone tells you, "You're almost finished; it's only one-tenth of a mile," and you draw what feels like your last reservoir of energy from a jar marked "save for last tenth," only to find that it's more like a half mile to go. The disappointment and disorientation drop on you like a thirty-pound lead jacket. In life, as in running, false encouragement—even well intentioned—can create friction within and sometimes without.

In that same race, I noticed that the course directors had dispersed groups of three or four teenagers (earning their community service hours?) to dot the edge of the course. Those who were vocal lightened our step. The others were like a bench of reserves talking about movies during the team's close game or a cluster of ushers talking during the sermon. Instead of lubricating the performers, it felt like they were dropping dirt in the runners' engines. You know the feeling, don't you, when you walk in to tell your partner or manager or spouse something really exciting and they never look up from the paper or the computer. Where does your energy go? It either plummets or is converted into a *different kind of energy*—one of irritation, or one that causes you to leave disappointed.

The power of good vocal praise is the reason why the Gallup Organization's authors suggest—based on enormously extensive survey research conducted among employees—that a great manager praises each worker at least once a week for something he or she has done well. Vocal energy matters. It takes energy to cheer, energy to produce energy.

One important endnote here: some people are gifted with praise-full-ness. My girls had a coach named Steve Finamore, and Steve was like a chattering machine. I was in awe. "Good job, Cece." "Beautiful." "Yes." "Way to work." "Forget the miss, you're doing great." "Awesome, Kate, perfect form." "Look out, Cheryl Swoopes." "Sweet." "Perfect." For forty-five minutes he sustained the praise. I got tired just thinking of being so encouraging. Steve had a gift. Most of us—especially those who tend to be introverted—don't have that gift. It takes work, it takes energy, it takes persistence, it takes intention, it takes stick-to-itiveness, it takes creativity . . . *it ain't natural!* This is just one of the many places where leadership takes work, and where it is about what *they need,* not about what *you want to offer.* You can do it. Build up. Take it on. Try it out. Go for it!

## Bringing the Energy

I have been a Bruce Springsteen fan for twenty-five years, and then last year I got to see him not just live but from the floor right beneath the stage. What a treat! I had come to love the leadership lessons of "the Boss" almost as much as I love his music, and this performance confirmed it all for me.

With due respect to Ben Wallace of the Chicago Bulls, Bill Clinton of the Democrats, Arnold of California and Superheroland, and Saint Peter of the Apostles, Springsteen is my human picture of leadership as energy. By the end of the second song his shirt was already soaked. Sweat was bouncing out of him like water shaken from a hosed-down dog. I self-consciously noticed that I was wearing a silly gleeful smile, but when I looked around I noticed rows of faces similarly mesmerized, many shaking their heads in disbelieving delight. Indeed, his guitar-playing wife wore this very look, smiling and repeatedly shaking her head "no," as if to say, "Boy, you are too much. . . . *Please* keep going!" His incredibly joyful energy produced a second huge effect: it seemed to encircle the band, which played as one. Some of the members have been together since the late 1970s, yet they showed an unmistakable enjoyment as they played, as though it were their first tour together. Who would know that they could "bring this," as Springsteen says in a filmed introduction of his band, "night after night after night after night"?

The first two songs and he'd unleashed sweat, joy, and inspiration! Now think about the first few minutes of your staff meeting—or of a retreat, a sales presentation, a recognition ceremony, or a review of your kids' report cards. Do your people get swept up in your energy, in your love for the work and your team? You've seen people who bring that energy. And you know that sometimes *you* bring more and sometimes less of it.

Springsteen's fellow musicians do not just take pride in Bruce. On top of his pure energy, he is astounding for the way he empowers and celebrates *them.* For instance, at this concert he shared the program with John Fogarty (of the sixties group Credence Clearwater Revival), the eighties group R.E.M., and a new band, Bright Eyes; each band played on its own, and then he brought them on to play with him. Whether it was the veterans Fogarty and Michael Stipe of R.E.M., or the young musicians of Bright Eyes, he introduced them with great reverence. When they sang together, it seemed that he could infuse their songs with more verve and flair than they could themselves, yet he seemed to stand back from the microphone, literally not upstaging them. He talked about how much he had learned from Fogarty, and he looked on Conor Oberst, the twentyish lead singer from Bright Eyes, as though he were Oberst's proud older brother.

Anyone who has seen "the Boss" knows this is the way he treats his own band. Each of the band members is a cog in the E Street Band, but Springsteen also gives them the opportunity to shine on their own. He introduces them with over-the-top, hyperbolic adulation. When his band members solo he looks on with an expression that, well, guess what his expression looks like? It looks almost exactly like the way his band looks at him when he's center stage: with the same quiet admiration and sheer delight. I hope I look on my teammates in that way, for who wouldn't want to "play" for a leader like that?

Is it that way with you? Really fine leaders let their people shine. Indeed, they delight in their "band members'" solos. They let their people perform a solo before the board, the big boss, or an important client. They know that by giving their team members an occasional and brief virtuoso solo, they likely heighten the willingness of these "backup" singers to do the less glamorous, day-in, day-out duties of good teammates, the duties that make the team great in the first place.

As kids, many of us stood before the mirror in the bathroom, or the full-length one in Mom's bedroom closet. We did our best Diana Ross or Elvis, Judy Collins or Sammy Davis Jr. (It wasn't me, I know, but I'll bet *somebody* was doing Leonard Bernstein, too.) We'd do well to perform with such passion. Sometime take a break from your job as the boss and do yourself a favor: watch the Boss.

## Great Competitors Raise Your Play

In the world of energy and challenge, you can hardly beat mano a mano (literally, "hand to hand"), and for that you have to love the world of tennis. The 2002 U.S. Open, the final Grand Slam tournament of the year, featured two incredible finals matchups. On the men's side, two "old" rival superstars met: Andre Agassi and Pete Sampras, thirty-two and thirty-one years old, respectively. The rivalry began when they played for the first time—when Sampras was not even ten years old. The 2002 match was the thirty-fourth time they had faced each other as professionals across the net.

"I played so well today," the victorious Sampras said. "Andre brings out the best in me every time I step out with him."

On the women's side, there was a similar story of rivalry but with two big differences: youth and blood. Venus Williams, only twenty-two, lost her title to little sister Serena (who was just shy of twenty-one). Venus's record that year was an unbelievable sixty and three—that is, if you excluded her matches against her little sister. Sixty wins and three losses is an extraordinary record in tennis because at every weekly tournament there is only one person who does not get tagged with a loss. But Serena beat her four times that year, and, get this, all four were for tournament championships. You want to talk about sibling rivalry!

Howard Fendrich, the tennis writer for the Associated Press, wrote about Serena and Venus, but the point he made applies as well to the Sampras-Agassi matchup: "It's often said about sports that the only way to improve is to play or practice against the best."

It applies to more than sports. In chess, in music, in law, in architecture, in medicine, in leadership, and in art of nearly any kind, being in competition with—or close proximity to—greatness evokes greatness. We rise or slip to the level of those around us. In football, Florida pushes Florida State, Michigan presses Ohio State, and Oklahoma elevates Nebraska. In business here in Michigan, there's the Big Three battling on the east side of the state (and battling the powers of the East), and on the other side of Michigan the furniture companies—Herman Miller, Steelcase, Haworth—are lined up, pushing each other to greater excellence. Our local pizza titans—Mike Ilitch and Tom Monaghan—made Little Caesars and Domino's national giants because they learned how to compete with each other in town after town around Detroit. And from pizzas to poetry and painting: the Italian Renaissance and the Harlem Renaissance produced individual giants but giants who grew and stretched as they were exposed to greatness all around them.

If you're all about generating energy for accomplishment in your office, team, or family, consider some implications that flow from the Agassi-Sampras or Williams-Williams rivalries.

> In sports or chess, in music, in law, in architecture, in medicine, in leadership, and in art of nearly any kind, being in competition with—or close proximity to—greatness evokes greatness.

First, personally put yourself in contact or competition with the best. Look for a mentor in action, someone who does what you do and does it really well. Watch him or her. Look for chances to see that person up close. If you're in their business—whether sales, sports, or music—look for a way to compete for the same business, play in the same arena, or act on the same stage. My wife found herself in her first really competitive political race, and it was the primary race for governor; she hadn't had a lot of chances to practice or make mistakes. And here she was going head-to-head with a legendary Washington congressman and a popular former governor. She survived, and she was a much stronger general election candidate as a result of that primary. Do you "play" with someone who really pushes you? A business rival? A business partner? A professor? A personal trainer? A coach or spiritual director? A spouse—okay, that one's a little risky if, like me, you've married a relentless achiever! But, if you can survive it, it sure makes you better!

Second, promote healthy competitiveness in your organization. I want to stress the "healthy" part, yet I'm not with those who condemn all competition. Some favor "collaboration" and see work as either collaboration or competition. I don't. For instance, I was highly collaborative with my business partners *and* I was simultaneously challenged by their excellence. When my partner M. A. Hastings did a great job introducing the Myers-Briggs instrument, I was both in awe and taking mental notes on getting better myself. When I saw our partner David methodically and indefatigably pursue sales leads, darn it, I wanted to do it, too.

Sometimes I even found there were strains of intellectual competition between a client and me, and that could be very healthy. A client might have the equivalent of a Roger Federer 135-mph serve; for instance, he or she might be exceptional at follow-through on new ideas. Seeing that talent pushes me, in the tennis metaphor, to improve my serve (e.g., as a consultant, I may strive to demonstrate similar speed in my follow-through on work I deliver). But I might also challenge that speedy client's quick turnaround on the work with alternatives that might show a little more depth and long-term value. With an executive I was coaching I might specifically challenge him or her to look at whether speed is everything or whether he or she might benefit from being a little more deliberative. The client pushes me to be quicker, I push the client to be more deliberate, and we learn from each other.

Leaders foster environments in which people see and value and emulate the strengths of their internal and external competitors. Leaders can foster environments in which the competition around ideas is rich and full and people really play the game with gusto. So look for the Serena-Venus combos where you work. Look for the Pete-Andre combos. When you have two such virtuosos it may take a lot of work to keep the two in the game and/or to keep others from getting discouraged by their prowess (or distracted by their battles). But such competitors can raise each other, and their respective teams, to entirely new levels of success. Your job becomes one of seeing and articulating the bigger picture—the beauty of the game, the importance of the team, the by-products of the competition, the greatness of all the players—and working to keep the participants and their fans from getting lost in the ego battles. But virtuosity has its value, whether it's two young interns, two seasoned managers, or two superstar creative types.

The third lesson that flows from the matchups of tennis greats is to match your junior people with those just ahead of them to help stimulate growth. I can relate to Venus. I was the oldest brother who pushed my younger brothers, who blew right past my levels of competence. One season they were begging me to let them play—the next I was begging them to play with me. One year my youngest brother, Jim, was begging Pat to hit with him; the next they were pushing each other as if they were Pete and Andre. We all pushed each other to improve. In so many occupations, we miss these opportunities for mentoring or sibling growth. We think that the boss is the only one who can bring others along and miss opportunities to pair people within or across departments on challenging assignments that will cause them to learn.

The same is true in schools, where for so long people acted like the principal or a department head was the only one who should observe and coach another teacher. Schools are slowly finding ways to get young teachers to watch the greats and open themselves to learning from the greats and those on their way to greatness. We can learn from our sages and elders, but we can also learn and grow with those who are just beyond our reach—as Venus *used* to be to Serena! You might look for ways to set up such vibrant volleys.

## Managing Your Own Motivation

I sense when people ask me to help them think about how to motivate others that they are totally focused on those "others" and are looking for tricks, techniques, and strategies that will *rejuvenate* their tired, cynical, bored, or apathetic workers. *Rejuvenate* comes from the Latin, *juvenis,* meaning "young"or "youth." So to rejuvenate is to make someone young again. The ideas I have been sharing on praising, lubricating, and stimulating competition function to make people young again, but the power of each of these strategies turns as much or more on who you are *being* than what you are *doing*. In other words: before you can successfully enter the side door to others' emotion/motivation, you had better check the mirror and look within. Looking to change others can cause us to miss the fundamental work of moving ourselves. Or, as the proverb puts it: "Physician, heal thyself."

Motivating others starts with continual attention to your own emotional intelligence. Indeed, when Daniel Goleman breaks down the dimensions of emotional intelligence, he *begins* with "*self-awareness.*"[4] In this he's echoing a thousand smart people from Socrates and the Oracle at Delphi (which put it simply: "Know thyself") to Carl Jung of Switzerland. It turns out that you'll lead most effectively when you develop two energy gauges—one for them and one to gauge yourself. And this gauge should give you not one but two readings.

First, the self-directed energy gauge must measure simply: are you highly motivated? I dare you to tell me about a leader whom you saw as a motivator who was not fired up. He or she may have shown it expressively, like Tony Robbins, the motivational speaker, or Herb Kelleher of Southwest Airlines, or with the quiet intensity of Mother Teresa or Bill Gates or the Dalai Lama. But if that individual was motivating others, I'll guarantee that he or she was personally motivated and radiating an almost palpable type of energy. The gauge would pick it up. Where *you* have best motivated others, I'll bet you were motivated yourself.

What is your awareness of your own motivation level as you read this? When was the last time it was strong? See if you can't develop within yourself a quiet observer, a little guy or gal with a measuring gauge to simply notice—without judgment—where your energy level is and how enthusiastic or passionate you are about your leadership situation. Then you can begin to notice the things that push the needle upward and make sure you are stopping at those refueling stations frequently. But not all energy is the same. So you're going to want to get a gauge that takes a second measure of the energy you are throwing off.

Here the measure you want to take is whether your energy

appears to be essentially positive or more negative. When a leader's energy is positive it is moving toward something, generally with confidence. Sometimes a newcomer to your shop brings it and wakes you up to the wonderful things present in the work and the great opportunities to achieve important things. On the other hand, sometimes our energy is negative, tainted with fear, skepticism, or irritation, often moving away from something (past failures, present conditions, or anticipated disasters).

Both types can move others to action. The negative energy will often motivate people in the short run, as children, for example, cooperate out of fear or to placate you. The dissatisfaction you are emanating may move others (especially those who get hooked on trying to save people), who will do anything to try to make you happy. People can get hooked on your guilt or sadness or fear. And it will move some of them for some time. But in the long run these are energies that don't renew people.

Daniel Goleman's call to self-awareness recommends a practice of great honesty about one's feelings. It is perfectly human to have negative energy, for example, worrying that something awful that once happened to you will happen *again* (to you or to your kids or your team). But allowing it to remain your dominant motivator will charge your work with a negative, "dissonant" tone. So pay some attention to these two forms of energy—both in the way you exude them and as you watch others lead. Become aware of how these positive forces create what Goleman calls "resonance" as people catch positive energy, or "dissonance," when that negative energy conspires to actually deflate people (and ultimately wear down the leader) instead of inspiring people to eagerly seize life's challenging work. And generate awareness with your personal energy gauge of what situations and activities and practices help you to create the kind of positive energy that will enliven you and resonate with others.

## Freezing People Out

In the world governed by physical laws, exposure to cold makes molecules slow down. In the world governed by constitutional law the Supreme Court looks harshly on laws that might create fear and have a "chilling effect" on people's freedom to speak. We don't want chilled or frozen politics but instead want a free *flow* of ideas. In the United States we want the cells of our political discussion—as well as our cells of scientific invention, business innovation, and artistic expression—to be vibrant, active, and alive.

The same thermodynamic principles apply in the workplace cultures we inhabit. If we want the energy of invention, creativity, experimentation, open communication, and nimbleness, then we have to work hard not to have a chilling effect on the environments in which we work. Most authorized leaders say they want openness and candor and innovation and want to see people initiate things! Many even boast of organizational values such as "innovation" or "creativity" or "openness." But it takes more than talk to create a culture of openness. And few authorized leaders realize the many ways in which they unwittingly chill the kind of speech and activity they claim to want.

Authority *naturally* chills. Just think of what happens when a teacher walks into a classroom, a judge into a courtroom, or a police officer into a bar. Here's what I have noticed happens to the tone of almost every meeting when the governor walks in: people sit up, their voices go down, and all random energy quickly seeps out underneath the conference room door. And this woman *works* to keep things open, warm, and light.

Authorized leaders can't possibly stay aware of the chill they necessarily emit. They inevitably lose sight of "the suit" they are wearing, as Governor Mario Cuomo called it.[5] Instead they frequently think they are just Jack or Jennifer or Jacques or George W. For instance, an authorized leader, like anyone else, might be inclined to kid, poke fun, or even ridicule on occasion. "Where did you get that goofy idea?" he might let out, with 80 percent mirth but 20 percent miffed, while thinking he was just being himself, just kidding around. Another boss might be feisty and combative by nature, "Come on, where's the data to support that?" he might thrust, as he has been jabbing back since a seventh-grade teacher tried to convince him of the existence of Santa Claus. Another authorized leader, who has risen based on his ferocious competitiveness, might talk about how "Tom completely smoked the rest of you slackards in sales this quarter." Perfectly human statements, genuine, without malice. Right? Yes and no.

Authority's speech is never just "another" opinion. The speech of authorities is always amplified—literally amplified, as he or she stands at a microphone. And even without a mic, when the boss speaks in a noisy room people hush to listen. Jennifer and I laugh at how an idle statement she makes one day, such as "It would be good to have some plants in this office," turns her office into a greenhouse the next. When the boss speaks, he is not just one of the guys. Shame, ridicule, sarcasm, and even seemingly good-hearted humor have added impact when they come from the boss and can all unwittingly chill free speech, particularly the type that is creative or questioning. It's almost impossible for an authorized leader *not* to constrain movement.

Authorized leaders are in a box on this one. For the paradox is that we *want and applaud* leaders who are powerful, compelling, speak in dramatic tones, act decisively and unequivocally, and help us clearly see enemies and heroes. Yet the leader who explodes with such dynamism can cause "followers" to shrink in utter fear of crossing or failing or disrespecting or undermining such a powerful leader. Especially when the authority figure is implicitly or explicitly seeking *loyalty,* or pushing us to speak with one voice or to stick to the strategy, it gets pretty hard to oppose him or her. Yet it's dangerous for such authorities to not have such voices, to chill productive speech.

As you lead with authority and seek not to chill but to warm and free the environment, here are four helpful considerations.

First, make sure you have naturally forthright people around you, people who call 'em like they see 'em. If you think about it, you can usually spot them. You might find them in their "first innocence"—in their late teens or early twenties—before they have really learned the cost of raising their heads in the herd. You see them taking on the principal, the dean, the coach, or their parents. They're *unconsciously* courageous. Remember the great story "The Emperor's New Clothes"? It was the "courageous child" who spoke the obvious fact that everyone else pretended they didn't see: hey, that guy's naked! I love having interns for just this reason, because sometimes they are the ones who blurt out the fact that the emperor has no clothes. We sometimes have to teach them the art of delicate speech, while they remind us of the value of candor.

You might also find these courageous innocents in their "second innocence," in their sixties or seventies, when many are largely free of the fear of being disliked by the pack. Or you can find them at any age at all, usually when they have experienced mortality in some significant way. Often people who have had a brush with death recognize that life is not permanent, and so things like money, fame, position, or prestige are even less permanent. They can't be made to feel safe or unsafe by anyone or anything outside themselves; their safety is in being authentic and honest. *They* are priceless.

The second thing you can do to counteract the natural chilling effect of authority is to continually ask for people's opinions. Everybody's got one . . . or two . . . or eight! When I came home from work one day a few years ago, I apologized to my son, who was three and a half years old, for I had left him at his preschool that morning while he was still really upset, before he'd had a chance to calm down. "Will you forgive me?" I asked him. He stood up on the chair he was on, wagged his finger as only an imperious toddler can, and said, "You should let me have a little juice before I go to school because I should have a drink before I go to school in the morning, and you should let me have a drink in the morning." "You're right, Jack. I'm sorry," I said. Meanwhile, a different voice, a tiny one in my head, asked, as if peering over my shoulder, "Do you think you should let this little squirt talk to you like that?"

At moments like that—when someone down the chain of command has the nerve to chastise the boss—it's pretty tempting to do a little chilling of that free speech! But I know that voice in my head was the Wizard of Oz voice, the terrified authority trying to silence the perceived rebels. The fact is that people—even the tiniest of 'em— have opinions. They're entitled to them. And *asking* for their opinions (which does not mean promising you'll follow them) hardly minimizes your authority. Instead it surely encourages them to share their thoughts, to get in the game. The irony is that you may have to walk away feeling a little beat up . . . to have them walking away feeling listened to, empowered, and reenergized. Just letting Jack talk warmed him enough to get back in the game and to play.

There is a third piece of antichill activity for leaders who have authority. Make it clear to *everyone* in the organization that when it comes to ethics your door is always open. Few things can do more damage to an organization than unethical or illegal behavior. So you have to be explicit: "On ethical issues, and issues that affect the heart of the business, I am *always* open, and open to *every* person on such issues." As with over-communicating the vision by a factor of ten, this point needs to be made repeatedly. You want people to be *sure* they can share ethical concerns, especially when something or someone in the environment may be intimidating them.

The final suggestion on keeping lines of communication open to you and throughout the organization is this. When you've been wrong about something, admit it. *They* know the boss is fallible, but they're glad to know *you* know it, too. The most powerful message this behavior sends is the message that it's okay to be wrong around here. In a world where we are bound to make mistakes, enormous value comes to those who can admit mistakes quickly and readjust. But when a culture is afraid of mistakes—symbolized by a boss who denies making them—then it may take a long time to redirect energy from losing propositions to hopeful solutions. Remember again the tale of the emperor in the new clothes. Wouldn't you rather admit or find out that you're naked before you're in the middle of the parade?

## Quick Strategies for Your People's Energy

You might be doing great things to motivate your team. But your folks may be up or down, energized or enervated by a lot more than the things that you say and do.

Maybe it's a Monday, and maybe it's gray outside. Maybe like a typical day a year or so ago.

- The polls show great concern about the war, economic conditions, and the budget.
- The stock market is decidedly bearish again.
- The fall days are shrinking, and the earth's tilt brings a creeping chill to the soccer fields.
- The rush of being back in school gives way to the doldrums of homework.
- The baseball season has ended, and for 90 percent of the major league cities their teams are not in the World Series . . . again.
- The National Weather Service has run out of letters to name

hurricanes, and it seems that another one is heading for Louisiana.

• The daily newspaper runs its typical headlines: Toxins Creep into Streams, Ford Threatens Layoffs, Mayor Won't Release Records. . . .

What's a leader to do when, because of the broader environment, his or her people are dragged down, weary, utterly unenthused?

When you find that you are just trying to create some energy out of nothing, consider using the following tried-and-true strategies.

1. Focus on successes—individual and collective. Successes past give futures hope. Trumpet achievements.

2. Set some very near-term *achievable goals*. Keep people focused on them. Don't shoot for the moon. With kids, try, with certain energy in your voice, something like this: "How much could you get done in the next ten minutes?" Then build from there.

3. Remind people of great *long-term potential:* "Here's what we'll do when the revenues flow again! But for now, let's see if we can just . . ."

4. Spend time being creative with those you lead. One thing groups do great is brainstorm. The very word is *energizing!* Pull them together and ask some relevant—and uncomplicated—questions such as: "How can we get a quick win? What opportunities are we missing? If there was one thing we could do as a team to achieve some success, what would it be?" No one may give negatives. Write down everything. Have the group pick a very few with potential and do them.

5. Be personally tenacious, just dogged, when it comes to facing the major underlying challenge to the business or organization or team. Let people know that you're taking it on and are unafraid of it.

6. Throw off routine. By late November in Michigan it feels like life is just slower. A trip to Florida sure helps. Short of that, move the staff meeting to a different room. Cancel an unnecessary meeting. Have a casual dress day. Have everyone work from home for a day. Move times and places.

73

7. Take measures to sustain your own energy, whatever they are, whatever it takes. I'll never forget a politician I interviewed, Kevin Vigilante, MD. He ran for Congress, he said, because he hated the idea that a Kennedy (young Patrick in this case) could waltz into town and become a congressman. He campaigned for about four hundred days straight, took Easter off and Thanksgiving; every other day he campaigned. It was uphill all the way, and he said the hardest thing was that he had to create his own energy, every single day. Even with his own family, he had to be "on," convincing them, bucking them up. He did whatever it took (and nearly won). So should you: maybe it's prayer, physical workouts, therapy, a good scream, a confidante, a day off, music, golf, massage, a long walk, or short naps. Know the fuel you run on, and don't leave home without it.

8. Reading this list probably gave you another idea. Write it down fast. Do it.

When people are dragging you've got to lead with your best self: set short-term goals, and act!

## Sapping Your Team of Energy in Seven Simple Steps

In the same way that there are tried-and-true ways to spike the needle on your energy gauge, unfortunately there are also some sure ways to send the culture around you into a deep freeze. I call these, with compliments to *Glamour* magazine, "energy don'ts." Now, I have done every single one of the energy don'ts that I offer below. I have had my reasons, and in some cases they have been *good* reasons. However, most of the time, behaviors like these are, at best, explainable but not really justifiable. Generally, they flow from one of two sources. The first is that we really do have some fear of empowering our people (and so, unconsciously, we're *trying* to slow them down); we make moves to maximize our control, to prevent them from threatening us or making our lives difficult.

The second source from which these energy don'ts originate is our peculiar disposition or style. We've all got our energy draining ways. Some bosses are just private people. Some parents just don't make decisions quickly. Some managers were just raised to be super-cautious. None of us is styled to motivate all of them all the time!

Whatever causes these behaviors, the energy don'ts operate on their own. Do them and—no matter how innocent, well-intentioned, or arguably smart they are—it is *guaranteed* that they will cause the energy level to drop among those you lead. So out of respect for this Newtonian-like reaction—bad behavior saps energy—I have written them down, as if you *want* to cut down on energy. So, yes, do these behaviors and you'll be sure to see measurable drops in drive, excitement, and energy.

1. Tell your team members that there is nothing you can do about their problems. Coleman Young was mayor of Detroit for twenty years. By the end, the city was the epitome of negative energy: homes and streets were literally falling apart, people were leaving, almost nothing new was being built. I found myself at a meeting at a neighbor's home to hear a man who was beginning to test the political waters in a race for mayor. The first question he was asked was the one on everyone's mind: "What are you going to do about crime?" And he began, "Look, a mayor can't do much about crime." Perhaps people admired his candor, for he was really just being honest with us about the work that neighbors would have to do. But, let me tell you, it was as if someone had sucked the oxygen out of that house—out of that whole proud but desperate neighborhood—when our great hope for mayor told us there was nothing he could do. He went on to talk about what a mayor could do, but the damage was done. He got a lot better on the stump, got elected, and did great things as mayor. But I'd recommend you not copy his candor in quite that way.

2. Take credit for things your team has done, or at least be sure not to give vocal praise to people who had the idea in the first place or did the hard work to get it done. Heck, they get paid for what they do. By the way, you'll just have to trust that this will suck their energy out. Because human nature is such that the vast majority of people won't tell you

how hurt they were when you passed them over or how they'll never work like that again for you. They will, of course, probably tell others. If, for some weird reason, you want to *increase* energy, act like Congressman Sandy Levin always does with his teams. He introduces them to audiences when he speaks, he always puts his arm around them and pulls them into VIP-only events, and he frequently asks them—at meetings that they shouldn't even have been at— to speak if it's an area where they have expertise. Those people are ready to scale walls for Sandy, but then why would you want to release that kind of energy? If you want to kill energy, you should instead:

3. Look for every perk you can for yourself and tell your team members about them so they'll be happy for you. Tell them about the World Series tickets you got (don't bother trying to get extras for them because then people will say you're playing favorites) and how you sat next to Tom Cruise at a White House dinner. They'll practically go running back to their desks with pride that they even know you.

4. Wait as long as you possibly can before making decisions and generally be as vague as you can, in case you need to change directions.

5. When you do make decisions, especially when you reverse those of your staff, don't feel you have to explain why. You don't. Live by the motto, "I'll share on a 'need-to-know' basis." If you really want to suppress energy—or even get people to take their energy somewhere else— renege on promises or, even better, claim you never said something that they say you did.

6. Micromanage. Be like your math teacher and make them show their work. See if you can't improve—even just a little bit—on every step of their work.

7. Make everyone communicate *through* you, so that things are perfectly coordinated. Think of yourself as the hub of the wheel, keeping all the players in perfect alignment.

I kid about the energy don'ts, but all of us do them and the result is that energy for action leaks out like hot air from a tear in a balloon.

No pharaoh ever built a pyramid, no coach pitched a shutout in a World Series, and no mom passed her son's chemistry exam. Leaders need the team's energy to get the job done. When a 17 and 0 Duke basketball team lost to Georgetown, Duke's Coach K said, "We didn't match their intensity." At some level, in all the sports we play, it's about raising that level of energy or intensity. Leaders *move* others to action. They do it starting with the energy and enthusiasm they personally exude and with their constant attention to fanning the flames of those they lead. Leaders are in the energy business.

# 4

# Get Yourself Together

THIS CHAPTER AND THE NEXT consider one of great leadership's most precious qualities—the quality of integrity. In chapter 5 I will invite you to envision a life *with* integrity, where integrity is about continually measuring yourself against some ethical standards. But in this chapter I invite you to imagine a life *of* integrity, where integrity is not so much measuring up to something outside yourself as it is a quality inside. People of integrity have it together. There is a full humanity about them. This integrity comes right out of the Latin roots of the word *integer,* for it is about being "whole" or, as we might say in the vernacular, about being a "together person." This chapter shows what some of the dimensions of that wholeness are. It explains that wholeness comes when we're not afraid to look inside and be honest about owning our faults and oddities and the negative consequences of even the most well-meant behaviors.

## Being Honest about Our Own Behavior

In the last chapter we talked about how great it would be to have a tool that could gauge the energy level in your group and another that could give you an instant read on your own energy level. Now, imagine that you had another tool, one that allowed you to get another instant read on yourself. This one would look into what I'll call your core and tell you the exact proportions of the drives that are generating your behavior. This gauge would tell you much more than what you tell others—or even tell yourself—about why you're doing and saying things as a leader. For let's be honest: what moves and directs our behavior is so much more than our conscious, rational, chosen words.

Our gauge would measure what's at the core that energizes and animates the thousands of nonrational moves you make (and thousands more moves you don't make). If we were to catalog our leadership behaviors, we would realize that people see so much more than the big leadership decisions. Here's a tiny sampling of what they see: smirks and smiles, fidgets of anxiety, stutters, behaviors of your parent or boss that you imitate without even knowing it, people you avoid, irritation you express but are hardly aware of, favorites you beam at, whines and "atta-boys" and exclamations of disbelief, second-guessings, sighs, detail obsessions or detail avoidances, and your baffling eloquence and baffled silences. First, then, we see how *many* behaviors are prompted by some core drives within us. And then, when we look at this list of behaviors, we realize: it is certainly not some rational, focused, analytical mind that's prompting those behaviors. Instead, my expressions are just sort of popping out of the strange amalgam of forces that make me who I am. So wouldn't it be cool to have a gauge that could give you a picture of just what drives or needs are directing those behaviors—especially the ones that are working at cross-purposes to the leadership vision, values, and goals you hold dear?

That quick list of leadership behaviors represents only a thimbleful of the complex of behaviors that others—our kids, coworkers, teams, and employees—see. It is a little sobering but potentially highly empowering to recognize that what our followers see is a composite of these behaviors and *not* the simple, unified picture of ourselves that we would like them to see and that we pretend or assume they do see. They do not necessarily take us at our best—like when we're at the team retreat, when we give an inspiring speech, or when we hand out bonus checks. They do not necessarily take us at our word when we espouse our values or philosophy. Instead, they see those countless behaviors, and they *do* have a sort of gauge that's telling *them* what they think is driving us most of the time.

Let me offer an example of the different inner drives that can be in play. I had a client, whom I'll call Larry, who sincerely articulated values of "respect, honesty, and excellence"; he spoke of them eloquently. Not infrequently, he was a model in action. He would have seen these values as the solid core of who he is and, like most of us, felt himself to be a person of integrity, oriented around and steadfastly adhering to those values. Yet at times his work was not steered by those values but was driven by his ego. For example, he was locked in an ongoing power struggle with another key manager, which resulted for their teams in anything but an obvious demonstration of respect or excellence. His drive for power (or was it fear of losing it?) seemed to be the driving force, as he would "forget" to get back to this manager or leave him out of the loop after a key decision was made or without explanation reject a reasonable suggestion.

This executive also had behavior patterns, going back to his childhood, that stemmed from his fear that he would never be good enough (despite, not unsurprisingly, overachieving!). As a result, he was always concerned about others' judgments of him, and so key initiatives—no matter how excellent—could linger for months if there was any serious opposition to them. The painfully slow decision making that resulted from his deep-down fear of not measuring up was also reinforced by his personality style, as he loved to get a little more data, take in one more view, read one last study. So his behavior strayed with some regularity from his professed values: excellence suffered from his long delays, and so did honesty, for he would say, "I'll let you know tomorrow," but his team would find that there were *many* tomorrows before a decision was reached.

This fellow was liked, respected, sometimes even loved by his team. He thought of himself as a person of integrity, for he had good values and tried to keep them in front of him, almost never *intentionally* misleading others. But, because of the way his unconscious forces were affecting his behavior, his team would not have described him as a model of integrity, and he lacked the power to move others that comes from solid integrity. They didn't jump to follow him unquestioningly— in part because they weren't sure if he was wholly behind anything.

Like all of us, driving his behavior were other things than his values and goals. For those gauging what drove him and how he might act in any given situation, there were all kinds of interpretations possible. This need not have been the case—at least not to such a degree.

Here is the alternative: people of integrity work at being "whole." They seem whole, credible, and "together" to others because they:

- Consciously put their values first, and *consistently* do so, as they
- Work to become aware of and integrate the often unconscious forces that drive their behavior.

Note the verb in the latter point: *integrate.* It has more than an etymological connection to integrity. We become more whole as we integrate the unconscious forces, for instance, those of our ego drive, our often hidden emotional pulls, and our particular style. This wholeness develops as we learn to see the behaviors that diverge from our values and as we learn to work with the unconscious drives that operate at cross-purposes to our conscious values and intentions. As we gain great awareness of these other forces, we can incorporate them and become more whole, more consistent and unified. Then our behaviors will make more sense, we will gain greater credibility, and our ability to lead will grow measurably.

## The Executive Is Not Whole

Personal integrity is not just personal—something nice to have but really just something between you and yourself, maybe a person you are dealing with, or your God. As the example of the executive presented earlier suggests, the lack of wholeness at the top can reverberate throughout the organization. Although we all have a tendency to ignore our dark sides, our shadows and compulsions, this may be especially true "at the top." For those who have arrived have so much to make them think they are home free.

One thing that gives them undue comfort is the leadership literature itself. For so much of the literature exalts, nearly deifies, great leaders. The literature praises these wonderful leaders and champions their "7 habits," "10 lessons," or "47 practices." The great leaders know what to do when "the cheese is moved." They are the ones who always have "crucial conversations." They are "servant leaders." They "win friends and influence people." Both the content and the tone of so many works on leadership suggest that the leader already has it together and just needs to do simple things to make *his or her people* do what the leader knows they need to do.[1] Parker Palmer, a teacher, writer, and activist, in his short and intensely insightful book, *Let Your Life Speak,* sets a different direction for us.

> We have a long tradition of approaching leadership via the "power of positive thinking." I want to counterbalance that approach by paying special attention to the tendency we have as leaders to project more shadow than light. Leadership is hard work for which one is regularly criticized and rarely rewarded, so it is understandable that we need to bolster ourselves with positive thoughts. But by failing to look at our shadows, we feed a dangerous delusion that leaders too often indulge: that our efforts are always well intended, our power is always benign, and the problem is always in those difficult people whom we are trying to lead![2]

Palmer implores us to look at the shadows, the inner shadows where light has not penetrated and the resulting shadows we cast that distract from the key messages we'd like to cast. He suggests that leaders must strive to integrate themselves—parts of them that they might rather ignore. This is about the leader but not *just* about the leader. For those large-scale leaders who don't acknowledge their mixed motives and drives, and somehow integrate those other aspects—their shadow side, their sensitivity or fear or unquenchable appetites—will find that those characteristics shadow the group they are trying to lead.

Here are some predictable ways in which whole organizations can end up living the consequences of their unintegrated executives' drives and obsessions.

- Show me a "political" executive, and I'll show you a culture of mistrust.

- Show me a "suspicious" executive, and I'll show you a culture that hides and lives with half-truths and self-doubt.
- Show me an executive concerned with appearances, and I'll show you a culture great at public relations but drifting from realities, especially the hard ones.
- Show me a risk-averse executive, and I'll show you a culture that loses both its imagination and its ability to decide.
- Show me an executive who never wants to leave his or her office, and I'll show you a culture in which people don't feel at home and don't stay long, where the central "policy" loses its connection with "practicality" in the field.
- Show me an impatient executive, and I'll show you a stressed culture, second-guessing itself, creating scapegoats, and feeling it never measures up.
- Show me an unsure executive, and I'll show you a culture that slowly loses its drive.
- Show me an executive who was never able to please his parents, and I'll show you a culture that can never please the executive.
- Show me an executive prone to tirades, and I'll show you a culture of fear, fights, and sickness.

I imagine you have one or both of two reactions: first, that I exaggerate, and, second, that in these descriptions you recognize managers or executives, or perhaps, sadly, a parent, whom you have known. As to the first point, the exaggeration is merely a product of the degree of lack of integration. For instance, where an executive has not even begun to realize and deal with the abusiveness of an obsessively critical parent, he or she may be more unbearably critical and may micromanage even *more* than I have suggested. On the other hand, in cases in which the executive has some clarity about his or her shadowy drives, the negative consequences will be less extreme than I have suggested in the "show-me" list. I exaggerate mostly to awaken awareness.

You probably do recognize real people in the show-me list: cases in which an executive has not begun to tame his or her demons and the culture suffers from the lack of wholeness. The remarkable way it works is that in large organizations the chief executive's shadow is cast well beyond the boardroom. And, where the executive is shadowed by neurosis or pathology, the whole corporate culture can be eclipsed in darkness. Since none of us is fully integrated, even the well-developed executive will cast *some* shadows across the organization. Personal awareness and integration by the executive create the opportunity to bring greater health and efficiency to the entire organization.

## Our (Un)Wholeness Affects Those We Lead

If executives shadow their far-flung cultures, how much more do managers, team coaches, or parents shadow the immediate worlds in which they hold sway? Marcus Buckingham and Curt Coffman, in their book *First Break All the Rules,* use a marvelous verb to describe the powerful influence of a manager. "Your immediate manager," they write, *"pervades* your work environment."[3] In direct, but perhaps more so in subtle ways your manager will infiltrate, shape, mold, and even dominate the way you experience your world. Most of us have had the delight of a well-integrated boss and the horror of one who was not so well put together. And, if it's true that a manager pervades your environment, it's just as true that teachers and coaches pervade their worlds. And parents overshadow them all.

Integrity by integrating thus becomes key. Take a simple example: most of us feel incomplete.[4] One of our versions of this feeling of incompleteness or unwholeness takes us back to our youth. There was something we didn't accomplish; for example, we weren't popular, were too serious, didn't make the varsity, or got too interested in boys. And we never fully came to terms with that. So, incomplete then, we still feel incomplete now. And we unconsciously play out *our* past in our children's *present.* We push them to have lots of friends (because we didn't), we go crazy when they score a goal (because we seldom did or our parents weren't there to celebrate it), or we keep them from dating until they are eighteen (because we were girl crazy at twelve). These are simple examples of a phenomenon the Swiss psychologist Carl Jung brilliantly described: "Nothing has a stronger influence psychologically on their environment and especially on their children than the unlived life of the parent." I might say the unlived and unintegrated life of the parent.

Take a concrete example from the world of work. I have managed like many ambitious young and midcareer people do. I bring great and positive aspirations to my work. I want to make a difference, do excellent work, and work toward accomplishing the vision. On the bright side I bring confidence and drive. Yet, on a much less obvious level, I fear failure and what it might say about me, and this has at times found its way into compulsive and controlling behaviors. If I'm not aware of this fear in me, and don't acknowledge it (at least to myself), then it becomes almost impossible for me to fully empower people. For instance, if I have not engaged and integrated my fear, then I am apt to delegate work but unconsciously communicate doubt about a staff person's ability or efforts to accomplish it. (And they, too, probably won't *consciously* realize I don't trust them, but, believe me, on a deeper level, one that really affects their performance, they'll sense that I don't believe in them.) Or, when my fear of failure is not engaged and integrated, I may delegate work, but then, before someone can reasonably finish it, I'll pull the work back, rationalizing that I need to get it right.

The results when fear is in control are numerous. I have lost time. I have lost the value others can add to the project. And I have succeeded in diminishing their confidence for future work. Notice the mirror effect: I failed to integrate my fear, and then I failed to integrate my workers and their work. I am working against myself, and I am working against my team. Further, what does my fear of failure generate in them? You've got it: a fear they are failing me. My incompleteness can fracture another person and the culture in which I am trying to lead.

It takes a lot to be a great parent or a great manager. The needs of your kids or your staff are always changing, and the environments in which they are operating are constantly generating new challenges for them. It is much to ask that we be present to assist them in doing great work. But the more our view of them and our work is clouded by the shadows of our unacknowledged inner drives, the less we are able to deal with those realities.

So what do leaders do who integrate, who strive for wholeness? The most important practice in the thinking of real leaders with integrity is the willingness to see themselves with eyes wide open. This is both an initial willingness to recognize that what they think and feel, especially at deeper, unconscious levels, impacts their work, and making a lifelong commitment to opening their view wider and wider to see it all. You might think of leadership as having two different domains: the domain of practice outside in the world with your business, team, or organization; and the domain of inner practice.

Great *outside* leaders are unafraid to learn about parts of the business that aren't working. They are continually reintegrating pieces that don't fit together or pieces that no longer fit at all with the needs of the outside world. They love to get anonymous feedback, to hear what a customer or employee or competitor sees about the business. In bigger organizations, these folks hold skip-a-level meetings so they can hear from employees layers down and won't get all their impressions filtered by others.

Similarly, great *inside* leaders never stop listening and learning about what's (not) working in themselves. They don't pretend that the image they hope to project into the world completely captures who they are any more than they believe that their advertisements or mission statements fully reflect the *reality* of their business. So they don't expect to be always in control, positive, vision focused, encouraging, and so on—as the leadership books would have them be. Instead, they are listening inside their own heads for the dissonance—for their own rebelliousness, cynicism, anger, doubts, or irritability—the darker stuff that doesn't fit the bright picture. Such an "inside leader" learns to listen to those voices within, much like the CEO who, while anonymous on a plane or at a ball game, listens with curiosity and without defensiveness when a middle manager from a key customer talks candidly about some of his frustrations with the CEO's firm.

Peter Drucker, the legendary business writer, says that effective executives don't just work "*in* the business"—making it produce and sell—but they also step back and work "*on* the business." A parallel exists when it comes to the leader of integrity. *Leaders with integrity* work "*in* the business" of themselves. Yes, they get stuff done. Yet they also work "*on* the business of themselves." They monitor their own performance and bring fresh eyes to the analysis. They have a flashlight that they seem to be willing to point inside at any time. And they open themselves to others' views, questions, and comments. When you are around people of great integrity, you sense that they have a powerful work ethic—not just in the way they relate to others but in the inside game. They're always getting better when it comes to their values and the way they walk the walk. They are open and checking their motives all the time; they are asking as much of themselves as they are of anyone else.

One of my weekly "Reading for Leading" readers is the CEO of a large not-for-profit organization. She shares my thoughts on leading with her whole organization and tailors my story and theme to the specific issues she is seeing in her organization. Often she is challenging, inspiring, and encouraging her team. In her field of health care, change and competition continue to increase, so she uses these e-mails to keep driving the pace. From time to time, she changes pace and shares with great candor the "inner game" that she and all great leaders play. In her case, she wrestles from time to time with impatience. Here's an excerpt that demonstrates how she shares that inner struggle: "I have to remind myself that everything in life has to unfold and most things cannot be forced—nurtured, yes—but not forced. I have to remind myself that this is the time of my waiting. I must hold myself back from tampering with the strategic plan to allow the seeds that have been planted to sprout and grow—confident that we planted the right seeds and have done the hard work that will produce a healthy, strong harvest." When a manager attends to the inner game—and even takes the added step of sharing that work with her team—she starts to *pervade* her world with an attitude of self-improvement, of growth and candor. The leader improves her practice and models the way for those around her.

## Integrating Our Powerful Emotions

In this inside game of integration, certain disciplines will serve you best. First, recognize that your leadership decisions and actions are driven at least as much by deeper and largely hidden *emotional* drives as by your rational, dry, analytical conscious explanations. This is not as easy as it sounds. For as we "matured," we were primarily taught *not* to be jealous, angry, sad, or afraid, and those emotions were pushed out of sight. (In many cultures, we also repress such emotions as joy, silliness, and exuberance.)

I have seen enough inner circles of high-level politicians and businesspeople to say with certainty that emotions drive all kinds of behavior. Occasionally, the emotions are right up front, as when a politician who has exacted revenge on a colleague admits to his inner circle, with a wicked grin, "I have a long memory." In such cases he holds on to resentments and acts on them without shame, punishing his enemies. Oh, there is an element of strategy, as he'll say, "I'm sending a message to all of them: 'Don't mess with me.'" But there is also irrationality, in that if someone says, "Are you sure? You might need his help later," the typical reply, often delivered with more powerful slang, is, "Screw him; I don't want his help, now or ever." In cases like this—where the emotion is right there on the surface—it can at least be argued out and potentially balanced against higher values or other realities.

More frequently, our emotions play out beneath the surface of our consciousness. Something happens that triggers a feeling. Our socialization and the environment tell us that it's inappropriate to express this emotion. So some part of our mind quickly snags the feelings right out of our conscious awareness. Then the suppressed or repressed emotions take shape in behavior, often way out of context and sometimes way out of proportion. Here are some examples; note that each begins with an emotion:

- Embarrassed at a meeting of our peers, we don't make the connection when we go back and chew out someone on our team.
- Frustrated that we lost a deal we thought we had, we go home that evening and ground our kid for something that the day before we would not have even noticed.
- Afraid our position is in danger, we look for scapegoats, shift the blame, hide the facts, and unquestioningly support a higher-up's idea that we know is misguided.
- Sad about our circumstances, we are like a vacuum, sucking energy out of our team or family. Unacknowledged sadness can give way to depression, which can confuse or immobilize a whole culture.
- Feeling small and unimportant, we unconsciously do things to bring our peers down.
- Hurt by being passed over, we don't find the energy to fulfill "minor" commitments to people we know can wait.

- Unresolved about our past, regretful, or resentful, we over-steer our children, unwittingly forcing the very rebellious behavior we are trying to prevent.

Perhaps you see yourself in these. We usually think lack of integrity comes from the conscious choices "bad people" make that carry them away from values such as honesty and commitment. But these examples demonstrate how unconscious feelings carry us "good people" away from our values and cause us to be innately disingenuous; we are not living up to our values and are also misleading ourselves and others.

It's just not true to say that our kid's bad behavior was the cause of his or her punishment or just not honest to say that we're making people wait because they don't need the information we promised right now. If integrity is wholeness, these examples prove how we are not one, not whole with our values, but are instead disconnected from our values, from the truth of our experience, and from the powerful emotions that are driving us. The most powerful cause of our behavior in these cases—all the examples above—is the powerful emotion we carry from some other experience.

Some of these examples touch new emotions, but usually they trigger old feelings. In either case, if we acknowledge to ourselves the presence of strong emotions, we can make choices about how to manage them, and reconcile them with the values we want to live. If we don't acknowledge them, they gain the strength to function on their own, apart from our values, and undermine the health and wholeness of our group.

*Integrity*—a word that sounds dry and analytical—in this case means being whole, being one . . . with our *emotions*. It means coming to terms with those unseemly feelings we were supposed to have put away years ago and not pretending to ourselves and others that we are doing things for rational reasons when we know we are prompted by powerful emotions. If we really want to commit to being a person of integrity, we must choose to incorporate those emotions. How we do this varies with each of us, with the intensity and frequency of the emotions, and with the particular situations we are in.

Perhaps *the* most useful thing we can do is to shift from judgment about emotions to engagement with them. As long as we strongly judge our emotions, we will remain unwhole, unintegrated. We will pretend to keep the emotion away when in fact it is within, just denied, or split off. For instance, as long as I believe that I should not feel anger or fear, I am consigning myself to a split self: the feeling is there, but I pretend it is not real or somehow not really part of me. Yet there it is (ready when it finds an opponent to fight or a place to flee). Integrity requires wholeness. To acknowledge (not "admit," as if it were a confession to have feelings) that I am angry or afraid does not mean to give in to the impulse the feeling creates but quite the opposite.

This work of acknowledgment and engagement with emotions is especially difficult for some of us. American men and managers have taken in ten thousand messages about looking cool and in control. And women who pay attention to this prevailing culture may feel even more pressure to prove *they* have their emotions fully in check. At a gut level we resist the idea that something so small as a little feeling of fear is moving us or that we even feel jealousy. Likewise, many people raised in Western religious traditions consume messages that would have us deny or fight emotions instead of acknowledging them.

If I were asked to raise a great *leader of integrity,* one of the first things I would do would be to help open that individual to the full reality of his or her feelings. Feelings have great power. That power will find a way to be expressed, and the question for the leader is: will it act without my knowledge and consent or will I find a way to engage with the emotion, to own it, and to make a choice about how to use it? The only way to fully reach this point of choice is to engage with the emotion, to know just what it is one is choosing.

## Our Achilles' Heel Can Lead to Strength

One of the great hero myths involves the awesome Greek figure Achilles. No modern American film hero could compare with Achilles, who was wise, handsome, and powerful in battle. Achilles fully emerged at a point where the Greeks were being routed by the Trojans, and he single-handedly turned the tide of war. Although his power and virtue were extraordinary, few remember this greatness, which Homer depicted with extraordinary detail and touch. Instead, when I say "Achilles" you say "heel." You might even recall how his mother dipped him in the River Styx, which extended invulnerability to his entire body but for the one place she held that grip. That point of vulnerability ultimately attracted Paris's arrow (guided by Apollo in a moment of divine jealousy) and sealed Achilles' fate and reputation for all time. Achilles will be forever remembered as a symbol of inescapable human vulnerability.

The paradox of integrity is that none of us is completely whole. Achilles shows the "hole" in our wholeness. Each of us has the shadows Parker Palmer talked about. We all have our soft spots, our dark spots, our gaps, our vulnerabilities. Our unengaged and darker emotions, and the limits of our leadership style, point to this incompleteness or vulnerability. And so the Achilles myth leads us to the edge of a new way of seeing. It leads us to the spiritual dimension—a necessary place if we are to find true wholeness. The grip on the heel represents both our vulnerability *and* the appropriate place to turn with that vulnerability: not to ourselves but to—how do *you* name it?—God, or the Divine, or the Spirit, or the Truth.

The vulnerable spot can be seen as a gentle invitation to be in the right relationship with power and truth and to leave to the gods what belongs to the gods: omnipotence, omniscience, and immortality. When we ignore the shadow and subtly take to ourselves those attributes that belong to the gods trouble begins.

Perhaps you are thinking: "Come on, who but the most arrogant CEO or politician thinks he or she is omnipotent or omniscient?" It sounds absurd, but managers and teachers and principals and parents frequently act just this way when they forget that they have this Achilles' heel of vulnerability or incompleteness. For example, some leaders really *want* to be omniscient when they insist on knowing every detail before they decide (or knowing every single place their teenager is going every single minute of every single day). But such knowledge belongs with God, or in the ideal world, not with any one of us. Who has a right to such certainty?!

For another leader, it is not omniscience but perfection that beckons. One who demands perfectionist detail from himself and everyone else is grasping after a judgment or quality that no one can seize and wield. Perfection lies with the gods. And perhaps the most natural Achilles-like challenge for leaders with authority is in dealing with their lack of power to snap their fingers and get things done. They expect omnipotence from themselves and their organizations, but there are always obstacles.

Take two polar examples. First, as a parent, we recognize early on that we can neither make kids do what we want nor even make them value things the way we want them to. From early on they assert control: we may force them to do some things, but, darn it, they'll control what they eat, they'll fight to stay awake, and they'll control (or not!) their bowels, no matter what we say. We learn that—big and smart as we are—there are very definite limits to our power. It's hugely frustrating, and most of us pray, "God give me patience." Sadly, some parents don't see and accept the limits of their power and instead, at the point of violence and to the detriment of everything good, impose their physical will and power.

Now consider an example from the other end of the spectrum: the governor. How grueling it has been for her. Our state is in a deep economic crisis and must transition from generations of dependence on manufacturing jobs to a new knowledge economy. She and her team have come up with creative answers and well-thought-out strategies, and she has brought a tremendous sense of urgency and the will to execute. But in our world of separation of powers between executive and legislature, and with the opposing party in power in that legislature, her will has long been thwarted. That has tested her character and her focus. She has had to manage her drive for power and accomplishment in order to work productively with those with whom she must share power.

An executive such as a governor has to want power, has to be totally willing to use power to accomplish things. Yet such executives must simultaneously deal with the fact that they can in no way proclaim, "Let it be said—let it be done." Instead, as in all human relations—starting with that defiant two year old who won't eat—they must share power and duel and dance with others who have power, too. If they fail to see the limits of their power they may abuse it (like an abusive parent) and fail to engage others' power effectively. They may also darned near drive themselves nuts—wanting to accomplish but always having to work with others. And when an executive is not in a healthy relationship with power—and its limits—it will be harder to focus and accomplish what he or she can.

For Jennifer, there was a certain liberation and much clearer focus when she did two things. First, she consciously realized that these legislators—no matter how frustrating she found them—were playing their role in a larger drama. Power IS shared in our system, and it is a good system. It helped her to respect that system, even though she felt little respect for the particular tactics and strategies being employed. Second, Jennifer always finds the greatest strength and focus to use the power she has when she goes back to her religious faith. Her faith tells her that she did not create all the circumstances she is in and isn't expected to resolve them on her own. Indeed, there is a certain hubris, an unnecessary and unhelpful pride, in thinking that it is all on her shoulders—that she bears the full responsibility and ought to have the full power. When she looks to God for guidance, she feels she has a clearer relationship to the power she does have and the purpose that guides her.

So beware the leader (in you!) that is often subtly tempted to think he or she knows it all, has it all, wants it all, deserves it all, and has found "the way." Integrity acknowledges that we are not "It." We may channel it, conduct it, share it, express it, voice it, or feel it. But It—the It of Knowledge, Truth, or Power, for instance—is a lot bigger than we are. When we can begin to spot the moment when we are about to cast our particular shadow—our impatience, indecision, fear of conflict, and so on—then we have a chance. The chance comes with awareness. Integration becomes possible with that moment of awareness and with the questions that follow from the realization, "I am not It."

So how do you relate to It? Do you have a place in life where you get back in true relationship with It? Where you are "just" you and "just" you is totally okay, with no need for obsession and restlessness and no need to impose, change, drive, create, perfect? Having such a "place" or "practice" helps us realize that we don't need to change others in the attempt to fill our shadow. It helps immensely to have a place where you can admit that the arrow in the heel hurts. It's liberating in the course of leading to find a place or relationship in which it's okay to say you hurt, to be messy, unsure, slow, imperfect, and so on. You might consider looking for a rabbi, a coach, a god, a mentor, a spouse, a place to cry, a shoreline to walk, a journal that's exclusively yours, a chapel, a forest path, a special chair, a mom, a brother, a sister, or a dad who doesn't need to know and control everything and can thus help create such a place, such a relationship, for you.

Great things can happen for a leader when he does find such a place in which to be made whole and genuinely himself, even in the sometimes painful incompleteness. There, freed from the parent or manager's pretense to complete knowledge and power, he becomes, paradoxically, a more whole leader and gives those around him a much better chance to be whole, to lead, and to accomplish.

## When Someone Has It Together

"People ask me all the time, and I'll tell you just what I tell them," said Scot Norris, of JoMar Construction, about why he had poured tens of hours and buckets of sweat into the Habitat for Humanity Blitz Build completed in Detroit in the fall of 2004. Norris, who supervised the construction of one house yet seemed to be known as a trusted adviser to every critical volunteer across the sixteen-house construction site, told the 250 volunteers celebrating the end of the Blitz Build: "I do it to make a difference." It's a common enough expression.

He went on to talk at some length about the assembled volunteers and the value we produced for the needy yet deserving families, neighborhoods, and the city for which we had all been working. But then he concluded his remarks with a surprise ending as striking as the spanking new homes on that formerly blighted city block. "I don't know for sure what it does for all of them," he said, "but I do it to make a difference in *me*. I am a better person for doing it. And *that's* why I do it."

I can't explain integrity better than that fiftyish 6 foot 3 inch, sun-baked guy in a hard hat did. Let me unpack just a little. First, everyone who was there knew Scot wasn't just a talker; he was a walker. He thus began his speech with credibility as obvious as the dirt under his fingernails. No one worked harder. Second, his honesty suggested personal wholeness: "This is just who I am," he seemed to be saying. "This is why I do what I do." There were no airs about it.

Sometimes such speeches are inflated with self-importance, sounding a kind of self-congratulatory tone of "Aren't we great for helping these poor, hopeless people?" There was no false humility in

Scot's tone; he wasn't pretending to be smaller than anyone, wasn't glamorizing the families and the work we were doing for them. Instead, he was recognizing the truth for him and sharing it with us: he was doing the work to make a difference in . . . himself. That was enough.

Integrity like that doesn't stop within the skin of the leader. It radiates out to create wholeness in those around him; he was whole with his people. He offered a basic truth for each of us: we want to make a difference, and working like this meets *our* need to do so. He not only cleared himself of any pretense, but he freed us in the sharing. Scot Norris offered a model of integrity: Do what is right, be honest when you talk about why you do it, take responsibility for your own motives . . . and others will follow. I believed in that guy, and I'd follow him about anywhere. I can't think of a more effective way to lead and have people believe in you, believe in the work they are doing with you, and believe in themselves.

A building with integrity withstands the mightiest winds. Leaders with integrity withstand the pulls from within and the intense pressures from outside that might blow them and their teams off course. Get it together to be a leader of integrity.

# 5

# Do the Right Thing

THE IDEAS OF "SHADOWS" AND "WHOLENESS" explored in the last chapter wander from the more traditional ideas we have about integrity. In the traditional view, if we had to choose one word for integrity, we'd probably say "honesty." In this sense of integrity, we mean obeying the law or a moral code. We mean doing the right thing—even when it's hard. We mean standing up for a principle, even when it's inconvenient or costly.

This kind of integrity—what the dictionary defines as "strict adherence to a moral code"—upholds and uplifts leadership. Living with this type of integrity gives you tremendous credibility. And it also gives you peace of mind. This integrity is more easily defined than the integrity of being a "whole" person, but if it's easier to talk about, it may be harder to achieve and sustain. This chapter begins with the horrific cost we suffer when leaders fail at integrity, but it is largely devoted to exploring usable strategies to help us achieve the kind of uprightness, the kind of integrity, that seems to elude us at great cost, whether we are front-page or less public everyday leaders.

## The Cost of Not Doing the Right Thing

Little does more to damage, even devastate, the trust between a leader and the led than a breach of integrity. In the last twenty years our society has been littered with those who have not "done the right thing" but have instead violated laws, rules, and mores: Wright and Rostenkowski and Gingrich and DeLay in the Congress, Ebbers of WorldCom and Lay of Enron, Cardinal Law in the Catholic Church, and Jayson Blair of the *New York Times*, to name just a few. In recent history one president resigned and another was impeached, in both cases over behavior that lacked integrity and a failure to be forthcoming and responsible about those lapses.

The costs in such high-profile cases are extraordinary. An entire country gets distracted, divided, and demoralized. Corporations implode overnight, taking with them employees, retirees, and duped investors. In the case of the Church, thousands of children were traumatized, billions are being paid in lawsuits, and the Church's credibility is deeply wounded. These individual failures to do the right thing cast their shadows across whole institutions. People wonder: Can I trust the Congress? Can I trust my president? Can I trust the media or my church or my employer? Are the leaders of these institutions watching out for me—and should I follow, support, and contribute to them? Or are they really pursuing their own comfort, safety, and well-being? Do they expect me to do the right thing when it's clear *they* don't?

These individual acts accumulate in people's perceptions and undermine nearly all authority. At a time when we face very serious problems—like global competition, terrorism, and drug abuse—and we need people in authority to use their leadership well to help us address them, we can't afford these deadly lapses in integrity. For instance, in my admittedly and extremely biased view, my wife is a person of *exceptional* integrity. She constantly holds herself to the highest standards, and on more than a few occasions—one of which I will share later—has shamed or inspired me to the high ground. Yet she operates in a field in which dishonesty is almost the presumption! So if she were to do any one small thing wrong you and I know what many people would say: "I'm not surprised. They're all crooks." Nor would such a reaction be without basis, for people have been treated to so many headline stories of fallen leaders.[1] The cost of this presumption of dishonesty is huge, for when people are asked by the governor to, for instance, make sacrifices in money or effort, many say, "Why should *we* sacrifice, when all these politicians do is take care of themselves?" Every time another political leader acts unethically, it makes it hard for the rest to *lead,* for it reinforces these cynical presumptions. There is almost no room for error for Jennifer if she wants to keep some moral authority to challenge people to do better and do more.

In October of 2005, the day before Delphi—the largest "tier-one" automotive supplier in America—declared bankruptcy, the company announced significant economic packages to protect its executives. Then, as the company filed for bankruptcy, it said it would ask the United Auto Workers to scale back average hourly pay from twenty-seven to ten dollars per hour. Now somewhere out there is a basic notion of right and wrong, and those two separate announcements from the same corporate leadership, examined together, seemed WRONG! To his credit, CEO Steve Miller, when questioned about it, scaled the executive bonuses back. Besides being RIGHT, this gave him much more credibility to go out and make the case he felt was necessary given global competition: workers would have to be part of the solution to saving this company. Personal integrity is essential at such times, when leaders in authority push their followers to accept painful truths.

It is not only at these top-of-the-pyramid places where governors and CEOs work that integrity matters. The power of integrity, and doing the right thing, impacts all of us everywhere we lead. When store managers supplement their paychecks by collecting coupons and sending them to the manufacturers for cash, *as if they had purchased the products,* do they really expect their employees won't cheat *them?* When a manager promotes a really good performer over a great performer because "there's something about that woman that bugs me," does he really think people won't see the unfairness, realize that performance doesn't really matter, and, if they are great performers, start to look for a better place to work? When people feel a leader has failed the integrity test and can't be counted on to do the right thing, behavior will change in many negative ways; for example, people stop sharing information, lower their personal standards, and just don't trust the information or teachings of the leader.

For instance, we tell our kids not to lie or cheat and to honor their word. But when they hear us on the phone telling people something they know is not true, or when they find out we have been cheating on our spouse—their mom or dad—for years, our credibility with them evaporates. And it's not just credibility they feel *we* have. Just as a lying congressman makes it harder for people to trust *any* member of congress, a cheating father makes it harder for his daughter to trust any man. I know this is not a popular or "politically correct" thing to say, for we fear offending by talking about the "wrongness" of divorce. But ask the psychologists if you don't believe me: children's hearts and minds are not formed as much by the nice things we say, by the talk we talk, as by the walk we walk.

When we fail to do the right thing—for instance, to do a painful thing such as divorce the *right* way—we cause those we lead to spend years of their lives trying to sort through what *they* did wrong and whether they have what it takes to sustain healthy relationships and make vows of their own with credibility. Leading can be a glorious thing, but when we wear a jersey that says "parent" or "boss" on the back we might remember the Hippocratic oath and strive "to do no harm," for when we do wrong in the role of parent or boss our wrongs are—like it or not—multiplied in magnitude.

So the effects of not doing the right thing are extensive when it comes to high-level authority figures, and the effects can be very *intensive* in the smaller worlds in which we lead. The impact of one person's bad acts as a member of Congress, corporate manager, or "just"a mom or dad can have sweeping effects on the institutions we represent. Yet, we are, after all, human, subject to errors, frail at times, sometimes highly emotional, and often operating under pressures and circumstances that bring out something other than our most rational or boy-scout-like goodness.

Any self-respecting account of integrity has to account for this complex humanity, prone not just to error but to guilt and shame, capable not only of doing great things in the world but of deceiving ourselves greatly! The following readings prescribe perspectives and strategies that might help complex and sometimes frail humans to do the right thing more often for the good of all.

## Paying Attention to Little Things

It was nearly twenty years ago, in the summer of our long-distance courtship, that Jennifer discovered the coin on the copier. She was clerking at a high-charging, silk-stocking, midtown Manhattan law firm. Dick Cullen, a partner who specialized in insurance law, stood in front of her at the copier, finished making a copy, put a nickel in the supply tray on top and turned to go. Never shy, ever mirthful, Jennifer deadpanned, "You mean you have to pay for copies here?" He smiled and said, "It's not law firm work; it's a personal copy" and walked away.

A lunchtime conversation with Mr. Cullen a couple of weeks later turned to the coin on the copier and to ethics and integrity generally. He said, "I believe that you take care of the little things and the big ones will take care of themselves." He would put a nickel on the law firm's Xerox machine if he copied something for home or his church just to keep himself square. It was a simple way to align his behavior with his values. Lawyers might need this practice more than most. For in a shop like Dick Cullen's lawyers keep meticulous time sheets, billing their clients in increments as small as six minutes. How easy it would be to routinely round up, to bill time spent thinking about a case while driving home, or to bill two clients while doing "roughly" the same legal research for both. And then, once one has tolerated "little" deviations on one's time sheets, how much easier to "slightly" misrepresent a client's position when you think he doesn't really understand but you don't have time to straighten him out. One can fall into small habits of cutting corners, blurring lines, and making assumptions instead of asking simply, "Is this the right thing?"

Rosa Parks offers an unparalleled example of someone taking a heroic stand against something that others have understandably tolerated for generations. On a much more everyday level, Dick Cullen offers the splendid example of building a foundation of solid ethics by handling the small things. Just as a pianist couldn't play Balakirev's *Islamey* without having practiced the scales a million times, so Cullen's behavior suggests that maybe we can't handle life's truly difficult, high-pressure moral dilemmas without first developing judgment and practice by repeatedly doing the right thing in matters quite small.

Sometimes when we think of ethics we think of "ethical dilemmas." We expect complicated questions such as stem cell research, abortion, euthanasia, or cloning. But frequently this is not the case. The coin on the copier is not about external, objective, hairsplitting ethics. Mr. Cullen

> When it comes to ethics, when you take care of the little things, the big ones will take care of themselves.

wasn't rehearsing complicated arguments, weighing, for instance, the cost to the firm of the personal copy versus what it would cost the firm if he extended his lunch by a walk to Kinkos. He was merely acting on a gentle reminder from deep within his personal core about what was his and what was not. He'd long had a code, which included respecting others' property, and this was a simple way to make his ideals and his practice consistent or "whole."

Cullen's act was like a million acts of integrity that happen at your work or away from it every day. They are simple, daily, largely unnoticed acts. He wasn't on a holier-than-thou moral crusade. He wasn't calling for an "integrity tray" on every copier. He was just acknowledging to himself how easily he as a human being could blur the line on things. He knew from his experience how easy it can be to go along with the "everybody does it" practices of the social environment and without knowing it leave behind his personal ideals. Cullen did not leave his personal ideals behind. Instead, he left a coin on the copier.

The point is not that Dick Cullen was *right* and the 99.9 percent of us who *don't* leave a coin on the company's copier are *wrong*. The point is to look for simple ways to practice what is right, so that when the tough ones come you have built up your capacity to handle them. Accept a little of the sting of conscience—in this case from Dick Cullen but in other cases from examining your own behaviors. Practice candor with your spouse, be scrupulous about what you put on your expense report, ask yourself, "Am I saying something behind someone's back that I would never say to his or her face?" These are the kinds of practices and habits that will strengthen your moral ability, lead you to the kind of moral greatness that will make those around you stronger, and give you credibility to lead.

The coin on the copier is a story about being attuned to your inner truth and practicing it in everyday ways. Twenty years later, I have not found a better small story of integrity. Its simplicity is why this puny tale offers so much in the context of our day, with its colossal collapses in integrity. Use the little things as small reminders of the greatness in living in the land of values and truth.

## Personal Reasons to Do the Right Thing

Paying attention to the little things and continually asking "what's the right thing to do?" goes a long way to promote integrity, but I want to suggest a twofold basis for really *wanting* to do the right thing. If we are not firmly convinced of the value of doing what's right, we won't lead that way consistently. For, face it, there's stuff on the other side of the scale tipping against doing the right thing. For instance, we may feel pressured to take a major shortcut around the rules when something important is at stake: money, job security, or our reputation or that of our institution. Of course, we *should* all do the right thing simply because it is the right thing. But that *should*, that moral weight, often does not weigh enough in tough circumstances. So we tell ourselves all kinds of things: that it's just easier, we don't *mean* ill by it, *we* have been treated unfairly and shouldn't even be in this position, or we will go back and fix what we're doing later. Or we allow our behavior by saying "Nobody will ever know." So what could be on the other side of the scale when it's tipping toward us doing what is against our values and our precarious sense of right and wrong?

There are two compelling reasons to want to lead by consistently doing the right thing. The first is the overwhelming cost when someone even alleges that you have violated legal or ethical norms. The initial humiliation and the enduring suspicion that many people will hold are painful for individuals, for those around them, and for the larger institutions of which they are a part. Perhaps there are many people who don't get caught (and it's true that some who engage in unethical and immoral behavior almost seem to love the risk), but as information is more broadly available and widely circulated, more and more people will get caught and the costs will be higher. In an information age in which the media thirst for sensational stories, it's simply foolish to think that secrets can be kept for long periods of time. And once the word is out it's like the genie out of the bottle—all but impossible to stuff it back in. We have witnessed this on the largest screen, where some of our presidents have led with intellect and courage and conviction but their moral lapses have brought extraordinary pain to them and their families—and thrown the entire country off track.

As individual leaders, and a society, perhaps, we need to reaffirm the basic message we were taught, that "crime never pays." We need to steep ourselves in the awful depths of the impact on our organizations when authority figures misuse their trust. If our goal should be to lead by vision, from time to time it may be worth looking not at the dream but at the terrible nightmare visited on organizations when their authorities betray them. Jennifer and I have played this nightmare card with our children, describing the awful price they will pay for bad judgment. We haven't wanted to scare them about the consequences of their behavior in a public world they did not choose. But we *know* that the near certain consequence of their engaging in illegal or rule-breaking behavior is that word will spread faster than a California wildfire and they, more than we, will bear the cost. Their reputations and their freedom to meet people on their own terms will be greatly curtailed by fast-spreading "news" of their activities. They will forever be "the governor's daughter who had that terrible problem with _____."

There is a second weight to be placed on the balance as we approach leadership and the importance of doing the right thing. That is the opportunity to secure peace of mind.

I mentioned that Jennifer lives by highly scrupulous standards and that from time to time she shames or elevates me to conform to them. Let me explain. I, like so many in my generation, grew up with a sense of economic scarcity and an abiding anxiety about what lurked around the financial corner. My parents experienced the Great Depression and inculcated a need for savings and caution. From the first minute I was old enough to deliver newspapers, I worked and worked and worked: multiple jobs through college and law school (where I cleaned an office building and did odd jobs to slow my mushrooming loan burden). I never sought to be rich; I was just about obsessed with making ends meet.

In the 1990s I left my work in public and social service and began working at a leadership-consulting business. The philosophy there was "eat what you kill," that is, we were all responsible for selling our services, and if you didn't sell you might not get paid. I learned the real meaning of "networking," as I tapped the many relationships I had developed over the years, and I was doing okay and signing up some good clients. At the time, Wayne County's airport was ranked in the bottom ten in the world, but a friend and former colleague of mine had been appointed director, and he was determined to turn things around. He invited me to put in a bid for the leadership development work they needed to do, and so my firm toiled for weeks, submitted the elaborate proposal, and won the work. At about the same time I decided to leave this business to start my own leadership firm. My departure from my firm was friendly, and after consulting with the airport client we all agreed that I should continue to work with my old firm, delivering the leadership development training on this project.

Just after this contract was approved by the county commission and as we were beginning our first meetings with the airport's leaders, Jennifer's decision about whether to run for governor was being pressed upon her, as a potential competitor was rattling his saber, ready to announce he was running. We talked about my work at the airport; as she knew, it would pay me something like thirty thousand dollars in a sales commission, which would be extremely useful, as I was launching my own business without the benefit of a nest egg or investors. She said, "I don't think you should do the work with the airport." I couldn't believe she was suggesting this. "You don't need it, and they are going to attack you and me about it." The fact was that years before Jennifer and I had both worked for the county that operated the airport, we knew the people involved, and the media were in the midst of an all-out offensive on the airport, the county, and the people who ran it. "Cronies" was the word of the day. I reacted strongly, arguing with her: I had obtained the work fairly and legally, we both knew that the airport director was trying to clean things up, and our firm would help them tremendously. Why should I give up something that I had earned fairly and would do to the absolute best of my ability? I continued my defense before my wife: I understand the public sector, I have the trust of the client so I can really challenge him and bring out his best, and you want me to just give it up because someone (probably someone who has it in for us) will say it's unethical?

She reminded me of the business of politics we had chosen for her and of how ugly the campaign would be—even without this. She said I would be attacked. I said it was unfair and I had done nothing wrong. She had the courage to say: "It doesn't *look* right, and that's all they need." She reminded me that my firm wasn't the low bidder; I reminded her that we were far from being the high bidder; that this was not buying nuts and bolts but a subjective, quality-oriented service; and that I had earned the trust the airport leaders were placing in our firm. She continued arguing, invoking language that lawyers know by heart: "Avoid even the appearance of impropriety."

My blood pressure must have been around 250 at this point. I was angry with politics, the media, and myself for not seeing how this could come back and bite us in the backside. Jennifer wisely reminded me, "I'm just a messenger, so don't get mad at me"—helpful advice because my frustration was surely in search of a scapegoat. I had all my baggage weighing on me, especially the baggage of fears of economic insecurity.[2] I was starting a new business, and this contract, which I had earned fairly, would let me breathe for a month or two. I was genuinely nervous about letting it go. What should I do?

I gave it up. I called our client. He was upset because he wanted me to do the work and also felt somewhat indignant that people would suggest I or *he* had done something unethical. I called my old firm and said I was backing out. We figured out the commission and, at this point of great economic uncertainty for me, I wrote *them* a check, returning the commission I had earned. It was the hardest check this hardworking, middle-class kid ever wrote. But I'm glad I did it.

I have suggested that there are two fundamental bases to help you choose to do the right thing: seeing the nightmare that could unfold if you don't, and choosing the peace of mind that comes when you do. To varying degrees, both reasons were in play in this example. On the downside, I wished I had clearly seen the nightmare that awaited me when I first pursued the work. If I had, I would never have sought the contract. And had I continued with the work we would have been dogged relentlessly with allegations of ethical misdoings.[3] We could have refuted them in a debate in front of an impartial jury, but in the leadership world you have no constitutional right to a jury of your peers. You are tried in conversations at the coffee machine, in the parking lot, in chat rooms, and on blog sites. Whether you are the mayor or the mom, CEO or vice president of this or that, you can be assured you won't have a fair forum, and even if it seems that on balance you have been "acquitted," you will still bear the costs. Understand: this is not a complaint. Well, perhaps it is, but the complaint doesn't alter the *fact*—or series of facts: your enemies will use your questionable judgment as grounds for attack, many business associates and acquaintances will now have doubt in their minds when they deal with you, and your good friends will be hurt by it. And, of course, almost everyone will be distracted from the issues and the work at hand. Let it go!

As I have said, the other weight that we can put on the scales to help us make the right choices is the opportunity to gain peace of mind. I hated letting go of that work. But I felt some real pride in the decision to hold our ethics to a higher degree of scrutiny. I gained a great sense of freedom by simply doing what was right. A strange irony lurks around the role of money when it comes to freedom. Many of us pursue economic success, and if we were pushed to articulate the value behind that pursuit, we would say: money will give me freedom—to make my own choices, to work or not, to travel, to be free, and to live without worry, with peace. The irony is that the need for financial success—and ultimately freedom and peace of mind—may do more than anything else to lead us to poor ethical decisions. When people embezzle, or even when they do the "smaller" things— padding expenses, using corporate resources for personal use, or cheating on their taxes—they cost themselves more in peace of mind than they are likely gaining. Going to bed feeling good in conscience is a highly underestimated value. Knowing that what you have earned *you* have earned fairly gives pride and ease.

I faced a second round of questions about ethics and appearance when Jennifer won that election for governor. If she had not, and if I had exposed her to even greater attack by not giving up that contract, I would have been haunted. But after her election I realized that I had a new dilemma facing me: how would I conduct my business in "her" state? After the anguish about the airport contract, and the frustration I felt that Jennifer was nevertheless attacked for my behavior, I wondered: how am I going to keep conducting my business without giving others ammunition with which to attack her? Prior to her election, I had chosen to work only in Michigan, as our children were young and needed me, and Jennifer's job was so hugely demanding. But now she was the governor, and her state budget and policies were impacting nearly everyone I had been or could be working with: school systems, hospitals, even auto suppliers. How would I know clients weren't giving me work to curry favor with her? How would I know how they might try to leverage their relationship with me? How would the media and her opponents react if one of my clients did well by the state?

I'll never forget meeting with Rick Wiener, Jennifer's chief of staff, a couple of weeks after the election. Rick is a model of integrity and solid ethical thinking. He had been a lawyer and lobbyist (those may not sound like the calling cards of ethical people, but there are some exceptional people in these, as in all, fields). Now he was going inside the state government, so he had to think through some tough issues, too. He told me, "For you, I figure that there are six circles of potential clients. In the inner circle is the state government itself, and under no circumstance should you contract with them." Then, he said, there were local governments, and they would probably be a problem, too. Then there's publicly regulated utilities and universities. I got lost somewhere around the third or fourth circle with him. "Rick," I said, "I just can't do anything. No matter who I work with people will attack me for it, and it will just get in Jennifer's way." So that was it. I kept one contract I had been doing for four years. I went from earning $150,000 to $18,000 annually. But I bought an *enormous* reservoir of peace of mind.

Now, we could argue the peculiar specifics of my situation. The governor is provided with a good salary and a house to live in, so you might say I had the luxury of not working. Totally true. At the other extreme of the argument, some in my circumstance might have suggested that it was almost wrong to "cave in" and give up my profession and that there was nothing, ethically, to make me quit *all* work in Michigan. I wouldn't say they are wrong. I am merely saying that for me the peace of mind was priceless. I have been able to support the truth of Jennifer's sound ethical practice. I have not allowed myself to be a distraction from the hard work she is trying to lead. If in some way I am an example of doing it right, that's okay, too. But that's way more than I am looking for. I am really just trying to do no harm, and that gives me great peace and allows me to focus without distraction on the ways I can lead.

I have witnessed at close hand how painful it is to be accused of ethical wrongdoing. I would not wish that nightmare on anyone. As opportunities present themselves to you to take shortcuts, to pass up doing the right thing, consider the price you will pay and the damage you might do to others. And, besides avoiding the nightmare, seek and enjoy the freedom and peace of mind that come with doing what's right. It's priceless.

## Acknowledging Our Appetites—So They Don't Devour Us

Nearly every one of the prescriptive strategies I have offered to help you lead with integrity suggests that you can think yourself into good behavior. I am urging you to adopt a mental framework that values doing the right thing, and I recommend that you build the small practices that support that commitment. But, I know from my own heart, experience, and study that issues of doing the right thing are not just rational. The appetites that drive us—like my anxiousness about economic insecurity, which made it so hard for me to give up that airport contract—are largely nonrational and require more than mere rationality.

At the extremes, those appetites are pathological, fully overwhelming all ethical and rational thought. Where people use their power to sexually molest children we know they have crossed some line. Likewise, when people are breaking the law—stealing, bribing, embezzling, or forging prescriptions—we know that rational, ethical thinking has been overwhelmed by appetites. In their case, it's clear that they are *not* thinking or, to put it differently, rational thought is not in control of their behavior. Something else is.

In this respect, for many if not most of us, even though our ethical failures are less black and white than child molestation or intentional falsification of financial statements, our rationality is *similarly* not in control. Although our appetites may be less demonic, and perhaps our victims may be less obvious, we, too, have experienced appetites or psychological needs driving us. We feel at some points so driven to succeed; to gain notoriety; to "get high" on some drug, sex, or risky behavior; or to feel valued or loved that our ethical thought processes are simply overwhelmed.

In such times or circumstances, we put our reputations and work, our families and the organizations we lead at great risk as we do things we know are not right. We put all our hopes in the "nobody will know" basket, as we change a few numbers on a sales report, use the company credit card, repeatedly visit a prostitute, share highly confidential information that puts a friend or client at risk, repeatedly berate an employee or child over whom we have power, or underreport the cash sales in our business to the IRS. We know we're doing it. But it's as if we have lost control. We feel we can't stop. We recognize that there's something deep, some need, some compulsion at work. We do the deed, try to get it over with quickly, and hope we won't be caught. We try to push it out of our conscious mind.

Some people will perhaps never reach this point of feeling out of control. Their overriding rationality may completely suppress or repress the kind of psychological needs that overwhelm others. Or their upbringing may have instilled such a powerful fear of being found out that they will stay forever on the straight and narrow. For the rest of us, at times we genuinely need—let me say it simply and clearly—help. We need to be able to air the need, the appetite, the compulsion with someone we can trust. For some, this someone may be God.[4] For many, it will require another human being—a friend, coach, counselor, therapist, or other person skilled in the ways of the heart and psyche.

Such persons may help us right then and there to get back in the driver's seat, to direct our behavior in the moment, and to make a choice consistent with our values and our sense of right and wrong. Or, in some cases, they may help us over a period of time to engage with the obsessive side of our personality, to understand the deeper need that is driving our behavior, and to find constructive ways to manage that deeper need. Are you put off that I keep writing about the "we" and lumping myself (and you?) in with addicted drug users, embezzlers, and such? To me, we are all on the same human continuum—some of us are blessed to be relatively free of such compulsions, but all of us from time to time have our freedom and rationality overshadowed by darker forces that drive us. Whether we have such times episodically or regularly, walling ourselves off and trying to go it alone is one of the worst things we can do.

Let me say this clearly: there is no shame in seeking help! Or, for persons who feel there is shame in it, let them only balance the weight of that shame against the pain and hurt they may be causing themselves and others. They should know that any wise counselor will easily get them through the shame part and on to managing the need that is at times running them. As the old fifties TV series declared, there are "eight million stories in the naked city." How sad that we discover many of them through tragedy, only after innocent people have been scarred, and only after the persons involved have been eaten away by a disease that could have been managed with a little help.

## Create a Culture of Openness

Just as openness is the key to individuals managing their appetites, it is also the key to individuals who are trying to create *organizations* in which integrity flourishes. Nothing does more to generate ethical behavior in a culture than openness. Conversely, when cultures are closed, rigid, or hierarchical then opportunities for misdeeds grow. One of the lessons of the scandals that have wracked the Catholic Church is that the lack of openness and the insulation of the hierarchy allowed problems to be hidden and to fester. There was no recourse at the parish level and no check on the authority of bishops. Problem priests, in some jurisdictions, were put in contact with children over and over again. When information is not available, when people can't ask questions, when authority is not open to others' views, then it becomes too easy for authority to be abused. The airtight seal and codes of loyalty that have historically been created in organizations such as the military, the police, and fraternities have allowed abusive behavior to be perpetuated.

If you seek an open and therefore more ethical culture, then open the doors. Openness comes from both a hard side and a soft side. Hard side openness comes when there are *systems* and *structures* that support people's candor. For instance, leaders who are serious about creating an ethical organization will create systems that allow for confidential reporting of ethical violations, and, where the company's size warrants it, they will appoint an ethics officer with high status. If ethics is important to *you*, then highlight it in newsletters and other communications, say what it means in practical terms, and celebrate success stories. We too often assume that people know what matters to us, but the instruction "over-communicate the vision by a factor of ten" applies not just to vision but to ethics as well. If you don't repeat it often, don't expect they will think it matters.

Perhaps the most important way in which those in authority create ethical cultures is that they expect it *uniformly*. This can be challenging. Challenge often arises in the form of a "take no prisoners" type of performer. Usually this character believes he or she is indispensable and frequently has others in the organization convinced of it. Every law firm has one. Every sales organization has two. Every creative force has at least one such *artiste,* who thinks he or she should operate under a markedly different set of rules than the others. These are the ones with great drive—to produce, to sell, to create. They are often quite passionate about their work, and, as they'll tell you, they "don't have time for any BS." They may, for instance, ignore the company policy on giving gifts to customers, find a way to sell in a colleague's territory, skip all meetings that they don't see immediate value in attending, periodically scream and holler at junior staff, routinely blow agreed-upon deadlines, or expect people to accommodate their creative style. They never apologize (or they apologize a lot, expecting that this will make their abuses go away). Sometimes they lie.

An organization that is serious about expecting ethical decisions and is committed to creating a culture in which integrity thrives will not tolerate such unethical behavior. The leaders of one firm I worked with had a crude but effective way of expressing their approach to it. They articulated and enforced a "no assholes" rule. If people did not treat others as worthy of respect, and not just means of production, they would be "called" on that behavior, and if they didn't shape up they were shipped out.

Some characterize matters such as this as the "soft" stuff. I have never really understood that characterization, as it's actually incredibly hard work—challenging from both an emotional and strategic standpoint. The managing partner who calls in the highest-billing member of a law firm to discuss his or her rude behavior toward a secretary is no wimp. For this rule breaker has little hesitance about running over people or rules and will very likely not respond with humility and penitence when confronted.

It is hard work to raise issues in the first place, difficult to constructively engage such a performer in the conversation. Denial and hostility are possible if not likely consequences. But the high risk can generate a high return: a better work environment and the possibility that an "asshole" can become more of a human being with their team, and perhaps their family, and themself. Of course, if such a gambit fails the leader will have to manage the consequences when this person leaves the firm. This is some of the hardest work there is in leadership. But having the guts to confront such behavior will say more to the rest of the organization than a thousand "messages from the CEO" or slogans about how "we value integrity above all."

The other great challenge on the so-called soft side of the effort to create openness and have it *uniformly* applied is this: Will the openness extend to the top? We have all been taught that authority carries with it the right to *not* be questioned. How many of us participated in or at least observed a dialogue like the following between an adolescent child and a parent?

> PARENT: If you don't watch your language, young lady, there
> are going to be serious consequences.
> CHILD: What? Why?
> PARENT: Because.
> CHILD: Because why?
> PARENT: Because I said so.
> CHILD: But you and Mom use that language all the time. Just
> yesterday, Mom . . .
> PARENT: That will be enough, young lady.

Depending on how sensitive the parent is about the issue the child is raising, the parent might well throw in a "How dare you talk to me about . . ." or a "Don't you *ever* talk to me about . . ." or a "Who do you think you are, asking *me* about . . ." It is as if an invisible fence has been erected around the personal behavior of the parent. The same kind of fence is extended to protect the schoolteacher, the principal, the boss, and indeed all the way around the authority world. Very early on, people quit testing to see if they will still get shocked if they get too close. You just don't talk about the personal (broadly construed) behavior of your parent, boss, or superior.

Great leaders, on the other hand, give up the privilege of living behind the invisible fence. They are willing to let anyone ask questions that have to do with the integrity of the organization—including the behavior of the top authority. This is not easy. It means, for instance, that the governor has to be willing to say, "Yes, I use the state plane." She may decide to hope people understand, or she may spend time explaining why it's cost effective for her to do so. Or she may decide that using the plane really isn't right, isn't in line with her declared values. If that's her conclusion, then the openness or transparency will cause her to lead with a more demanding ethic. Likewise, the boss who is playing golf while his or her team is in assembling a project on the weekend has got to be (at least willing to be) open about it or accept that this behavior is establishing an example of pretense for the team to follow. If it's really not right for the boss to be playing while they're working, then he or she can expect that they will not always do what's right, that they will instead follow the authority's lead and conceal their departures from the straight and narrow.

Openness by the authority establishes openness as a value for others. And it serves as a check on leadership behaviors, prompting leaders to hold themselves to the same standard they expect of others. If we want to protect our organizations from the ravages of unethical or even illegal behavior, we are well advised to declare a commitment to doing the right thing, talk about that a lot, apply it—even in hard cases—and live it like an open book!

## Getting Back on Track: Mistakes and Apologies

Sometimes we don't ask why we're doing questionable things, and we don't seek good counsel and keep everything open and transparent. And sometimes we actually know what we should do, but then our actions betray our best intentions. To err is human. Then the questions quickly become: What do we do about it and can we get back on track? We can learn from watching others speak about their mistakes and missteps. In the span of about two weeks in early 2004, a variety of admissions and apologies captured the news.

- "We were almost all wrong," announced David Kay, the former U.S. senior weapons inspector, when it became undeniably clear that there were no widespread weapons of mass destruction in Iraq.
- "We took an approach that I now realize was wrong," Bill Gates said of his company's decision to ignore the Web search market. "But," he added pointedly, "we will catch them." (Look out, Google!)
- "I again offer my apologies to those who have been victimized and for our failures to address this matter appropriately," said Detroit's Cardinal Adam Maida on the release of a report detailing sexual abuse by priests in his archdiocese.
- "I apologize to anyone offended—including the audience, MTV, CBS, and the NFL," said Janet Jackson about her offensive dance move during halftime of the Super Bowl. (The Columbia Broadcasting System, Music Television, the National Football League, and fellow performer Justin Timberlake had already "apologized" for the incident.)

Error is inevitable. But when we lead, unchecked error can be corrosive of our credibility. There is a simple leadership-integrity test that can help us here. In the strange dance between the leader and the led, this is what it takes to have those you lead follow you again.

- Be truly contrite, and apologize fully.
- Genuinely and credibly commit to acting differently in the future.

The first sets a standard of unadulterated honesty about the past; the second offers a genuine commitment to the future. Followers expect both. Some will place more emphasis on the past or the future. Similarly, some will be more focused on the repair of feelings while others will be almost exclusively concerned about understanding *why* it happened and why it *won't happen again*. Our job as leaders is to sense who needs which emphasis but assuredly to accomplish both.

Just as followers will place different emphasis on the past or future, so also leaders may be naturally better at *doing* the first or second. For instance, in my case, I almost always do well with the first—feeling and conveying remorse—but I constantly have to work on the second by fighting habits and patterns that tend to prevent me from going forward. And if I am not credible about the future, the apology about the past will become hollow. At some point my sweet sincerity about the past will start to taste bitter if those who follow me suspect that I have failed them again. I know, as a follower, that my heart likes the apology for the past, but my head and hands crave the genuine commitment to the future. When leaders admit *and* apologize, and commit to realistic ways of doing better, people are generally quite ready to forgive and move on.

It's rare to see a flurry of apologies like those offered by Janet Jackson, David Kay, and the others. In some of the cases, the apologies were much less effective than they could have been because they came late. But often they don't come at all. Instead of apologies we get denials and cover-ups, which are often much more offensive to followers and more damaging to leaders than the initial offense.

If there's one good piece of advice on the apology it's this: get it done! At the time the Monica Lewinsky/Bill Clinton situation was unfolding, I was conducting an interview with Doug Sosnick, an adviser in the West Wing of the White House. We were talking about politics and character. With some exasperation, he talked about how amazing it was that so many people in Washington thought they could hide mistakes or cover them up: "I don't know why most of them do that because once you sort of cough it up, you say it, you apologize, it's over. The American public is pretty forgiving of indiscretions, although there's a point where they're not forgiving . . . for a lot of indiscretions, they're pretty forgiving. *But they're unforgiving if they think you've been dishonest or deceptive about it.*"[5] Our pride makes it hard, but our pride will take a walloping hit, and our credibility an even bigger hit, when we *don't* come clean.

Apologies are full of paradox: on the one hand they are so simple, and on the other they are so hard and become so complicated. I find apologizing to be one of the most challenging acts of human behavior. In *principle*, it is simple: take responsibility for what you have done. Simplicity generates effectiveness. The simpler and clearer the apology is the easier it can be accepted and the past left behind. The other person might say, "Really? You mean it?" And you say, "Yes." Yet our overwhelming tendency is to start with an apology but manage to merge it into, "But if you hadn't . . ." or "But I really had no choice. . . ." The gift of apology they thought they were getting begins to give off an odor.

It's not always simple, even when we do it well. If we have caused hurt, people may need to express some of it. It might help to realize that had they not trusted us they would not have been hurt. And now we are moving toward regenerating that trust. They may express hurt, anger, and even lingering mistrust—"I appreciate the apology, but I'm just not sure I'm ready to go back to the way things were." Most of us will want to jump in then and defend ourselves or give the justifications that we have at the ready: "Well, it's not like you didn't have something to do with this . . ." or "I think you're being a little unfair." Our very best bet is to accept the feelings—feelings, after all, that we helped to generate. There is a completion that is necessary, and letting others express their feelings is a necessary part of closing that circle on the past.

Then the future beckons. The most powerful apologies put in place a commitment to the future. Generally, this means more than good intentions. The Catholic Church, for instance, to its credit, has established a lay board to advise the bishops, instituted a "zero-tolerance" policy, and promised "transparency" in the settlement of abuse cases. When we have failed to do the right thing, we also need to identify specific things we will do to allow ourselves to move forward with credibility. This may demand much of us as leaders. To take the example of the Church again, its credibility remains shaky because some of the deeper issues in its institutional character remain. Not long after the lay review board was formed, its chairman, Governor Frank Keating, was pressured to resign after making an inflammatory remark; and so questions of openness were again at the forefront. A sincere commitment to doing better means we have to engage with the rough human edges that led to our shortfalls in the first place. And that's the inner work of leadership.

Ed Riley, a youth basketball coach, offers in summary some lighthearted but well-fashioned advice: "Don't let your ego or pride keep you from admitting a mistake. When you screw up, hold your hand up in the air and admit it. (It's good exercise for your arms.) Learn from your mistakes and go on with life!"[6]

And, oh yes, try not to foul out of the game!

## When Strict, Steadfast, and Moral May Be Way Too Much

In summer jobs in Ford-UAW (United Auto Workers) plants in the late 1970s, I don't remember ever hearing anyone talk values and high moral standards. Neither quality nor respect was played up; neither fairness nor hard work nor cooperation was a watchword. Oh, a few "Safety is Job 1" posters were up, but otherwise it was a values vacuum. And at the grassroots level, without leadership calling us to higher values, the lowest common denominator of self-interest prevailed. A vast number of workers had no care for quality, teamwork, or any higher values. They did the minimum, punched out, and went to the bar—or, in some cases, went to the bar, punched in, and did the minimum. I have witnessed how things have changed markedly. Good thing.

Organizations without high standards lose quality and direction. When the leader of a business, family, union, work team, or church offers little teaching of and adherence to moral standards, it is only a matter of time before chaos and dysfunction will begin to arise and eat away at those organizations. On the other hand, leaders who speak of high ethical standards keep teams together and elevate behavior.

Many in society today—in church, politics, and community— crave higher standards. They are begging for them. And some leaders are eager not just to champion these standards, but to preach them, push them, and even impose them. There a new danger arises. For rigid standards preached without the balance of wholeness practiced do not create integrity in the individual or health in the organization. We can see the false promise of overly strict adherence to moral standards in high-profile cases. And, if we are honest, we can see the same dangerous tendencies in our own leadership.

In educated America in the early twenty-first century, we are completely justified in our gut instinct suspicions of this steadfast moral adherence stuff. Too often it is plastered upon us. Our gut tells us that the Dr. Lauras and Pat Buchanans of the world are just a little over the top with their strict moral prescriptions. They seem to stampede through people's legitimate differences, refusing to see the true gray in complex issues and prescribing a rigidity that we abhor in "fundamentalist" or "radical" religious states. Rigidity comes at a high price.

Further, there seem to be more than a few righteous Jim Bakkers, whose "steadfast and strict" talk are not matched by a steadfast and strict walk. Our skepticism about strict-talk leaders in the Catholic Church (to which I belong) seems warranted when we read of the ongoing revelations about the behavior of some priests. Their behavior defies their explicit vows and mocks their impassioned preaching. Likewise, a number of the bishops who blare their views about moral behavior from the rooftops refused to come to grips with the immoral and dangerous behavior of these priests in their own churches. So, too, we wonder about the strict talk on morals or "virtues" coming from William Bennett when we read about his gambling practices, which seem anything but moral, strict, or steadfast. How can we believe these messages about "steadfast moral adherence" when the messengers repeatedly demonstrate the opposite?

Now, there is a place in the world for a prophet, a place for one who aches with the hurt of injustice and will not be silenced. We are served by those who echo the cry of the poor, those who sound the cry of a stressed environment, or who ask us to adhere to the highest standards of uncompromising truth. They pierce us with an arrow of righteousness, stimulating guilt and a motive to action. But in my experience, in real life, many prophetic calls of raging indignation ring hollow. Their sound is not pure. They sound a little off-key, strident, like the adolescent who rages against all authority but has only seen it from one side or the rich white guy who champions a color-blind society without really countenancing the unfairness of racial prejudice. Whether on the "left" or "right," these champions of adherence to (their!) cherished values seem to have some other agenda at work, some dissonance in their voice, as if all is not what it seems. Methinks the lady doth protest too much.

I don't think we think of these superrighteous people as people of integrity. Integrity is missing, not because there is no "moral code" but because there is no wholeness.

These people often oversimplify the world to cut it into convenient slices of truth. For example, religious adherents of various faiths would seem to wish or will that people of all other religious faiths will one day wake up and forsake their ways for the religious adherents' dogmatic truths. Why is that not colossal arrogance? Did these "prophets" bearing their high standards consider the depth of the others' faith and teachings before they championed their own? Not likely. So there is a one-sidedness, a lack of wholeness, about their picture. The same is true of the labor or management advocate who is absolutely *sure* what the other side needs to know and do differently without fully listening to the others' point of view and without fully challenging *his or her own* point of view.

Yet we don't have to go to political and religious extremes to see the limits of a view of integrity that rests solely on strict ethical or moral codes. Instead we will find, if we are honest, that what limits our integrity is *our* unwillingness to look at the *whole* world of truth out there and, perhaps even more, our unwillingness to look at the whole truth *within* ourselves. Just as some Christians vividly see the shortcomings of Jews, some Democrats ridicule the mistakes of Republicans, and kids indignantly uncover all their parents' faults, so also most of us see others' failure to adhere to high standards but fail to notice our own. The people I have known about whom I would say, "Now that person really has integrity," were people who saw the world broadly, and they viewed *themselves* from many angles and with courageous openness.

So, when I hear myself speaking righteously, when I start to get up some momentum with my talk of others' failings, and when I can feel some heat rising in my judgment, then it's probably a good time to see if *I'm* not feeling a little out of control. In the simplest case the mom who "can't believe what a mess your room is" might just be feeling like *she's* having a hard time keeping her life and all its responsibilities neat and clean. Or the dad on his soapbox about the importance of "discipline if you're ever going to accomplish anything" should perhaps get up from watching the Red Wings and finish that part of the landscaping project that bores him.

Often hyperrighteousness seems to mask our insecurities. It masks them from others. For instance, in an interview I once asked one of the most righteous politicians I had ever witnessed, "How do you know whether what you're saying is really on target and helpful for the political dialogue or whether you're just on your high horse?" I honestly did not mean it as an attack but as an inquiry to a person I considered quite thoughtful. He shot back, as with a .38 caliber, "Do *you* think I'm on my high horse?" The intense righteousness seemed to be part of an attitude of defensiveness. It worked with me; I wasn't about to answer that question. I laughed nervously, and the interview moved on.

The danger in our tendencies toward absolutes is that the world is largely *not* made up of absolutes. When we cast it that way, it usually means "We are right, and they are wrong." Such righteousness usually means two things. First, we have given up on our own improvement, for we are right! That's a dangerous place to be. Second, we are losing our grounds to work with others. For, when we make others wrong or bad, their natural defense is to block us out of their thinking, close themselves off from our opinions. We make ourselves into the Arabs against those Israelis, the Protestants who have nothing to learn from those Catholics, the religious who have nothing to learn from those sinners. We won't learn from them, and they assuredly won't learn from us.

So, when we lead, we walk a line when it comes to what is right. We must suggest it, declare it, set it up for others to react against. But it's dangerous when we too closely align ourselves with what's right and confuse ourselves with the ideals we are articulating. When we think we *are* the message, we have probably crossed a line, and we ought to go back and see how we got there and whether we left some of our true humanity behind.

# 6

# Authority

"Hey, who's in charge here?" The answer sets the context. For though we can lead—whether we have authority or not—the perceptions of authority will always affect leadership. And perceptions about authority are often loaded with emotion and expectation. To the child, the parent has all power. The adolescent's perception is that authority threatens. And those of us who have any amount of authority know that its powers are often exaggerated.

Watching my wife, close up and personal, has been replete with lessons about the limits of authority. She has been "checked and balanced" in our magnificent system by the legislature and judiciary (both in this case controlled by the opposing party). She has been checked again by factions within her party and the branch she ostensibly controls and balanced by collective bargaining agreements. And, perhaps most of all, she has been checked by a great array of public views and perceptions. So as this book goes to press she's in the middle of a campaign to win a second and final term. She wages that campaign like Odysseus, steering between the Scylla of all those who want to hold on to what they have and the Charybdis of those who demand change. It's a tight passage, and the currents never rest.

Meanwhile, Jennifer and I are attempting to sail our teenage daughters between the dangers of parental authoritarianism—which will block them from developing their own compasses and their own confidence—and parental permissiveness, which will expose them to greater risks than teens need encounter. Our authority, which seems supreme (and sometimes irrational!) to those children, seems closely circumscribed to us. Use too much and it backfires, too little and it could be tragic.

As authorities we have huge responsibilities. We keep the lights on, keep away outside attackers, keep people within from going at each other, and manage the present while anticipating a fast-approaching future. With such responsibilities come even more complex perceptions and expectations. We can't lead well without a good sense of how our authority gives us responsibility and power but also makes us vulnerable to a complex and often conflicting set of perceptions. Much of our leading comes when we have positions of authority, so it's good to see how authority plays into the leadership context.

## Having a Target on Your Back

"How did it go?" I asked my wife at the end of the day.

"Oh, my gosh," she said. "Never let me do that again!"

"Are you kidding? Was it really that bad?" I asked. She was pretty used to audiences that were riveted and appreciative.

"I couldn't believe these kids," she replied. "I know law is pretty boring stuff to them, but they were just so . . . rude. I didn't mind the ones who were falling asleep in their seats, but so many seemed, well, almost hostile."

Jennifer's experience in that auditorium of tenth graders was not unusual. They were hardly upset with the job she was doing as attorney general; she was simply an "authority figure." They didn't treat her a whole lot differently than they would any other adult. Indeed, if anything, the more "important" the authority the more they would have pushed the limit. Similarly, when a governor or mayor throws out the first pitch, it's all but guaranteed that boos will sound out from the crowd. When you have authority, you wear a target on your back.

In that school auditorium or on opening day at Comerica Park, the crowd creates a cloud of anonymity that lets individuals give voice to feelings they generally keep hidden from those in authority. They can vent their feelings and holler their irritation without having to explain it, be accountable for it, or face recrimination for it. Although it's seldom so vocally expressed, resistance to authority is universal. In classrooms, kids *whisper* their frustration with teachers. And workers, at the water cooler, at lunch, or after working hours, quietly grumble about the boss. I know that my kids tell their friends, "You won't believe what my dad did this time. . . ."

Step into the role of authority. Before you even start the hard work—enforcing bedtimes, administering a tight budget, assigning homework, and choosing sides when staffs offer competing solutions—you put on the suit with the target. We can trace it all back to the archetypal relationship at the root of all other relationships of authority and power: the parent-child relationship. Every worker or team member or constituent was affected by parent(s) who made questionable judgments and used their power in more or less arbitrary ways. Consequently, who among us did not think, utter, declare (or hear a sibling cry out) in rage at a parent: "I hate you!" And who does not carry forward conscious and unconscious frustration and skepticism toward those in control? Authority engenders deep feelings.

In Michigan, as GM aggressively negotiates with the UAW (and its suppliers, dealers, and others), workers wonder, "Why do they hate us?" They point to the severity of the proposed cuts, and they complain that they have already negotiated concessions. They are not stupid; they understand that GM is losing money, that foreign competition is fierce, and that there is overcapacity that must be addressed through *some* layoffs. But a fundamental mistrust of authorities is also fueling their discontent. Their mistrust is part of a long story, and they bolster this feeling with plenty of evidence. Their parents, teachers, bosses, and GM itself have had to make good but tough decisions that have affected them badly. Then, too, there have been times when these authorities have undermined the legitimacy of their authority—for instance, acting unethically or communicating poorly. Some of the evidence of untrustworthiness is objective and credible, and some is just the accumulated disappointment with the tough decisions of authority. And, because authority evokes deep, irrational resistance, GM will fairly or unfairly wear the target.

Here's how an upstart business magazine took aim. On the cover of its August 2001 issue, the editors of *Fast Company* challenged: "Raise Your Hand If Your CEO Gets It." This screamer was accompanied by a picture of a blue-suited CEO with his hand high, flanked by six others with their hands at their sides and expressions that said, "I can't believe he's so out of touch." The story inside outlined the ways in which CEOs are unaware of the strengths and weaknesses within their own companies.

The analysis was solid. Some CEOs really are badly out of touch. But the cover story underscores the point: resistance is unavoidable. Every parent, teacher, supervisor, manager, or CEO alive, *no matter what they do or how well they do it,* will generate dissension and resistance. Those we lead think we "don't get it," even while they are pretending to be playing along with us. Sometimes it's visible and workable; sometimes it's a cowardly voice you can never address, like a bad song you just can't seem to get out of your head. But make no mistake: the resistance is always there.

## Using Your Authority—Not Letting Yourself Get Used

We can lead with or without authority—as mayor or citizen, as manager or employee, as teacher or student. In either case, when we lead we are usually seeking change—change that will allow others to work and live better. Those with authority have a title or have been elected or have legal authority. Leaders with authority also have the advantage of tools at their disposal: they have carrots, sticks, and often control of some space and the pace with which things are to be addressed.

On the other hand, as we have just seen, authority makes its holder a target and evokes in others deep feelings, including resentment and anger. If authority is a target for arrows of steady resentment and outbursts as strong as rage, more often it is a target for manipulation. One of the tricks of *leading with authority* is that groups have an uncanny ability to get *you* to do *their* work.

I was asked to speak to a group of students at one of our state universities. They were in a special leadership program, a part of which was the study of leadership theory. I was geeked up to engage these young adults and hear what they were thinking. So within the first few minutes I asked them excitedly, "Who do you like? What thinkers or books have captured your interest?" As I did, a tiny nagging voice within me said, "Geez, I hope it's something I'm familiar with since I'm supposed to be some kind of expert here." Not to worry, for they stared back at me, rather blankly, and then they stared back at me some more, still blankly—as if it were my turn to talk. And then they stared back at me some more.

The game of the leader with authority—in this case, the visiting "learned" speaker—could often be called the game of "turn the tables." The easiest thing to do would have been to plow ahead. I could have shifted into, "Here's my favorite author." I'd have looked smart. They would have been relieved. And, best of all, I wouldn't have those blank faces looking at me! Instead, I had to turn the tables. If I could fight through the painful silence, I could give them a fantastic opportunity to test their own thinking, to express themselves and try on the ideas they had been learning. They could walk away with pride and remember offering their thoughts about leadership to two professors, the program administrator, and the governor's husband. I offered a few more specific questions to jump-start them, but I also used my authority and a lot of self-discipline to *not* speak, thus forcing them to do the work that I could not do for them.

So how do you use your authority and not let them turn the tables on you? When you recognize them trying to use or manipulate you, you might consider these strategies:

- Know you're being played. Cultivate the awareness of how those you lead want you to do their work.
- Realize that leadership is not about *your* success but theirs. To be really successful you want to build their capacity to learn and resolve issues. Although they are trying to manipulate you, and will unconsciously play on your feeling that you're supposed to figure everything out, in the long run your job is about *their* fighting through *their* fears, not you trying to meet their every need.
- Give them a little help but recognize that you're doing it. In some measure the more you help the more you are undermining your goal: their success, expertise, thinking, and so on. It may take multiple efforts; you may have to assist, but by all means keep giving the work back.

- Realize that you're asking people to take risks, to step out of the safety of dependence and passivity. So emphasize that risk taking is a great thing (e.g., that it takes courage to speak first in class, or to come to a resolution on a tough issue with a coworker in which you fear you may be the one giving far too much).
- Recognize that this is an art. You are pushing them to "grow up," yet you are simultaneously helping them along. Even though you may feel frustrated with them—and even a little angry—your success is tied to your positive belief that they can rise to the task.

If you struggle with this balancing act, you are surely not alone. Year in and year out, one of the most requested *Harvard Business Review* article reprints is one entitled "Management Time: Who's Got the Monkey?" by William Oncken Jr. and Donald Wass.[1] It was first published in 1974, and the authors argued compellingly that managers often walk into meetings or discussions with staff and walk out with "monkeys on their backs." Managers accept the work that rightfully should be done by their teams. Oncken and Wass advise: don't accept the monkey! Let your team figure out what it needs to figure out and ensure that you are doing the work that only you can do.

How often do you accept monkeys? Do those you lead get you to do their work? Do you wonder, "Whose work is this anyway?" Do you maintain your belief in them, even when their passivity is driving you nuts?

Use your authority to turn the tables in order to generate work, build confidence, and develop skill within your teams.


## You're Wearing a Suit

Through Brian Mulroney, former prime minister of Canada, I bring you a subtle but powerful idea that could widen the paths of your leadership. The context will take a moment to set.

I have watched how my wife, as governor of Michigan, is like a kind of magnet, attracting people's deep feelings about many things. It's as if she wears a suit (adorned with a target, of course) that attracts many strong feelings. In this suit people see her variously as a representative of women, Democrats, politicians, authorities, and any number of other categories about which they have strong feelings. Most important, she represents Michigan itself. Every Michiganian has powerful, sometimes irrational, and often unconscious feelings about our economy, schools, environment, past, and future. And they connect these to her. So people are attracted, almost magnetically, and they approach her with letters, phone calls, and in person to share their joy, hope, anger, frustration, pride, and worry about all that she seems to represent. Now take that up one giant step.

In June 2004, Jennifer and I occupied a remarkable position in the west balcony of the National Cathedral for the state funeral of President Ronald Reagan. On this occasion *others* were wearing the suit. Before the ceremony began, it was Jennifer and I who were drawn from our balcony seats to the floor by those magnetic forces to shake the hands of Presidents Carter, Ford, and Clinton and their wives. (The Bushes had not yet arrived.) Each wore suits threaded with the fibers of hundreds of stories of hopes, expectations, regrets, and triumphs that Jennifer, I, and all of America saw in them.

During the memorial service, Prime Minister Mulroney remembered President Reagan. He said, "I always thought that President Reagan's understanding of the nobility of the presidency coincided with that American dream." He then spoke of what François Mitterrand had said to him about President Reagan.

> "Il a vraiment la notion de l'etat." Rough translation: "He really has a sense of the State about him." The translation does not fully capture the profundity of the observation: What President Mitterrand meant was that there is a vast difference between the job of President and the role of President. . . . [N]o one could more eloquently summon his nation to high purpose or bring forth the majesty of the presidency and make it glow, better than the man who saw his country as a city on a hill.[2]

So you and I are not the governor, let alone the president. Still, the lesson applies to us: there is a vast difference between our job and our role. You do a job but wear a suit. People see their authorities— parent, priest, rabbi, imam, teacher, boss, shop steward, as well as

CEO or mayor—as so much more than people doing a job. And it is what you do in relationship to the role, the suit—and the complex expectations around it—that matters as much as or much more than execution of the job.

As a parent you feed your children, put them to bed, save for college. That's the job. But the role, or suit, is so much more. Do you bring "forth the majesty" in the role of parent? Do you "glow" in your role as parent or in the role of child caring for an aging parent? Do you imagine your family as a "shining city on a hill?" People long for such a vision of greatness. As head of a work unit or a labor local, what's the suit you wear for it? Do your people feel you're with them, proud of them, that you wear their jersey? As a school principal it's not just smooth schedules and instructional insight but pride in the place and the possibility of the people. Do you beam at what you see they can be?

President Reagan loved the suit. Prime Minister Mulroney's assessment was brilliant. Reagan wore not just the suit of the presidency. He always seemed to know that he was wearing the suit of America. As you wear the suit of boss, parent, or teacher, try to remember that to others you're wearing the suit of the team, or of the family, or of the classroom of kids they care deeply about. It's *their* suit! Wear it well.

> It is what you do in relationship to the role, the suit—and the complex expectations around it—that matters as much or much more than execution of the job.

## Catch-22: Opposing Your Own System

The suit of authority is, of course, not an enchanted robe. We kid ourselves when we think—and we do—that people in positions of authority can wave their magic wands to solve our problems. They face resistance and are manipulated to do the work of the group. In addition, they face the forces of inertia and tradition and just the weight of routine that plagues all organizations. The demands on your authority that come with your position can box you in.

In my first job out of college I taught at Tampa Jesuit High School, a college preparatory school much like the one that had prepared me well. What I saw early on was that many of the boys in my class were just not ready to work hard. So they got homework and quizzes back from me, and with red pen blazing I sought to wake them from their adolescent slumber. Results: minimal. So at the end of the first quarter I seized the major tool at my disposal, and I blasted about 15 of my 140 students with Ds and even a couple of Fs. I would not have described it this way at the time, but what I was doing was using my authority to leverage work.

What I could not have predicted or expected is that I had unleashed other forces. Remember the Oncken article about how workers try to put the monkey of work on your back? Well these monkeys were the flying variety, and they were all landing on my back. It seems that everyone thought *I* was the one with the problem. Parents were challenging me. Students were working harder at recalculating their averages than they had worked on any assignment I had given. Fellow teachers were raising their eyebrows and turning up their grins, as if to say, "I was young and idealistic once, too; you'll relax and lower expectations." Most surprising to me was the principal asking me in to his office (the first time he had all year) to figure out what I was up to. He never told me—in so many words—to relax my standards, but he focused on my behavior and not on the kids' work habits or how to light a fire beneath their academic behinds. The authority I had was legal, and I used it, but a more powerful force of *culture* was at play. While I was pushing for more and better work, the system was pushing me to relax and play along. I was learning how hard it is to bring about change.

While many authorized *leaders* hope to stimulate change, they face systems and structures that work to slow them at every turn. These obstacles to those who lead from positions of authority were identified in a book appropriately entitled *Why Leaders Can't Lead*, written by Warren G. Bennis in 1989. After ten months serving as president of the University of Southern California, Bennis says he found himself at his desk at about four in the morning and realized that he had been doing a thousand tasks but had yet to even begin the work of change that had drawn him to accept the post. In describing this frustrating moment, he coined his first Law of Academic Pseudodynamics: "Routine work drives out non-routine work and smothers to death all creative planning, all fundamental change in the university—or any institution."[3]

On the most basic level, every organizational head I know has routine demands that would fill about three times his or her working day. The systems conspire, seemingly in a benign way, to keep leaders from getting to the bigger picture. And sometimes the institution itself—a university, a department, a company, or even a family—was built for circumstances that no longer exist. What I mean by this is that the market may have fundamentally changed, the skills of labor changed, the competition changed, or the children grown in such a way that their risks and challenges are altogether different than what they once were. In other words, the authority—the head—has the prime responsibility for running the organization, but the organization is set up for a world that quite literally doesn't exist, so that continuing to run it "as usual" is to allow it to malfunction or die.

Here are a few simple examples. Our unions were built to check unbridled corporate power, yet today the larger problem in manufacturing is not the company bosses but the lack of effectiveness in facing the challenge from global competitors and the reduction of jobs due to robotics and technology. Likewise, our schools were built when 90 percent of their students lived on farms. The agrarian calendar persists despite the fact that today only 1 percent of students live on farms. Even when union and school leaders see the need to change and *want* to change, the pressure on them is enormous to conserve and protect. As Machiavelli wrote five hundred years ago: "There is nothing more perilous to conduct or more uncertain in its success, than to take the lead in a new order of things. Because the innovator has for enemies all those who have done well under the old conditions, and lukewarm defenders in those who may do well in the future."[4]

The pressure on authorities to preserve their present systems—even dysfunctional systems—is clear even at the family level. Anyone who has been through it knows how difficult it is for adult children to begin conversations that will lead an elderly parent to accept that he or she can no longer live alone. Avoidance can go on for years—despite enormous risks and costs. And at the other end of the spectrum parents know how easy it is to avoid the difficult teenage questions about drugs, alcohol, sex, and relationships. How easily the old "routine work"—preparing the meals, paying the bills, and getting to games—pushes out the critical work of leading young people into a whole new world in which they will live.

Every status quo is by definition a response to prior conditions. So the authority inherits a system set up for yesterday, with enormous pressure to continue it today, and is thus handcuffed to lead into tomorrow. The bottom line is that leaders are heavily pressured to be conservers and protectors while they may need to be revolutionaries! They may need to break the very system that brought them to power and expects their protection.

Leading from a position of authority requires skepticism about the role and the power and sometimes the adulation that comes with them. Persons in authority would do well to regularly ask themselves to what degree their groups are causing them to protect people, procedures, practices, or programs that they should instead be challenging? Leaders almost need to set themselves against all that they are there to protect and to maintain a critical eye on the hard systems and soft habits that were built for a different time. The practice of asking why to maintain ethical practice becomes useful here to examine organizational habits.

Why are we doing that?

*Well, we always have.*

But why did we start?

Why do we still do it?

Why can't we change?

Leading with authority requires a fierce commitment to viewing reality as it is, paying attention to facts that some might want to ignore: the kids are not calling home as we had agreed they would, Wal-Mart is not competing with us the way Sears did, or we are going to have a raft of retirements in the next five years. Paying attention to realities may require that we make changes necessary to stay vital.

As leaders gain greater awareness of how they may need to oppose the very systems they are supposed to uphold, an interesting

131

question arises: "How can I use and maintain the power the system is giving me while fighting the system I am expected to protect?" The tools of authority allow leaders to turn the system toward its difficult work of renewal. For instance, by continually drawing attention to the vision of success, leaders can persuade people to determine whether current practices are supporting attainment of that vision. Likewise, by using the ability to communicate successes, a leader can point people toward ways in which the system can adapt that are necessary for its long-term success.

In short, groups expect authorities to protect them—even from the hard work that those groups must perform if they are to survive and thrive. So leaders must suspect the groups they are supposed to protect and continually challenge the systems and structures that were built to do the work. Leading with authority is much more difficult than telling folks what to do and doing what your predecessor did.

## How Your Authority Can Attack You from Within

There is yet another way in which authority is less easy to wield than it appears. The actions of William Bennett, Rush Limbaugh, and President Bill Clinton invite us to explore how this is so. For their excesses seem closely linked to the authority they possessed. Although they are wildly high profile, their public behavior still has lessons for regular folks who gain authority, status, and power in organizations. You've followed their stories—how could you not in the mass media culture that loves heroes almost as much as it loves to see heroes crash. Bennett reportedly lost eight million dollars on slot machine gambling, Limbaugh became addicted to and illegally purchased prescription painkillers, and the former president had his infamous affair(s). They are, of course, a thimbleful in an ocean of public figures whose personal behavioral storms left a wake of hurt, confusion, and pain. Examples like these cause you to wonder:

- Why is it that those afflicted with this ambition for power seem totally unsatisfied with rather huge amounts of attention but instead drive on for further excitement, thrills, and power, whether through sex, gambling, or drug-induced highs?

- Why, in particular, do the "righteous" people seem to end up betraying their own talk? President Clinton inspired and uplifted his followers generally and was and is a great advocate for women. Limbaugh and Bennett are two of our culture's most notorious champions of the Right, speaking frequently of morality and virtue. How, then, do we explain the behavior of these men? Are they doing their highly public preaching in some measure as a way to try to tame their own private demons?
- Do they gradually become inflated in self-importance and think they are the authors of the laws they are enunciating and somehow not necessarily subject to those laws? Their behavior certainly recalls the myths of ancient Greek heroes and gods. When mere mortals would begin to talk and act with hubris, the so-human Greek gods would inevitably become jealous and rain down a sentence of shame and infamy.[5]

Bill, Rush, and Bill—I use their first names to emphasize that these are human beings just as we are—may seem distant from and irrelevant to your leadership experience. But on one level they are simply people with authority. In the previous chapter I wrote about doing the right thing generally in the world of leadership. But let me emphasize here the ways in which *authority* plays into those questions.

First, just as I have discussed gauges of energy in other contexts, it is worth thinking about a similar gauge here. This gauge would measure the energy flow between the authority and the followers. Around authority figures energy rises. Anyone who has approached a judge at the bench, a bishop in his or her robes, a senator, or a president has *felt* the energy that comes with authority.[6] This energy can electrify others—in good and bad ways—charging them into action. But it seems that the energy does not merely point outward, as if the authority figure is a neutral entity that does not *conduct* any of this energy. In fact it courses through him or her.

Take positive and negative examples. When a school board president fields an hour and a half of angry citizen comments on the board's decision to close a local school, that board president will leave feeling like he or she has been hooked up to thousands of kilowatts of energy. Conversely, at times when I have spoken and tapped people's hopes and indignation, had them excited and appreciative, I know I can physically feel the energy. And the sensation after such an experience speaking is that you want or need to be reconnected or become grounded again. There is just too much random energy going through you.

These are "live" examples. But anyone who has had authority knows that pressure (which is another form of energy) comes with it. Anyone who has had a baby has some sense of, "Wow, I'm now really responsible for something more than me! A child's life is depending on me." Business owners who have had to lay people off know the pressure of others' livelihoods depending on their decisions. And people who have led others—through pressure and uncertainty—to great success in business, politics, sports, or other fields know that the energy the leader conducts is intense, stressful, and yet for some quite addictive. When I read about a CEO arrested for driving 140 miles per hour or a politician involved in an extramarital affair, I am slow to judge, because I expect that the pressure such people are conducting may be more than I can possibly imagine. And who are any of us to judge others' resilience, vulnerability, or makeup? I am not saying we should condone the act, but we should appreciate the pressures around authority that generate these sideshows.

Knowing that authority tends to bring this intensification of power, we need to be honest about a second fact. The conferral of authority, and with it some power, fame, or wealth, almost always brings privilege and separation. The three high-profile men mentioned earlier had, of course, extraordinary privileges, and a zone of protection was erected by those closest to them. They had aides, dark limousines, private planes—the ability to be physically secreted away. Likewise pedophiliac Catholic priests and abusive CEOs have been insulated by those around them. They were given leeway because of their authority—privilege and separation—to do as they wished in their worlds. Although you might not think so, it's similar for anyone elevated to a position of power. Even a first-line supervisor gains new privileges and esteem; he or she has access to information and people and money. And perhaps the most significant privilege of nearly anyone with authority is some significant ability to be exempt from questions, to be allowed separation, and to be given deference.

In even the very best organizational cultures I've seen, it seems that the taboo against going into your parents' dresser drawers has carried over into a taboo against questioning your boss's judgment. You might question facts, or even interpretations, but not the boss's judgment and certainly not issues related to his or her character or personal behavior. In the rare instances when those questions are raised, people at the staff table gasp in disbelief. Those questions get people fired. Sometimes kids have the guts to question a parent's judgment or personal behavior—generally after the young person has become thoroughly fed up with being dominated by the parent. As I suggested in the last chapter, parents are inclined to strike back, sometimes physically, or in a much less evil way, with such words as, "Who do you think you are? What right do you have to question me, young lady? I should . . . Don't you *ever* in your life say such a thing to me." Such responses erect a wall of protection.

Those in authority are especially insulated from questions about things in their private spheres, including their potentially disastrous personal judgments. It is difficult enough to raise tough issues with a sibling, a peer, or even a child; we are *highly* unlikely to challenge a "superior." Yet our human frailties follow us up the authority ladder, don't they? Indeed, as I have suggested, the pressures of authority can make us more susceptible to lapses in judgment and the attractions of alcohol, fast driving, a comforting or exciting person outside our marriage, or some other downfall. These lapses are not exclusively caused by the responsibility of raising children or having a city's or company's welfare depend on our decisions, but authority certainly heightens pressure . . . even as it insulates us from help.

One of the toughest things for managers, and it gets worse as they climb the hierarchy, is that they lose peers along the way. They feel uncomfortable treating those who now report to them in the same way as when they were peers. They feel guarded when it comes to confiding in peers, not wanting to look vulnerable or disclose confidential information. And as they rise there is an expectation that they will be more and more capable of handling pressure and will be under control all the time. Where is the release valve for the pressure? Home? Friends? Often not.

The reality of executive leadership in the early twenty-first century doesn't lead to a very optimistic answer about help at home. For the sheer workload, and often the extraordinary travel demands, will weigh heavily on home and friends. A spouse or significant other may have plenty of feelings of sadness or even anger at the sacrifices he or she is required to make to support a partner's career. Instead of getting support, the busy executive gets more grief. And the effect is to further isolate the authority. Now he or she is conducting even more currents of energy. Somehow it becomes critical to offload some of this tension.

So authority can be difficult to wield because it can generate great pressure inside. The pressure combined with the privilege of isolation can put a person at great risk. When we lead with authority we would do well to choose not to allow the isolation but instead to encourage candor with those close to us. Recognize that you are operating amid social expectations that will make others very hesitant to approach you, especially about issues in any way personal. And, as I suggested in chapter 4 and will return to in the final chapter, retaining an executive coach may be the best investment ever made for those in high-pressure work.

## See the Authority You Have

I have touched on some of the pitfalls of authority—the ways leaders are hemmed in and the internal pressures and risks authority generates. I have done so because, in general, both authorized leaders and their followers are naive about what the mantle of authority brings with it and expect leadership to be much easier than it is. But, of course, authority does create plenty of opportunities, too. I am at heart a 1970s egalitarian who has always believed that anyone can lead. I have often felt that authority can be a distraction and deterrent to maximizing the group's work. One consequence of this egalitarian bias is that I have been slow to see how authority creates opportunity. I offer a simple story, especially for others of like mind.

As I began to think that I would run the *Detroit Free Press* Marathon, I wondered how I could use my running for some good. I thought maybe I could help promote the marathon itself, and I also wanted to promote Think Detroit, a nonprofit organization that "builds character in young people through sports and leadership development." One day I noticed on the marathon Web site that the race had partner charities, and I thought it would be great if Think Detroit could gain that prominent status. So I tried to reach Patricia Ball, the director of the marathon, to see if I could assist in her efforts and also to see if she could help promote Think Detroit. I left her a bumbling message about how I was married to the governor, was going to run the marathon, and would love to speak with her.

She called and left me a bumbling message in reply. The next day we connected. We talked for fifteen minutes about Think Detroit, marathon training, and our shared passion for the revival of the city of Detroit. It was a nervous call. It reminded me of being fourteen and calling a girl for the first time, but it had nothing to do with gender stuff. It had everything to do with authority. You see, I was pretty surprised that Pat had any time for me or any interest in what I had to say about the marathon. She was the expert, the marathoner, the race director, the big cheese. I was a little nervous about imposing on someone that important, and I was taken off guard by her enthusiasm about collaborating with me.

What I found out later is that Pat had wanted to contact me when she heard that the governor's husband was going to run the marathon, but she didn't want to bother someone who was that important. She didn't want to impose on my position. So the nervousness I felt was fueled by the nervousness she felt. I have seen such peculiar, mutual nervousness when Jennifer has met someone like Ahmad Rashad or Aretha Franklin or Bill Gates, and in those cases the nervousness generally seemed mutual. People used to being invested with a little (or a lot) of fame and authority in *their* domain feel quite small with someone who has authority from some other sphere.

I learned from my experience with Pat Ball that I really did have some authority, which to some readers may seem obvious. To me, it wasn't. I have had that experience many times with people whom I initially hesitated to contact or challenge. The fact is that *many* of us—if not all—have more authority to open doors than we think. A parent has inbuilt authority to address a child's school. A line supervisor has authority to speak to a CEO about what is happening in a company—at the most important point of all—where the product or service meets the customer. A citizen has the authority to submit a letter to the editor.

The point is that we fail to lead sometimes because we think we do not have the *authority*. But that is often no more than a self-perception. The fundamental right to lead—our essential authority—flows from our humanity, yet it can often be strengthened from worldly authority that we have and that we underestimate. Many of us have a kind of unused capital, an authorization that we need to draw down—as citizens, taxpayers, students, customers, and even spouses. If you go to the *Detroit Free Press* Marathon Web site and click on "Run for a Reason," the first charity you will find is Think Detroit. Sometimes you just have to pick up the phone and see whether you can get through.

## Truth Is: We're All Leading from the Middle

Pat Ball, the marathon director, and I got over our hesitance about using the authority that came with our respective roles. One day we gathered in the *Free Press* offices to talk about how we could combine our efforts to achieve our vision of a great marathon. I found that Pat was aptly named, for she was a five-foot-tall ball of energy, full of enthusiasm, ideas, and, as I would find out, humor, too.

Mike from Think Detroit asked her how fast a local celebrity runner was, and she said, "Oh, he's not fast at all." Now you have to understand that Pat spends a lot of time courting, following, and promoting the elite runners who move at incredible speeds—you know, these men and women will pound out twenty-six straight five-minute miles. Mike smiled and said to Pat, "I just wanted to make sure Dan [that would be me] could keep up with him." Pat clarified about the celeb: "Oh, he only runs a at nine-minute-per-mile pace." Just as she was saying it, she and I shared a look of hope: she was hoping that I was fast, and I was hoping she would say something like "The guy runs a twelve-minute pace." So our look of shared hope quickly turned to one of mutual embarrassment, as it was now my turn to come clean. Drawing on my small supplies of humility and self-deprecating humor, I said, "I'm hoping to tear the course up at a . . . well, a nine-minute pace." The truth was out, and I had to accept it: I'm slow!

Actually, Pat's comment helped me accept that I'm stunningly average. During that summer I had run a couple of timed races, and I checked out the results. In my first half marathon I finished 126th out of 170 in my age group. And in a race on Mackinac Island I was 15th out of 29—the perfect midpoint. With Jennifer as governor I had been learning that you can lead from behind. Now it seemed I was learning another valuable life lesson: you can lead from the middle, too!

The truth is: the middle is where most of us find ourselves all the time. As I suggested at the beginning of this chapter, even a powerful governor like my wife is more accurately seen as in the middle than on top. Everything she does to lead occurs in a milieu in which she is pressed by the legislature, the opposing party, the media, and even competing thinkers and advisers in her own circle (including her husband and kids). Although she has some genuine clout, she is—among these competing constituencies, values, and power sources—leading from the middle. Sometimes a president can leverage his authority to push through a war effort. Just as often, he has to wage his own insurgency to secure, for example, reform of social security. He knows he can't declare it; he must marshal a thousand allies about him to get it done.

Often we in the middle act as though leadership must come from the top, despite observing that those at the top are waging *grassroots* mobilizations to support their efforts to achieve change. And so we miss opportunities. Many who begin to move up the corporate or political ladder spend far too much time wondering how they'll climb *higher*. And, busy with our moves to *increase* our authority, we miss opportunities to lead with the authority we have.

From the time we were children, we avoided full responsibility by hiding from our parents, blaming our teachers, or occasionally angrily defying the system. It is exciting to watch a great community organizer who is able to mobilize opposition against those in power but has the negotiating skills to know that authorities are protecting genuine interests. A great organizer helps the authorized leader to save face. Such an organizer is not naive about authority. Indeed, he or she sees that authorities rule from the middle; the organizer needs to tip the balance, not tip the whole thing over.

Some seem never to realize that they may be in the middle of the pack yet they still have the ability to be on top of their game. It is more challenging and fruitful to lead from where we are than to grouse about where we're not. In the end, in one way or another, we are all in the middle.

So, as I write this, it is unclear whether Jennifer will be reelected to her position of considerable authority. Perhaps she will find herself where former senator Tom Daschle was in early 2005, when he joked that it took him a few minutes sitting in the backseat of his car to realize that there was no longer anyone to drive him and he had better get behind the wheel to make it happen. Authority is temporary, increasingly so in our political and business worlds. It behooves those who have it to use it, as a way to lead from that middle that appears to others as the top.

One more point should be obvious to those who lead most frequently from the top. The challenge, when your own authority will always be checked and balanced—and when the bureaucracy may well outlive you—is to get the masses in the middle to realize that the organization will move forward only to the degree that *they* feel empowered to lead. James Kouzes and Barry Posner brilliantly observed that "credible leaders accept and act upon the paradox of power: we become most powerful when we give our own power away."[7]

Great authorities lead from the middle, even as they empower those around them to lead as though *they* are at the top.

## Acknowledging the Middle, the Source of Your Power

I have tried to show in this chapter how authority is not what it appears. Authority unleashes both internal and external pressures that threaten and box it in. In our culture, almost in spite of ourselves, we focus on authority—on the extraordinary individual. I have watched Jennifer experience this as governor (and from afar viewed Governor Arnold Schwarzenegger experience the same). There was a time when she could do no wrong, and was viewed as a kind of savior, with astronomical approval ratings. Then, as our economy struggled with changes that were historic and global—as our unemployment rate rose to the highest level in the country—the latent, long-quiet skepticism about authority erupted to the surface. And skeptics who spoke for that restless public, which so desperately wanted quick and effective answers, zeroed in on Jennifer's vulnerabilities.

The truth is that those in authority are locked in a strange dance with those they manage. Parents have significant control, but, in ways their children can't perceive, the parents also follow the children's lead or else they lose influence and control. Pastors preach from the pulpit, but they also depend heavily on volunteers and are vulnerable to those who vote with their feet, emptying pews and collection baskets. Authority works best when it constantly gauges others' commitment and involves them in supervising the effort. It would be hard to underestimate the interdependence of authority and those subject to it. So let me return to the story of my first marathon to close this chapter.

A marathon surely seems like a solitary or individual experience: there's just the runner on his or her own, right? Only two feet can fit in those shoes. But for me, and for many other runners I've compared notes with, this is a huge misconception. In the lead-up to the race, I had shamelessly exploited my position as first gentleman to call attention to my marathon effort. I seized on the marathon and my position to take every chance to show how I was being a role model for healthy living, reflection and re-creation, goal setting, focus, and discipline. If you had heard me on the radio or at a speech, you would have thought I was—and considered myself—some solitary American hero. The truth, as you will see, is that I was anything but *the* leader, and people on the sides, at the back, and in the middle led me throughout.

First, Suzanne and Mike Thomashow became my mentors. My first marathon was their eighth and sixth, respectively, and they are both on the verge of qualifying for the biggie, the Boston Marathon. For months, they encouraged me, repeatedly telling me in exactly these words, "You're gonna do it." They said it in a way that made me believe it. They also taught me a hundred little things to build me up—literally and figuratively—from Web sites on running to blister care to Gu (the high-energy gel that helps you keep from "hitting the dreaded wall"). They, like most who lead from the middle, held no formal leadership positions; instead, they were simply powerful and proactive peers. Mike and Sue's leadership of me prompts this question of you: how often do you tell your junior colleagues, younger siblings, teammates, or spouse, *"You're gonna do it"*? In great workplace cultures, people don't get praise only from the top; instead praise is generated throughout the culture.

The second way in which I was not alone is that my family and others on the course pulled me through. My wife and daughters ran the last 2.2 miles and told me, "You're looking strong, Keep it up, You're gonna make it." Twice on the course a woman—I couldn't see her either time—yelled, "Go, first gentleman, the Y loves you." If you're reading this, dear woman: Thanks! Lots of other voices, faces, and signs picked me up. My kids and the woman from the YMCA were "leading up." They were supporting someone of some stature, someone you would think would not *need* encouragement. Their participation and support cause me to ask: how often do you say the simple words of encouragement that will not receive even a word of thanks but may help someone—even an authority who shouldn't *need* your help—attack a problem with renewed energy, find patience with his or her kid, or just take a deep breath? Most great executives I have known are frequently led by an executive assistant who continually watches out for them.

On race day, Suzanne and I laid down the first ten utterly joyful miles. The race start was a predawn thrill of humanity. Corktown, where the Irish settled, and Mexicantown, with the smell of fresh tortillas, came alive around us. The Ambassador Bridge, on which we crossed to Canada, offered up an exquisite Sunday morning sunrise. And the three miles along the Detroit River in Windsor, Ontario, were peaceful and gorgeous. Just past halfway, Suzanne and I split—a normal marathon move in which one partner moves ahead while the other keeps the pace. Just about that time, Mike Tenbusch, the extraordinary CEO of Think Detroit, joined me with the four Kendle girls, two sets of identical fifteen-year-old twins who play soccer for Think Detroit. Their kindness buoyed me. The girls dropped off as planned after a mile or two, but Mike stayed with me.

Mike stayed with me. And, stayed . . . until at mile seventeen, I said, "Mike what's your plan?" He said, "Well I had been planning to run a mile and then join you at mile twenty-two, but if you want me to I can hang with you." "Really? You would? That would be great!" I quickly said. Mike had planned to run four one-mile stints. He ran almost thirteen miles—solid! It wasn't until that evening that I realized he was probably less well trained for that distance, and more exhausted, than I. For fifteen years, I have been Mike's mentor, yet on this day he carried me for almost thirteen miles; I fed off his every tip or word of encouragement. At one point, when he heard me groan as I missed grabbing a cup of water while coming out of a water station, he circled back to grab a glass for me, doubling his pace to catch back up. He was the embodiment of servant leadership.

Finally, there was a job of leadership equal to Mike's, and that was the work of Cornelius, Marvin, Jason, Sylvester, Will, and DeDe—more Think Detroit youngsters—who came in with their soccer coach, Tim, at mile 20, where "the real marathon begins," as fatigue creeps into every cell. They were to run a mile. They ran 6.2. Tim arranged them like geese. They ran in a V formation, breaking the wind and drafting me like Lance Armstrong's teammates pulling him through the Pyrenees. They grabbed an extra cup of water through aid stations. They lightened the mood by joking about how peppy they would not be in their soccer game that afternoon. They slowed down when their speed was discouraging me, and they happily sped up on the rare occasions when I asked them to pick up the pace.

Those eager kids remind me of the tens, if not hundreds, who work for my wife (and so many others I see supporting their "top dog"). They stand up front and break the wind, taking the shots from angry constituents or customers. They ask people to do more with less and lead by example. They are delighted to serve close to the governor (or president, coach, rabbi, etc.), and so they constantly generate energy and enthusiasm for the boss. They work into the night, neither for more pay nor expecting special thanks. They laugh with each other when they wonder why they're doing what they're doing. And they do a million simple things, like the kids who brought me a glass of water when I was flat out empty. In other words, they lead—from the middle.

Now I had to finish that race; no one could do it for me. In the same way, leaders in authority do some things that no one else in the gaggle can do. But, when those around them work like my "geese" did, then the authority can truly give his or her very best. The authority may take the bow, make the announcement, decide on the strategic plan, give the sermon, or cut the ribbon, but the members of the team and a humble authority know where the power was stored and how it was expended. So I acknowledge my leaders—Mike, Tim, the Kendle girls, my wife and girls, and the soccer geese—and encourage you to acknowledge and exult in the people who often lead your flight.

In the end, authority is conferred by the group. The better we keep their interests at the forefront, the more they will both work for us and allow themselves to be led by us. When we think our authority and power are of our own creation, and that others are there to serve our needs, then it is sure that our downfall will follow; it is only a matter of time.

# 7

# Inclusion

AUTHORITY GIVES US THE OPPORTUNITY to grab people's attention, and authority comes with conditions and at a price. When there is authority, there are always boundaries. So our authority may exist within a building or inside the lines of a division in a company, a city, or a family. Those boundaries mean that people within them will see themselves in a special way, differently than outsiders do. And often, even within the boundaries, there will be insiders and outsiders.

Great leaders become expert at helping groups to be inclusive. Those who include as they lead tap whole new sources of ideas, energy, and goodness. They give new life to those who feel marginalized, and by including individuals they build the organization's strength and capacity. The concept of inclusion has become popular, especially within "diversity" work, which is being done in companies and other organizations across the country and around the world. Sometimes people equate inclusion and diversity with categories such as race and gender. The following readings are informed by and touch upon those aspects of inclusion. But they also reach beneath and well beyond race and gender. In many, many ways, leaders vigilantly work to include.

## The Nature of Group Pressure

Sometimes we are too caught up in the color and specifics and personalities in our businesses and institutions. We think our situations and our groups are different from everyone else's. We don't realize that common patterns are stamped out over and over again when people form working groups. So consider a simple organization, stripped down to its basics. We'll give it two founders, call them John and Mary, who come together with some shared values, interests, and ideas. Things go pretty well, and so they decide to expand. They bring in a new person, Kathy. This figure illustrates the basic dynamics that are already present. Even in this simple system, we can see the (oft-dreaded) triangle. Kathy finds herself somehow an outsider, at times, to the founders. On the other hand, with no detail added but gender, we can also see that John may be the proverbial "third wheel," as there may be ways in which Mary and Kathy align. Or perhaps Mary is pushed out by John and Kathy.

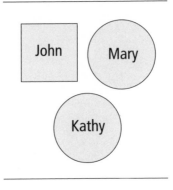

Where there was one relationship between John and Mary, you can now count six different configurations of relationships.[1] But all is going reasonably well, indeed so well that John and Mary decide to grow yet again and now add a fourth person to the team, Ann.

Now there is a little better *balance* to the system; like a good, solid table, you can have three different sets of "two pairs," with no one left out. Of course, there is now a large majority of females, which means . . . well, any number of things, for example, John is more powerful, or . . . less powerful. There is now more balance between the founders and the newcomers, which may be good, or . . . not. There is potentially

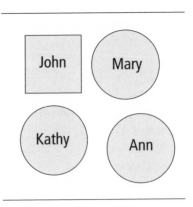

a new dimension of competition, too, between Kathy and Ann for the favor of Jack and/or Mary. And, where we started with one relationship—Jack to Mary—and then had six different relationships among the three on the team, we now have eleven different relationships (when all four are present and more if someone is absent for a while). On any given issue—of small or large importance—the group could split in many ways. And, life being what it is, there will be many, many, many issues, and so different typical patterns will tend to develop over time; for example, John is the odd one out or Kathy acts to solidify her "lead dog" status among the new players or Mary tends to tip against Kathy to be more fair toward Ann.

To this seemingly still-simple system, let's just make some minor additions, as the organization prospers and adds Dan and Mary Sue. Now, with the simple addition of two more players, the organization

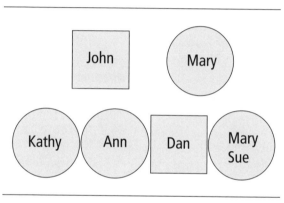

has become entirely different and much more complex. For instance, the founders are outnumbered. The women dominate two to one. There is perhaps a favorite son. Whereas John had been in a three-to-one minority, now Dan is—among the newcomers—in a three-to-one minority, for good or not. And perhaps there is an even split between the two newcomers and the first two who were added on. Questions, problems, and opportunities may well be dealt with based on common sense and the basic values in the system, but there will *always* be undercurrents, won't there? So beneath the surface of nearly every issue percolate questions of who is in control, who is in (or out of) favor and with whom.

If you are like everyone with whom I have ever walked through this stripped-down scenario of the growth of a group, *you* could have guessed at both the strange and natural fault lines that would develop. I withheld much from this picture—formal job descriptions, ideology, beliefs, age, personality, ethnicity, expertise, social status, experience, and so on—*all* of which could have created even *more* fault lines. Yet, in my most basic articulation anyone who has ever been in a group can see the likely divisions. It's as if our minds unavoidably create and observe these fault lines, these splits—who's in and who's out, who's with or against him or her. As the human animal, we seem incapable of not creating and perceiving in-groups and out-groups.

Our scenario could describe a business, nonprofit, or club. In fact, the names and order of growth reflect the family in which I was raised. And I cut the story short. Three more kids came along—Pat, Jim, and Sheila. So, in addition to the basic dividing lines between the kids and the parents, and the natural pushes and pulls along gender lines, there was also a divisional hierarchy created—the "big kids" and the "little kids." Like small, medium, or large organizations, these group divisions made for insiders and outsiders.

The fault lines and boundaries didn't only appear at the group level; they profoundly affected individuals as well. There were roles: the Oldest, the Artist (a rebel, of course, who challenged the system), the Nurturer, the Favored (and resented) firstborn son, the Redheaded Hell-Raiser, the Joker, and of course the Baby. All of these roles were like boxes. They all had *some* basis (e.g., the Baby was a baby but of course only for the same duration as the others had been babies). The roles or boxes that had some basis endured long after they were useful (e.g., the youngest was babied long after she quit being a baby). Most were unspoken roles. No role was created to *hurtfully* box someone in. All the boundaries were tremendously hard to redraw. And all of us—some much more and more often than others—felt at times like our box was restrictive, hemming us in and sealing us off.

As in all groups, the authorities set forth values that created enough order to hold the group together, yet those values also ensured that some kids would appear troublesome, different, and at times unwelcome. So in our environment, where my folks exalted book learning, the kids who were not academic overachievers felt undervalued. And in a three-bedroom ranch with seven kids, those who were messy or slow or demanded extra attention felt pressured. And, as with all systems (except those in a state of active rebellion), those kids who actively challenged the rules, the authority, and the values felt the weight not just of the authorities but of the whole group. And, if a person was in conflict with the group's values and needs on multiple levels, watch out. So, for example, my most artistic sister was in a near-continual battle in a culture that did not have the time and space and energy for someone who thought, dressed, acted, and spoke differently than our quite conventional Catholic parents (and the lead male and female children, who reinforced those values). We were (and are) a wonderful, often-envied, loving family. Still, the differences, divisions, and resulting difficulties were continual . . . and remain so to this day.

I start the chapter with family for two reasons. First, it offers a stripped-down example that we all understand: groups *always* draw boxes and boundaries that continually shape the relationships and the work. Family is just an accessible example. But the second reason I begin with family is that it is not "just" an example. For family informs—maybe *in-forms* would be more visual and accurate—all of us. In family—of whatever shape—we wrestle with the power, rules, and values of those in authority. We seek independence, yet we also seek approval. We want to be unique, yet we want to belong. We want to create identity: "We are Mulherns."[2] And our exercises in power, affiliation, and identity inevitably draw some *into* the circle, or closer to its center, and so they frequently push others out.

When we lead, especially with authority, the game of "who's in and who's out" is always at play. For people are constantly replaying the fundamental games of family. We jockey for position; we love and hate the values that help us get along but create outsiders and hierarchies. And we all struggle both for uniqueness and to belong.

## Leadership Necessitates Vigilant Inclusion

By second grade, the same dynamics at play in the family are now wildly in evidence in schoolrooms and on playgrounds. Teachers have their sets of values (conscious and unconscious), and hierarchies inevitably develop around them. The boys and girls have their own sets of norms and values, and they form their own hierarchies and in-groups. Such words as *weird* or *cool* become the most powerful ones in

149

school, with souped-up descriptors for those at the center and on the edges (e.g., *totally cool* or *totally weird*). Vast amounts of emotional energy—sometimes explosive and dangerous—will be spent in drawing and redrawing these lines. Great leaders—adult or peer—will know that these types of boundaries, divisions, and hierarchies are in play all the time.

Group forces, unchecked, will hold some kids down, push some out, or make some psychologically down and out. Productivity of all kinds—academic, athletic, artistic, and social—will turn on school leaders' abilities to continually work to include. Creativity will be pinched in the push for order and simplicity. And, although we grow into adults, become more sophisticated, and overcome *some* of these tendencies to classify, oversimplify, divide, and exclude, we remain human animals. Our youthful sibling rivalries, peer pressures, and other inevitable tendencies to create in-groups and out-groups—cheerleading captains and geeks and greasers—morph and mask but do not go away. Humans act to exclude. Great leadership fights to include. At a fundamental level leadership embraces a view of diversity that says: difference from the prevailing norms is often enriching, and I will make room for it. Because groups innately push people out, leadership necessitates vigilant inclusion.

Here I mean *diversity* in its broadest senses. There is race, certainly, because it remains a huge piece of America's unfinished work (and recently has reared its ugly head in Europe and Australia), and gender, too. Diversity also includes age, religion, sexual preference, and certainly class. Yet I also mean diversity and inclusion in terms of those whose ideas, styles, perceptions, and philosophies challenge the dominant group cultures in which they live. Maybe you have been a member of one of *these* minority groups.

- The bean counter in a world of designers
- The pragmatist in a shop of idealists
- The introvert in a family of extraverts
- The radical in a moderate party
- The moderate in a radical party
- The jock in a family of bookworms
- The scientist in a family of poets
- The innovator in a conservative business or church

- The Hispanic in a city dominated by white-and-black ideology and politics

In all of these cases, people "feel" excluded. But don't think for a minute that this is just mushy, touchy-feely stuff. For you don't just lose someone's warm feelings; instead you often lose their expertise and contribution and commitment. Inclusion gets pretty pragmatic in the real world. When I first entered politics I learned the no-nonsense expression for this pragmatism: "Keep your enemies closer than your friends." That's not easy because your friends indignantly ask why you're rewarding your enemies, giving jobs or appointments or credit to those who fought you. But you know they have energy, wisdom, and connections—all of which can help you or could be used to hurt you if you don't bring them inside.

Leadership necessitates inclusion because if you don't include others they may kill you—through a well-executed shot when you're vulnerable or an agonizing death of resistance. The unincluded child rebels, takes the car keys, and causes you to pay the price. The aggrieved and ignored worker exacts a price in productivity. The constituents you thought were the *last* ones that would ever feel like they weren't a valued part of your team decide that since you don't need them they won't play.

> Great leadership fights to include. At a fundamental level leadership embraces a view of diversity that says: difference from the prevailing norms is often enriching, and I will make room for it. Because groups innately push people out, leadership necessitates vigilant inclusion.

If you include, you may preempt attacks from those who are alienated. And the gains of vigilant inclusion are far greater than the avoidance of attack. But the prevailing group generally has instinctive fears about such inclusion. Its members worry that including strangers (perhaps immigrants, gays, reformers, or evangelical Christians) will lead to the loss of their dominant norms and values or their jobs and opportunities. In fact, well-managed inclusion does not diminish the whole but expands and strengthens it. Inclusive leadership is constantly resisting the tyranny of the zero sum, where people presume that more for "them" means less for "us."

What sense does that zero-sum presumption make in most cases? Consider some examples of how "majority" groups worried about invasion of their territory. Did sales of rhythm and blues reduce those of rock and roll in the 1960s or did R & B offer wholly new sounds, positively influence other forms of music, and create a *new* demand for music across the board? It didn't steal a slice from the pie but enlarged the pie. Consider inclusion of children with disabilities. Talk to any family or school that has been "forced" to expand its boundaries and change its culture to accommodate a developmentally disabled child and you will always hear the same thing: enlarging the system had positive benefits *for everyone*. Or, to take a third example, the inclusion of women as automotive engineers and designers has led to new ideas in design and a closer connection to the marketplace, as women are increasingly the ones making car-buying decisions.[3]

Those "on the outside" often have much to bring to the "mainstream" culture. In the places you lead, you might well ask, "Whom have I/we excluded?" They're not always vocal, and the exclusion is often subtle and unconscious, so it might help to ask, "Who has the hardest time being heard in my company, shop, or family?" That takes you to the threshold of an important inquiry about what *they* may be losing, and what *you* and your group are losing by having them on the sidelines or at the edges.

## Inclusion because It's Good and Right

I think I was five at the time. Dad took me on an errand with him to a colleague's house. I was introduced to his daughter, Mary, who was a few months younger than I. We began to play tag. I ran for my life. Mary had been in a house fire and had very bad scarring and bumpy skin grafts all over both legs. She laughed joyfully. I laughed fearfully. And ran. And ran frantically in my own thoughts.

I was both a good little Catholic boy and too introspective for my own good, so I felt excruciating conflict. I felt a primordial horror and fear of her disfiguration, as if I "thought"—with some residue of my inherited, ancient animal brain—that her scarring was contagious. She was alien to me (far more than most girls, who all had cooties anyway), and I was disturbed and frightened. The good Catholic boy, who felt terrible for wanting to deny her the simple kid pleasure of a good-faith game of tag, was working overtime. I tried to put on a good face, although I felt pretty sure the adults could see my shameful fear and harsh judgment. Even then I had some inkling that the really grotesque one was not Mary but me, or the instinct in me that would prefer that she not have to be treated as "one of us."[4] There, in this odd memory, lies the powerful tension: the social instinct to exclude and some nobler impulse toward compassion and inclusion.

Great leaders look to include because it's the right thing to do. The psalmist says, "The Lord hears the cry of the poor. Blessed be the Lord." So, also, blessed is the leader—whether in authority or not—who "hears the cry of the poor or marginalized." Blessed is the leader who hears the *silent* cry of the poor. The poor may be the new kid in class who feels tortuously alone; the blind woman who the embarrassed, sighted people pretend not to see; the black child in an all-white class; or the mixed-race child whose perspective is ignored.

It is beautiful to behold a high school senior consciously approaching a frightened freshman, a congresswoman really engaging with a citizen who has become alienated and hopeless, or a Big Brother or Big Sister drawing a withdrawn child from the edges of the classroom or play or family back into the stream of life. How extraordinary when Michigan's award-winning Cascade Engineering company bucks family, society, and marketplace and says to mothers on welfare, "We're going to do everything we can to get you back in the game, to draw a circle that does not isolate you in a modern-day leper community but instead includes you among us."

In the United States, it has not been an unbroken path toward inclusion, but the rightness of the struggle to draw a wider circle is beyond question. Our initial founding—"no taxation without representation"—said everyone matters. The Emancipation Proclamation, Reconstruction, and civil rights successes are examples of goodness and justice prevailing over our smaller instincts to push people out of our community. Women's suffrage was good and just and beautiful. It behooves us all to be grateful for the ways in which America's freedoms have been a blessing to us, a gift bestowed by leaders (initially those *without* the authority to do anything about it), the fruit of sacrifice and courage. Grateful for that gift, and knowing of the beauty and goodness of inclusion, we each need to recommit, as a friend put it, to "lifting as you climb." When you lead you never lose sight of the possibility that all can climb, and you're ever watchful that you're offering a chance for people to do so.

I first saw this poem, written by Pastor Martin Niemoller, at Yad Vashem, the Holocaust museum in Jerusalem. It still gives me chills.

> They came for the Communists, and I didn't object—
> For I wasn't a Communist;
> They came for the Socialists, and I didn't object—
> For I wasn't a Socialist;
> They came for the labor leaders, and I didn't object—
> For I wasn't a labor leader;
> They came for the Jews, and I didn't object—
> For I wasn't a Jew;
> Then they came for me—
> And there was no one left to object.[5]

We can disagree about the best *means* of creating justice, but it is hard to argue with Pastor Niemoller's verse, which speaks to both our tendency to exclude and our universal obligation to include. A sense of rightness, of community and connection, comes to leaders who vigilantly work to include. Every day in our worlds there are opportunities for us to open doors that may feel closed to others. We should. It is simply the right thing to do.

## A Message to Men: What You Don't See Can Hurt

The act of including uplifts those who include. And inclusion of "minorities"—whether of race, gender, philosophy, sexual orientation, style, or religion—is not merely "nice" or "just" but fundamentally complements the "majorities" and strengthens the welfare of the whole. Predictably, those people who benefit most from the in-group and out-group lines often protest most harshly when people challenge the existence or fairness of the lines that have been drawn. I belong to one of those groups of people. I think guys like me need to speak up.

American circles of power remain dangerously populated by straight, white, Christian guys. Don't get me wrong. Some of my best friends are SWCGs![6] But let me offer a quick example of the danger.

At the *American Woman* car awards held at Detroit's world-renowned North American International Auto Show a couple of years ago, the room was filled with two important constituencies: women with big buying power and women's media folks with a great ability to reach female car buyers.[7] Now, when the awards were being given—Academy Awards style—the car company representatives came forth to accept their prizes and offer their thanks.

After about the eighth of the ten awards, my wife whispered, "Can you believe this missed opportunity?" I started to ask, "What do you mean?" and realized as I was saying it that only two of the eight recipients designated to accept on behalf of their companies were women. In the end Ford sent up three women; the other seven sent up men in gray or blue suits. How could they have missed the opportunity? How could they have been so short-sighted? And why did it take someone whispering it for *me*, considering myself to be Mr. Enlightened, to see? The story proves the overall point of this chapter: it takes vigilance for the majority—in this case, as is often the case, white guys—to include as they lead.

At the same charity kickoff to the Auto Show, you would have had to wonder what it was like for Detroit's young mayor, Kwame Kilpatrick, to walk on the stage, the only black skin in a sea of black tuxedos. It sent my mind to a line from Plato: "It takes a contradictory impression to awaken reflection." You had to reflect: what's wrong with this picture?

This is the kicker for us SWCGs: we live so often without that "contradictory impression." Blacks in America (or at least in those integrated domains of America) discover themselves, because reflection is awakened by contrast, by the questioning about difference. They learn to navigate two cultures. Women in American business must learn two languages, two sets of rules, two ways of being. Gays, Jews, Arabs, Hispanics, and Muslims likewise face the contradictory impression that awakens their reflection. Sometimes it is just difference. Too often it is also subtle exclusion, misunderstanding, distancing, and an expectation that "you should learn my ways; I don't need to learn yours." The "twofers" and "threefers" are often immeasurably more adept than we SWCGs. For instance, a gay black man learns to navigate in multiple cultures, and black females likewise are doubly challenged.

So many of these non-SWCGs have so very much to teach SWCGs. I would go one step further: if you are an SWCG who wants to lead—especially in a rapidly changing American demography and a multicultural global economy—then find a place to be a minority. Get abroad long enough to learn another way. Join a group that doesn't look like you. Worship for a long time at a church that expresses its faith in a different way. Experience what it feels like, in a prolonged way, to be out of power and displaced, the different one. Blacks and women, especially in the upper echelons of business, don't get to choose this; they live it every day. And it's not easy.

This kind of displacement fosters empathy. For example, in my role as "first spouse"—traditionally a woman's job—I have a hundred times thought: "Geez, this is what it's like to be treated like you're part of the background, the scenery. I can see why women get tired of this all the time!" I knew it in my head before, but the *experience* of being on the outside hits at a deeper level. As they say, the fish does not know it's been in water until someone pulls it out. I recommend sustained displacement, for experience heightens empathy and empathy stimulates vigilance.

Ironically, SWCGs don't just need this to learn to gain awareness of our privilege and to be more inclusive and humane with the power we have. This kind of displacement gives *us* a new opportunity to appreciate our gifts and also to choose who we are and what we will stand for. When we swim in the fairly safe waters of our dominant culture, there is not that much to "awaken reflection." I have always been struck by the promise of the Jesuit Volunteer Corps, which places young adults in poor neighborhoods, on subsistence wages, and in communal housing. This experience of radical displacement teaches them an enormous amount about "how the other half lives," and in so doing it teaches them a great deal about the many assumptions they have made about themselves. They gain as much as those they serve.

So, especially for my brother SWCGs, I ask: when have *you* experienced being a minority? Was it a long (and/or difficult) enough experience to really begin to see the larger group's norms and think about going with the flow of a different culture? How might you intentionally put yourself into a minority experience that would heighten your awareness of how diversity works? If you work in a culture in which you are the majority, how might you more actively invite the full participation of others and the "wisdom of the group" they bring?

## Inclusion Is Personal, but It's Also Systemic

In the prior examples, I have been focusing on the broad social and cultural dimensions of inclusion and exclusion. Now let's shift our attention to a highly specific form of exclusion—the literal exclusion that occurs when someone is fired or otherwise pushed out of a work environment.

Beginning with our playground days, we feel exclusion as a very personal matter. Anyone who's been left out or left behind knows it sure feels that way. Persons left off the team—whether it's the varsity team or the management team—often feel the exclusion in a deep and personal way. Their families, spouses, friends, and coworkers feel it with them. The hurt can endure for months, years, and even decades, directly and indirectly shaping the very course of people's lives. It can impact their career decisions and reverberate through their personal lives.[8] Given this real, human pain we owe it to them to make our best efforts to help them succeed and to approach their departure with humanity, honesty, and compassion. And yet leaders must also assess issues of exclusion through a lens entirely different from this highly personal one.

Although exclusion feels deeply personal to the excluded one, a leader also has to see it as impersonal or transpersonal. It's not just about Joe or Mary. Instead, in a wide array of cases, Joe or Mary *represents* issues or ideologies or perspectives that the system just doesn't know how to handle or wants to push out of the picture. The classic example of this is the so-called Saturday Night Massacre, in which President Nixon fired Attorney General Elliot Richardson. Richardson had refused to fire Archibald Cox, the special prosecutor who insisted that he needed the recorded presidential tapes. It was no doubt hellish for Richardson and Cox—although in their highly unusual case they received public sympathy if not adulation. But the exclusion was not fundamentally personal, not about these two particular men. Instead it was systemic; it was all about trying to dispose of a tough issue by disposing of the people raising it.

In explicit cases, we might describe this as shooting the messenger. So, for example, some companies will repeatedly turn over the same position. They churn through budget or human resources or communications directors because the company does not want to hear what *any* self-respecting professional in that field feels bound to tell them: "Houston, we've got a problem!" Sometimes they're fired. Sometimes they leave on their own when they can't take the frustration of being the only one who seems to care about an issue that threatens the company. Good leaders watch who is leaving. They especially watch when good talent is heading out the door. They are skeptical when people tell them, "It was just a personality issue." Instead they keep their eye out for systemic reasons that are leading to exclusion. Sometimes a firing or a repeated turnover in a position is like a body rejecting a transplanted organ; the problem is not with the organ but with the system that is hostile to it.

I was impressed with the thinking of a statewide elected official who called me for some coaching.[9] She said that her highly talented chief human resources (HR) person was quitting. The behavior of this HR person's boss seemed to be the main cause of her departure, and this same administrator was having personnel problems with other staff members. Here's what I was impressed with: this elected official said she was concerned that they had lost some talented people and was concerned about this senior administrator. But when good people are leaving like this, she told me, "I am concerned about the culture of our whole leadership team—starting with me." In other words, she saw through the first, seemingly "personal" issue of the HR person. And she was inclined to look through the second personality issue: where some would say, "Let's fire the chief administrative officer; she's the real problem here," this official was suspicious of excluding another problem person. Instead she was asking: "What's going on in the culture (starting with me) that's making it hard for good people to work with us?" Brilliant!

So, to lead well, we need to look past the personality issues and ask: what does this person *represent* that's so difficult for us to hear, appreciate, and manage?[10] I remember one management team I worked with. It was full of big-picture people—that is, all but one person. I was brought in to coach that one woman, and before my four-month coaching engagement was half over they had fired her. The rest of the team couldn't agree with or understand many of the issues she was raising, and they felt she wasn't "on board" with their strategies. To some degree, they all told me, "She just didn't fit in." But I always suspected that the major reason she was terminated was that they just didn't want to hear the difficult, practical issues she was raising. They were more interested in concepts, theory, and strategy. It was easier to lose her than to sift through the really tough issues she was raising. They wearied of her language of the practical. But much of what she was saying they *needed* to hear. She was closer to the customer and line staff, and her *resistance* was not nearly as much the result of her unique personality as of the genuine pressures and experiences of those she was managing. When she left, they lost a vital connection to reality, practice, and necessary detail.

Good leaders look beyond the personal to ask: what does he or she represent that *we* are having a hard time hearing? They consider the very real possibility that when he or she is gone they will have the same difficult issues staring them in the face. So, as much as you think you see a problem individual, I'd urge you to ask: what would I see if I *assumed* that the issue was systemic rather than personal? You may gain a great opportunity to change many things for the better.

## Vigilance across and inside Groups

Leaders vigilantly include because exclusion is painful and when we exclude people we often avoid the important issues they represent and the contribution they can bring. And we know that beneath these two reasons to vigilantly include there lies a third: great leaders work to include because the *exclusion of groups is our most costly human fail-*

*ing.* One can only hope that we will begin to shape a twenty-first-century leadership that can instill a fundamental bias toward inclusion.

This chapter began with the premise that *individuals* seek to belong. And quickly from the individual wanting to belong groups or classes arise that seek to generate identity within themselves and status, safety, and strength relative to outside groups. Even in the most basic family story we find separate groups appearing—parents and children, males and females, and older and younger kids.

I was noting to my teenage daughter the tough irony that we save some of our worst behavior for those we love most. She smiled and paraphrased a novel she was reading that said with family you can get away with showing your ugly side because in the long run those closest to you will accept you. Then her face lit up, and she asked me if I remembered the time when she was five and her sister Cece was three and Katie, their babysitter, sent them to their respective rooms as punishment for fighting with each other. "Ten minutes later Katie came upstairs, and we were playing cards in the hall together as if we had been having nonstop fun." She laughed telling the story. Then she commented, "The minute you and Mom are mad at the two of us for something, we'll be totally tight with each other." That's the sweet side of group identity and strength. Common enemies create strong bonds within.

Unfortunately, in groups the strong bonds within can lead to savagery directed toward those outside. What an excluded individual feels as a sad sense of hurt or victimization, for example, can in a group be whipped into a virulent sense of outrage. In a group, too, we can lose our moral sense, our belief, for instance, that we are responsible for any unintended consequences of our group's behavior. And so the twentieth century may well stand for millennia as one of our most technologically advancing but tribally regressing centuries. Whether we look at the intentional extermination of one-third of the world's Jews, the tribal genocide in Africa, the Armenian holocaust, the terrorism in Northern Ireland or southern Lebanon, or the brutal clannishness of the Klan, the map and the century were blanketed with the disease of tribal warfare. It seems that as fast as the cold war thawed the world overheated with new spots of faction and border friction.

What does *this global stuff* have to do with little old us? Well, in some measure we can actually affect global struggles, while in other cases these highly visible divisions provide us with a metaphor for understanding our more "local" worlds. Some of us *can* reach to the international level, for instance, with the "sister cities" movement, which connects people in towns, cities, and villages across the world and makes it harder to view them as fundamentally "alien." Those who support Amnesty International or volunteer for the Peace Corps, Doctors without Borders, or other humanitarian programs help send a message of our shared and common humanity. Those who drive these and other diversity and peace programs, and those who participate in them, help to create a stronger bond with our shared humanity than with our clan mentality.

I always admired the work of David Gad-Harf and Ishmael Ahmed, one the director of the Jewish Community Council in Detroit and the other the director of the largest Arab American group in the area. These two men were tireless advocates for their own communities and tenaciously fought all forms of stereotyping or bias against their respective communities. At the same time, they also built a strong personal friendship. Ish could see that he and David were in many respects fighting different versions of the same problem: blind group consciousness, bias, and exclusion. As their friendship developed they began to do more and more work to build bridges *across* communities.

When 9/11 came, and on its heels the Patriot Act, which cast a wide net in Detroit's substantial Arab communities, the city passed through the experience without incident.[11] It is not a stretch to say that the friendship between David Gad-Harf and Ishmael Ahmed radiated widely throughout the community and created a backdrop of tolerance and understanding that helped it weather a difficult time without blame, scapegoating, and avoidance of tough issues.

When David Gad-Harf left Detroit in 2005 to work in the Jewish community in New Jersey, his friends gathered in typical reception style, standing about and talking about him and his wife and how they would be missed. But, while the well-wishers commiserated about the loss of David and his wife, Nancy, there at the back table was a cluster of Jewish, Christian, and Muslim leaders plotting their next moves in community building. It was as if no one had told them there was a party going on. "Have you seen *Children of Abraham* yet?"

one asked me excitedly. They were sponsoring a play written by Christian, Jewish, and Muslim kids who recognized their shared beginnings and emphasized their unity in diversity. David's legacy was coming alive.

As members of a world family that breaks down into fierce family divisions, we can all help—by building bridges as David and Ishmael have to other communities. And *inside* our communities we can fight blind loyalties and thoughtless tribalism. I was once facilitating a session of a Jewish welfare group—wonderful people doing outstanding work to help people down on their luck. When someone in the group joked about another ethnic group's stereotypically dogged work ethic, Gerry Acker quickly broke in, "Hey, I don't appreciate our indulging in comments like that, and I think they'd be offended. Let's stop." When he struck this chord, audible tones of agreement emanated from members of the group, many of whom had lost relatives in the Holocaust. Gerry exhibited *vigilant* inclusion, fighting what some would see as innocent clannishness. Like all good leaders, he moved people to be their best.

There is work to do within our groups and in building bridges to others. In my hometown of Detroit there are a million daily opportunities to exercise these two sides of vigilant inclusion when it comes to issues of race relations. People have a world of opportunity to build bridges *out* of their segregated worlds, and they have countless opportunities to lean against the tribalism *within* their worlds. We no longer see these issues of racism and exclusion as "big city" problems or, as we used to pretend, as a problem in the South. Exclusion is widespread and endemic. Indeed, at the end of 2005 in Paris and Sydney violence erupted as people of color struggled to be treated as first-class citizens and members of the majority groups fought to protect their clans' perceived borders. The year 2006 ushered in a major struggle over American policies of inclusion and exclusion of Mexican immigrants.

We can learn from these continuing global struggles about the tribelike tensions that obscure our vision and our thinking in the smaller worlds in which we live. "We" stereotype and blame "them," blithely lumping people into supposedly tight and uniform groups. Every day at work, these tribal oversimplifications distract us from fully seeing problems or fully grasping opportunities. These are some of our modern day, business world tribes: it's the central office versus the field, labor versus management, the longtime partners versus the new associates, the reformers versus the conservatives, the engineers versus the sales teams, the administration versus the teachers, the mayor versus the council, the city versus the suburbs. Are there substantive differences between such tribes? Sure. But the oversimplifications often make the differences appear much more stark than they really are.

Perhaps worst of all, exclusion and division almost always make the problem somebody else's. Again, the most powerful, universal example: home! How many kids continue to commiserate about their parents' mistakes, even as the "kids" enter their forties, fifties, sixties, and seventies? And how many parents complain to their fellow parents about "kids these days," seemingly incapable of hearing the echoes of Archie Bunker, Spiro Agnew, Rev. You Name Him, and, of course, of their own parents. Kids sweepingly blame parents, and parents sweepingly blame kids. Blacks blame whites, and whites blame blacks. Great leaders gently turn their teams to the hard work *they* can do. They reach out across boundaries to reveal common ground. They're grateful for the strength they get from belonging to their clan, but they don't pretend that the clan is the full measure of their humanity.

In a world sure to continue to experience the natural but deadly tendency to form groups of us versus them, what role do you play? Leaders look for ways to continually reach out beyond their groups and to check the arrogance and even violence within them.

## Protecting the Ear and Voice of the Ethical

Nowhere is it more important for a leader in a position of authority to "vigilantly include" than in the realm of ethics. Because leaders need help with ethics. Now, nearly every authorized leader I have ever met, and those I have observed as well, would bristle at the insinuation that they are not ethical or need help to be so. But let's just be honest about positions of authority and power and what it takes to get there and stay there.

The fact is most leaders in positions of authority got there in part because they have a nose for power. They understand *realpolitik*. They sense what can realistically be accomplished and the trade-offs necessary to make that happen. They also know what (and who) protects their power and standing, and so they pay attention to keep themselves and their organizations strong. After all, the car manufacturer who wants to put out a perfectly safe or environmentally friendly car will go out of business in a heartbeat. The politician who sees every issue as an issue of principle on which he or she cannot compromise will never be elected. The doctor who insists on giving every patient his or her very best diagnosis will never see enough patients to keep the lights on. To gain positions of authority people have to prove that they will keep their institutions funded, staffed, safe, and well lit. And once they *get* such positions the pressure to produce real world results only intensifies. They know they must move the bottom line, get the troops in line, or make sales regardless of some of the collateral damage along the way. Good organizational leaders are always dealing with shades of gray, trading off one "pretty good" for one, hopefully, "slightly better." They consciously but also quite instinctively work to protect their power and the existence of their institutions.

Precisely because authorized leaders must work in just such worlds of short-term pressures and real trade-offs, the voice that asks, "But is it right?" becomes a vital one to hear. As pressures mount, ethical concerns can gradually fade into the background; a question is raised once at a management meeting, gets half an answer, and then people move on, thinking, "Well, I guess it's okay since no one else is raising it again." Yet one of a leader's most essential jobs is to protect his or her integrity and that of the organization. So he or she is well advised to figure out who will consistently ask (the team or the leader directly), "But is it right?" Especially in pressured times, the leader must vigilantly include such a voice, for the pressure in the system will work to exclude it. The organizational body will experience this voice as a threat—for example, triggering the fear that we can't handle the costs of doing what ethics (and perhaps even the law) require or fear that we will be publicly (and legally) exposed for things we have done or feel we need to do now to survive.

So where were such ethical types at Enron, Arthur Anderson, Kmart, among the Catholic bishops, or at the prison in Abu Ghraib? It doesn't seem possible that the issues were raised and aired and these leaders just came to the wrong conclusions. So what happened to the ethical voices? This is a tough question because we know they were there! We know Arthur Anderson had tremendous people of high character, we know the military takes its rules very seriously and expects people to follow them, and we know the Church hierarchy has no shortage of people concerned about ethics and morality, right? Human nature tells us that they just weren't vigilantly included. Some were squeezed out long ago for raising vexing questions. Some may have raised issues but were at the periphery. And the others? Were they overtly silenced, covertly silenced, or just ignored? Why didn't the authorized leaders hear them out fully? At some level, one can only believe that the group's survival (or perceived survival or survival of its reputation) simply trumped its willingness to hear the voice of questioning, the voice of ethics. And the top leaders didn't protect and demand such questioning.

Group identity is powerful, and those voices that challenge the identity will most often be experienced as threatening. Although we *all* possess the "still, small voice" we call conscience, for most of us it gets stiller and smaller as groups become larger and when the group is fearful for its survival. Yet for some the ear for the ethical is always sharp, and a very few of these are willing to speak up. I'll bet you've met people with just such a voice of integrity, who ring as clear as a well-struck bell.

You've got to keep that voice within earshot. It's not easy. Such questioners may appear to the group to be dangerous, a wild card, or a loose cannon. They're the type who ask embarrassing questions or seem self-righteous; they're not easy to have around all the time. Their sense of justice or honesty, or their insistence upon courage, can rage and fire. They may take a stand on an issue and be virulent about it, altogether certain and a bit extreme. The language of the moralist, the prophet, the editorialist, or the rebel tends to be hot. And so, as leader in charge, we face two difficulties. First, we want to douse their flames, for they may singe us with embarrassment or fear or hurt. We want to crush the resistance. It's overstated and cutting edge—like the cry "Dad, you're a hypocrite" from a teenage child—which makes us especially eager to silence them.

The second difficulty we face is as bad or worse. You may be a highly ethical authorized leader and feel no such need to muzzle the questioner. That doesn't mean others won't. Often the chief's lieutenants and sergeants will take great offense at such a renegade, and they will counsel retribution. They will encourage you to see the danger in this "loudmouth whiner," and you may go ahead and transfer that person to a less public position, even against your own best instincts. And in large organizations the group will carry out retribution against troublesome ethical challengers without the authorized leader ever knowing. Vigilance is the word. A strong ethical leader—especially in a system under survival pressures—must vigilantly listen and be ready to question and slow the group's instinct to silence the always-appropriate inquiry about "what is right," what is best in us.

Imagine if Ken Lay at Enron or Cardinal Law in Boston had had a trusted, though perhaps irritable and demanding and self-righteous, voice of morality at their sides. Imagine if they'd held off the pressure to move such persons to another job or to silence them somehow. Imagine the damage they might have saved their organizations—and the many innocent victims. So how hospitable is your home, office, or church to a challenging—and perhaps strident—voice? Michigan remains proud of our deceased senator Phil Hart, after whom one of the U.S. Senate's office buildings is named. Senator Hart was known by his colleagues as "the conscience of the Senate." Wouldn't it be great if every organization formally or informally knew who was "the conscience of the group" and accorded such a voice the attentiveness it deserves and the organization needs!

## The Subtlest and Most Powerful Form of Exclusion

In groups, every day, individuals are quietly *nestled*. They possess knowledge or judgment of extraordinary worth. Sometimes it's ethical. At other times, it's creative, for the group is thinking in black and white yet they see things in Technicolor. Sometimes it is just the "minority view" about strategy—for sales, design, theology, child rearing, communications, you name it. Two largely different views were at some time discussed, and theirs "lost" in the overall scheme of things. They still see that other way. Again, they're *nestled*, by which I mean they're right there, ready for the taking. But they have been stilled, stifled, quieted. And we're losing their value.

Probably the most costly forms of exclusion in organizations operate like this. People are just nestled, right there in the organization. But here's what's surprising about their exclusion from the key conversations. The authorities have not told them to be silent. No one has overtly silenced them. Instead what's causing their exile is the power of *self-exclusion*. Take a simple example.

> Ever had this feeling? You are in a group and you have something to say, but, while you think it's pretty important, you feel sure the others don't want to hear it. So you sit there and think: "Should I say it? No. Should I say it? Yes. No. Yes."

There were five of the governor's senior staff members in the room with her political adviser on the speaker phone to discuss the coming year's State of the State speech. And talk about "speech"—I felt like I had lost my faculty for it! I was nestled like the others I have described. We had worked as a team on past years' speeches, and this was our first meeting for the 2006 speech. The discussions were about the standard topics: the economy, values, education, and health care. The new twist was that we were also talking about how the speech would impact the upcoming election. But, while they were exploring these central themes, one thought and one reaction to that thought kept cycling through my mind. The first thought was that Jennifer should go to Iraq and visit the troops. And the thought that kept forming in reaction to it was: this idea is just weird and probably would not be welcomed by the group.

They were talking issues, budgets, programs, and policy, and I was talking about something largely spiritual and symbolic. It didn't fit. The idea was out of the box, and as a result *I* felt out of the box. Ever have that feeling that you have something worthwhile to say but it's kind of off track from where everyone else is? So you go back and forth: should I say it or shouldn't I? You think, "I don't want to waste their time. I don't want to throw them off their agenda." And, forget about them, you think, "I don't want to look stupid."

That's the subtlety of exclusion. It works on people's sense of belonging. Don't bother looking for a heavy-handed censor imposing the norms and values of the leader. This is not Stalinist Russia. Instead look to the self-censors that are tied to our feelings of wanting to belong, of not looking odd or different or "sounding stupid." So, for example, a brilliant engineer hesitates to raise a problem about a new engineering design when everyone else is crowing about it and the chief of engineering is beaming. Or an operations person grows quiet, nestled right there in the room, as the "big picture" folks propose a whole new approach that he or she expects will be met with cynicism and resistance. Or a freshman's parent doesn't say a word about the baseball coach's schedule with two doubleheaders during exam week, even though it seems to totally conflict with what the principal has said about the school's philosophy on sports and academics. No one says the parent can't talk, but he or she figures that it must just be the way they do things around here.

The upshot is clear for leadership. Leaders with authority have to *pull* people out of their nestling places; they have to solicit opinions, invite dissent, and protect creativity. They have to constantly break down the walls that stifle openness and work to exclude. They have to challenge the statements that are full of assumptions, and they have to lead the way by asking "stupid" questions so others can do the same. Great leaders have to get out and visit those nestling places and find out what people are really thinking. They have to convene the new workers, who don't really want to totally fit in but slowly (or not) learn to conform and not rock the boat. They have to celebrate the rule breakers, the voice raisers, the ones who come out of their nestling places.

It also seems a sad but true fact of organizational life that we have to create back channels through which people can communicate to leaders in authority. In the fall of 2005, I received the results of my "MI-360"—an anonymous survey of my boss, peers, direct reports, and other individuals who observed me leading. One question on the survey asked what one thing a leader could do to lead more effectively. In reading the responses, I read things from members of my own team that they had *never* said to me. Now, I run a very open ship, where anyone can raise any question. Yet clearly some people hadn't. They had self-censored and needed the anonymity of the 360 survey to share really helpful feedback with me. Because people self-censor it's necessary to give them clear channels through which to talk.

A final lesson of nestled folks and self-censorship should be obvious: we all have to find our courage! I am almost *daily* struck by stories of people in the large bureaucracy of the state government who self-censor. The censoring occurs despite an administration in which the governor and her employees have explicitly pronounced "inclusion" and "teamwork" as two of their core values. It's not rational. That is, the level of hesitance in this and every organization I have ever been in far exceeds the likelihood that speaking up will lead to negative personal consequences. And those who self-censor completely miss the opportunity to contribute (and not infrequently be rewarded). Great leaders absolutely treasure those who lead without authority, who hear the self-censor and say, "Thanks for the caution, my dear self, but I am going to share this idea!"

I waited and waited at that meeting on the State of the State speech and finally said, "This may sound crazy, but I think we should look for an opportunity for the governor to go to Iraq." The first wave was one of silence, then some questions, then a shared sense that this *might* be a good idea. Quite by coincidence the Department of Defense called a couple of weeks later and asked Jennifer if she would visit the troops with three other governors over the Thanksgiving break. She went on what was treasured by the troops and one of the most humbling and inspiring experiences of her life. It all would have happened independent of my intervention, but it taught me the lesson again: don't worry about looking stupid; say what you've got to say, man!

## Leaders Say, "It's My Place, and All Are Welcome"

Perhaps the most striking quality of great leaders comes into prominence when they act to include. Actually, two qualities come together to impress us. First, great leaders *act like they are responsible for the whole*—whether on the playground, at the front of a classroom, in the pulpit, or leading a movement. They do this whether anyone has authorized them to or not. On a local level, we generally admire them for jumping in and making things work. (I say "generally" because, human nature being what it is, some may say, "Who does she think she is?!" when her active leadership ruffles feathers or gains her notoriety.) In my official capacity, I champion volunteerism across the state of Michigan, and I regularly see inspiring stories of teenagers or senior citizens or housewives who respond to events—from childhood cancer cases to hurricanes to war—as if they have been given some official mandate to make something happen. They are just filled with initiative.

If it's true in our smaller worlds that leaders just jump in and take responsibility for the whole, how much more true is it of the leadership greats? Martin Luther King Jr., Lech Walesa, Alexander Solzhenitsyn, Mohandas Gandhi, Elizabeth Cady Stanton—I mean, who appointed *them?* They just decided that their countries were capable of more and that all of their people deserved more. It was as if they said, "I may look like I don't own this place, but I LOVE it, so I will fight to keep it open, just, beautiful, and good." They invite all of us to ask: do I act like I own the place, the company, the church, or the country and act for its best benefit?

Of course, these leaders are symbols of proactive ownership behavior. The second striking quality of their leadership is, of course, what this whole chapter has been about: their vigilant inclusion. Although each of their situations was unique and nuanced, this much was common: they fought to give everyone a right to participate more fully. Their conditions were dramatic: throwing the British out of India, lifting the chains of communism from Poland, or throwing open the doors to women's suffrage. But the *nature* of their impassioned struggles is *no different* than what fine leaders do all the time on less dramatic scales.

In families, cities, businesses, churches, and schools throughout this world, great leaders include and empower people every day. They don't let people of talent just nestle. They don't accept unequal and segregated schools. They keep a vigilant eye out for opportunities to invite people with disabilities to fully participate. The challenges of inclusion are more subtle and masked than they were with slavery, for instance, or the right of blacks or women to vote. But they remain quite real. And they are *not* just about civil rights, about politics or race or gender. For the *civic* struggles are of the same essential quality as the *business* struggles and the *family* struggles.

People get pushed out to the margins. Sometimes the most important voices to hear are just not heard or are left to speak with such stridency that the message can't be heard and assimilated. Often,

170

in time, they silence themselves. Particularly in our large institutions—corporations, unions, state governments—it is precisely the rebels who need to be heard if these organizations are to remain vibrant and the least bit nimble. We need creativity and involvement and commitment from everyone. We can't afford *not* to have everyone in the mainstream. The twenty-first-century leader will fight for genuine inclusion in all these settings.

We can expect that there will be heroic leaders in the twenty-first century. Whether on the dramatic scale of Jefferson in the eighteenth century, Lincoln in the nineteenth, or Martin Luther King in the twentieth, we can predict that their legacy will revolve around creating a world that is more fair and open. And in the millions of smaller domains where each of us lead, our heroism will also flow from the degree to which we can get people fully in the game. See what kind of difference you can create when, on the one hand, you always see it as *your* place to lead and, on the other, you believe it ought to be a place where *everyone* can fully participate.

# 8

## Ego and Team

I came from the people
They need to adore me
So Christian Dior me
From my head to my toes
I need to be dazzling
I want to be Rainbow High!
They must have excitement
And so must I.[1]

BROADWAY'S EVITA, EVA PERÓN, sings ego unabashedly. It's all about Evita, movie star and model, living large as Argentina's first lady! Evita's story confirms our legitimate fears of ego in leadership. We want to say: "Wait! Leadership is about *them*, not about you. Great leadership is not about what you can *get* but what you *give,* not about *your* accomplishment but about what *they* can accomplish when they are well led." Evita's bold-faced "They need to adore me" shows our deserved suspicion of ego, but it also conceals two other truths about ego that this chapter will explore: Ego is not just a problem of the rich and powerful, and it's not always a problem at all; it can be one of the best things we have going for us.

We all have ego—a deep need to "be somebody," to be seen as special. Perhaps our ego craves glamour or power, but it also pursues many other ways of being seen as special. When Evita sang, "I came from the people," she might as well have added, "And so I have an ego—just like you do." Ego is not a problem of egomaniacs but a universal human characteristic.

Thanks in large part to the energy of ego, the real Evita led a short but absolutely explosive life. Thanks to the drive of her ego, she built homes and schools, wasn't afraid to alienate the military and wealthy elite, nearly became vice president, supported her husband (Juan Perón, president of Argentina), was beloved for championing *los descamisados* (literally, "the shirtless"), and transformed the world's idea of what a first lady could be and do. Ego unleashes energy, and, as we've seen, leadership demands energy.

This chapter offers new ways in which to see the great possibility of ego, as well as its well-known risks. Most of the chapter is dedicated to giving you new tools to get ego's best without being undermined by its largely me-centered hunger.

## Ego: The Good and the Bad

*Ego* in Latin is simply "I." Nothing's wrong with that. At the most fundamental level, it is the sense of "I" that moves us. Could Joe Montana have led the San Francisco Forty-Niners back from the edge of so many defeats if he did not think he really was somebody? Mustn't Tiger Woods think, "I *belong* at the top"? It takes no shortage of ego to say, as Tiger has, "I am the toughest golfer mentally." Could Doctor King have asserted himself against all the forces arrayed against him if he did not have a strong sense of self? Could Rosa Parks, who certainly stood for a principle, have accepted that she was going to be arrested, charged, and jailed without also possessing a powerful sense that she was somebody? Could Bill Gates have dropped out of Harvard without some grand sense that he was somebody? Could Abraham Lincoln have lost eight elections and yet persisted to reach the presidency without a powerful sense of *Ego sum!* "I am"?

There are problems with *unchecked* ego. In a moment you'll come across some ready examples. But perhaps the biggest problem when it comes to the three-way intersection of ego, the challenges we face, and the need for leadership is not *too much* ego but *too little!* As Marianne Williamson, the popular spiritual writer, has so eloquently written,

> We ask ourselves, "Who am I to be brilliant, gorgeous, talented, fabulous?" Actually, who are you not to be? You are a child of God. Your playing small doesn't serve the world. There's nothing enlightened about shrinking so that other people won't feel insecure around you. We are all meant to shine, as children do. . . . And as we let our own light shine, we subconsciously give other people permission to do the same. As we're liberated from our own fear, our presence automatically liberates others.[2]

Great leaders are full of just such a sense of "I can do," and it's contagious. Powerful *egos* can generate powerful *teams.* When we think of the challenges we face—eradicating hunger and disease in the world, fighting racism, or succeeding in a fiercely competitive global economy—who could possibly say we need less ego? We have HUGE challenges that demand huge confidence to take them on.

Ego drives. But unchecked we all know that ego, that very sense of "I can," can drive teams into all sorts of trouble. Sometimes ego becomes "all about *me*" at the great cost of *us!* Which of these have you experienced?

- A boss who is so intent on achieving the heights he thinks he deserves that he is paranoid about any kind of criticism or difference of opinion
- A boss so confident of his intellect that he insists on learning every inch of everyone's job and is constantly telling them how to do it
- A choir member who loves his or her voice and is always trying to be heard above the rest, bringing down quality as fast as the choir's morale
- An aggressive CEO who, despite coming up through the finance side, is telling the design teams what their products should look like—at great cost to quality
- A boss who comes to a three-year assignment with huge

goals and seemingly great enthusiasm for the system but then gets a better offer and leaves with three days' notice.

- An elected official who thinks that the system exists to serve him or her—commandeering staff, perks, and public resources—creating ill will and mistrust among other officials and citizens
- A football player who cares so much about his personal statistics that he demoralizes the team with his halfhearted play when making an effort doesn't seem to hold any advantages for him

You could go over that list and notice two results of unchecked ego in every single example: a drop in both morale and quality. It makes sense. If the system is being asked to meet one person's needs—even if it's the needs of the boss—the effect will be to drive down morale and create an imbalance in the system's work. You could probably double or triple the length of this list of ego gone amok, and your examples would likely show the same assault on morale and quality: bosses who take all the credit—deserved or not— and teammates who think they are so good that they don't have to help with the "grunt" work. These all tend in the same direction— against the team doing its best work.

The other thing you might notice about these examples is that— especially in the case of a boss or other person in authority—no one is likely to say anything about the causes or effects of this behavior. The ego drive is obvious (to everyone, perhaps, but the boss), but the topic is off-limits. Teams almost always silently bear the unproductive consequences. So when we lead, our awareness of and response to our own behavior are the only things that are likely to help us lead past ego.

## Nice Guys (and Girls) Have Egos, Too

Maybe you don't think this ego thing applies to you, that you've pretty much got it under control. You don't have a "big ego" at all. Maybe. Or, maybe . . . not. Ego is universal, but it's trickier than we usually think. It wears disguises that fool us. Let me clarify. Ego is not just indicated by the desire for praise and power. Those desires to be at center stage are merely the most obvious manifestations. Instead we all have an ego, some *identity, which each of us has cultivated by adulthood, that drives us to meet certain needs.* In the same way that we each crave different types of food or entertainment, so also we each seek our own sense of being special. Deep down we live to establish an identity. It is the way we want to be perceived, what we want noticed about ourselves. The drives are rooted deeply in our unconscious, and we recognize them by watching our behaviors and figuring out the appetites that lie behind the behaviors. Deep down they come from fairly elemental forms. So, for instance, we want power or we hunger to be admired. And from those deep-down depths, huge amounts of energy are made available for us to achieve and protect that specialness.

We recognize the ego of a Trump, Steinbrenner, Schwarzenegger, or Gates. I doubt that's you! But this driving need for identity can be just as insistent, even when its ends are much less notorious. For instance, some are very intent on being seen as suffering servants; it's as if they are not happy, don't feel like themselves, if they're not paying a price for their hard work and sacrifice. While some people's egos must take the stage, others must be there *after* the show, meticulously packing everything up while insisting they don't need people to know that they haven't slept in thirty-six hours. This is not to say that such service is not laudatory (indeed, the fact that ego drives Trump and Gates hardly makes their accomplishments insignificant). The point is that ego is at work, even in those who appear to be acting selflessly. Deep human needs for identity drive us all.

Two things are important to notice about this broad picture of how ego works. First, ego takes the shape of a driving, personal, human need to be "identified" or recognized in a particular way. If the need goes unsatisfied, people will feel uncomfortable, not themselves; they'll be agitated, restless, and compelled to change things in order to get what they need. Ego is highly personal in its nature, and it powerfully affects the way we operate in groups. Inner drive leads to outer behavior.

Second, no one is without such ego drives—the enduring desire to sustain a consistent identity. In this sense it's not really accurate to say, as we do in the vernacular, "He has a huge ego." Instead it would be more accurate to say, "His ego is hugely *apparent*." That's because his ego is probably caught up in power or fame, and those needs by definition are played out on the IMAX theater screen of life. But other people's unique needs, which drive their egos or senses of identity, can be every bit as powerful; their aim is simply less obvious, aggressive, or public. They, too, "want to be" or "need

> **No one is without such ego drives—the enduring desire to sustain a consistent identity.**

to be" something; just not in a high-profile way.

Great leaders get a pretty clear sense of their own "want to be" drives. They feed off the energy that pushes them to establish their identities. What might your drives be? What is essential to your identity? Here are some of the most popular ego drives among people I have seen in leadership work. Some:

- Want to be perfect
- Want to be respected
- Want to be loved
- Want to be in control
- Want to be creative and original
- Want to know everything
- Want to be harmonious
- Want to be powerful
- Want to be attractive
- Want to be certain
- Want to be the best

I say "want to be" because it doesn't sound especially bad or foolish to *want* to be something "powerful" or even "perfect." But in truth these ego drives are not mere "wants." Instead, it is as though the unconscious were saying, "I don't just *want* to be powerful, darn it, I *need* to be powerful." Life, of course, will not consistently accommodate a need for "power" or "harmony" or "certainty," but the ego's drive for these does not go away.

Let me reiterate that the ego drive makes us get up and go. Just as Adam Smith wrote about the "invisible hand" that generates growth in a market economy, so also ego acts like an invisible engine driving activity in the leadership domain. Those seeking to distinguish themselves, to be seen, to establish an identity, will in various domains create, produce, sell, and lead. But in the blind service of ego, that is, when people really don't understand what's driving them, they will unfortunately also do these things in ways that damage their teams, groups, and families.

We have all seen how an unchecked ego drive, for instance, the drive for power, will compromise the needs of the group. In a legislative body the ego's drive for power will generate competitiveness that will erode trust. In a business setting such an unchecked drive will alienate colleagues inside and stakeholders outside. Set two power-driven egos against each other in a labor-management dispute and they will subjugate the needs of the workers and shareholders to their personal need to win. Again, that's the kind of ego drive whose cost is obvious to us because its aim is so open and notorious. Yet the seemingly "good" ego drives can function in equally troublesome ways. For instance, in the same labor-management dispute you might have two negotiators who both need to feel harmonious. Because of their need to be harmonious and to be seen as likable, they may well cut a deal that fails to address the legitimate but difficult to resolve issues of their stakeholders.

Take another example of how the hidden ego can keep someone from giving the group what it needs. I had an executive client whose ego was caught up in his need to be loved. Repeatedly, as I held coaching conversations with him or as he met with his managers, he would become clear about the difficult steps he was planning to take. He would then tell me or his team just what he was going to do. But a week later we'd find that he had not had the tough conversations or had begun them but backed off when he started to meet resistance. So initially people left meetings with him feeling good, understood, and clear. But later they would wonder if he had been serious with them and why he hadn't done what he said he would. He always seemed to make everyone feel good in the moment, and his intentions were always good. Meanwhile, the tough issues just weren't being addressed. His need to be loved was painfully trumping the needs of the group.

These "softer" needs of the ego deserve our attention (the ego needs for power, wealth, and control are almost always in our critical sights). Here's why the soft needs matter. One of the surest legitimate requirements to lead well is the willingness to raise difficult questions and challenge people to adapt, especially in fast-changing environments. Whether we are raising children, challenging employees in a tough marketplace, or trying to "lead up" in an organization, challenge and conflict appear all across the landscapes of leadership. So the softer ego needs—to be liked or loved or admired or at peace or unthreatened—create a problem for us. And this is *especially* true in the close and intimate circles where most of us lead. The hardest place to bring tough news—the kind we fear others might judge us for—is in business partnerships, in the relationship between manager and employee (whether managing "up" or "down" in that relationship), and in our close personal relationships.

Many of us short-circuit the kind of candid communication that can give these relationships a stronger life, a firmer ground. The ego's need to be loved and its fear of being rejected cause us to just swallow stuff. We resort to passive-aggressive comments, symbolic protests, or attempts at manipulation to get people to give us what we or the rest of the team need when our ego images of ourselves will not allow us to simply say, "Hey, we need some help here! What you're doing isn't working." By not giving associates, partners, siblings, or spouses a chance to understand the impact of their behavior, we handicap them in carving out a workable solution for us and the rest of the group. On top of that, our discomfort is likely to play out in unproductive ways for us. Instead of addressing the apparent problem, we may become discouraged and lose our own energy, play out the conflict in some safer place, or find that the conflict is affecting our mental and even physical health.

> Those leaders whose egos need love and peace almost always create confusion because they suppress the natural differences that arise when important stuff is at stake. Ironically, by avoiding conflict or not resolving it fully, these leaders end up creating not less but more stress and discomfort.

So you don't have to be an apparent egomaniac to have your good leadership tripped up by what *functions* as an aggressive ego. Even the kindest people—those who *need* to be kind and viewed as kind—can (softly) elbow people out of the game; passive aggression is aggression nonetheless. They find ways to hold off people or strategies or issues that might cause pain. They work to avoid any hurt to others, even though some stress and hurt are often necessary side effects in the process of change and growth.

Unchecked ego affects every dimension of leadership we have discussed in prior chapters. Ego can eclipse the best efforts to articulate a *vision* when, for instance, people say, "Our CEO says we will always put our customers first, but everything about this place—from pay to privileges—says we put our CEO first." Ego can get in the way of *ethics,* for example, when my need to be seen as brilliant gets in the way of my saying, "We have made a big mistake and must apologize." And ego can taint *communication,* as the stories that are generated are those "I need" rather than those the group deserves. If I have not dealt with ego needs—for example, for power or order—it may be very difficult for me to be *inclusive,* taking on views that may create waves around me. And, when I have driving ego needs—for example, to be perfect or admired—I may be overly cautious or self-absorbed when I *coach* someone. If we wish to lead well, we have to account for ego and its ability to craftily put our identities first rather than seek first what is in the best interests of the group.

The bulk of this chapter will offer thoughts on how to get a handle on this thing called ego, which we see so easily in others yet see so dimly in ourselves. Hopefully this beginning has given you a sense that we all possess ego and some thoughts about what your ego drives for. Ego is a great source of fuel for attacking the job of life and leadership. And, as we'll see next, it's also a necessary source of strength for fighting off the inevitable attacks on us and those who lead.

## Ego under Attack

To this point I have been talking about how the ego can cause us to be on the offensive, expecting or taking things that we need and distracting us from the needs of the group. Yet ego comes into play not just on offense but also on defense because when we lead we will inevitably feel attacked.

In leadership, and especially when one is in authority, the ego is under regular assault. For instance, as parents we're attacked by our kids, especially teens, who can say the harshest things, including, "I hate you. I wish I wasn't your daughter." Our ego identity—whether we need control or order or wisdom or love—is under assault. Coaches are savaged on Monday morning talk shows and have their firings blared not just in the sports section but across banner headlines on the front page. That hurts.

Your ego may have been assaulted when a competitor at work was behind the scenes telling false tales about your work. Or the project you poured your heart into was taken away and given to someone else. Or you ran for city council and discovered that fliers—anonymous fliers—were sent around claiming, falsely, that you were guilty of sexual harassment. Near the end of Jennifer's first campaign for governor, a political hack sent out a mass mailing (which the newspapers picked up) that said my wife could not be trusted because she was married to me and I came from a family of crooks. It is a painful and helpless feeling to have your "reputation"—the great treasure of the ego—slammed in the mass media.

I believe the following is, however, about the hardest ego shot of all the ones I have seen. In November of 2002, federal agents swept into the Wayne County offices of friends and former coworkers of mine. They suspected "corruption" of some kind. Their names and photos were printed on the front pages of the Detroit papers. Nearly four years later, as I write this, one person has been charged. And no one has been publicly exonerated. They dangle—suspended, named, exposed, and wounded. They were all public servants. Some were idols of mine, people whose work ethic, dedication, and integrity were superlative. But as long as this cloud hangs above them their identities, their egos or sense of self, are exposed and assailed. People talk and wonder and judge. People hesitate to hire them. And, perhaps worst of all, although they chose public service, now their *public* commitment will always be suspect.

I will offer a number of general strategies for managing the ego, but the question of managing *attack* deserves specific attention. How can we respond to these "slings and arrows of outrageous fortune"? Three options exist, two of which I recommend. The first we could call the DeLay response, in honor of the former Speaker of the House Tom DeLay of Texas. And I don't mean *delay*, meaning "wait." In fact, I mean the opposite: counterattack, fast, hard, and relentlessly. DeLay's response to his indictment by a grand jury in Texas was to furiously attack the motives and actions of the prosecutor. It's one way and perhaps a way that works for those who love to fight and love the attention . . . and don't care what kind of attention they get.

I do not recommend this strategy, however, when one is under the kind of attack that is aimed at character. Whacking back doesn't work when you're in a scrap with a bully, for, as the old saw goes, "Never get in a mud fight with a pig because you'll both get dirty . . . and the pig loves it." You may get some temporary emotional relief from firing back, but you're certainly inviting further attacks. This is particularly true if it gives the media or onlookers a "juicy" story. Responding keeps it alive and in most cases causes other people to repeat the attack on you, ensuring that more and more people will hear about it and guaranteeing that you and your staff, your family and friends will hear it again, too. Follow a "scandal" story in the paper sometime. What you will often find is that the papers write week after week, with each new story introducing often tiny bits of "fact," which justify a new headline, while 90 percent of the story is filled with "as we reported earlier." For the most part, there's nothing new. But to casual readers it looks as though you have done *another* awful thing.

In this vein it is worth remembering that it's all but impossible to fight the news media, for, as another old saw goes, "Never pick a fight with someone who buys his ink by the barrel." As you learn in politics, when you're attacked your best bet is to tell the full truth quickly and hope it's "a one-day story." Can you fight back against a prosecutor? Prosecutors can bring charges and subpoena all your records. You can't. Or a boss? Bosses can fire you or make your life miserable. You can't. Even in the family, aggressive self-defense has limited value because most of us ultimately want peace and coexistence, and if *our* ego wins round one whose ego will win round two?

This is not to say that there may not be good reasons to wage a strategic defense or launch a counterattack, especially if those reasons are rooted in the good of the team. And the nature of authority is that sometimes when you are personally attacked it reflects on the entire organization, so you may have to fight for others (or is this mostly ego's rationalization?). But only one impact is guaranteed from the natural ego response to strike back to protect *itself*: further attacks will come. And getting into that kind of fight—besides getting you muddier and muddier—nearly always takes your focus away from the needs of the team and takes the team's focus away from the work at hand. Everybody loves a circus—allegations against the president, CEO, or priest—and the amount of work declines as the circus atmosphere gets rolling.

So if the DeLay strategy of denial and counterattack doesn't often work, what strategies will work when you're under attack? Each of the next four sections will outline a strategy for managing yourself through both attacks on the ego and the ego's own potential attacks. An especially important strategy for dealing with attacks is to begin by gaining self-awareness—especially emotional awareness—of the impact the attacks are having on you.

The most helpful way to think about "attacks" is to know that there is a type of "law of conservation of mass and energy" at work in the world of human emotions. The whack you take necessarily produces reactions. When you're hit, there is impact and energy is released. If you're brittle emotionally, you may crack. If you're coiled and tight, you may strike back instinctively. If you're already deflated, you may further absorb this attack into your body and spirit (or others in your system, such as your spouse or kids, may unfortunately feel it for you in the form of your rage or shame or sadness). Some get sick. No one *decides* to have ulcers or headaches or back trouble, but this may be how you absorb such hits.

It's vital to know that the blow to ego is often *not* happening at a conscious level. By the time you're an adult, you have "learned" not to show the effects of attacks on you—especially if you are a man or a strong woman who recognizes the male culture's preference not to deal with emotions of hurt, sadness, or fear. Indeed, many are trained to not even think they're *feeling* attacked. Others are socialized to forgive when they are attacked. But the ego is not very impressed with conscious fearlessness or the moral impulse to forgive; your conscious, moral mind may forgive, but your ego still feels the hurt. The ego is not easily fooled. It registers the attacks. It keeps count. It looks for ways to recover and protect itself—to fight back or to absorb the attack and flee to avoid further attacks.

Some people are gifted, like boxers trained to deflect the full force of punches. Some, like my wife, Jennifer, have remarkably thick emotional skin; they don't cut easily. But the shots wear. For instance, the shots of adolescents wear on you. The first and best thing you can do is be honest about the hits and effects—the hurt or anger or fear you may feel. Honesty with self is a hallmark of great leaders. They see the retribution they'd like to mete out or they recognize their desire to flee. Because when you're hit you sometimes get an intense "screw this, I'm quitting" feeling.

When Michigan's favorite sensationalist attack journalist was characterizing the governor's residence as a terrible drain on public resources and its inhabitants (our family) as living high off the taxpayers, Jennifer and I felt attacked (our egos were tied up in our reputations for integrity). We spent one evening laying out plans to abandon the house. We reasoned that we didn't enjoy living in an institutional setting in the first place, and if we were going to be attacked for it, heck, let's just get out and move into a normal neighborhood. That is the kind of Newtonian reaction that attacks can cause. The reporter's shots caused us to think seriously about the insane idea of moving our family out of the historic governor's residence at a time when our lives were filled with the complexity and pressure of her leading the state and while our kids were in the middle of school. It was all ego hurt talking. Fortunately we didn't listen for too long!

Whether you are leading your kids, leading a team at work, or in a high-profile position such as mayor, governor, or CEO, you've got to be able to gain awareness of the ego's reactions. This usually means that you must get some distance from the battlefield to process the attacks and your thoughts and feelings honestly. You might be able to manage this work on your own. The hurt or frustration may be at least partially unwound through activities such as journal writing, yoga, aerobics, basketball, playing an instrument, or going for a long walk or run or swim. I emphasize these body activities because they allow us to almost physically sweat out the internalized hurts and to breathe at a deeper level in order to loosen up. Prayer and other spiritual practices are, for some, a way to let go of the negative; the hurt evaporates like the smoke of incense rising.

If these solitary processes work for you, then exploit them. Use them often. Expand your openness to see just how honest you are being about the most basic levels of give-and-take, attack, fight, and flight. And monitor the impact that these releases have. Are you really able to "let it go" and move on the way you want to? I have my doubts about whether the attacks on the ego can be well managed in just these solitary ways. In the following sections I'll explore other ways to manage both the attacks on ego and ego's own tendency to dominate our leadership behavior.

What is the point of all this awareness talk? It is twofold. First, you can deal with what's really affecting you. Without conscious awareness, your sadness, anger, or hurt is as likely to be turned on someone else or yourself as it is on the problem that generated your feelings. Awareness helps stave off road rage, cat kicking, or self-medicating, for instance. When we actually engage the feelings head-on, they have a way of working their way out and dissipating. Second, as we realize that we are hurt, angry, and so on, we can actually separate this feeling from the overriding situation. For example, if Jennifer and I had announced that we were moving out of the governor's residence, we would not have addressed any ethical issue that might be there for us, nor would we have handled the public relations issue well at all. Decisions we make when we are hurting—especially when we don't know we are hurting or why—are generally not balanced and prudent decisions. Dealing with the emotions lets us later return to the issues with objectivity and thoughtfulness (instead of irritation or annoyance, desperation or rage).

Awareness thus offers the first step in managing ego in a way that allows us to lead well.

## Humor—Antidote to Ego's Excess

We called him Butta (*butter* with a down-home pronunciation). Our family and everyone on our team weren't kidding about this sergeant of the State Police Governor's Security Detail when we said, "Everything goes betta with Butta." He did stand-up comedy in his spare time, and, like a lot of good comics, he loved to take aim at those silly human peccadilloes that we pretend we have evolved beyond. Butta could see through stuff and so make you laugh at it. He'd joke about someone "secretly" picking his nose, or he'd laugh at a politico pretending he wasn't looking at that pretty woman in a meeting. He'd chide me when we got back in the car, and say, "I saw that look of disgust when that reporter asked the governor whether she had overreacted on an issue. He hit your button, man. You were *mad*." "I was?" "Are you kidding? Man, you were beet red mad."

Butta had an eye for ego. In fact he was like an ego detective, and if you were close to him he was an ego antidote. Remember that ego's drive is to establish some identity, to prove to yourself (and whoever else is watching) that you are somebody. And every once in a while we give others (and ourselves if we watch) clues about when ego is overly in charge. Ego generally likes titles, position, reputation, and media coverage because these seem to establish *proof* that "I *am* somebody." And some egos seem almost insatiably driven to prove that they are somebody.[3]

We can see traces of this ego drive or ego need when people talk about themselves in the third person. Butta would laugh about how a football player would say about himself, "If they think they can stop Sam Jones, they've got another thing coming. Cuz nobody stops Sam Jones." Was there another Sam Jones on the team? No. He was just helping create his own celebrity. Or Butta would mock the candidate who says about herself, "When Mary Major is elected to Congress, things will be very different. Because Mary Major won't be beholden to special interests." Can't you almost hear the echo of the three year old bent on proving her identity who says about herself, "Monica's not going to bed. Monica isn't tired. Mommy can't make Monica go to bed." Similarly, we see the ego driving to prove "I am somebody" when the executive who is pulled over for speeding or the elected official who is told that he or she does not have a reservation asks indignantly, "Do you know who you're dealing with? Do you *know* who I *am*?" A good question in response might be, "Yes, you're the one in the Ferrari who was going 150 and endangering lives, including your own, and so a better question might be, 'Do *you* know who you are?'"

Ego also shows itself in more everyday lives, as when a frustrated parent says to a fourteen year old, "Young man, do you know who you're talking to?" An accurate (albeit highly inappropriate) answer might be, "You are a parent who doesn't want to just discuss things person-to-person but needs to prove that he or she is smarter, stronger, wiser, and more powerful than your kids." Of course I am not suggesting that a parent doesn't have authority or shouldn't use it. I am saying that when we feel ourselves attaching closely to power and position we might be wise to take a step back and see whether *our need* for recognition is truly necessary for us and especially whether it's helpful for those we are dealing with.

In all of these examples people are mighty serious about the connection between themselves in reality and their ego picture of who they are. You could see this seriousness in all the examples of ego drive listed earlier. To take just a few examples: those whose egos are bent on looking perfect will try to explain away every imperfection in their work or will blame the defects on someone else. Those whose egos are bent on being seen as attractive will go to great lengths— including criticizing others' looks—to lay claim to what the ego wants. If their egos need to be in control, then they will resent or attack whatever seems to be diminishing that control. Those folks could use a little Butta about now.

Humor works on this drive to connect the way our ego *wants* us to be seen with the sometimes conflicting *realities* we face. John Morreall, a world-renowned expert on humor, says that he has "a theory of humor which has a fancy name but it's not a hard idea." Here's how he describes it.

> It's the incongruity theory of laughter. Incongruity is a mismatch between my ideas and my experience. It's a discrepancy between what I expect and what I get. So humor is based on experiencing something that doesn't fit your idea of how stuff is supposed to go but somehow enjoying it. There are two parts to it: first, you're surprised, you get something that doesn't fit your expectation. But secondly you somehow get a kick out of it; you enjoy it. So humor is the enjoyment of incongruity.[4]

In my own case, my ego has driven me toward power and accomplishment. I worked hard and was lucky enough to get into good schools and have great opportunities and some success in my professional efforts. Because I am so close to my wife and played a part in her electoral success my ego gained satisfaction there. Her success supported my identity. But it is at times difficult to link my ego needs for significance with the role of supportive spouse.

Butta provided an antidote that helped me get a kick out of the incongruity between ego and circumstances. I'd tell him how this first gentleman stuff often reminded me of Brendan Sullivan, Oliver North's attorney during the Iran Contra hearings. Sullivan insisted on objecting incessantly, to the utter consternation of North's interrogators. When pressed on this behavior Sullivan shot back that he was North's *lawyer,* and famously crowed, "I'm not a potted plant." Butta loved to tell me what a fine potted plant I made. Or he'd tease me with his other name for me, A. G., which stood for "and guest," as in "We cordially invite Governor Jennifer M. Granholm and guest to attend . . ." Butta made me laugh about—instead of being connected with deadly seriousness to—my ego's need for power and importance.

The ego's need for power and control is a major issue for first-time supervisors and every-time parents. We tend to want to oversteer, to demonstrate that we know what we are doing. Unfortunately this tends to generate what Isaac Newton described as an "equal and opposite" reaction: the harder we push the harder the others push back (though the push back may not be openly defiant and may well be delayed or displaced). "Control" seldom works for long with big or little people because what we *really* want is their free will, their choice, their commitment, and these can't be compelled or controlled. Again I am *not* saying that kids (or employees) don't need constraints, rules, and guidelines, because they do. And rules—from "time outs" with little ones to withheld driving privileges with teenagers—need to be enforced. What I am saying is that we have to continually gauge whether the instinct for control is to satisfy *our ego need* for (apparent) order and control or is really based on the needs of the child and family under the specific circumstances and reality before us. When we're taking ourselves deadly seriously, it's a little hint that we might be advised to loosen the grip of ego and loosen up on them.

We know from research that humor and laughter diminish the physiological effects of stress. We also know from experience that humor and levity often make teams perform better. An ego-bound boss with no sense of humor can cast a shadow across everyone's work, while a boss who engages in genuine, self-deprecating humor can help create an environment in which people take risks, cooperate, and enjoy themselves more. One of the most successful businesses in American history, Southwest Airlines, stands as the best example of the power of a lighthearted culture, and it starts with the ego at the top. Herb Kelleher began his testimony before the National Civil Aviation Review Commission in 1997 by introducing himself in this way: "My name is Herb Kelleher. I co-founded Southwest Airlines in 1967. Because I am unable to perform competently any meaningful function at Southwest, our 25,000 employees let me be CEO. That is one among many reasons why I love the people of Southwest Airlines."[5]

Kelleher is a huge believer that his human, and humorous, culture leads to much better results. He told an interviewer, "A ramp agent from Oklahoma wrote me one time and said: 'Herb, I'm on to what you're doing.' He said: 'You're making work fun—and home work.'"[6] Workplaces aren't often fun when ego is on the loose!

We're not all Herb Kelleher, and we may not be funny, but we all have the capacity to laugh when the world doesn't seem to take seriously whatever grand plans our ego seems driven to fulfill. We could all use a little Butta to give us a good laugh at ourselves with our cravings for order, power, fame, or control. It takes a real adult to just go with the flow sometimes.

## The Wisdom of People with Wisdom

Sometimes we can sense that ego is in control and not happy. We may even take a second step and want to step away from ego and choose instead the welfare of the team, organization, or family we are leading. We may even want to laugh, try to laugh, but still be in the grip of self-serious ego. We may feel frustrated in the grip of an ego that wants its needs met and a reality that's not delivering. For instance, we may be laboring in a job in which we don't get credit or in a home where conflict is high and support is low. Or we may be frustrated with a boss who just doesn't see things our way, who seems to want to overcontrol us, or who makes the environment more competitive than we like. The needs of ego—for accomplishment, recognition, control, or peace—are real, and they are affecting us. And we're not sure what to choose among the basic options: try to change ourselves, fight for what we need, or leave.

Humans are innately social. The ego is hurt or deprived, in the social, *by* people, *in front of* people, and *with* people, and so when it's wounded it almost *requires* an honest airing with another human being or beings to be restored. In these conversations, where we ask, "Is it the job or me?" we figure out who we really want to be. "*Can* I get what I need here? Or can I let go of what I think I need?" So it has been my experience that a real, honest wrestling with the ego becomes most real and productive when it is shared. You may be able to sort it out with a confidential friend, a mentor or minister, a lawyer or trusted girlfriend or boyfriend. With someone we trust, we will almost always get both an understanding of the inside of ego—our thoughts and feelings—and a better understanding of the reality we perceive. We can give voice to the assaulted ego yet also begin to put it back into a healthy relationship with reality.

Three groups of listeners deserve special mention here: therapists or counselors, spiritual directors, and personal or professional coaches. I believe our leadership quality would soar if leaders—moms and dads, teachers and coaches, managers and religious leaders—all chose to work with such guides. In my experience with each, I have been able to be more honest about myself. Not just honest in an intellectual way but emotionally as well. So often we pretend we are playing objective "policy games," whether it's the policy of teens being in by 11:00, the policy of who becomes a partner in the firm, or health care policy. Yet beneath the surface are "political games," that is, people games, such as: how to prove (to my ego and the world) that I am not an imposter, how to show somebody that I'm not going to be pushed around anymore, how to make sure someone doesn't criticize me, and how to hold off my fear that my kids are going to make the same stupid mistakes I am still embarrassed about making. Getting to this level of self-honesty almost always requires a special, skilled, independent listener.

I will never forget Susan Roth, a social work counselor I saw when I was twenty-three years old. I was full of bravado but a little over my head as the executive director of a neighborhood center with nine full-time employees and nearly a hundred volunteers. She helped me see how much emotion lay beneath the surface and was holding sway over me. My ego was *way* more involved than I knew or could possibly have learned on my own. Let me give an example of what I mean.

In one session with Susan, I was discussing a situation in an antipoverty coalition I was part of and how I thought it was off-track. She asked me if I felt anger toward Bill, a man I'd mentioned who was the informal leader of that group. "No, I don't think so," I said. "Well, what if you pretended he was sitting here and you really told him how you felt about him?" she said. "Are you willing to tell him what you think of him—without censoring anything? It's safe here. Just tell him." I let go of my ego need to appear in control and unruffled and I began this task. I can still feel the embarrassment and the huge amazement I felt, as I told the imaginary Bill sitting there, "You think you're such hot !@*!^. You make me sick." I was on a roll, my voice rising. The language, emotion, and intensity all caught me by surprise. It was the really wonderful *energy* of ego, but it had been all plugged up until she helped me to let it loose. I saw that I was human and that trying to be perfect wasn't making me perfect.

This is not an unusual case of ego playing its games beneath the surface. Like many people in competitive office environments, I was not aware of how strongly I felt about Bill. And I had no idea how it was affecting my ability to see with any real objectivity and to contribute in a positive way. My ego needs then were to be seen as smart and humble. Because I had these needs, I saw this man mostly as a threat to my ego: *he* was the smart one, and I felt patronized by him and competitive with him. My ego need to be seen as smart kept me from appreciating his ideas or responding to them in a very rational way. Because of this crazy inner game, I wasn't seeing Bill's strengths or the issues and needs of the team with any clarity. It really was (though I was not aware of it until that counseling session) all about me! But when, and as, we see ego as just ego, it has an amazing way of finding its appropriate place again. I could see this guy was just this guy, Bill, a good-hearted and bright lawyer who was on the "same team" I was. Now we could get on with the business of working for justice instead of the business of feeding my ego.

It is difficult to this day—twenty-five years later—to write of that moment in Susan's office, for it's personal, raw, and human. But I share it because that's the point: if we can go to safe places with people who can help us be honest about ourselves, we can be much more honest about our situations. There we can say what it may be hard to say anywhere else: "I don't know why, but I can't stand this vice president; I cringe every time he talks" or "I want to run for county commissioner, but I'm really nervous" or "I am so intent on getting this project right that I can't sleep, and I'm jumping all over my toddler just for doing toddler things." Are there people or projects or situations about which you have really *irrational* feelings? Sure there are because we're all more than rational beings. When we talk to someone skilled in the ways of ego and its hidden drives, we can see our world more clearly and bring energy to the task at hand. We can see what we need, or what we think we need, and make choices about how to get our needs met without compromising relationships, work, and honesty about what's happening around us.

The emerging field of professional coaching provides an outstanding venue in which to work through issues of conflict between ego needs and our perceived reality. This is particularly true of people in CEO or executive-team positions. The nature of these positions is that people in them almost always have to project confidence. This is something that ego is supremely suited to do. A candidate cannot raise money or convince voters if he or she doesn't believe "I can!" A CEO cannot move Wall Street or local investors if he or she does not exude confidence. And a senior vice president will never get sufficient resources to do the job if he or she comes to the boardroom table shaking and uncertain. They *must* show strength and energy. And it's hard to do this—hard to even fake it—when the ego is wounded. The wound may cause them to want to fight; or the executive may expend badly needed energy containing or concealing his anger or later papering over it. Or the wound may cause another deep hurt—for instance, from a bad opinion poll, a bad quarter's results, or a reorganization that reduces an individual's role. These people will expend great energy forcing themselves to come out of hiding and hide the sadness or anger. Executives must generate energy and confidence.

The other complicating rule for executives is this: it's lonely at the top. It is tough for a CEO or executive director, a governor or mayor to look to anyone on their teams when it comes to these very personal ego issues. For one thing, even their closest advisers are looking to them for confident leadership. It's important to be candid, but that doesn't mean sharing every doubt all the time. In addition, sometimes the toughest ego issues involve those close advisers. Is my senior vice president being a team player? Is my chief of staff really getting the job done, or is my irritation with him or her mostly caused by my own ego and the criticism I am getting? Is the finance chair of the board trying to send me a message, and is he or she "on my side" or not?

A coach brings an outside perspective—a sounding board for inner feelings and outer perceptions. And a coach is indispensable when it comes to that toughest question: am I taking this action because it works for me, makes me feel comfortable, and supports my ego need or is this really the right thing to do? A coach can be an indispensible source of understanding.

A third guide that works extremely well for those few who choose it is a spiritual director. Spiritual directors generally listen and give counsel from a spiritual or religious perspective. In many spiritual-religious traditions religious leaders themselves are required to have a guide, teacher, or mentor. Buddhists strongly recommend having a teacher. Jesuits all have an assigned spiritual director. These two and other traditions recognize that there is a kind of craftiness about the ego and its ways and that it is enormously helpful to work with a guide who can help you assess whether you are fooling yourself.

I recommend coaches, spiritual directors, and counselors because they bring three assets. First, you get the peace of mind that comes from having a dependable confidentiality agreement; word will not leak out. Second, you get someone without another agenda, someone completely uninvolved in the situation. And, of course, you get someone whose skill is in knowing the wily ways of the ego and the hidden secrets of the human heart. In my experience their guidance has been immeasurably valuable.

Perhaps some can sort out ego's drives through solitary activity.

But it's good to recognize that ego is designed to fool you about this as it insists, "I can handle this. I'm not weak. I don't need help." The vast majority of execs would be very well served by periodically turning to one of these wise people. Finally, in the next section you might explore the most consistently positive strategy of all: put ego in the greater context of serving the needs of the group.

## Lift Every Voice

Let's look at what happens when a leader brings an intense commitment to a team or group. Good leaders ask, "What do *they* need?" not just because it is kind and thoughtful to do so but also because good leaders know that they depend on others to produce results, especially truly remarkable achievements. Consider a rather simple example. When my daughter Kate was ten years old, she sang in concerts in Canterbury, London, and Paris with her grade school choir and five other children's choirs from across the United States. My mom and I shadowed the tour.

Kate was the youngest of the girls in her choir. Her voice, as far as I could tell, was pleasant but could not honestly be described as exceptional. Indeed, although there were some skilled and well-trained singers from our choir, there were certainly no Luciano Pavarottis nor Cecilia Bartolis in the group. Yet when they sang in Westminster Hall, together with the other children's choirs and the Virtuoso Symphony of London, I was in awe and in tears.

What opened me up was seeing and experiencing a chasm of spectacular depth. On one side of the chasm was my little girl: young, average in voice, a child like you'd see in any school pageant. And on the other side of the chasm was music that was absolutely gorgeous. It seemed crazy and utterly incongruous: my little girl was an integrated part of otherworldly harmonies, clarity, pitch, pacing, and passion. That chasm of opposites opened a chasm in me. Hearing them was like experiencing a great canyon with a rushing river below; it literally took my breath away.

These were all pretty regular kids, average singers. I do not say this to disparage them. I say it to heighten the contrast: the performance was anything but average. It was deeply moving, totally gorgeous. No individual, no handful, nor even handfuls could have come close to creating that effect. The beauty was in the numbers and the way that they worked together. When each sang her part, she had to sing well with others on that same line. And when each sang her part she had to sing with and against those singing a line of harmony. Every single one was in relation to every other one. Now you could have taken any one child out and never have known the difference (even if you were her parent). Yet every child was part of the fullness and richness of the sound. Each one contributed.

Face it. Our world obsesses over Bono and Alicia Keyes, Tiger Woods, Jack Welch, and Bill Clinton. And we forget how spectacular the teamwork of ordinary people can be. Humans have always loved outstanding individual achievement. Yet the accomplishments of groups and teams wildly surpass what the greatest of individuals can accomplish. For all the brilliance of a Henry Ford, Bill Gates, or Franklin Roosevelt, their accomplishments came through the innovation, cooperation, and achievement of thousands who both led with and followed them. When it comes to achievement, the group reigns supreme, and for that reason a great leader goes beyond what he wants and focuses incessantly on what the group needs.

Would it surprise you to know that Susan Lindquist, the choir instructor from my daughter's school, paid extraordinary attention to each child? She made each one feel enormously special, and she continually built group identity by telling them how special they were and how special the trip was. "Do you know what an honor it is," she would tell them, her small fist clenching and shaking the paper she was holding, "to sing in Westminster Hall?" And would it surprise you to learn that after months of planning, rehearsing, inspiring, teaching, and cajoling Susan handed her choir over to a lead conductor who led the melded choirs in concert? She was literally not even on the stage. She had done her work of taking care of the needs of each of her singers and prepping them as a whole. And then it was thoroughly about them, wholly *not* about her . . . except for what had to be her ecstasy at their spectacular sound. Who wouldn't want to be *that* leader?

Susan paid attention to the choir members so that they could do as a group what neither she nor any of them could do as individuals. With her marvelous leadership they did, as the black national anthem proclaims, "Lift *Every* Voice." And the whole was spectacular. We lead in large part to create such efforts. Anyone on a great team—athletic or life—knows that the whole far exceeds the sum of the parts. And the leader whose ego shrinks enlarges the whole.

The children's choir offers a wonderful metaphor. For we can imagine our team as a choir and ourself as a conductor. Like Susan's kids, there are times when teams do not yet know the music, times when it seems like they'll never know it, times when their rivalries and jealousies seem more important than the work they are performing, and times when they seem to have lost all focus. Yet each face in that choir of your leadership team is an invitation. Each is a mystery. Each needs something from you as conductor to evoke his or her best music. And all of them need you to be "all about them" so that they can feel the tremendous invitation to sing as a group.

The spectacular concert is one of life's most enduring riches. Let them sing! How blessed we are when we have the opportunity to conduct. What extraordinary joy when they experience the beauty of making music together. What a thrill when different parts of your organization are contributing their best. How awesome the results when the foundation that the bass section brings uplifts the tenors' creativity and the sopranos' exquisite soaring.

In our everyday leadership we can seize the greatest opportunity of life: to lead with our best self so that others can achieve greatness they may never have imagined possible.

# NOTES

CHAPTER 1

1. John P. Kotter, "Leading Change: Why Transformation Efforts Fail," in *Harvard Business Review on Change* (Boston: Harvard Business School Press, 1998).

2. You remember from the story that Moses sometimes had a passionate conviction that his vision would be realized. At other times he was weary, burdened, and doubtful. Like so many other extraordinary leaders, Moses tapped the deepest source of energy we know to support his own confidence and effort.

3. Martin Luther King Jr., "I Have a Dream," Estate of Dr. Martin Luther King Jr., Intellectual Properties Management.

4. Julia Cameron, *The Artist's Way: A Spiritual Path to Higher Creativity* (New York: G. P. Putnam's Sons, 1992), 66–67.

5. The annual issue of *Fortune* dedicated to the "100 Best Companies to Work For" is a wonderful source of creative practices at award-winning companies.

6. This and other great lessons of public speech are revealed in James C. Humes's book *The Sir Winston Method: The Five Secrets of Speaking the Language of Leadership* (New York: William Morrow and Co., 1991), 45–46.

7. You can sign up to receive "Reading for Leading" by going to www.danmulhern.com

8. Robert Fritz, *The Path of Least Resistance: Learning to Become the Creative Force in Your Own Life* (New York: Fawcett Columbine, 1984). I refer to this as "structural tension" because that is Fritz's term for it. Peter Senge, a colleague of Fritz, has popularized the notion but refers to it as "creative tension" in his books *The Fifth Discipline,* and *The Fifth Discipline Fieldbook.* Senge spends much more time than Fritz expounding on the role of personal and shared vision, but I have referred to Fritz here because he first offered the idea of vision and structural tension.

9. Not to worry! To paraphrase Jesus, "Reality ye shall always have with you." We will discuss this directly in the next section.

10. By writing "you can't always do such fully inclusive work," I don't

mean to suggest that working on a shared vision is something good leaders can take or leave. Groups that hope to work well together and achieve greatness can't afford *not* to find the time and space to do the work of articulating a shared vision. When you get people on the same page, a page with a big bold title that declares the vision, you save enormous time and energy down the road by acquiring the energy and clarity that come from buy-in and alignment.

11. This is emotionally challenging because employee resistance can be filled with negatively charged emotions. They may be disdainful of your "flavor of the month," your "psychobabble," or talk cynically about your "touchy-feely nonsense." Leaders, at times, benefit from the carefree attitude of Don Quixote, who tilted at windmills as though they were his enemies in battle. The ability to appear foolish and naive can be developed and serve a leader well.

12. Max De Pree, *Leadership Is an Art* (New York: Doubleday, 1989), 28.

13. George Bernard Shaw, *Man and Superman* (London: Penguin Publishing, 1903), from the dedicatory letter to Arthur Bingham Walkley, 32.

### CHAPTER 2

1. Jeanie Daniel Duck, "Managing Change: The Art of Balancing," in the *Harvard Business Review on Change* (Boston: Harvard Business School Press, 1998), 61 (originally published in the *Harvard Business Review*, November–December 1993). Duck is especially speaking to the importance of managers talking about the whys of change and strategy and not leaving this to the professionals, the human resources or communications folks. So she's not only saying that you have to communicate *all the time* but that *all of you* have to communicate all the time.

2. The references are to Jack Canfield and Mark Victor Hansen's series, which began with *Chicken Soup for the Soul: Living Your Dreams,* and to Robert Fulghum's *All I Really Need to Know I Learned in Kindergarten.*

3. Like any honest leader, she also had moments when she wondered whether her efforts were futile, whether fate would offer a break, or whether she was the right "man" for the job. Her strength of conviction about both reality and the story flowed precisely from being honest about this part of reality: there were moments when she felt frustrated and defeated.

### CHAPTER 3

1. Benjamin Zander, *The Art of Possibility: Transforming Professional and Personal Life* (Cambridge: Harvard Business School Press, 2000), 74.

2. Daniel Goleman, *Primal Leadership: Learning to Lead with Emotional Intelligence* (Boston: Harvard Business School Press, 2002) ix (emphasis added).

3. I first saw this exercise led by M. A. Hastings, who was working with adults in a training session. She would have a volunteer write any phrase, for example, "leadership requires attention," as many times as he or she could on

a flip chart and then repeat the action with a cheering crowd. Not only does the exercise prove the point about performance improvement; it also gives the audience a palpable sense of what energy *feels* like. The idea of having an instrument that gauges energy becomes transparent, as everyone can sense that something has swept through the room.

4. The field of "emotional intelligence" is quite new, and in academic circles at least three theories are quite hotly debated. Goleman (with Richard Boyatzkis and Annie McKee) has gained notoriety for his EI models, see, e.g., *Emotional Intelligence: Why It Can Matter More Than IQ* (New York: Bantam, 1995), while Reuven Bar-On, see, e.g., *The Handbook of Emotional Intelligence: The Theory and Practice of Development, Evaluation, Education and Implementation—at Home, School and in the Workplace* (co-authored by James Parker) (San Francisco: Jossey-Bass, 2000), and Peter Salovey, and David R. Caruso, see, e.g., *The Emotionally Intelligent Manager: How to Develop and Use the Four Key Emotional Skills of Leadership* (San Francisco: Jossey-Bass, 2004), offer two other frameworks. I have chosen to focus on Goleman, not because of in-depth comparison and study on my part but because he is widely published and quite accessible (in print and ideas). If you want to read about this emerging field and the three varieties of approach, see http://eqi.org/real_ei.htm.

5. Lest you think this is all very simple, and that the governor or other leaders should make everything informal, think about how much respect you had for the teacher who wanted to be one of the guys and expected no order, rules, or standards. Good, authorized leaders know they must wear the suit and that the suit has vital properties that they must uphold and protect.

### CHAPTER 4

1. One wishes that the leadership literature did a little more of the job that I have heard journalists and preachers take on: "to comfort the afflicted and afflict the comfortable." Much of the leadership literature comforts the comfortable.

2. Parker Palmer, *Let Your Life Speak* (San Francisco: Jossey-Bass, 2000).

3. Marcus Buckingham and Curt Coffman, *First Break All the Rules: What the World's Great Managers Do Differently* (New York: Simon and Schuster, 1999), 34 (emphasis added).

4. The sense of incompleteness is a fundamental tenet of nearly all religious and philosophical thought systems.

### CHAPTER 5

1. I would be remiss if I failed to point out that there are many more stories than there are indictments or convictions. One of the most agonizing aspects of living a public life is watching exceptionally good people splattered with attack ads, false headlines, and even wide nets of criminal investigations that were intended to "make somebody (anybody!) talk." There are people I *revere* whose names wrongly ended up in the papers and who will *never* see a

headline that reads, "Sorry, We Were Wrong about X: Facts Prove She's Exceptional."

2. Another piece of my baggage was what I would call a stubborn righteousness. I can almost look for a fight when I think there is a principle involved. Here I was feeling that I was the one being wronged, so I was ready to fight that unfairness.

3. Giving up the contract did not spare us attack. As if to prove the old adage "No good deed goes unpunished," Jennifer and I were treated to campaign attack ads about her unseemly connections to Wayne County and I was exhibit A. Newspapers feeling the obligation to report "the news" also ran stories about the contract. In a strange way, my giving money back was seen by some as proof that I *must* have done something wrong. Had I stayed on the job with the airport, I am convinced the attacks would have been even more relentless, but I wish I had appreciated the potential nightmare awaiting me from the outset.

4. One of the most effective systems ever invented to manage obsessive behavior is the twelve-step process that is at the heart of Alcoholics Anonymous. The steps involve an acceptance that the individual has lost control and a commitment to turn to a higher power, "God as we understood him," as the organization puts it. The twelve-step process, which can be found at alcoholics-anonymous.org, offers insight and guidance for people dealing with any number of obsessive behaviors that threaten their freely choosing to do the right thing.

5. Doug Sosnick, assistant counsel to the president, interview with the author, March 1997.

6. Ed Riley, http://www.powerbasketball.com/2ndyear-21.html.

CHAPTER 6

1. William Oncken, Jr., and Donald Wass, "Management Time: Who's Got the Monkey?" *Harvard Business Review* 18, no. 6 (November 1974). The William Oncken Corporation declares that the "monkeys" article "has consistently been, over the years, either the most or second *most requested* reprint in the history of the *Review*. This material is, as Harvard has stated as recently as the Fall of 1997, one of the *most 'influential'* subjects they have ever published." www.Oncken.com.

2. Brian Mulroney, eulogy of Ronald Reagan, http://news.bbc.co.uk/2/hi/americas/3799881.stm.

3. Warren G. Bennis, *Why Leaders Can't Lead* (San Francisco: Jossey-Bass, 1989), 14–15.

4. Niccolò Machiavelli, *The Prince,* translated by William J. Connell (New York: Bedford/St. Martin's, 2005), 56.

5. It would not be intellectually fair if I failed to point out that it is overwhelmingly men and not women leaders who are so afflicted. It makes you

wonder: will it simply be a matter of time before women are similarly compromised? Or do we need to learn how to raise our men a little more like we raise our women?

6. I specifically am not offering this explanation of the *energy* around a figure of authority as merely a metaphor. I mean that this energy exists in the physical world. Although we do not have the tools to measure it, this does not mean it is not there, any more than the fact that we did not have powerful microscopes meant that cells did not exist. It makes sense, especially when we have much authority and power, to treat this notion quite seriously.

7. James M. Kouzes and Barry Z. Posner, *The Leadership Challenge,* 2nd edition (San Francisco: Jossey-Bass, 1997), 285.

### CHAPTER 7

1. There are three one-to-one relationships. And there are three different two-to-one relationships possible.

2. "We are Mulherns," true. But from the beginning of the formation of family we were Mulherns and not Sanitates, my mother's family name. So a boundary—arguably necessary, certainly simplifying—was drawn about our identity. My sweet daughter Cecelia Granholm Mulhern asked me when she was about eight years old, "Dad would you be sad if when I get married I keep my Granholm name but drop my Mulhern name?" I smiled at her sweetness (and laughed inside at the absurdity of carrying four thudding syllables into a marriage) and said, "That would be fine, sweetheart." Drawing the lines of identity is often as benign as it is necessary.

3. A 2004 JD Power and Associates survey found that women made or influenced the car-buying decision 59 percent of the time. Study cited by Joan Helperin in "What Do Women Want in a Car? The (Automotive) People's Choice Awards: Women vs. The General Public," published by Edmunds.com at http://www.edmunds.com/advice/specialreports/articles/104829/article.html.

4. I have wondered whether in some cell in my brain I connected Mary's skin condition with the Bible stories about "lepers" I had probably already heard in church. Jesus visited lepers despite their contagious sores and communal isolation. Our collective conscious and unconscious are filled with examples of such isolation, often with some grain or more of medical truth. If the biblical story was indeed in my head, it would have exaggerated both sides of my conflict: fear of Mary but also the impulse to ask, "What would Jesus do?"

5. Attributed to Pastor Martin Niemoller (1892–1984).

6. Indeed, I am an SWCG.

7. *American Woman Road & Travel* magazine sponsored these awards. In 2004 the magazine changed its name to *Road & Travel,* and it continues to focus on women and to name the International Car of the Year at the Detroit International Auto Show in January of each year.

8. When you're excluded from something that matters, from somewhere you *expected* to be, you can imagine that path denied as part of your "unlived life." Perhaps it's this type of exclusion, then, that helps us see the rationale behind Carl Jung's powerful intuitive statement, "Nothing has a stronger influence psychologically on their environment and especially on their children than the unlived life of the parent." The authority's power to exclude can endure far beyond anything he or she imagines.

9. This official was not from Michigan.

10. Ronald Heifetz offers marvelous insights into the way leadership requires looking beyond apparently "personal" problems. See, for example, *Leadership Without Easy Answers* (Cambridge: Belknap Press, Harvard University Press, 1994), 38.

11. I am referring to intergroup conflict, but I have perhaps overstated the case. For the fact is that the Patriot Act allowed the government to investigate and detain many Arab Americans. Revelations late in 2005 made it clear that the federal government made some very wide determinations of who was potentially dangerous and that these were almost exclusively related to ancestry and religion.

CHAPTER 8

1. "Rainbow High," by Tim Rice and Andrew Lloyd Webber © 1976, copyright renewed by Evita Music Ltd. All rights in the United States administered by Universal Music Corp./ASCAP. Used by Permission. All Rights Reserved.

2. Marianne Williamson, *A Return to Love: Reflections on the Principles of a Course in Miracles* (New York: HarperCollins, 1993), 190–91. Let me hasten to add—as is certainly implied in this oft-quoted passage from Marianne—that she is not exalting personal power or speaking of personal power in a vacuum but sees it very much in relation to fulfilling the greatness God intends for us. On this I agree with her. However, I suspect that much of the immense popular power of this quote (which is often inaccurately attributed to Nelson Mandela) comes from the way Marianne has put her finger on a seemingly universal hesitance to rise to our full stature. We don't stand, speak, risk, or create in the same way that those with powerful egos and great self-confidence do.

3. One could argue convincingly that persons who possess such egos—even those *most* intent on proving that they are somebody—are reacting to some deeply buried fear that they are *not* important, not somebody. They may move mountains and accomplish extraordinary things yet never shake the fear that, at bottom, there is nothing there.

4. John Morreall, "A Healthy Workplace Is a Humorous Workplace," *William and Mary News*, 2004, http://www.wm.edu/news/?id=3686.

5. Herb Kelleher, testimony before the National Civil Aviation Review Commission, May 28, 1997, http://www.library.unt.edu/gpo/NCARC/testimony/swa-te.htm.

6. Herb Kelleher, "Herb Kelleher on the Record," *Business Week*, December 23, 2003, http://www.businessweek.com/bwdaily/dnflash/dec2003/nf20031223_5702_db062.htm.

Text design by Mary H. Sexton
Typesetting by Delmastype, Ann Arbor, Michigan

The text face, Palatino, was designed by Hermann Zapf for the
Stempel foundry in 1950. The graceful and highly legible Palatino
is one of the most widely used typefaces in the world today.
     —courtesy adobe.com

The display font is Frutiger. In 1968, Adrian Frutiger
was commissioned to develop a signage system suited to the
architecture of the new Charles de Gaulle Airport outside Paris;
he designed a simple, clean, robust sans serif type that is highly
legible. In 1976, Frutiger completed the family for the
Stempel foundry.
     —courtesy adobe.com

*Burpee Basics*

# annuals

## A Growing Guide for Easy, Colorful Gardens

### Emma Sweeney

Macmillan • USA

MACMILLAN
A Simon & Schuster Macmillan Company
1633 Broadway
New York, NY 10019

Macmillan Publishing books may be purchased for business or sales promotional use. For information please write: Special Markets Department, Macmillan Publishing USA, 1633 Broadway, New York, NY 10019.

MACMILLAN is a registered trademark of Macmillan, Inc.

BURPEE is a registered trademark of W. Atlee Burpee & Company

Library of Congress Cataloging-in-Publication Data

Sweeney, Emma.
    Annuals : a growing guide for easy, colorful gardens / by Emma Sweeney.
        p.   cm.   (Burpee basics)
    Includes index.
    ISBN 0-02-862223-5 (alk. paper)
    1. Annuals (Plants)   I. Title.   II. Series.
SB422.S84      1998
635.9'312—DC21
                            97-38115
                              CIP
Manufactured in the United States of America

10 9 8 7 6 5 4 3 2 1

Book design by Nick Anderson

Photography Credits:
    W. Atlee Burpee Co.: 28, 60, 71, 98, 101–102, 104–106, 107 (bottom), 108–109, 111–115,
        117–118, 120 (bottom), 121–123, 125, 127–128, 130–131, 133 (top), 135, 136 (top),
        137, 138 (bottom), 139–140, 142 (top), 144–145, 148–150, 152–159
    David Cavagnaro: xiv, 34, 37, 67, 68 (left), 120 (top), 124, 126, 129, 132, 133 (bottom), 141,
        142 (bottom), 143, 147, 151
    Ernst Benary Seed Growers Ltd.: 138 (top)
    Saxon Holt Photography: frontispiece, 103, 107 (top), 110, 134, 147 (bottom)
    Pan American Seed Co.: 136 (bottom)
    Roger Straus III: 42, 88 (right), 116, 147 (top)
    Royal Swiss Seed Co.: 119

To the memory of my brother

Burpee Basics: Growing Guides for Easy, Colorful Gardens
Down-to-earth handbooks for beginning gardeners

## Available from Macmillan Publishing

*Burpee Basics: Annuals,* by Emma Sweeney
*Burpee Basics: Perennials,* by Emma Sweeney
*Burpee Basics: Roses,* by Mary C. Weaver
*Burpee Basics: Bulbs,* by Douglas Green

### To order a Burpee catalogue:

order toll-free 1-800-888-1447
email www.burpee.com

### or write:

Atlee Burpee & Co.
300 Park Avenue
Warminster, PA  18974

# annuals

# Contents

# Foreword

Gardeners have been looking to Burpee for basic information about how to garden, as well as the seeds and plants to implement their dreams, for almost 125 years. In one or the other of the six different catalogs we publish each year, a gardener can find just about any kind of plant his or her heart desires. Our big annual seed catalog, the *Burpee Annual,* has become a gardening bible. (If you've never had the pleasure of paging through one, there's information in the back of this book about how to get your own free copy.)

What you hold in your hands—one of our new series of concise gardening guidebooks—is a continuation of that proud tradition of giving gardeners the essentials they need. These handy little books have a great deal in common with seeds: Each one contains all you need to start a wonderful gardening experience, one that will grow year by year. Successful gardens are built upon a constant reworking of the fundamentals. Season after season, even the most experienced gardeners attend to the basic practices that you'll find so skillfully explained in these guides.

If you're a novice gardener, *Burpee Basics* will help you quickly find the information you need to get started. More seasoned gardeners can use the books as invaluable reference tools for reminders of when to start the marigold seeds or divide the anemones, how to cut back the roses, or determine the right amount of fertilizer for daffodils—all the details needed to keep plants at their best.

We've made these books conveniently sized as well as easy on the eyes, hoping they'll find a valued spot not on your coffee table but on the shelf above your potting bench or in your garden workroom, right next to your seed packets, where they'll become as well-worn and comfortable in your hand as a favorite trowel or trusty clippers.

George Ball, Jr.

# Acknowledgments

This book, like most books, was really created by a team of people. I feel very blessed that the team behind this book is especially creative and talented.

My deepest thanks to Laurie Barnett for the opportunity to write the book and Richard Parks, my agent and friend, who is always supportive, smart, and kind. And to Barbara Berger, my editor at Macmillan, who carefully edited the text and photographs, oversaw the project, guided and cared for it and me, and had wise suggestions throughout. I'm grateful to have a talented editor and consider myself very lucky to have one who is also a brilliant artist. And to Roger Straus III, photographer, for the beautiful photographs he contributed and for his generosity, friendship, and abundant good advice; and Gregory Piotrowski, for his astute technical editing. My thanks also to Susan Clarey, publisher.

I'm also grateful to Mac McDermott, Janice Potter, Doris Straus, Julia Sweeney, Emily Lewis, Mary Phipps, Marilyn McLean, Ann Torrago, Kati Killam, Alice Peck, and Caron K. for help along the way.

And thanks to the team at Macmillan, including Sharon Lee, Nick Anderson, Laura Robbins, and Candace Levy.

# Introduction

My first garden was a testing ground of sorts: Could someone who had never dug and cultivated a bed, never planned or planted a plot grow a pretty garden with a minimum of fuss? Could I have a garden as colorful as the one in my imagination? Or would I stand by, hopeless, as my plants suffered and succumbed to diseases and insects and as small animals feasted on the wreckage? Would my lack of experience be evident in drooping stems and unopened buds? Would I spend countless hours in the garden unhappily tending to the needs of these plants, because all I ever wanted was a few pretty flowers?

The summer of my first garden I fell in love. I gazed admiringly at my pretty pink cosmos rising up on bright ferny foliage, marveled at the bright bursts of sunny colors in zinnias and marigolds, was fascinated by the great deep blues in my lobelia. My fears were never realized. Why? Because I filled my garden that year with easy annuals, plants I could enjoy and admire. I'm forever grateful to those annuals for making gardening easy.

Annuals are wonderful plants for the beginner gardener. You'll want to continue to use annuals every year in your garden. In *Burpee Basics: Annuals,* you learn how to plant, grow, and care for annuals. You learn what annuals need—good soil(!), sun, and climate—and you learn how to design your garden using colors, shapes, and textures.

To get your first garden with annuals up and growing, *Burpee Basics* encourages you to think about these three principles:

### 1. Start small, think big.

The best way for a beginner gardener to begin is with easy and reliable annuals in a small and manageable garden. As you learn more about gardening, you may decide you want to build bigger gardens. But start small.

Remember, too, that the big picture includes the environment. Even the smallest garden creates an ecosystem; and a balanced and healthy ecosystem is good for the soil, good for the plants, and good for the environment.

### 2. Soil is everything.

Start with good soil, and you're on your way to guaranteed success. Some things can be fudged in life, but not the soil. Every plant needs the right kind of soil.

### 3. To grow it is to know it.

Plants are great teachers, and every plant you grow will tell you what it needs. Learn from your plants, and take notes on their likes and dislikes. Also, keep using the plants that work for you. I continue to grow cosmos, marigolds, and lobelias; and each year I discover new reasons to like them. Don't be afraid to try new annuals. As the garden grows, so do we.

Carry these principles with you into your first garden, with a list of what you want from your annuals. Don't be surprised if your annuals give you what they gave me: abundant flowers, glorious color, and a love of gardening.

Emma Sweeney

# getting the basics

## The Essentials

- Defining Annuals
- Soil Is Everything
- What All Plants Need
- Tools and Supplies for the Gardener and the Garden

# Defining Annuals

Plants are categorized by the length of their life cycles, and annuals are plants that complete an entire life cycle in one growing season. They germinate, flower, set seeds, and die all in the same year. Unlike plants with longer life cycles (for example, perennials, which live for more than one growing season, and biennials, which take two years to complete their life cycle), annuals devote their brief existence to the production of seeds. Beautiful flowers are a wonderful by-product of this process.

## *Hardy, Half-Hardy, Tender*

Plants are further categorized according to their ability to withstand cold and frost. It's helpful to know whether an annual is "hardy," "half-hardy," or "tender" so you can plant it and grow it accordingly. In general, hardy annuals can withstand repeated cool temperatures below 32°F. Hardy annuals, such as snapdragon (*Antirrhinum majus*) and pansy (*Viola × wittrockiana*), provide color during the winter months in the Southwest, Gulf Coast, and southern coasts of California, where frosts are rare. In colder climates, the seeds of hardy annuals are sown directly in the ground in early spring, just as soon as the ground has thawed.

> **HARDY VERSUS TENDER PLANTS**
>
> Don't make the mistake of thinking *hardy* means the plant is tough, pest resistant, or disease resistant or that *tender* means it is fragile, sensitive, or temperamental. These terms refer only to a plant's resistance to frost or freezing temperatures.

Half-hardy annuals, such as cosmos (*Cosmos bipinnatus*) and zinnia (*Zinnia angustifolia*), can take a slight drop in temperature but are subject to freezing in the coldest winters. Tender annuals, such as black-eyed Susan vine (*Thunbergia alata*) and moss rose (*Portulaca grandiflora*), won't survive freezing temperatures, but you'll find these plants holding up beautifully in the heat of the summer. Half-hardy and tender annuals are sown after danger of all frost.

## Plants Grown as Annuals

Sometimes you'll come across the phrase *grow as an annual* or *treat as an annual,* which refers to using longer-living plants, such as perennials and biennials, for just one year. This is common practice when growing plants that cannot withstand freezes in winter in colder parts of the country or, conversely, the heat of summer in more temperate regions. To grow any plant as an annual, simply enjoy it for a season or two (spring through fall, for instance); then discard it after the first frost when it is killed naturally by the cold. Gardeners in warm climates can plant in the fall, enjoy the blooms through the winter and spring, and discard the plant in the summer.

## Some Annuals Self-Sow

Although all annuals produce seeds, many annuals, such as cleome, centaurea, calliopsis, and rudbeckia, do so with such great enthusiasm that the seeds they produce sow themselves into the ground. These "self-sowing" annuals return to your garden year after year.

### LIST OF SELF-SOWING ANNUALS

Bachelor's button (*Centaurea cyanus*)
Black-eyed Susan (*Rudbeckia hirta*)
Borage (*Borago officinalis*)
Calliopsis (*Coreopsis tinctoria*)
Cosmos (*Cosmos bipinnatus*)
Flossflower (*Ageratum houstonianum*)
Forget-me-not (*Myosotis sylvatica*)
Larkspur (*Consolida ambigua*)
Nigella (*Nigella damascena*)

Pansy (*Viola × wittrockiana*)
Petunia (*Petunia × hybrida*)
Poppy (*Papaver rhoeas*)
Snapdragon (*Antirrhinum majus*)
Snow-on-the-mountain
   (*Euphorbia marginata*)
Spider flower (*Cleome hasslerana*)
Statice (*Limonium sinuatum*)
Sweet alyssum (*Lobularia maritima*)

## Learning from Annuals

Annuals allow us to experiment and learn about gardening and our potential gardens. You can use annuals to learn about flower colors that appeal to you

*Cutting gardens are ideal for gardeners who want to enjoy their flowers indoors.*

and to understand the types of plants that may work best on a more permanent basis in a new landscape. There's no need to worry about the long-term effects with annuals—at the end of the year, you can decide whether you want to continue with the same plants and color schemes or to try something entirely different the following year. But you won't want to grow these versatile plants for the learning experience alone; the bright and energetic bursts of flowers each year make annuals some of the most desirable plants in any garden scheme. In Part Two, "Planning the Garden," you'll find many suggestions for where to plant annuals in your garden.

### *Instant Gratification in the Garden*

Annuals grow quickly, providing the garden and the gardener with instant gratification. Shrubs and perennials are often slow to establish themselves—they are busy underground developing root systems—and it may be years before they will flower the way annuals will the first year they are planted.

## Soil Is Everything

Knowing your soil is fundamental to gardening. Its texture, composition, and fertility are key issues for the gardener, making soil preparation the most important factor in growing a healthy plant. This is particularly true with annuals, because they have only one year or growing season in which to mature and flower. You'll want to give your plants good, healthy soil; and to do so, you must first understand the type of soil you have.

Plants have scientific names and common names. Although the scientific names (usually Latin) seem complicated, they really aren't once you've decoded them. Here's the basic information you need to understand this system:

- Plants in the binomial system have two names: The first name is the *genus* name; it tells you the plant's genus or type (a noun). The second is the plant's *species* name (an adjective describing the noun). Both names are in italics, as in *Viola odorata.*
- A multiplication sign (×) between the two words indicates a hybrid (the crossing of two genera, species, or cultivars), as in *Viola × wittrockiana.*
- A capitalized name in single quotation marks tells you the plant is a cultivar. A cultivar is a cultivated variety, which means it was selected in cultivation, not in the wild. These plant varieties are usually named for the person who propagated the plant. An example is *Viola odorata* 'Rosina'. 'Rosina' is the name of a cultivar within that species. Cultivar names can also describe certain characteristics about a plant and sometimes are quite playful, as in *Torenia × fournieri* 'Happy Faces'.

As you see, this system is both informative and useful, particularly when you are shopping for a specific plant, because a genus can be quite large. The violet genus, for instance, has more than five hundred species. One of the common names for these plants is "pansies"; but to get the exact plant you want, you should use the scientific name. Otherwise, you may end up with the wrong plant.

Soil has three layers: topsoil, subsoil, and bedrock. The topsoil layer is where plants' roots absorb water and nutrients. We can enrich the topsoil layer with organic matter and nutrients. The subsoil contains fewer nutrients and few soil organisms. To see the difference between topsoil and subsoil in your own garden, take a shovel or spade and dig straight down into the soil. You'll notice a marked contrast in color and in the size of the rock particles between the two layers. The subsoil has a lighter color and tends to contain bigger stones, because it is closer to the bedrock.

## Sandy or Clay?

Learning about your soil's texture is a good starting point for determining how to improve it. Soil types are defined by the size of the soil particles and range from sand, which has the largest particles, to clay, which has the smallest, even microscopic, soil particles. Between the two is loam, the healthiest soil, which has a balance of large and small particles. Loam has a rich, dark brown color. It is composed of weathered rock and minerals (have broken down over eons of geological of years), water, air, and organic matter that is teeming with helpful microorganisms.

Find out what kind of soil you have by digging a hole a few inches deep in slightly moistened soil and squeezing a handful of the dug-up soil. If the soil has a gritty texture and falls apart easily, you have sandy soil. There are some advantages to sandy soil: Plant roots will spread easily through the light soil and drainage is good. Also, it will warm up faster in the spring. On the other hand, sandy soils drain too quickly to allow nutrients to be absorbed and are consequently not very fertile.

You've got clay soil if your soil ball is sticky and easy to mold or if it is dry, hard, and practically impossible to scoop out. Clay soil won't crumble or fall apart the way sandy soil will. Heavy clay soil contains extremely fine textured particles that hold moisture in and take the air out of the soil. Although they are often fertile with nutrients, clay soils have very poor drainage, and, as a result, plant roots have a hard time establishing themselves.

Both sandy and clay soils can be improved with organic matter,

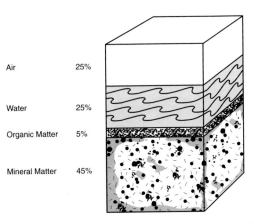

Air               25%

Water             25%

Organic Matter    5%

Mineral Matter    45%

*Ratio of air, water, organic, and mineral matter in a soil with good structure.*

such as well-rotted manure, leaves, and compost (see page 8). In addition to changing the structure of the soil, each application of organic matter will add nutrients. You want to build up your soil to create a rich, dark brown, fertile loam, which has a crumbly texture, forms a ball easily in your hand, and falls apart easily when you tap it. Loam retains moisture and nutrients, and contains a balance of organic matter.

It's best to prepare the bed well in advance of planting in it. Ideally, you would want to prepare the bed in the fall and plant in the spring. At the very least, you should prepare the bed not less than one month before planting, to give the soil time to settle.

## Alkaline or Acid?

Another factor to take into account is the pH (potential hydrogen) of your soil, which is a measure of the soil's relative "acidity" or "alkalinity." If your soil is extremely acid or extremely alkaline (low acidity), the nutrients you give your plants won't reach them, as most plants are unable to absorb nutrients under these conditions. Places where the pH tends to be extreme are deserts, where soils can be highly alkaline, and woodland areas, where soils can be highly acid.

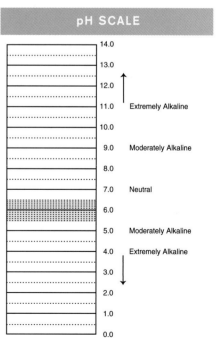

The pH scale runs from 14 to 0: 14 indicates a high-alkaline ("sweet") soil; 0 indicates a very acidic ("sour") soil. Neutral pH is 7.0, halfway between the extremes. Although most annuals prefer a pH level of about 6.5, slightly acid, on the whole a garden soil with a neutral pH is best. Plants are best able to absorb nutrients in a neutral soil.

To test the pH of your soil, purchase a soil-test kit or meter from your local hardware store or garden center. Or have your soil tested by your local Cooperative Extension, an agency within the

Department of Agriculture. The soil test may be free or cost a nominal fee, and you'll receive recommendations for improving your soil's fertility in pounds of nutrients per 100 square feet. A Cooperative Extension office is located in each county in the country, and you can usually find the phone number under the name of your local college. It may also be listed under the county name. Whether the pH test is something you do once in a lifetime or every four or five years, the information the test yields is of great value.

## Improving the Soil

Once you've determined the type of soil you have, you can work on building up its structure and fertility with organic matter. When added to the soil, organic matter will alter its structure, improving both sandy and clay soils. Sandy soils are improved with peat moss and manure mix, because these materials help regulate the amount of moisture and increase the availability of nutrients in soil. Organic matter, such as peat moss and sawdust, can be added to clay soils to lighten it up.

In addition to improving the texture of the soil, organic matter will improve its fertility. Compost and aged manures contain nutrients, such as nitrogen, phosphorus, and potassium. Each of these elements contributes to the plant's overall health. Nitrogen develops the plant's green color in the foliage and stems; phosphorus is very important for developing the flowers, seeds, roots, and fruit production. Potassium helps the plant's overall development and makes the plant's stems strong.

Organic matter is comprised of chemicals, just as inorganic fertilizers are. They are both available in different forms and are labeled with codes that refer to the percentages of nitrogen (N), phosphorus (P), and potassium (K) contained in the bag by weight. A code that reads "20N–20P–20K" tells you that this fertilizer contains 20 percent nitrogen, 20 percent phosphorus, and 20 percent potassium—a "balanced" fertilizer. Other fertilizers are high in one element and low in the other two. For instance, you've probably noticed lawn fertilizers are high in nitrogen and very low in phosphorus and potassium. This is because nitrogen will develop the green color in the grass; the other elements are less important. Organic fertilizers, as you can see from the table on pages 10–14, tend to be lower in nutrient value than synthetic fertilizers but are useful for improving the soil.

The goal of composting is to turn green matter back into organic soil, and, although it may take time to get the process right, it's worth trying, because the benefits are great. You'll save money in the long run on fertilizers for the garden.

The organic materials you put into the pile create what's called "humus," decomposed plant and animal matter. Humus is high in nitrogen, carbon, and microorganisms that break nutrients into a form usable by plants.

**WHAT TO USE**

| High-Nitrogen Materials (*The Green List*) | High-Carbon Materials (*The Brown List*) |
|---|---|
| Grass clippings | Leaves |
| Sod | Prunings from shrubs |
| Stems and stalks of annuals | Straw |
| Vegetable peelings | Ashes |
| Fruit pulp | Newspaper |
| Eggshells | Shredded bark |
| Coffee grounds | |
| Cow, horse, sheep, and chicken manures | |

**WHAT NOT TO USE**

Meat scraps
Dairy products
Weeds and plants treated with chemicals
Pet excrement
Woody stalks

Either buy a compost bin or make one with chicken wire and stakes. Always alternate layers of brown materials and green materials, and occasionally moisten the layers with water from a hose. Turn the pile over and mix it up. The more often you turn your pile, the sooner the ingredients will have composted, leaving humus. This process should take about six months.

# NATURAL FERTILIZERS AND SOIL AMENDMENTS

Fertilizers and soil amendments are not the same thing, but many organic materials fill both bills. All of the items listed here are organic; the table also includes the N–P–K fertilizer value (the percent of nitrogen, phosphorus,

| Fertilizer | Source | Fertilizer Value |
|---|---|---|
| Bat guano | Made from the aged manure of bats; expensive; fertilizer value varies with the source; rich in nitrogen and phosphorus; odorless | 8.0–4.0–1.0 |
| Blood meal | A by-product of the meat-packing industry; high nitrogen content; works quickly; may burn plants, so use sparingly and carefully | 12.0–1.0–0 |
| Bonemeal | A by-product of the meat-packing industry; sold as a powder; has a mild odor; high in phosphorus and low in nitrogen, thus it is most helpful for producing flowers, seeds, and roots | 0.7–4.0 to 18.0–34.0 to 0 |
| Chicken manure | Fast, strong nitrogen fix | 6.0–4.0–3.0 |
| Compost | Decomposed plant material; a gentle, slow-acting fertilizer; make your own or purchase it | 1.5 to 3.5–0.5 to 1.0–1.0 |
| Cottonseed meal | Made from the hulled seeds of cotton; ground up after the oil has been extracted | 6.0–2.5–1.7 |
| Dairy manure | Dairy cattle are pen fed so the manure has fewer salts and fewer weed seeds than steer manure | 0.25–0.15–0.25 |
| Fish meal | Distilled from the inedible parts of commercially caught fish; thick, brown liquid; fishy smell; slow-acting source of nitrogen (released slowly to the plant roots) | 10.0–4.0–0 |
| Humus | Rich, dark, uniformly textured substance; made from the decomposition of plant and animal matter in the final stages of decay (unlike compost, which is only partially decayed) | None |

and potassium) and the soil amendment value. (Note: Topdressing refers to the application of a dry fertilizer to the garden soil; side-dressing should be applied specifically around the plant, as close to the roots as possible.)

| Soil Amendment Value | Best Uses |
|---|---|
| None | Use as a topdressing or mix with water; good for container plants |
| None | Use as a side-dressing; sold as a powder—dilute and apply as a liquid; add to compost pile to speed decomposition; its unpleasant odor may deter deer |
| None | Good for side-dressing but expensive; steamed form is recommended over the raw form |
| Improves soil texture | Better for leafy vegetables than for flowering plants; use as topdressing |
| Improves soil's ability to hold moisture and nutrients | Apply each spring as a topdressing and work into the soil |
| Improves moisture retention | Highly acid; best for acid-loving plants as a topdressing; avoid applying to seedlings and small plants, as they can be burned by its direct application |
| Loosens soil; improves drainage in clay soil; adds texture to sandy soil | Use to improve organic content in soil; apply in spring as a topdressing and work into the soil |
| None | Dilute the concentrated form and spray on leaves for a foliar feeding |
| Improves soil aeration and allows water to penetrate more easily in clay soil; improves sandy soil's ability to retain water | Work into soil to improve both sandy and clay soil |

continues

| Fertilizer | Source | Fertilizer Value |
|---|---|---|
| Leaf mold | Nearly decomposed compost of tree leaves | 0.8–0.35–0.15 |
| Lime | Becomes chalk in its softest form and marble at its densest and hardest; an almost pure source of calcium carbonate, which acts to de-acidify soil | None |
| Manures, general | Commercial types include steer, dairy, llama, and elephant manure and even zoo poop; fertilizer and soil amendment values vary with the source; llama manure is high in phosphorus and potassium, has no unpleasant odor (the llama has three stomachs so food is completely digested and converted into a great fertilizer); read labels for fertilizer content | Varies |
| Mushroom compost | Easy and inexpensive in areas where the mushroom-growing industry thrives | 0.4 to 0.7–60.0–0.5 to 1.5 |
| Peat | Also known as peat mulch, sphagnum peat moss, and sphagnum peat; dried and decomposed plant debris from wetlands; fibrous or powdery texture; can be difficult to wet | 1.5 to 3.0–0.25 to 0.5–1.0 |
| Seabird guano | Aged manure of seabirds; great source of phosphorus and calcium, which promotes strong roots and stems and improves disease resistance | 1.0–10.0–0 |
| Seaweed extract | Also known as kelp, kelp meal, and liquefied seaweed; rich in minerals and won't burn plants | 1.0–0–1.2 |
| Sewage sludge | Created from municipal sewage and aerated in a special process; looks like a rich soil mix and does not smell; popular brand name is Milorganite; some products may contain pesticides and heavy metals—read labels carefully | 5.0–3.0–7.0 |
| Steer manure | Not the best available manure; often high in salts and full of weed seeds | 0.25–0.15–0.25 |

| Soil Amendment Value | Best Uses |
|---|---|
| Improves soil's moisture and nutrient retention | Use as a mulch and dig into the soil after the growing season to improve organic content of soil |
| None | Use primarily to raise a soil's pH; good sources include dolomitic limestone and mushroom compost; use as a side-dressing |
| Loosens soil, improves drainage in a clay soil, and adds texture to a sandy soil | Incorporate into the soil in spring; some manures may deter deer |
| Loosens soil and improves drainage in clay soil; adds texture and volume to sandy soil | Highly alkaline; don't use around acid-loving plants; use as a side-dressing to improve soil's pH balance |
| Loosens clay soils and helps sandy soils retain water | Work into soil to improve it; don't use peat when it's dry; once wet, it will retain water better than any other amendment |
| None | Use as a topdressing |
| Stimulates growth of soil microbes and earthworms; expensive | Apply to the garden as topdressing each spring and fall; good source of trace minerals, plant hormones, and vitamins |
| Improves sandy soil's ability to hold moisture and nutrients; loosens heavy soils | Add to gardens as a fertilizer and soil conditioner; may deter deer |
| Loosens clay soil, improves moisture and nutrient retention in sand | Dilute to make a "tea" by steeping it in water, then dilute again to be sure mixture is weak; it can burn plants if not diluted properly |

continues

| Fertilizer | Source | Fertilizer Value |
|---|---|---|
| Wood ashes | Taken from a fireplace or wood stove; similar to limestone in alkalinity; ashes from hardwoods are more alkaline than ashes from softwoods | 0 to 5.0–7.0 to 2.0–3.0 |
| Worm castings | Worm manure; high in nutrients and microorganisms | 0.5–0.5–0.3 |

Organic and inorganic fertilizers can be applied in a number of ways. Inorganic, or synthetic, fertilizers afford you the greatest number of options. They can be applied as a liquid or dry powder and come in time-release formulas. You can choose which fertilizer to use based on your needs. For instance, time-release fertilizers are more expensive than the other two but are worth it if it's easier for you to make just one application of fertilizer. Liquid fertilizers work well—just mix with water and apply every few weeks or according to directions. Dry powders are applied to the soil, around the plants.

Inorganic fertilizers are very useful, particularly for annuals, which benefit from the application of a balanced fertilizer such as a 20–20–20 mix. If you don't have the luxury of a compost pile, you may want to use chemical fertilizers as a low-cost alternative to buying more expensive organic matter.

## Potting Soil (for Plants in Containers)

Soil in your garden and potting soil for containers are two completely different substances. The best potting soils are actually soilless and usually consist of two parts peat moss, one part perlite, and one part vermiculite. The peat

### NOT FOR CONTAINERS

Don't use ordinary garden soil in your containers—it won't drain well, and the plants' roots may rot. Also, if you decide to bring them indoors for the winter, you'll risk bringing in diseases and insects.

| Soil Amendment Value | Best Uses |
|---|---|
| Can improve a sandy soil; can harm a clay soil by making it even heavier | Dig into garden in late fall with lime to raise soil's pH; don't apply more than once every 3–4 years. |
| None | Use as a side-dressing for plants in beds and containers |

moss gives the soil its body, the perlite helps with drainage, and the vermiculite allows this mix to retain water. You can buy potting soils at a garden center or make it yourself by combining these ingredients in approximately the two to one to one ratio. Potting soils have no fertility (no teeming microorganisms here), so nutrients must be added.

# What All Plants Need

In addition to requiring a soil or some medium to grow in, most plants share a basic need for sunlight and adequate water. The majority of annuals require average soil, full sun, and regular waterings; but there are annuals that are tolerant of less water and a shadier environment. It's important to know the needs of the plants you are growing as well as what your environment provides for the plants. What kind of soil do you have? How much sunlight will your garden receive? Does your area receive adequate rainfall in the growing season?

## The Sun

All plants need light, and where you place your new garden will determine how much sunlight the plants will receive. You can assess the amount of sunlight that will reach your plants by observing the patterns of sunlight in the morning, at midday, and in the afternoon. You have full sun if your garden receives at least six hours of direct sunlight. The garden may receive shade for some of the time between 8:00 A.M. and 6:00 P.M., either in the early morning or the late afternoon. Partial sun or partial shade is the second possibility. Here you have sun half the day (about four hours) and shade half the day (four hours). This kind of shade may be filtered or dappled, such as that beneath limbs of trees. Last, you may have a shade garden, which receives fewer than four hours of sun per day. This is the shade you find in woodlands, underneath dense, overhanging trees, or by a building or wall that blocks the sun. Another name for plants that do best in this kind of light is "shade tolerant."

Keep in mind that the available sunlight in your garden will differ by the time of day and season of the year. Full sun in the morning and full sun in the afternoon are not the same; and morning sun is the more preferable of the two, as it will dry the overnight dew on plants quickly, reducing their susceptibility to diseases. Morning sun followed by afternoon shade is ideal, in that the shade in the afternoon gives plants a respite from the heat of the day and helps them cool down for the evening.

## ANNUALS FOR SHADY SPOTS

Here are some annuals that are sun loving but will still bloom in partial shade:

Black-eyed Susan vine
  (*Thunbergia alata*)
Five-spot (*Nemophila maculata*)
Geranium (*Pelargonium × hortorum*)
Larkspur (*Consolida ambigua*)
Lobelia (*Lobelia erinus*)

Nicotiana (*Nicotiana alata*)
Love-in-a-mist (*Nigella damascena*)
Pansy (*Viola × wittrockiana*)
Spider flower (*Cleome hasslerana*)
Sweet alyssum (*Lobularia maritima*)

Finally, you may find you have more sunlight in the spring, before deciduous trees have leafed out, than you do once the trees have their leaves. This is important to keep in mind since spring is probably when you'll be planting.

While most annuals need full sun, there are some annuals that actually prefer shade or partial shade, for example, impatiens, browallia, begonia, caladium, forget-me-not, and torenia.

## Water

If the environment doesn't provide your plants with enough water, you'll have to provide it for them. Gardeners in arid parts of the country, where rainfall is consistently low, may prefer to site the garden in shade where plants will need less water or to use plants that are drought tolerant. Gardeners living where rainfall is heavy face the problem of waterlogged soil, which prevents plants from growing properly by asphyxiating the roots. Thus good drainage is key in areas of high rainfall.

Whether your area gets little rain or buckets, your soil should be free-draining: neither too clayey nor too sandy. You'll see the phrase *a well-drained soil* a lot, particularly in the "Plant Portraits" section of this book; it refers to the ability of water to travel through soil at an average rate, neither too quickly nor too slowly. You can tell how well your soil drains by digging a hole about 1 foot deep and filling it with water. If it drains in under 1 hour you have quick-draining soil; if it takes a few hours your soil is well-draining; if drainage takes longer than 3 hours, your soil is slow-draining. Soil amendments can improve drainage. If watering your plants on a regular basis is difficult, consider using an irrigation system with automatic starters. Determine how much water your plants need and be prepared to make watering them an essential part of your gardening chores.

## The Zones and Your Climate

Finally, you'll want to know about "hardiness zones" and learn which zone you are gardening in. Although most annuals do well in all climates and zones, you may decide at a later date to add perennials and shrubs to your garden; then knowing your zone will be more important.

The USDA Zone Map (see page 160) breaks down the United States, Canada, and Mexico into eleven climate zones; the coldest zone is 1, and the warmest is 11. Although temperature is a factor, so are rainfall, snowfall, and the number of hours of sunlight. Some plants are hardy in the coldest climates and perform poorly in the heat; other plants do well in heat and can't take the cold.

Bachelor's button (*Centaurea cyanus*)
Baby's breath (*Gypsophila elegans*)
Black-eyed Susan (*Rudbeckia hirta*)
Candytuft (*Iberis umbellata*)
California poppy
  (*Eschscholzia californica*)
Calliopsis (*Coreopsis tinctoria*)
Cosmos (*Cosmos bipinnatus*)
Creeping zinnia
  (*Sanvitalia procumbens*)
Dahlberg daisy (*Dyssodia tenuiloba*)
Dwarf morning glory
  (*Convolvulus tricolor*)
Four o'clock (*Mirabilis jalapa*)

Globe amaranth (*Gomphrena globosa*)
Love-lies-bleeding
  (*Amaranthus caudatus*)
Mealy-cup sage (*Salvia farinacea*)
Mexican sunflower
  (*Tithonia rotundifolia*)
Moss rose (*Portulaca grandiflora*)
Nasturtium (*Tropaeolum majus*)
Snow-on-the-mountain
  (*Euphorbia marginata*)
Spider flower (*Cleome hasslerana*)
Treasure flower (*Gazania rigens*)
Verbena (*Verbena × hybrida*)

## Other Climatic Factors

Plants on south-facing terraces in high-rise buildings, near the ocean, and on exposed hilltops can suffer from damaging winds; the soil will dry out quickly under these conditions. It's best to use plants that tolerate such an environment, or try to provide your plants with a protective windbreak.

These plants are good when the weather is a little chilly, in fall and spring in the cooler climates and during winter in the more temperate regions.

Nicotiana (*Nicotiana alata*)
Ornamental cabbage
  (*Brassica oleracea*)
Pansy (*Viola × wittrockiana*)

Snow-on-the-mountain
  (*Euphorbia marginata*)
Spider flower (*Cleome hasslerana*)
Thorn apple (*Datura meteloides*)

Additional factors to consider are pollution and humidity. Many plants cannot withstand poor air quality, although Madagascar periwinkle (*Catharanthus roseus*) is one that does not seem affected by heavy pollution. If you think smog may be a problem, try to find plants that do well in your area by investigating nearby gardens. Plants that do well locally are your best bet.

If you live in an area where humidity is very high in the summer, be aware that the moisture in the air can cause some plants' leaves to retain more moisture, encouraging diseases. The best defense in these cases is to know in advance how to detect the diseases, and then deal with them immediately.

# Tools and Supplies for the Gardener and the Garden

Shopping for tools and supplies can be an overwhelming experience for the beginner gardener—there are tools for garden maintenance, supplies for the soil, soil conditioners, protective clothing and equipment for the gardener, products for pest and disease control—the list seems endless. Then there are the decorative and useful items for the garden itself such as containers, planters, pavers, trellises, statuettes, benches, fences, and gates. Although you'll never need all of these items, it's good to have an idea of what you will need and a basic understanding of the necessary gardening tools and supplies.

## *Gardening Tools*

When you garden, you want to perform the basic chores—such as weeding, digging, pruning, cutting, watering, and caring for growing plants—with relative ease. By purchasing solid, well-built, long-lasting, high-quality tools and using the right tools for the job, you'll make caring for your garden a pleasant exercise rather than hard labor.

Good tools, such as a high-quality gardening spade, can last for more than twenty years. It's always worth it to buy the best. You should get tools that are steel-tempered because they last longest, and be sure to purchase the right tools for your size and weight. Try each tool out in the store, making sure it feels comfortable in your hand.

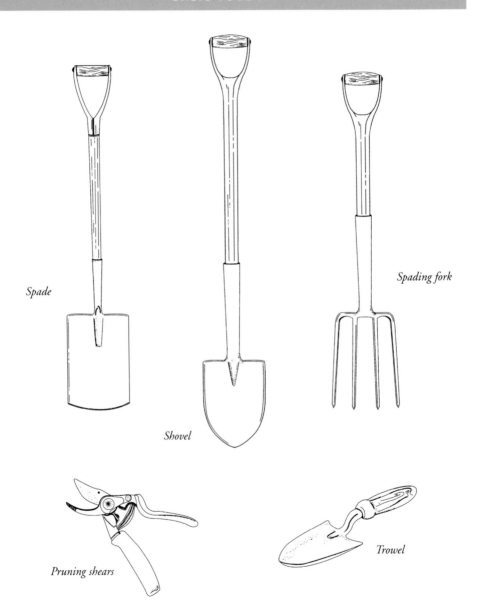

Spade

Shovel

Spading fork

Pruning shears

Trowel

Tools are designed to handle specific chores in the garden. For instance, the fork, spade, and shovel will allow you to prepare and plant the bed and to lift out rocks from the garden. The trowel is smaller and is ideal for planting seedlings. The hoe, or cultivator, will help you in your weeding efforts as well as in "cultivating," or preparing, the ground; the rakes are necessary for smoothing the topsoil and cleaning up leaves and other debris. Edgers are very handy for making a neat garden edge (you can also use a square-pointed spade for the same purpose), and shears will be useful for cutting back and cleaning up plants.

## Spading Fork

Spading forks are useful for turning over soil, lifting medium-sized plants, forking in manure, and spreading mulches. You'll use this tool most often while preparing your garden bed.

## Shovel and Spade

Shovels and spades come in a variety of sizes and styles, and each is designed for a particular purpose. The shovels with long handles and rounded tips are used to dig holes, scoop soil, and move plants; they have a long shank to provide better leverage. Square-pointed shovels are best used for scooping gravel. The shovel you will need is commonly called a "garden shovel" and is somewhat smaller and lighter than the other shovels. It has a round point and its light weight makes it ideal for digging in the garden.

Spades come in a variety of shapes for different functions. The two most commonly used for the small garden are the square-end spade and the transplanting spade. In general, spades are like shovels in that they are also used for scooping and turning over the soil, but their smaller sizes make them more useful in the garden. The square-end spade can be used for digging, cultivating, edging, or breaking up soil.

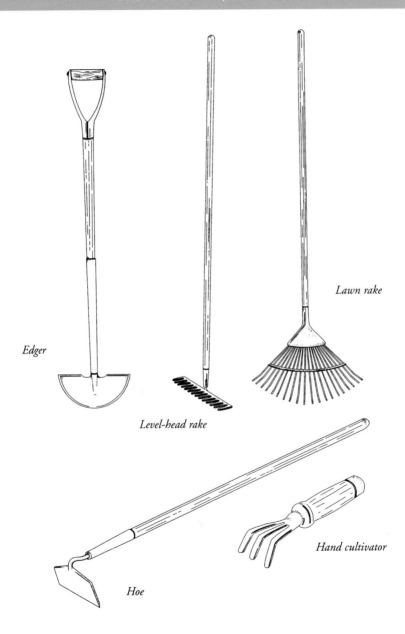

Lawn rake

Edger

Level-head rake

Hand cultivator

Hoe

## Trowel

Small-scale tasks are best done with smaller tools, such as trowels. These narrow metal scoops with curved or padded handles are ideal for planting seedlings and other small plants and working with plants in containers. This is an item you won't want to skimp on: Get the best! Some trowels come with lifetime guarantees. You can't imagine how many trowels you may go through (in a lifetime) if you don't buy one that is built to last. It's a good idea to paint the handles of small tools with bright colors so you can easily find them in the soil.

## Hoe

There are many different types of hoes. Hoes, or cultivators as they are also called, can be hand held or attached to the end of a long shank. They are used for weeding and cultivating the soil and are available with diamond-shaped heads, flat heads, and forks with three or four tines.

## Rake

Lawn rakes and level-head rakes (sometimes known as tined rakes and flat-head rakes) are both important in the garden. The lawn rake is useful for raking leaves, twigs, grass clippings, and other light debris. Rakes made of bamboo are not as expensive as metal rakes and do the job as well. Besides, the natural feel and smell of the bamboo is nice. Be sure to store a bamboo lawn rake in a dry place.

Level-head rakes are useful for making a level surface on new garden beds and seedbeds. If you decide to get just one rake, get a lawn rake, which you can use in the garden in a pinch.

## Edger

The semicircular edge on the edger is about 8 inches wide and attached to a long handle. Edgers are ideal for cutting sharp edges along the garden or lawn walkways, driveways, and sidewalks. Stainless-steel tends to slice through sod more easily than do other metals.

## Pruning Shears

Also known as pruners, hand pruners, and secateurs, pruning shears look like pliers with a spring in the pivot point and two sharp blades. Good-quality shears will have small shock absorbers, and the best ones will reduce wrist fatigue. Shears are an essential tool for the gardener, and you'll use them to prune woody and green stems up to about $3/4$ inch thick.

## Watering Tools

Get a durable, flexible, and weather-resistant rubber garden hose fitted with brass couplings that won't leak, a nozzle, and plastic watering cans.

---

### EXPANDING YOUR TOOL KIT

Garden supplies you may want to think about getting later:

- Twine for securing tall stems to stakes
- Stakes
- A soaker hose, which allows the water to be evenly distributed in the soil
- A dandelion weeder
- Labels for plants
- A barometer—it's always good to watch the weather
- A wheelbarrow

---

## *Supplies for the Garden*

When you shop for your garden supplies, you'll see all kinds of amendments and conditioners for the soil as well as potting soils, seed-starting kits, mulches, and pest and disease products. Before you purchase any of these items, learn about your soil type and decide how you want to grow your annuals (indoors, directly in seed beds or as nursery transplants). Please see Part Three, "Digging In," for further information on these topics.

You may also be intrigued by the selection of attractive planters and pots, and it's worth knowing the differences between natural and synthetic materials so that you can purchase the right containers for your needs.

## Containers

A large terra-cotta container will cost much more than a plastic one the same size; is the terra-cotta container better? The answer is yes, if your priority is aesthetics—the plastic one will never look as good. However, if you plan to use the container by a swimming pool or on a flagstone patio where reflected heat is strong, you may want to get the plastic one; your plant will need fewer waterings. Terra-cotta is porous and dries out faster than its counterpart. You may also want to consider some of the newer materials on the market that look remarkably like the real thing: Therma-Lite™, for instance, looks just like heavy concrete or clay but is a synthetic. Not only does it retain moisture better than terra-cotta, but it weighs much less and is easier to move around.

If you plan to use lots of containers, you may want to consider buying them in large sizes: plants in small pots require more water than those in large ones, and you may tire of watering so many different containers.

---

### COMPARING CONTAINERS

Porous materials, such as clay or concrete:
- Drink up water
- Crack from freezing and thawing
- Need to be brought indoors in winter in areas where it freezes

Synthetic materials (Fiberglas, Thermo-Lite, plastic):
- Are very lightweight
- Are long lasting
- Are fairly inexpensive
- Are nonporous
- Are winterproof

Wooden containers, including window boxes:
- Are natural looking
- Are often lightweight
- Can be made of easy-to-find whiskey barrels, available at nursery centers

## Equipment for the Gardener

Protective clothing and gear is important in the garden. What you'll need and what you may want:

- A wide-brimmed hat
- An apron with pockets for hand tools
- Gardening clogs or boots
- A blank book to record notes about the garden
- A basket or bucket to carry tools in
- Sunscreen
- Garden gloves—cowhide for cooler months and bigger jobs and cotton or rubber for light tasks in the summer months

---

### SHOPPING CHECKLIST

- Get solid, steel-tempered or stainless-steel tools: spading fork, spade, shovel, trowel, hoe, hand cultivator, steel rake, tined rake, and edger.
- Get the right accessories—hat, gloves, clogs/boots, sunblock. Wear light-colored, lightweight clothing in the summer.
- Think about soil amendments, fertilizers, and mulches.
- Think about containers, trellises, and benches.

# planning the garden

## The Essentials

- Dream a Little
- Garden Styles
- Using Colors, Shapes, and Textures
- Making the Most of What You Have
- Planning and Mapping the Garden
- Seven Easy Garden Plans

# Dream a Little

Every garden begins with your idea, dream, or vision of what a garden should be. For many of us, the most perfect garden we will ever tend is the one in our imaginations—no doubt it's free of pests and diseases and in vivid Technicolor. It almost doesn't matter that in the end the *real* garden is vastly different from the one we envisioned: It's our dream that matters. With the dream, we begin the process of creating the garden we want.

Imagine your perfect garden. What does it look like? Is it a private retreat with cool blues and grays or is it a bright burst of sunny colors? Look for inspiration for your dream garden in books, magazines, seed catalogs, everywhere around you, and begin building your garden by dreaming it. Eventually, you may even come close to creating a garden that looks like the one in your imagination.

## The 10-Minutes-a-Week Garden: When It's All About Ease

As you consider your garden, think about how much time you want to spend tending it. You may have other commitments for your time or simply prefer a garden that is low-maintenance. Either way, you'll want to choose annuals that require very little care. You can plan a garden around your lifestyle and still let it reflect your personality. Plant a wildflower garden with poppies, calliopsis, and bachelor's buttons or grow moss rose and nasturtium along the

---

### THE VERY EASIEST OF THE EASIEST ANNUALS

Black-eyed Susan (*Rudbeckia hirta*)
Calliopsis (*Coreopsis tinctoria*)
Cosmos (*Cosmos bipinnatus*)
French marigold (*Tagetes patula*)
Impatiens (*Impatiens wallerana*)
Love-lies-bleeding
  (*Amaranthus caudatus*)

Madagascar periwinkle
  (*Catharanthus roseus*)
Moss rose (*Portulaca grandiflora*)
Nasturtium (*Tropaeolum majus*)
Pot marigold (*Calendula officinalis*)
Spider flower (*Cleome hasslerana*)
Sunflower (*Helianthus annuus*)
Zinnia (*Zinnia angustifolia*)

---

driveway. Low-maintenance plants are very important for the gardener with limited time, and luckily, annuals provide a diverse group of easy-care plants from which to choose.

## The Weekend Warrior as Gardener

On the other hand, if your garden is quickly becoming your new obsessive hobby, then let your dream garden reflect your quest for perfection—garden with gusto! This is an opportunity to bring all your creative talents and energy to the fore. Rise at dawn to water, feed, mulch, or inspect the plants for overnight insect and pest damage. Love your lobelia and worship your pansies. And, most important, plan more gardens.

## Back to the Practical

Once you have an idea of the type of garden you want, focus next on the practical considerations, such as where to site the garden, how much sunlight the site receives, and what you will need to do to prepare the soil.

### Siting the Garden

The most useful place for your garden is where you'll most enjoy it. Beyond this basic premise, site your garden in the most level area in your yard where the plants will receive adequate sunlight and where a water source is near at hand. It's best to place the garden within 50 feet of an outdoor water faucet.

The site of your garden may have been chosen for you if you're reviving an existing garden or working in a small space. Some of the outdoor space may already be designated for other activities: the middle of the lawn won't be a good place for the cutting garden if it doubles as a baseball diamond. Often the best place for a new garden is also the most practical place: close by the house or along a fence, even along the driveway.

However, don't feel you have to use annuals in a garden design at all if that doesn't suit your style. If you prefer your gardens to provide food for the table, combine annuals with vegetables and herbs for a pretty potager or French kitchen garden. If you have an unsightly fence you want covered, use a quick-growing annual vine like morning glory (*Ipomoea purpurea*) to clothe it.

- Use low-growing annuals such as alyssum (*Lobularia maritima*) and cottage pinks (*Dianthus chinensis*) to fill in bare spots between shrubs and perennials and for edging paths.
- Use all sizes of annuals in pots, planters, window boxes, bed, borders, cutting gardens, and vegetable gardens.
- Use large annuals like spider flower (*Cleome hasslerana*) and sunflower (*Helianthus annuus*) for temporary hedges.
- Use vines like morning glory (*Ipomoea purpurea*) to cloak a fence.

## Each Garden Is a Room

Think of each garden you create as a "room." Whether your new garden is on a city terrace or in a large backyard, plan it with the idea of creating a finished look to that part of the landscape. For instance, in the small backyard, you may want to create a simple woodland garden beneath a large shade tree. A house in the country may benefit most from a pretty and practical cutting garden. When you create garden rooms, the entire landscape begins to look pulled together, coherent, and balanced. In future years, you can always add on by extending the garden.

Finally, first-time gardeners will want to keep their gardens small. A garden of fifty or sixty square feet is plenty of space. Don't invite disappointment by creating a garden you haven't got time to tend, and don't create a labor-intensive situation that will have you swearing off gardening for the rest of your life.

## Your Garden, Your Ecosystem

Although your garden may seem small, it is a vital part of an ecosystem. Keep your plants in good health, create a habitable environment for beneficial insects, and choose plants that are well-suited for your particular landscape. Your first garden may be small, but if you think of it in the larger picture, it isn't small at all.

# Garden Styles

The style and mood of any garden is determined by its overall shape and the types of plants within it. Before considering what shape of garden you want, consider your landscape as a whole and where your garden will fit in. Your garden should suit you and your home, so you should design your new garden with these thoughts in mind. Think about whether you want a bed or border, a garden that is formal or informal, or a shape that is circular, rectilinear, or free-form.

The basic difference between garden beds and garden borders is that beds tend to be more formal, adhering to stricter geometric patterns (rectangles, diamonds, circles) whereas borders are usually more informal: They border or are backed by a tall hedge, wall, split-rail fence, or other defining feature. The fronts of borders are often free-form, shaped to imitate contours as they appear in nature. That said, there are curved beds and rectangular-shaped borders; there are no hard and fast rules in garden design.

If you're not sure what kind of garden would best suit you, take a look at your house. Formal houses—Georgian designs and many ranch-style homes—are defined by their use of symmetry and angles. These houses usually have a kind of "boxy" architecture and classical or traditional elements, such as front doors framed by round or square pillars and pediments. Formal gardens work best with homes that require symmetry.

Informal houses, on the other hand, such as rambling colonials and California bungalows, are likely to be more informal; the appeal of these houses is in their meandering layouts and open floor plans. When a house's architecture is based on a rambling design, or a design that is very modest and understated, like a cottage at the beach, you'll want to continue the theme into the garden, especially if the garden is close to the house.

## Neat and Tidy or Organized Disorder?

A formal garden has an overall look of neatness and tidiness about it. The principles underlying its design are symmetry, order, right angles, pattern, and repetition. Annuals with neat habits of growth—such as cottage pinks (*Dianthus chinensis*) and flossflower (*Ageratum houstonianum*), which are low

*Informal garden*

and round—are particularly well suited to creating a patterned formal bed design. Such annuals were used extensively in the great Victorian gardens that resembled enormous carpets (the gardens were called "carpet beds").

An informal garden has a curvilinear or free-form shape; and the plants within it spill, flop, and sprawl. You won't find a formal hedge around this garden. Plants in the informal garden tend to have a relaxed habit about them, like daisies, or those with tall, feathery plumes. Cosmos (*Cosmos bipinnatus*) is a favorite in these gardens, with its colorful, daisy-like flowers atop tall stems, as well as spider flower (*Cleome hasslerana*), a tall plant with graceful stems that bend in the wind. Mealy-cup sage (*Salvia farinacea*), black-eyed Susan (*Rudbeckia hirta*), and bachelor's button (*Centaurea cyanus*) are native American wildflowers that provide the kind of informal, relaxed feeling just right for this kind of garden.

## AESTHETICS IN THE GARDEN

Don't forget to add a bit of whimsy to your garden plan. Consider installing some garden art, such as animal or human figures, birdbaths, gargoyles, Victorian gazing balls, sundials, a well-placed rock, or a weathered wheelbarrow.

# Using Colors, Shapes, and Textures

Some of us firmly believe that in nature, no colors clash, and certainly, we would like that to be true, but everyone has a different opinion. Some say that pink flowers must never be planted next to orange, while others feel that pink and orange are a perfect color combination. Although you should try to avoid obvious clashes that put both colors at a disadvantage, keep in mind that the use of color is very subjective. The best guideline, really, is to know what you like.

It may be helpful to understand some basic principles about using color when designing a garden. For instance, color is only as good as the light it appears in. A bright color such as red or orange looks vibrant in sunlight, while a pastel color will appear washed out or weak. On the other hand, those pale colors will show up well in the shade. White is a wonderful color in shade, and will look almost luminescent by moonlight.

A backdrop can make an enormous difference in the way a flower color appears. A backdrop of green, for instance, in a hedge, will bring out the colors in a garden design, particularly the lighter and paler colors.

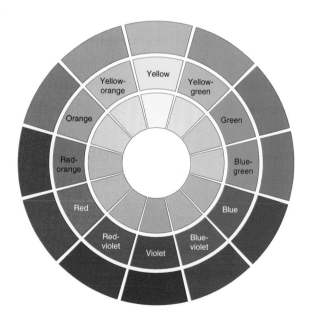

*The color wheel shows primary colors (red, yellow, blue) and the colors that connect them (red-yellow, or orange, for instance). Hues are pure colors; shades are made by the addition of black, and tints by the addition of white.*

The way you combine colors in your garden is an important consideration, one that will affect the overall mood. For instance, using varying shades of one color (known as a monochromatic color scheme) evokes a feeling of restraint that can enhance the symmetry of a formal garden. White is often used this way to elegant effect. In the polychromatic color scheme, different colors are combined to create a less static, more dramatic look. Placing colors of different values—blues next to yellows next to violets—may be a challenge for the garden designer, but the results can be wonderful. A riot of color is exciting.

Any two colors that sit next to each other on the color wheel, such as yellow and orange, are said to be "harmonious." The use of such colors in the garden paints a restful picture: the eye can take in both colors at once without refocusing. The opposite effect is attained when we use "complementary" colors such as yellow and violet, which sit across from each other on the color wheel: The eye is constantly refocusing to adjust to the different hues. A complementary color scheme can be dazzling, and allows both colors to be shown off to their advantage.

## USING COLOR

Rather than combining two complementary colors of the same value or intensity, use one true color and the other in a tint or shade. For instance, instead of using violet with yellow, use blue/violet with yellow, or a strong violet with a softer yellowish cream. This subtle use of color will provide an ever greater contrast between the two colors, showcasing both of them.

### Complementary Flower Colors in the Garden

**Blue and Yellow Mixes**
Light blue flossflower (*Ageratum houstonianum*) with bright yellow pot marigold (*Calendula officinalis*)
Bright blue mealy-cup sage (*Salvia farinacea*) with soft yellow nasturtium (*Tropaeolum majus*)
Light blue bachelor's button (*Centaurea cyanus*) with bright yellow calliopsis (*Coreopsis tinctoria*)

## The Values of Hot and Cold Colors

Warm colors seem to appear closer and larger than they actually are and are said to advance, while cool colors appear more distant and are said to recede. You can use this phenomenon in your own garden to make it appear larger and closer, or smaller and farther away than it actually is.

Hot colors—reds, oranges, and yellows—evoke passion and excitement and work best around pools, tennis courts, play centers, and other "high-energy" areas. These colors tend to look their best in large spaces they can't overwhelm and in bright, sunny settings.

On the other side of the color spectrum are the relaxing, calming, cool colors: blues, purples, and greens. These colors create a restful, peaceful garden perfect for unwinding and listening to the birds sing. Cool colors, even in a hot climate, make the sun feel a little less intense. They give the illusion of space, making a small garden appear bigger.

## Using White

White flowers are very useful in the garden. When white is added to color it lessens the intensity of that color. Red becomes pink, yellow turns cream, purple softens to lilac. Pastel colors in the garden are very soothing and can be enhanced by a dark green background. White or cream-colored flowers can be used to tone down very hot colors, such as red. Scarlet sage (*Salvia splendens*), with its bright red spikes, looks pretty with white cosmos (*Cosmos bipinnatus*) next to it. White looks magnificent when used in big splashes. Or sprinkle it throughout your garden to give the space a feeling of unity and movement. A shrub border really stands out when white impatiens (*Impatiens wallerana*) are planted underneath.

*White gardens don't have to use only white flowers: This garden makes use of blues and grays and a bold splash of orange.*

## Shapes, Textures, and Sizes

The shapes of plants and their flowers play a large role in garden design. Flower clusters, or "inflorescences" as they are called, come in many sizes and forms, including composite (daisy), raceme, spike, umbel, and panicle. Combining plants with different flower shapes can be striking—try planting a daisy-shaped flower next to a spiked flower. If the color contrast between the two plants is strong, too, such as with a white cosmos (daisy-shaped) and a red salvia (spiked), you have a winning combination.

The colors, shapes, and textures of plants' foliage vary from the big, bold, multicolored leaves of a fancy-leaved caladium (*Caladium* × *hortulanum*) to the blue-green, fernlike foliage of cottage pinks (*Dianthus chinensis*). It's good to use a mix of foliage textures and colors in the garden. For instance, the glossy purple leaves of purple basil (*Ocimum basilicum* 'Dark Opal') and the woolly, silvery leaves of dusty miller (*Senecio cineraria*) complement each other well.

Finally, think about situating your plants according to size, but don't be dogmatic about it. In general, taller plants are placed in the back of a border or toward the center of a bed, and smaller plants are used as edgings, but simply arranging plants from shortest to tallest can make your garden appear dull and uninspired. Try putting a taller plant toward the front just to break up the order. Weave a plant throughout the garden to create a flowing feeling. Design concepts come in handy when you're working out the plans for your garden. (See page 41, "Planning and Mapping the Garden.")

# Making the Most of What You Have

We aren't all blessed with a perfect combination of space, sun, rainfall, and great soil. Make the most of what you have, whether its a small space, a dry garden, or an area with unusable soil or no soil. Here are some ways to get around your property's problems.

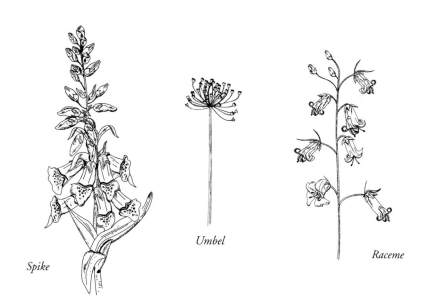

Spike

Umbel

Raceme

Panicle

Composite

## When Space Is at a Premium

If your garden is in a small space, consider the following:

- Enhance the vertical space with hanging plants that are at eye level.
- Add trellises for depth and dimension.
- Keep color to a minimum.
- Use plants with large leaves and height.
- Don't think that small spaces require small pots: On the contrary, a large ornamental pot or two in a small space will catch the eye.

## The Dry Garden

Gardeners in the desert and semiarid regions of the United States have to make the best of low rainfall and prolonged drought conditions. Water restrictions because of climate, cost, or conscience can mean watering is not always practical or possible. The solution is the Xeriscape™ garden, "landscaping for water conservation." The principles of the Xeriscape (*xeri* means "dry" in Greek) garden are:

- Make use of plant species that require little, if any, water beyond what naturally occurs as rain or snow. Good garden design can reduce waterings. Avoid planting at the top of a slope, because water will naturally run off. Try not to plant in windy areas.
- Give your garden a soil that can retain water, one that is neither too sandy nor too clayey.
- Minimize turf grasses.
- Put thirsty plants in one area of the garden, plants that require less water in another. Take into account microclimates, making the best of naturally cool spots such as north-facing walls and shady areas.
- Use a mulch to keep your soil cool in summer and help retain moisture in the soil.
- Water only when absolutely necessary. Transplants, however, need watering, and attention to new plantings is crucial to the success of the garden. Drip irrigation with a soaker hose is the preferable method of

watering, but it must be used properly. Mist sprinklers can waste water, and a faulty sprinkler system is also wasteful.

- Maintain the garden and your irrigation tools. Deadhead, cut back, fertilize, and weed; clean sprinkler systems.

## The Great Solution: Containers

Containers are excellent for growing annuals and can be especially useful when a garden in the ground is not an option. Some tips:

- Give the plants what they need: sun, water, and fertilizer.
- Elevate larger containers to expose drainage holes. Bricks work well.
- Cram the annuals into pots and let the foliage spill over the sides; the more the merrier. You want a lush effect.
- Plant annuals that will trail or cascade from the container, such as edging lobelia (*Lobelia erinus*).
- Add a wire trellis to a container for height and an annual climbing vine, such as a morning glory (*Ipomoea purpurea*) or hyacinth bean (*Dolichos lablab*).
- Move the containers around if they are getting too much sun, not enough sun, or if the soil dries out too fast.
- Use colorful pots with discretion—let the plants make the statement.

For more about containers, see page 25.

# Planning and Mapping the Garden

The first step in designing a garden space is to lay out the shapes of the future garden in your yard. You can accomplish this with measuring tape and string to map out a formal bed design; use a garden hose or rope to replicate the sinuous lines of a curved bed or border. The next step is to draw two maps: The first is a sketch of the site, which you'll make outdoors, and the second is a garden plan, which you'll draw using the information you gathered outside.

## Planning

After choosing a site and shape for your garden, sketch it in a notebook. The first step is to make a legend in the lower right corner of your paper, indicating the scale you are using, such as 1 inch = 1 foot. Next, outline the shape of the garden. You should feel free to be as basic as you can: Just draw straight lines to indicate where the borders of the garden are. Draw curved lines if the bed has a curved shape.

Next, assess how much sun your new garden will have by determining the polar directions. Where is your garden when you face north? Note on your sketch the direction north (it's easiest if you designate this on the paper with an arrow facing up, making north up, south down, east to the right, and west to the left). If you're up to it, include other relevant features in your sketch, such as your windows, doors, existing gardens, paths, fences, etc. You can, and should, make this drawing as simple as possible. Finally, note how much sun your garden will get: full sun, shade, or partial shade. This survey will provide you with a record for years and will help you design and plan new gardens. It's a good idea to update your survey as trees grow, fences are put up, or other significant changes are made in the landscape.

### MAKE A RECORD

You may also want to take photographs of your garden site at this time. If you left something out, the picture will remind you. Before and after photographs are also great incentive builders and will no doubt encourage you to create more gardens.

Your survey could turn up some surprises. Perhaps you thought your garden was in full sun and learn that, in fact, a portion of the garden is in partial shade. You may have forgotten an existing large shrub and now have to decide

*Facing page: Arrange your containers to show the flowers and pots off to their best advantage. This arrangement, with its bright and hot colors, is particularly effective against the cool white background.*

whether to incorporate it into the design, resite the garden, or get rid of the shrub. Preparing a map is a great exercise for helping you learn about your site. It will also help you determine the number of plants you will need for the garden. Annuals, in particular, have specific spacing requirements (except when they are in containers), and your garden will look best if it is planned and planted with accurate spacing in mind.

## Mapping the Garden

The next step is to draw up a garden plan. Translate the sketch of your site onto graph paper (or use a ruler on plain paper). Have on hand a list of the plants that you want to use in your garden design; read through Part Four of this book to help you choose which plants to grow.

Start with a legend, as you did with the sketch. Draw an arrow facing up and write *north,* and note the scale. Graph paper makes this part very easy. Outline the garden according to scale, and start planning the space.

When deciding on the number of plants to incorporate into your design, remember to take into account the spacing requirements of each annual— chiefly, how much space to allow between plants in your bed or border. This is determined by the size of the plant when full grown. As a general rule, smaller plants should be spaced approximately 6 inches apart; middle of the border plants, 8 to 12 inches apart; and tall plants at the back of border, 18 to 24 inches apart. Labels and seed packets will give you all the spacing information you need.

---

### CHECKLIST FOR PLANNING THE GARDEN

Consider all of the following when planning your garden:

Sun and shade requirements          Shape of foliage
Soil requirements                   Plant height
Water requirements                  Spacing requirements
Flower color

---

Be as precise as you can with spacing requirements at this point—you'll avoid making costly mistakes later on when shopping for the plants by getting too many or too few. Remember to employ some of the concepts of color and design discussed earlier: Use color to achieve your desired effect; mix shapes and textures; and weave plants throughout to give the garden a unified, or tied-together, feeling. Finally, record the name of each plant you want to use in the design as well as its height, spacing requirements, and color.

The plan you create on paper may not look like any garden you've ever seen, but it will look similar to other garden plans and the plans that follow at the end of this chapter. These two-dimensional maps have their limitations (there's no sense of depth or texture), but the overhead perspective of the garden gives you a good sense of the overall picture, and this stage of planning is a valuable step in the process of creating a garden.

Remember, refining and editing are important parts of the process, and every good plan allows for as much modification as necessary.

## Seven Easy Garden Plans

If designing and planning a garden at this stage is less attractive to you than jumping right in and starting to dig, consider using one of the seven garden plans that follow. You can choose from a very low maintenance garden, shade garden, moon garden, self-sowing annuals garden, cutting garden, container garden, or mixed border. Each has its advantages: the moon garden might be best enjoyed by the gardener whose favorite time (or only time!) to relax in the garden is in the evening; the shade garden will brighten up a shady nook; the sunny summer border may be a challenge for some first-time gardeners, but it's well worth the effort.

# The Ten-Minutes-a-Week Gardener's Garden

The rectangular shape of this bed is easy to measure out and the pattern of zinnias and geraniums, bordered by alyssums is simple and elegant. The design of the bed also makes getting in and out of the garden easy, and maintenance is a breeze with ten minutes a week of deadheading.

**Step 1:** Choose a sunny site in the middle of your lawn and measure out a space 4 × 10 feet.

**Step 2:** Prepare the bed, incorporating organic amendments.

**Step 3:** Purchase zinnias and marigolds as healthy nursery transplants in six packs or flats. You can start the alyssum by seed, planting according to the directions on the seed packet.

**Step 4:** Water and feed throughout the growing season; deadhead the zinnias and marigolds as necessary. The alyssum will self-sow, so you can leave those plants in the ground. Discard the zinnias and marigolds.

**PLANT LIST**

A  Marigolds (*Tagetes patula*), orange (18)
B  Zinnia (*Zinnia elegans*), red (9)
C  Sweet alyssum (*Lobularia maritima*), white (24)
D  Sweet alyssum (*Lobularia maritima*), rosy pink (24)

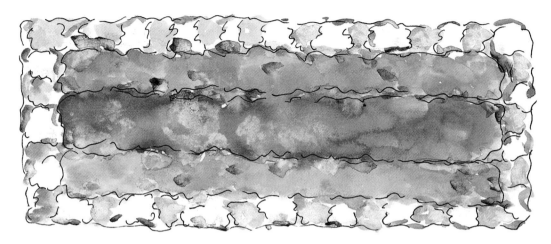

*Design for a 4 × 10-foot easy garden bed*

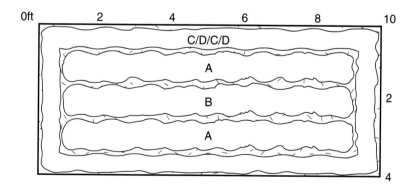

# Made for Shade

This garden is designed for a shady spot under a large deciduous tree, such as a maple. It may seem like a larger garden than some of the others (at more than 60 square feet); but since its center is a large tree, it occupies less space than you think.

**Step 1:** Choose a location in partial shade. Measure out 1 foot from the tree and mark out the garden around the tree, placing the tree in the upper left corner.

**Step 2:** Prepare the bed. You will probably have to add soil or humus to the garden so that the plants' roots are not competing with the tree's roots for water and nutrients. Simply mound the soil—about 8–12 inches high—around the base of the tree, being careful not to disturb the tree's roots.

**Step 3:** Water as needed throughout the growing season. If you've added enough compost, the plants should need only one feeding at the start of the growing season. There's no need to deadhead these plants. In the fall, simply discard the annuals in a compost bin.

**PLANT LIST**

A  Nicotiana (*Nicotiana alata*), white (4)
B  Coleus (*Coleus × hybrida*), foliage (3)
C  Browallia (*Browallia speciosa*), blue (4)
D  Forget-me-not (*Myosotis sylvatica*), blue (18)
E  Impatiens (*Impatiens wallerana*), white (10)
F  Caladium (*Caladium × hortulanum*), foliage (6)

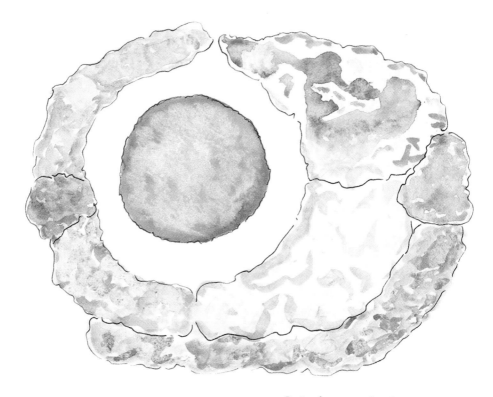

*Design for a 7 × 9-foot shade garden*

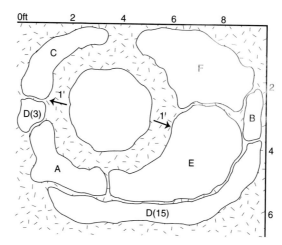

# Moon Garden

This garden uses white and silver plants, which become luminescent when the moon rises, and fragrant plants to enjoy in the evening. It's the perfect garden for those who are away from home all day—a haven in which to wind down after a hard day's work.

Step 1: Choose a sunny site for the garden and measure out a garden bed 4 × 10 feet. Install a trellis along the rear side of the bed for the climbing moonflowers. You may want to put the trellis against the south-facing side of your house or another building. If you don't want a trellis, simply remove the moonflower from the list. Provide a place to sit and enjoy the garden in the moonlight, such as a bench or pergola.

Step 2: Prepare the bed.

Step 3: Plant the annuals. All the plants on the list can be started with seeds. Sow the sweet alyssum and poppies directly in the garden. You could also start with nursery transplants for everything but the poppies, which resent transplanting.

Step 4: Water and fertilize throughout the growing season. Deadhead plants as necessary.

Step 5: In the fall, discard the stock, snapdragons, dusty miller, and zinnias; let the other plants set seeds for next year's garden.

**PLANT LIST**

A  Shirley poppy (*Papaver rhoeas*), white (3)

B  Scented stock (*Matthiola incana*), white, lavender (3)

C  Snapdragon (*Antirrhinum majus*), white, pink (6)

D  Nicotiana (*Nicotiana alata*), white (2)

E  Sweet alyssum (*Lobularia maritima*), white (16)

F  Dusty miller (*Senecio cineraria*), foliage (3)

G  Common zinnia (*Zinnia elegans*), white (3)

H  Cosmos (*Cosmos bipinnatus*), white (6)

I  Moonflower vine (*Ipomoea alba*), white (5)

J  Mexican zinnia (*Zinnia angustifolia*), white (3)

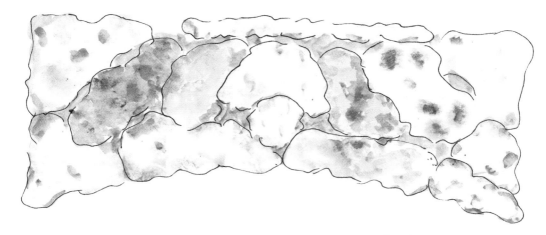

*Design for a 4 × 10-foot moon garden*

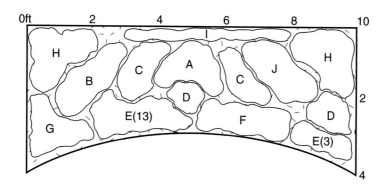

# Self-Sowing Annuals

This garden uses annuals that will reseed themselves into the soil each year. The garden may look raggedy in a year or two when plants come up where you didn't expect them, but the cottage garden charm and informal, haphazard arrangement of flowers can be very appealing.

**Step 1:** Choose a sunny site and lay out the 5 × 12-foot bed. An open area is best; a meadow would be ideal.

**Step 2:** Prepare the bed.

**Step 3:** Plant the annuals. Purchase healthy seedlings in six packs or flats, or start with seeds. You'll need to sow the poppies directly in the bed.

**Step 4:** Deadhead and water throughout the growing season. You may not need to fertilize if you incorporated a lot of organic material into the soil when you prepared the bed.

**Step 5:** In the fall, let the plants remain so they will self-sow. In the spring, enjoy your garden all over again!

**PLANT LIST**

A  Shirley poppy (*Papaver rhoeas*), mixed (8)

B  Gloriosa daisies (*Rudbeckia hirta*), yellow (3)

C  Spider flower (*Cleome hasslerana*), pink (8)

D  Johnny-jump-up (*Viola tricolor*), purple, yellow (9)

E  Love-in-a-mist (*Nigella damascena*), light blue (9)

F  Bachelor's button (*Centaurea cyanus*), purple (6)

G  Sweet alyssum (*Lobularia maritima*), white (20)

H  Calliopsis (*Coreopsis tinctoria*), yellow (3)

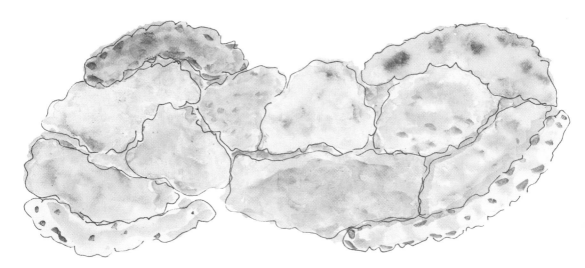

*Design for a 5 × 12-foot garden with self-sowing annuals*

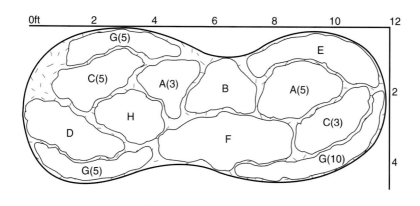

# A Garden for Cutting

This is a garden that makes use of flowers that are great for cut flower arrangements, because they are long-stemmed, or last a long time in water. Gardens designed specifically for cutting flowers should be no wider than about 4 feet so that you have enough room to get in and out of the garden easily.

**Step 1:** Choose a sunny site and lay out a garden 4 feet wide by 12 feet long.

**Step 2:** Prepare the bed, incorporating plenty of organic matter into it.

**Step 3:** Plant the annuals. Purchase healthy seedlings or start with seeds. Cutting gardens look best when colors are grouped together: the reds in one part, pinks nearby, blues in another section.

**Step 4:** Cut flowers to enjoy indoors. It's best to cut flowers in the morning when it is still cool. Always bring shears and a bucket of cool water with you into the garden and place the cut stems immediately in the bucket of water. Provide fresh water for the cut flowers in a vase by changing it daily.

**Step 5:** In the fall, dig up annuals and discard in a compost heap. Start a new cutting garden in the spring, altering the arrangement of the flowers within the garden.

## PLANT LIST

A  Spider flower (*Cleome hasslerana*), pink (6)

B  Pot marigold (*Calendula officinalis*), yellow (3)

C  Scarlet sage (*Salvia splendens*), red (8)

D  Globe amaranth (*Gomphrena globosa*), scarlet (4)

E  Bells of Ireland (*Moluccella laevis*), foliage (4)

F  Nicotiana (*Nicotiana alata*), white (2)

G  Snapdragon (*Antirrhinum majus*), mixed pastels (3)

H  Scarlet sage (*Salvia splendens*), violet (3)

I  French marigold (*Tagetes patula*), yellow (9)

J  Cockscomb (*Celosia argentea* var. *cristata*), red (6)

K  Cosmos (*Cosmos bipinnatus*), white (6)

*Design for a 4 × 12-foot garden for cutting*

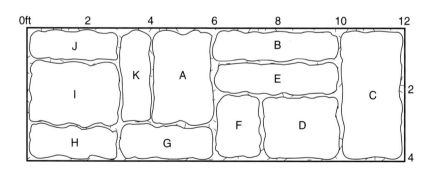

# Container Garden

This is a garden design just for containers. Choose your containers—whether plastic, terra-cotta, concrete, or wood—for their practicality and their looks. They shouldn't upstage the plants! Also make sure that your containers have drainage holes and are elevated on bricks.

**Step 1:** Prepare four containers—make sure they are clean and place them in a sunny location.

**Step 2:** Prepare the potting soil and pot up the annuals. Move the containers around to show off all plants to their best advantage.

**Step 3:** Water and fertilize throughout the growing season. Remember, annuals in containers need more water and fertilizer than do plants in the ground, because the soil has little or no nutrients.

**Step 4:** In the fall, bring the geraniums indoors to winter over. Cut plants back by half. In the spring, move them back outdoors.

**PLANT LIST**

**First Container**

A  Geranium (*Pelargonium* × *hortorum*), salmon (3)

B  Common zinnia (*Zinnia elegans*), white (3)

C  Verbena (*Verbena* spp.), purple, pink (6)

**Second Container**

D  Fountain grass (*Pennisetum setacum*), foliage (1)

E  Petunia (*Petunia* × *hybrida*), purple (6)

F  Gloriosa daisy (*Rudbeckia hirta*), yellow (1)

**Third Container**

G  Pot marigold (*Calendula officinalis*), gold (6)

**Fourth Container**

H  Angel's trumpet (*Datura meteloides*), white (1)

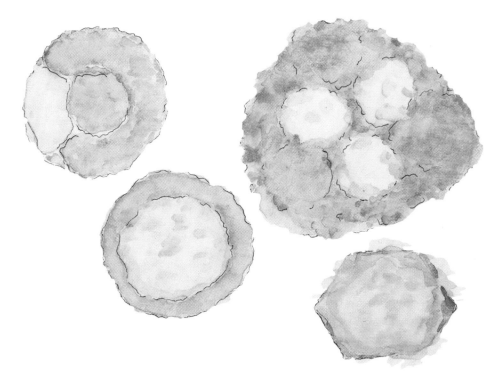

*A container garden*

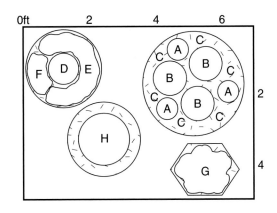

# Sunny Summer Border

This garden is designed as a border for full sun, with brightly colored annuals (yellows, oranges, reds) that are at their peak in the hot summer months. It may be a bit more challenging than the other gardens, but the reward of brilliant color all summer long will make it worthwhile.

**Step 1:** Choose a sunny site for this border against a fence or wall.

**Step 2:** Prepare the 5 × 12-foot garden bed.

**Step 3:** Plant the annuals. Purchase seedlings from a nursery or start with seeds started indoors or sown directly in place. You can sow directly into the ground the Mexican sunflower, sunflower, marigold, nasturtium, creeping zinnia, and moss rose. Purchase globe amaranth, gloriosa daisy, Mexican zinnia, and love-lies-bleeding as seedlings.

**Step 4:** Water, feed, and deadhead regularly. In the fall, discard annuals in compost bin.

**PLANT LIST**

A Mexican sunflower (*Tithonia rotundifolia*), yellow (3)

B French marigold (*Tagetes patula*), orange (8)

C Nasturtium (*Tropaeolum majus*), mixed (3)

D Creeping zinnia (*Sanvitalia procumbens*), yellow (2)

E Sweet alyssum (*Lobularia maritima*), white (6)

F Mexican zinnia (*Zinnia angustifolia*), yellow (3)

G Gloriosa daisy (*Rudbeckia hirta*), yellow (3)

H Cosmos (*Cosmos bipinnatus*), white (3)

I Love-lies-bleeding (*Amaranthus caudatus*), red (3)

J Sunflower (*Helianthus annuus*), yellow (3)

K Globe amaranth (*Gomphrena globosa*), scarlet (5)

L Moss rose (*Portulaca grandiflora*), mixed (9)

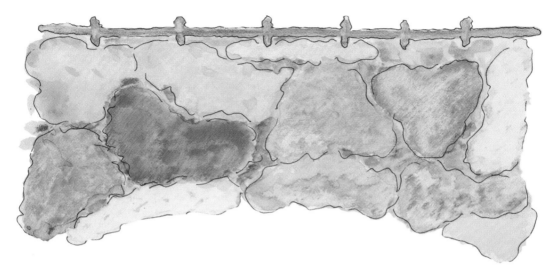

*Design for a 5 × 12-foot sunny border*

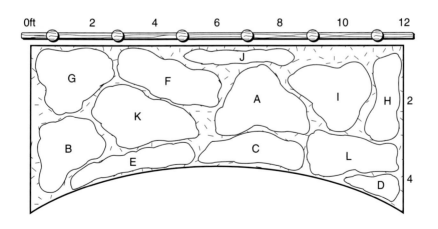

# digging in

## The Essentials

- Preparing the Garden Bed
- Planting Annuals
- Soil Skills: Watering, Feeding, Weeding
- Ordinary Chores: Pinching, Deadheading, Staking
- Wintering Over
- A Course in Container Gardening
- The Natural Way to Healthy Plants

# Preparing the Garden Bed

You've selected the site for your new garden, decided on a garden design, and chosen your plants. Now you need basic information on planting, watering, feeding, and caring for your annuals.

One of the most important tasks is the preparation of your garden bed—annuals need 8 to 12 inches of good soil in which to grow. It's best to prepare the bed and improve the soil when the weather is cool, and fall is the ideal time for this chore, followed by a spring planting. Preparing the bed well in advance of planting gives the soil time to settle. Lay a mulch of compost or shredded leaves over the new bed to protect the soil from exposure to strong winds and rains during the winter months. In the spring, use your spade or fork to incorporate the mulch into the soil before you plant. As an alternative, you can prepare your new bed in the spring and wait a few weeks (a month would be best) for the soil to settle. If you plant too soon after the ground has been tilled, plants can easily suffer from root damage as the ground settles around them, exposing their roots to sun and wind.

The job of preparing the soil can be done in three easy steps:

## Step One: Removing the Sod

The first step in creating a bed is to remove all grass and weeds. It's tempting to rush through this part of the process, but don't! You'll be plagued by pernicious weeds for years to come, and it's actually not a difficult job. Your diligence now will pay off in years to come when you're happily doing something else in the garden besides weeding.

New garden beds that are in the middle of a lawn are the easiest to prepare: Just remove the sod and till the ground. Where the land has to be cleared of shrubs, large rocks, and brush, the job gets a little harder.

### PROTECT YOURSELF

If you think you might be getting into poison oak or ivy, wear a long-sleeved shirt and gloves. In areas of the country where ticks are a problem, wear light-colored pants tucked into socks.

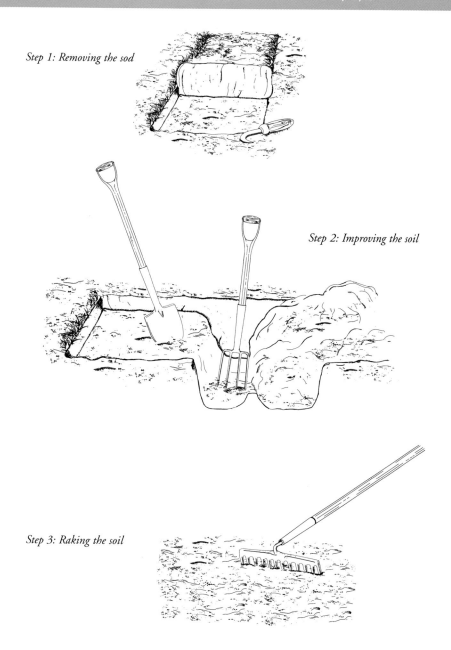

*Step 1: Removing the sod*

*Step 2: Improving the soil*

*Step 3: Raking the soil*

## Rolling Up the Lawn

The easiest way to carve a rectangular garden bed out of an existing lawn is to slice the sod, much like the way you cut a carpet and roll it up.

First, outline your garden area with stakes and string or lime. Using a sharp knife (a linoleum knife, which you can buy at any hardware store, works best), cut into the sod as you would a carpet, very carefully pulling the knife back toward you. Following the outline in the sod, cut down the length of the garden bed about 4 feet long, then cut a parallel line about 2 feet away. Next, make a cut at the top that connects the ends of those two lines, forming three sides of a rectangle. Work your fingers into the connecting cut and under the sod, gently tugging at the grass. You'll feel it pry loose. If it doesn't come up right away, take your spade or edger and gently loosen it. Once you get a few inches loose, roll back the sod. You can continue this process throughout the bed, working from the top to the bottom. Be sure to shake as much soil from the pieces of sod as you can into the garden bed. It's good topsoil and worth keeping. Pieces of sod can be put into a wheelbarrow or on an old sheet nearby and either thrown in the compost bin or placed on bare spots in the lawn where they may reroot.

## Smothering with Plastic or Newspaper

One way to get rid of weeds and grass is to lay sheets of black plastic or sections of newspaper on the potential garden area to smother them. This method works well only when it's hot—you'll need to wait until early summer for the heat to kill the growth. Cover the garden plot entirely and anchor the plastic or newspaper with rocks. The grass or weeds should begin to die within a week or so, after which time you can remove the plastic or newspaper and lift off the dead grass and weeds.

However, persistent perennial weeds won't be killed so easily; they will have to be removed by hand. It's easiest on days when the soil is neither very soggy nor very dry and hard. Don't move on to Step Two ("Improving the Soil") until you feel confident that all the perennial weeds and every inch of their long roots are gone. Otherwise, when you chop up the soil with your spade or rototiller, you'll also be chopping up and dispersing the weeds, and they will return with a vengeance.

## Step Two: Improving the Soil

Once you've removed the debris and vegetation, you can begin improving the soil by tilling it (that is, through cultivation) and adding amendments. You may want a rototiller for this part of the job, which you can rent at a local hardware store. Rototillers are machines that can dig about 8 inches into the soil, making your work a lot easier.

Start by loosening the soil in the bed to a depth of 6 to 8 inches with your spade, fork, or rototiller. Wait a week or so and work the soil again, this time adding 2 to 4 inches of leaf mold, well-rotted compost, or peat moss. You can add the amendments to the top of the soil and use your spade and fork to incorporate them.

### AVOIDING HEAT STRESS

Do the strenuous gardening jobs, such as lifting and digging, in the early morning; drink plenty of liquids such as water, iced tea, and fruit juice; wear light-colored, lightweight clothes (including a hat); wear sunblock; don't do too much too soon—gradually lengthen your exposure to the sun.

Organic matter will break down slowly over time, so it's practically impossible to add too much. Remember, organic matter differs in the amount of nutrients it contains (see "Natural Fertilizers and Soil Amendments," pages 10–14). If you are using a synthetic fertilizer as an alternative to organic matter, add it the day before you plant because it breaks down quickly.

## Step Three: Raking the Soil

The final step in soil preparation is to smooth and grade the soil with a rake. This should be done immediately after Step Two. Use a rake with a level head to even out the soil, then turn the rake around and use the flat surface of the rake to tamp down the soil and remove any air pockets. Allow the soil to settle, which takes several weeks. However, if you're in a hurry to get your garden started, you can help the soil settle by watering the newly prepared ground. At the very least, wait at least a week between smoothing and grading the soil and planting in it.

After you've dug your garden bed, give it a clean edge with natural materials, such as bricks or stones, or a synthetic material, such as black plastic. The least expensive edging is the one you create yourself with an edger or a flat-edged spade where the grass meets the soil of the bed.

You can create the most precise guidelines for a rectilinear bed by tying string tautly to stakes placed at opposite ends of the bed. Or simply use your eye to determine a straight line. Either way, work down the length of the bed cutting into the sod about 3 inches deep with your edger or spade as you face the garden, and follow the line. For a curved bed, use a garden hose to outline the shape, and follow the outline as you would for a linear bed, making smaller cuts in the sod and overlapping where necessary to form the curve. Shake any loose topsoil from the sod into the garden bed and smooth the topsoil into the bed.

# Planting Annuals

There are basically two ways to start a garden with annuals: You can plant seedlings or nursery transplants or sow the seeds yourself. Although starting with seedlings from the nursery has definite advantages (it's often easier to do), starting annuals by seed offers you a greater variety of plants you can grow and costs much less than purchasing plants begun at a nursery. For gardeners where the growing season is short, however, transplants can bring color into the garden before seeds have even emerged.

## *Buying Good Seedlings*

Nursery transplants are available in flats, cell packs, and individual pots. Seedling flats are large boxes with no partitions between the plants; this lack of division often causes the roots to become entangled. Cell packs are preferable; these individually molded plastic containers with 4 to 6 seedling plants offer the least risk of transplant shock. The third option is to buy 3-inch or even 5-inch individually potted annuals. These seedlings provide instant results and are great for a quick fix—they look like they were planted weeks earlier. Remember, whether you buy your seedlings in flats, cell packs, or bigger pots, space plants in your garden according to the directions on the labels.

## A Healthy Seedling Plant

When you shop for seedling plants, keep in mind what a healthy seedling should look like:

- Make sure that it's been properly pinched; it should have a full shape with lateral growth. A tall stem with sparse growth indicates that the seedling was not pinched.
- Watch for yellowing leaves around the base of the plant, which can indicate the plant is suffering from a pot that is too small. Leaves that are wilting or brown mean the plant could be suffering from too much or too little water. Look for green leaves.
- A mass of roots growing out of the drainage holes tells you the plant has long outgrown its pot and is "root bound."

*The look of a healthy seedling versus a leggy seedling*

The day before you plant:

- Get the soil ready—turn it over, grade it, level it, and help it settle by watering it.
- Check your garden plan; make any last-minute changes.

The day you plant:

- Make sure you have all the plants as outlined in your plan.
- Keep annuals in small containers moist and in the shade.
- Bring your trowel, spade, gardening bag or wheelbarrow, flat-head rake or lawn rake, scissors, labels and pen, hose or watering can with you to the garden.

*Newly planted garden*

## Planting Day

Before planting seedlings from cell packs, water them and trim off any roots showing through the drainage holes in the bottom. Be careful not to hurt the seedling's young top growth; it's okay to touch the leaves—they will grow back if broken off—but take care not to break any stems.

It's best to plant seedlings in the morning or late afternoon on a cool and cloudy day when the temperatures are around 50°F. It shouldn't be too windy when you plant.

If you want some help in properly spacing your annuals, make a grid in your garden similar to the one on your plan. Measure out every foot in your garden, dividing the bed into square feet. You can draw a line with a stick or use lime if you have it. At first your newly planted annuals will look pretty far apart from each other, but proper spacing will ensure they grow into healthy plants and fill in just right. (See "Mapping the Garden," page 44, for more on spacing.)

*Plant your seedling at the same depth at which it was planted in the container.*

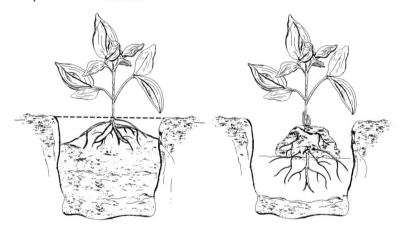

Plant your seedlings at the same depth at which they were planted in their containers. Use a trowel to give them a hole that is slightly bigger than their root ball, and place them in gently, replacing the soil around the roots. Tamp down the soil to carefully remove any air pockets. Water the transplants, and place their label nearby. When all the plants are in the ground, give them a good, deep soak.

## Starting Seeds Indoors

If you can provide the right germination conditions for seeds, you might want to start your garden with them. Certainly, for gardeners in colder climates with shorter growing seasons, starting seeds indoors brings color to your garden earlier. When you start seeds indoors months before you plant them, you get bigger plants sooner by extending their growing season. Some annuals have to be started indoors before being moved to their permanent locations, such as begonias, geraniums, impatiens, and petunias, which all require long periods after germination to grow to sizable plants.

| EASIEST PLANTS TO START FROM SEEDS | |
|---|---|
| Pot marigold (*Calendula officinalis*) | French marigold (*Tagetes patula*) |
| Cosmos (*Cosmos bipinnatus*) | Nasturtium (*Tropaeolum majus*) |
| Love-lies-bleeding (*Amaranthus caudatus*) | Sunflower (*Helianthus annuus*) |

Be sure to give yourself plenty of lead time to start annuals indoors; most need to be sown 6 to 8 weeks before the last frost date. You can check for the frost date in your area by looking at "Average Dates of First and Last Frosts in the United States," pages 167–178.

You can start seeds in containers you purchase at a nursery center, such as flats or soil blocks, peat pots, or peat pellets. Peat pots are very useful containers in which to start seeds. These are made of peat and wood fiber, and many have soluble fertilizer added. They are biodegradable, so when it's time to transplant the seedlings you simply set the pots into the soil. When using peat pots, be sure to plant the pot below soil level—the dry peat at the rim can act as a wick, absorbing all moisture and keeping water from reaching the plants. You can also use seed-starting trays, which have water trays beneath them to ensure that plants are watered properly.

All plants have specific germination needs, and their needs vary. For instance, most seeds require a high level of humidity and an average temperature of about 70°F, though some seeds, such as sweet peas (*Lathyrus odoratus*),

*Seed-starting trays*

*Soil block molds*

*Fertl-Cubes*

*Peat pots and pop-up pellets*

thrive in a cool 55°F. Some seeds also need strong light to germinate, where-as others require darkness. Always check the seed packet for the individual requirements of the seeds you sow.

Always use clean containers for starting your seeds. Diseases, such as damping off (a fungus that occurs when the soil is too damp and the air too humid), can develop as a result of microorganisms lurking on the sides and bottom of the container. Wash all recycled containers, such as plastic crates, with a solution of ten parts water to one part household bleach to kill off germs.

You can decide whether to use a sterile, soilless growing medium or a "live" medium. A sterile medium has the advantage of reducing the possibil-ity of damping off disease. However, with a soilless mix, plants are being grown in an artificial environment and will have to adjust to real soil. You'll have to repot them into individual pots, introduce them to soil for a couple weeks, then move them outdoors.

Sowing in a live medium will introduce the seedlings faster to the envi-ronment they will eventually grown in—that is, soil—so you can move the seeds directly outdoors after hardening off (see below). Gardeners who prefer a live medium often use a live mix containing equal parts compost, peat moss, and builder's sand. Either way, you can purchase most types of grow-ing media at your local nursery, along with the other supplies you'll need for starting seeds indoors.

To begin sowing seeds, moisten the sowing medium in a large pan or bowl, then fill the seed container with the potting mixture. Don't fill con-tainers to the top; leave $1/8$ inch or so of space between the soil and the lip of the container. Follow the seed packet instructions on how deep to plant the seeds. You can press small seeds right into the growing medium, and make holes the right depth for larger seeds with the eraser end of a pencil. After seeding, water with a mister or other means of gentle overhead watering. Keep the soil evenly moist, but don't let it get waterlogged.

The first leaves to appear from germinated seeds are really "false" leaves, called cotyledons, which are actually food storage cells that just look like leaves. When the seedlings have developed their true leaves, you can begin to add a liquid fertilizer at about one-quarter strength.

If you chose a sterile medium in which to grow your seeds, you'll have to move them into a live soil when they develop true leaves by transplanting them gently into their own individual pots filled with ordinary potting soil. Gently prick them out of the containers when they have two or three sets of true leaves. Be careful not to damage the stem, which will cause the seedling to die. Don't worry if you tear a leaf or two.

The easiest way to get the seedlings out is with a pencil or other pointed object. Hold the stem between your thumb and forefinger and carefully prick out the roots with the pencil tip. You can then place each seedling into its individual pot and carefully firm the soil around the roots. Water the seedlings after transplanting, and keep the newly transplanted seedlings out of direct sunlight for the first few days to reduce shock.

The final step before moving your seedlings out to the garden is called hardening off, which is the process of acclimating them to the outdoors. Young plants will need as smooth a transition as possible from indoors to outdoors. First, move them outside to a sheltered, lightly shaded position for an hour or two each day for the first two weeks. Always bring them indoors at night. Gradually expose them to direct sunlight, a little more each day.

Keep watering as necessary. This process should take a few weeks, after which time your plants are ready to be transplanted (or, with peat pots, simply planted) in the garden. The same techniques for transplanting home-grown seedlings also apply to nursery-grown seedlings.

## ANNUALS YOU CAN SOW DIRECTLY IN THE GROUND

Baby's breath (*Gypsophila elegans*)
Bachelor's button (*Centaurea cyanus*)
Cosmos (*Cosmos bipinnatus*)
Gloriosadaisy (*Rudbeckia hirta*)
Four o'clock (*Mirabilis jalapa*)
Larkspur (*Consolida ambigua*)
Nasturtium (*Tropaeolum majus*)

Poppy (*Papaver rhoeas*)
Pot marigold (*Calendula officinalis*)
Spider flower (*Cleome hasslerana*)
Stock (*Matthiola incana*)
Sweet pea (*Lathyrus odoratus*)
Sunflower (*Helianthus annuus*)
Zinnia (*Zinnia angustifolia*)

## Sowing Seeds Directly in Place

Sowing seeds directly in place is a wonderful way to start your first garden—it's both easy and gratifying. Some annuals, such as sunflowers (*Helianthus annuus*) and cosmos (*Cosmos bipinnatus*), can be started directly in the soil after the last frost. Other annuals prefer to be planted directly where they are to grow because they don't like to be moved. Simply plant the seeds according to the directions on the seed packet (always check to be sure the seeds are fresh by looking at the expiration date on the package).

When you sow directly in the soil, you need to be sure the right germination conditions are met by sowing them at the right time and watering as often as necessary. Be careful to water gently, as a rush of water can wash the seeds from the soil.

Sowing seeds in place can be done either by "broadcasting" or by sowing the seeds in place at their correct depths. Seeds that germinate early can be sown by broadcasting: Sprinkle the seeds over lightly raked soil, cover them with a very thin layer of soil, and gently water. Seed sizes vary, from the very smallest alyssum (*Lobularia maritima*) and moss rose (*Portulaca grandiflora*) seeds, to the largest, about the size of small peas, such as sunflower (*Helianthus annuus*) seeds. The tiny seeds are easier to work with if you mix them first with a little builder's sand. Seeds are planted at different depths, depending on their size. When planting any seeds, follow the directions on the seed packets and plant at the right depth.

## Thinning Out Seedlings

Thin your seedlings when they are 3 to 4 inches tall and there are two true leaves on the plant. Seedlings will need to be thinned to give space to the remaining plants. Be careful not to crowd annuals, as it will only result in them all being unable to get enough sun, water, and food. Thin seedlings, depending on their size and spacing requirements. Lower-growing annuals should be thinned to 6 inches apart, medium-height annuals to 12 inches, and taller annuals should be thinned 12 to 24 inches. You can thin either by cutting the seedlings you are eliminating at ground level or by pulling them up from the soil. If the soil is disturbed around the remaining seedlings, firm it in.

Many annuals, such as begonia, coleus, and pelargonium, can be propagated easily by cuttings from the plants. The best time to take cuttings is in the middle of their growing season. Select a few strong, healthy shoots and cut them off at their bases. Place the cuttings in a well-watered sterile, soilless, rooting medium (such as perlite and vermiculite). Keep the medium evenly moist. Give the cuttings bright light and a temperature of about 70°F. You may need to place them in a plastic bag to provide sufficient humidity.

You'll know your cuttings have formed roots when you tug gently at the stem and feel a resistance. After about two weeks, when the roots are a few inches long, you can repot the cuttings in ordinary potting soil.

Annuals that propagate by self-sowing appear in your garden in early to middle spring (along with weeds, so it will take some time to learn to identify them as annuals) and are a wonderful addition to most gardens. These seedlings are also known as "volunteers." You can decide whether you want the volunteer to stay where it has sown itself into the ground or transplant it to another location. The only plants you shouldn't relocate are those that resist being moved because they develop long taproots, such as poppies.

# Soil Skills: Watering, Feeding, Weeding

Young seedlings and transplants will have to be watched closely. Check them every day for the first week or so to be sure they have enough water. Firm the soil around them if it is loose.

## *Watering*

Climate and soil type influence how much water you'll need to give your plants and how much water will be retained in the soil. Because sandy soils dry out more quickly than other soils, they need to be watered more frequently than clay and even loamy soils. Plants that need a lot of water will need even more water when grown in a hot climate than when grown in a cool climate.

Check the soil's water content with a small hand tool, such as a trowel. Stick it in 1 to 2 inches and loosen the soil. If the soil appears moist, it's fine; if it's dry, give it water.

It's always best to water in the mornings or evenings, when the temperature drops. Try not to water in the middle of the day when it's hot outside. You should also water deeply to encourage the plant to dig deeply into the soil, creating healthy roots. A plant that gets most of its water from shallow waterings will develop shallow roots, and it won't survive drought and other stressful conditions as well as a deeply rooted plant.

## Feeding

Many annuals respond well to regular applications of a balanced fertilizer such as 20–20–20. However, annuals that don't need feeding or much watering—such as moss rose (*Portulaca grandiflora*), nasturtium (*Tropaeolum majus*), and love-lies-bleeding (*Amaranthus caudatus*)—will respond to fertilizer by producing more foliage at the expense of the flowers. (The "Plant Portraits" in Part Four provide specific information about which annuals need fertilization.) If you've been able to prepare a garden bed that is rich in compost or well-rotted manure, your plants will get all the nutrients they need in the growing season from the soil and may not require an application of fertilizer (plants in containers have very different needs; read "A Course in Container Growing," page 83). Don't overfeed your annuals or you risk burning their root systems.

Fertilizers come in different forms: water soluble, dry, and time release, and the application method depends on which one you choose.

### Water-Soluble Fertilizers

Water-soluble fertilizers are applied in their dissolved forms. Simply add the fertilizer to water and pour on. Instructions accompany the fertilizers, but you can make weaker solutions by increasing the ratio of water to fertilizer. Apply every three weeks or so during the growing season.

## Dry Fertilizers

Dry fertilizers are small granules that are directly applied and cultivated into the soil. Scatter the granules around the base of the plant and "scratch" them into the soil with your hands or a trowel.

## Time-Release Fertilizers

Time-release fertilizers feed the plants over a period of several months or an entire growing season. They can be very easy to use, but they're expensive. Time-release fertilizers are a great alternative for gardeners who can't feed their plants on a regular basis. These too are applied to the soil around the plant and scratched in.

## *Weeding*

Weeds compete with plants for water, nutrients, and sunlight and usually win: They can edge out any plants in their way, making weeding an essential garden chore. All weeds need to be dealt with, and it's best to get rid of them when they are young—before they grow stronger roots. Perennial weeds, such as dandelions, will return unless you remove the entire root system.

## Hoeing, Hand-Pulling, and Mulching

The best way to handle weeds is to dig them out by the roots when they are still young. A cultivator or hoe will help. When you are finished weeding, be sure to dispose of the weeds. If you let them lie around on the ground they may reseed themselves and you'll have to dig them out again.

Mulch is ideal for weed control. By placing 2 to 3 inches of an organic mulch on the soil, you'll stifle any weed's chances of growing through.

Add a layer of 2 to 3 inches of mulch to well-weeded garden soil in the late spring, taking care not to cover up your plants. Mulches help the soil maintain an even temperature. Summer mulches keep the soil from getting too hot in the middle of the day and keep the soil cool even when temperatures rise on unseasonably warm winter days. Personal taste can determine what kind of mulch you use, and so can your pocketbook. Some mulches, like buckwheat hulls, are expensive, whereas a synthetic mulch, like plastic

## THE BEST MULCHES

Here is a list of natural mulches. Choose a mulch that will suit your specific needs. Most mulches can be purchased at your local garden center or found around the house or yard.

| Mulch | Description |
| --- | --- |
| Buckwheat hulls | Tiny, dark brown, lightweight, disk-shaped hulls; expensive; retains moisture well |
| Cocoa shells | Rich brown color; chocolate aroma that disappears quickly; expensive |
| Compost | Natural looking; water retentive; free if you make it yourself; can be purchased from the nursery |
| Evergreen boughs | Good winter mulch; easily available from prunings of evergreen trees or Christmas decorations |
| Grass clippings | Free; decompose quickly, making them a good mulch choice |
| Leaf mold | Made of rotted leaves; one of the best mulches; full of nutrients; will break down and improve the structure of your soil; soft brown color looks natural; available free by making your own or from your community |
| Leaves, chopped or shredded | One of the best mulches for adding nutrients and structure to the soil; make by running your lawnmower back and forth over the leaves until they are chopped |
| Peat moss | Not recommended as a mulch |
| Pine needles | Light and airy; look natural; easy to collect if you have pine trees |
| Salt hay | Made of dried salt marsh grasses; available in coastal parts of the country; more expensive than straw, but it is seed-free |
| Sawdust | Not recommended; free or inexpensive |
| Stones (pebbles, gravel) | Can be very attractive, particularly in an Asian garden design; natural looking |
| Straw (hay) | Not recommended as mulch; easily available |
| Tree bark | Commercially available as chips, shredded, and ground; shredded bark is one of the most commonly used mulches and is available in coarse and fine grades; very attractive |

## Best Uses and Pitfalls

Spread 2–4 inches on a level bed; can easily be blown away in very windy areas

Spread 3–4 inches on a level bed; don't use on slopes where it may wash off; too much moisture may cause mildew and mushrooms to sprout

Spread 3–4 inches on garden beds; may contain weed seeds

Place one or more layers of evergreen boughs over and around tender plants in the winter after the ground has frozen; in the spring, remove the layers slowly over a period of weeks; good for erosion control; not recommended for summer, since dry boughs can be a fire hazard

Spread 2 inches on garden beds; use only when dry, since wet clippings can breed flies; dry a day or two before using; may contain weed seeds

Spread 3–4 inches on garden beds

Spread 4–6 inches on garden beds; don't use whole leaves, as they will mat and trap excess moisture

Use only as a soil conditioner; used as a mulch, it prevents water from passing through to the soil beneath

Spread 3 inches around acid-loving plants; useful on slopes; refreshen often, since dry pine needles can be a fire hazard; highly acidic

Spread 3–4 inches around plants; good winter mulch for tender perennials and bulbs

Unattractive; can be a fire hazard

Spread 1 inch around the garden bed, being careful not to set any too close to plants' stems; very useful in desert plantings; safe for arid regions subject to wildfires; does not add nutrients to the garden

Use on pathways to keep weeds down; best when well-rotted; don't use in gardens because it contains weed seeds; look for weed-free straw

Spread 2–3 inches on garden beds; chips are better suited for larger plants, such as those in a shrub border; if you have the space to store it, purchase bark by the truckload and apply it to garden beds throughout the summer sheeting, can be quite cheap. Just be sure that any mulch you add to your flower bed improves the look of your garden. Coarse, nuggetlike chips of bark mulch look out of place in an annual garden, because the chips are bigger than the flowers. Shredded bark and leaf mold are two mulches that are ideal in the flower garden.

# Ordinary Chores: Pinching, Deadheading, Staking

Many plants have basic maintenance requirements: deadheading, pinching, staking, and other routine chores. As often as you can, get into the garden with shears and a bucket. Examine your plants for signs of any potential problems and remove dead or broken branches. You'll probably also find some new flower buds—cut a few to enjoy indoors.

## Pinching Back Annuals

Pinching is a method of pruning seedlings to create a fuller plant with more stems and flowers. Annuals may grow weak and leggy if they are not pinched

*Pinch back your plants to keep them growing compactly and to encourage fullness.*

back several times during the growing season. When plants are young, use your forefingers (or scissors) to snip off the stems' growing tips back to the closest set of leaves.

Be sure to read about each annual you're growing in the "Plant Portraits" in Part Four to see which ones need to be pinched back (not all annuals do). Poppy (*Papaver rhoeas*) and pansy (*Viola × wittrockiana*), for example, do not require pinching.

## Deadheading

Deadheading is a technique for removing flowers that have faded; this prevents the plant from producing seeds and allows it to devote its energies to the production of flowers. Deadheading also neatens up the appearance of the plant and often encourages it to bloom longer. When you see a faded or brown blossom, remove the flower with your fingers or scissors. You don't have to wait until the flowers are completely faded to deadhead them; if you cut blooms while they're fresh, you can enjoy them indoors and still be helping the plant. For purely aesthetic reasons, you may want to cut the flower to the base if there are no other flowers or leaves on the stem or, if there are

---

### ANNUALS THAT DON'T NEED DEADHEADING

Some annuals, known as "self-cleaning" plants, don't need to be deadheaded because their faded flowers drop naturally. Here is a selection of low-maintenance annuals that don't need deadheading:

Blackfoot daisy
  (*Melampodium paludosum*)
Dahlberg daisy (*Dyssodia tenuiloba*)
Dwarf morning glory
  (*Convolvulus tricolor*)
Lobelia (*Lobelia erinus*)
Impatiens (*Impatiens wallerana*)

Madagascar periwinkle
  (*Catharanthus roseus*)
Mealy-cup sage (*Salvia farinacea*)
Moss rose (*Portulaca grandiflora*)
Statice (*Limonium sinuatum*)
Sweet alyssum (*Lobularia maritima*)
Verbena (*Verbena × hybrida*)
Wishbone flower (*Torenia fournieri*)

leaves, to the next set of leaves. Don't deadhead plants that you want to encourage to self-sow in the garden, such as poppy (*Papaver rhoeas*), bachelor's button (*Centaurea cyanus*), and pansy (*Viola × wittrockiana*).

## Supporting Plants

Some annuals, such as tall-growing dahlia and climbing sweet pea, need to be staked or given support on which to grow. Bamboo stakes are great for single-stemmed annuals and are relatively inexpensive. Simply tie the plant to the stake by looping a string around both the plant and the stake. Try not to let the plant and stake touch.

*When you see a faded or brown blossom, remove the flower with your fingers or scissors.*

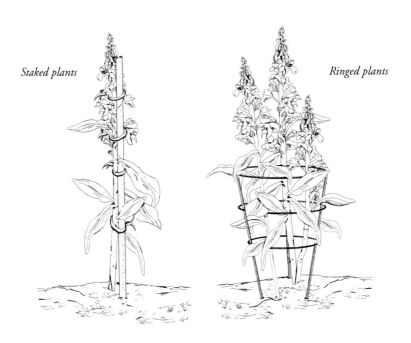

*Staked plants*

*Ringed plants*

Hoops work well for plants with multiple stems. These are round rings with wire legs, usually made of metal. Plants grow through the metal supports. You can also make your own hoop-like structure with a few strong stakes and string: Place the stakes around the plant and run the string from stake to stake. This kind of support works well with plants that sprawl, such as calliopsis (*Coreopsis tinctoria*) and cosmos (*Cosmos bipinnatus*).

# Wintering-Over

In the fall, after the annuals have died with the first frost (some annuals, such as snapdragons, will keep going for a while) just pull them out and bring any you want to winter-over into the house. A few plants that make good houseplants are begonia, coleus, and pelargonium, which you can bring indoors in the fall and take back outdoors the following spring. If these plants are growing in containers, simply bring the plants indoors before the first frost, being careful to accustom them gradually to the warmer indoor weather. Plants in the ground will have to be dug up and potted in sterilized containers in a soilless medium. You don't want to bring garden soil into the house for the winter, where the warm conditions will attract insects.

Cut your plants back by one-half to stimulate growth and place them in a sunny window. Remember to let them acclimate to the indoor temperatures gradually, getting them used to their new environment a little bit more each day.

In colder climates, you should bring in all containers made of natural materials that shrink and expand in the cold, such as terra-cotta and glazed clay. You can, however, leave very large clay and ceramic containers outside during the winter if they are emptied, the soil is removed, and the pot is covered with a plastic sheet and a board to keep snow from caving it in.

# A Course in Container Gardening

When you're ready to pot up your containers with annuals, remember that plants in containers are treated a little differently than those in the ground.

Annuals in containers may need to be watered more frequently than do plants in the ground. The size, placement, type of container, and kind of potting soil you choose will all influence how much water your plants will need. In general, clay and concrete pots dry out more quickly than synthetic materials; small pots dry out more quickly than large containers; and containers in the sun dry out more quickly than those in shade.

## Preparing the Container

Make sure your intended container has drainage holes in the bottom to allow the water to drain through. If you want to use a particular pot that does not have holes and don't want to drill them, place a slightly smaller pot (with holes) within the larger container. Add stones to elevate the smaller pot.

You can purchase potting soils at the garden center or, if you need a large amount of it and want to save some money, make your own with peat moss, vermiculite, and perlite. Peat moss gives the soil its body, vermiculite holds the water in, and perlite aids in the drainage and keeps the mix lightweight. You may also want to add organic matter, such as compost, to give the soil some fertility.

It's best to mix and moisten the soil before putting it in the container. This makes it easier to work and prevents settling. Let the mixture sit for a half hour or so, to give the soil time to settle and allow the air bubbles to escape, then mix the ingredients again. Place your plants in the container, moving them around to get the desired look. Don't be too quick to plant them. Take a few minutes to decide which plants look best toward the edge and which ones look best toward the middle. Try to squeeze as many annuals into the container as you can fit. Your only guideline should be to keep all roots well-covered with soil. You don't want to expose them to the drying effects of wind and sun. When you cram plants together, their foliage and flowers will burst out of the pot, creating the lush look you want in a container.

Elevate large containers (those larger than 3 feet wide or deep) on bricks or 2×4s, so that the drainage holes are exposed. The size and weight of them often prevents drainage, especially if there is only one central drainage hole.

## Feeding and Watering

Feeding annuals in containers is important. They should be fed with a liquid fertilizer about twice a month during the growing season. Give them a thorough soak in the morning and allow the plants to absorb the water throughout the day; collect the excess in a pan beneath the container. In the evening, empty any water still in the pan. Don't let your container plants sit in water for long periods of time or the root tips may rot and cause the plant to die.

## REVIVE A WILTING PLANT

A wilting plant in a small pot on hot summer days is a sorry sight, but before you give it the last rites, try this technique for quick resuscitation: Place a cloth over the top of the soil to hold it securely in place. Plunge the container into a large bucket filled with water, immersing the entire container. You'll see bubbles rise to the surface. When the bubbles stop, pull the container out and let it drain. Give the plant a gentle spray of lukewarm water and keep the plant out of the sun for a day.

# The Natural Way to Healthy Plants

The first step in dealing with a damaged plant is to correctly diagnose the problem before it gets out of hand. Usually, we have only the damaged plant as evidence of infestation or disease: the insects that have been nibbling away are not always visible, and the symptoms of a disease begin to appear after the plant has been afflicted.

It's important to first consider every possible reason for the damage we see and to rule out factors such as underwatering, overwatering, sun scorch, wind, and other climatic factors. However, a munched leaf here or there is no cause for alarm. And take an environmental approach to dealing with pests and insects in the garden. Don't reach for chemicals: We have learned the hard way how devastating the effects of harsh pesticides on the environment can be.

## Common Diseases

In this section you'll learn about the symptoms of diseases and various remedies. Not all garden problems are caused by diseases or pests; damage may be

Today many gardeners favor the use of Integrated Pest Management (IPM), developed by the Council on Environmental Quality, when dealing with insects and diseases. This is really just a new name for an old practice, and one that makes a lot of sense.

The goal of IPM is to use biological and cultural remedies before resorting to the prudent use of pesticides. The IPM program is built around the use of pest-resistant plants and shrubs, good maintenance of those plants, and careful monitoring of plants before pest and disease problems arise.

The building blocks of IPM are as follows:

1. Don't create problems in your garden. Take steps to avoid "bad" gardening habits, such as overwatering, overfeeding, and crowding plants, that can result in encouraging pests to gather and reproduce in your garden.

2. Select plants, flowers, trees, and shrubs with care. Use plant varieties that are proven to withstand insects. Some plants are not as attractive to pests as other plants are; check with your nursery or garden center to find out which plants are the most pest-proof for your location.

3. Examine plants routinely and carefully. It's very important that you learn to identify insects and diseases when they first appear. It may not be easy at first, if you can't tell a good bug from a bad one, but you can begin to learn which ones are harmful and should be controlled.

4. Use natural predators, such as ladybug beetles, green lacewings, and earwigs.

5. As a last resort only, use an appropriate pesticide.

the result of sun, wind, heat, cold, and even water. And you shouldn't worry about your plant if its overall health is good. A stressed or wilted leaf is not cause for alarm. Plant diseases are easier to understand if we think about them the way we think about our own illnesses—they are classified similarly. We get fevers and blisters, which can be symptoms of a cold; plants get wilts, blights, and rusts, which are the names of the visible symptoms for their ailments.

Plant diseases can be caused by a virus, bacterium, or fungus. Fungal diseases tend to be the most common and are most likely to occur when growing conditions for the plant are either too wet or too dry. Viruses are the most destructive to plants, and once they infect a plant there is little that can be done to restore it.

Some common plant diseases you may see are described below.

## Botrytis Blight

Botrytis blight is a fungal disease that appears as a grayish powder on buds and flowers. It can be a problem with petunia and geranium plants when humidity is high. Remove and discard all affected flowers.

## Damping Off

Damping off is a disease that occurs at the soil level of young seedlings and causes them to wilt and die. It appears as blackened soil at the base of the plant and can be the result of the soil remaining wet for a long time, poor air circulation, or poor soil. To avoid, use sterilized soil and clean pots, and don't overwater or overcrowd seedlings.

## Leaf Spot

Leaf spots are caused by various fungi and bacteria and appear as white, brown, yellow, or black circles. The best way to prevent leaf spots is to maintain good air circulation between plants. Discard the diseased foliage to control its spread.

## Mildew

Powdery mildew is a fungus that appears as a gray or white powdery substance on foliage and stems. It is most often a problem toward the end of summer when humidity is high and nights begin to cool. To prevent powdery mildew, plant cultivars in your area that are not susceptible to this disease, do not overcrowd plants, and give your plants good air circulation. As a last resort, use horticultural oil according to the manufacturer's directions.

## Rust

Rust is a fungus that appears as powdery orange or brown spots on foliage, especially on the undersides of leaves. Cut off the diseased portions of the plant and spray the remaining plant with a fungicide.

## Wilt

Wilt is a term used to describe a number of fungal and bacterial diseases that cause plants to wilt. If the entire plant has wilted, discard it. Don't worry if one or two leaves wilt—the plant probably will recover.

*Powdery mildew*                              *Leaf spot*

## *When Insects Come: Prevention and Solutions*

You can usually identify the kind of insect that's eating your plant by examining the wreckage. Take a good look at every plant, checking tops and undersides of leaves, stems, buds and flowers, and bases. Note all leaves that are partially eaten, covered with webbing, or are a different color. Look for blackened, wilted, or chewed stems, sticky substances, or discolored flower buds. You should also look for clues in the surrounding soil surface, such as loose soil mounds.

## SIGNS OF PEST DAMAGE

| Damage | Pest(s) |
|---|---|
| Leaves with holes | Caterpillars, grasshoppers, and beetles leave a kind of leaf skeleton and may chew away the surface leaf tissue |
| Seedlings cut off at ground level | Cutworms |
| White pathways on leaves | Leaf miners |
| Oozing, sticky sap | Borers burrow into stems and branches, leaving oozing, sticky sap or sawdust |
| Wilted, twisted, yellow, spotted, or curled leaves | Aphids, mealy bugs, scale, and whiteflies suck the sap from plants |
| Sticky, shiny substance called honeydew on leaf surface | Aphids or scale |

## Hand Picking

Hand picking is the first choice of remedies. Remove and crush the insects. You may wish to wear gloves to avoid an allergic reaction. If enough insects are hand picked in the spring and early summer, succeeding generations may be severely reduced.

## Biological Controls

Natural predators of harmful insects are extremely useful in any garden. Many beneficial insects can be purchased in egg form from mail-order catalogs and released into your garden. Or you can attract them to your yard by growing the plants they like. Many of them are lured to flowers with an umbel shape, such as Queen Anne's lace and dill, which allows them to get into the nectar easily. Garlic chives and all members of the mint family are also attractive to ladybug beetles. Other plants beneficial insects tend to be attracted to are cosmos, sweet alyssum, and chamomile.

You can order ladybugs in half-pint and quart batches (a quart is enough for a half acre). Ladybugs devour many times their own weight in destructive insects. Praying mantis egg cases are also available; these insects devour huge quantities of aphids, flies, beetles, and other damaging pests. Unfortunately,

## OUR ALLIES IN THE GARDEN

Nobody wants to eliminate destructive pests from the garden more than the gardener, right? Wrong. Voracious insects, such as those listed here, along with bats, reptiles, and other predatory creatures have the same desires (albeit

| Garden Allies | Characteristics |
|---|---|
| Bugs | Assassin bugs, big-eyed bugs, and damsel bugs; about $1/2$ inch long; among the most effective predators |
| Dragonflies | Pretty as they are useful |
| Earthworms | Beneficial because their digestive activities increase available phosphorus and potassium in the soil; they are almost always a sign of healthy, biologically active soil with good structure |
| Fireflies | Inhabit open areas where the grass is tall. |
| Green lacewings | Delicate; bright green with lacy green wings; adults and larvae are voracious predators of aphids; sometimes referred to as aphid lions (although the larvae look like little grayish alligators) |
| Ground beetles | Range in size from $1/8$ to 1 inch long; most are black, but some blue-black or green; night feeders |
| Ladybugs (ladybug beetles) | The most beloved of beneficial insects need no description; partial to warm, sunny gardens; will fly away if they aren't happy |
| Parasitic wasps | Nonstinging, tiny wasps that lay eggs in other pests' eggs; types include chalcids, ichneumons, and trichogrammas |
| Praying mantises | One of the most voracious insects; eat anything and everything; not recommended |
| Robber flies | About 1 inch long with large heads and slender abdomens; they like sunny, open fields and pastures |
| Spiders | Voracious consumers; some are deadly (the black widow and the brown violin), most are just annoying; types useful in the garden are daddy longlegs, jumping, and crab |
| Tachinid flies | Adults look like large houseflies; frequently seen flying around plants or on the ground; lay their eggs on other insects |

they desire the pests for dinner) and can be extremely helpful in controlling the pest populations.

| Pests They Prey On | Where You'll Find Them |
| --- | --- |
| Aphids; leafhoppers; small caterpillars; spider mites | Nature |
| Mosquitoes; midges; gnats | Nature |
| None | Nature; mail-order nurseries |
| Larvae of pest insects; slugs; snails | Nature; keep grass on the tall side to encourage them |
| Soft-bodied insects such as aphids; thrips; whiteflies; small worms; scale insects; eggs of other insects | Nature; eggs are available from mail-order catalogs; 1,000 eggs are enough for 500 square feet of garden |
| Cutworms; snails; slugs and their eggs; tent caterpillars | Nature |
| Aphids (one of the best biological controls); leaf miners' eggs; scale; spider mites; root worms; weevils | Nature; live insects are available from mail-order nurseries |
| Become parasites of whiteflies, cutworms, aphids, caterpillars, moths, and other pests | Nature; available from mail-order nurseries; 5,000 wasps are enough for a large garden. |
| Everything, including your plants; indiscriminate feeders | Nature; egg cases are available from mail-order nurseries |
| Horseflies; bees; beetles; butterflies; moths; leafhoppers | Nature |
| All pest insects; indiscriminate feeders | Nature |
| Become parasites of cutworms, beetle larvae, caterpillars | Nature |

they then devour everything else in sight, and their usefulness today is the subject of great debate. Praying mantises are sold as eggs in cartons and shipped when dormant. The eggs hatch after two weeks of warm weather. Green lacewings and their larvae, another beneficial insect, feed voraciously on aphids, spider mites, thrips, moth eggs, caterpillars, leafhoppers, and whiteflies; they are also sold as eggs. One half-pint of green lacewings can control pests on about an acre.

*Green lacewing*

Beneficial parasites, such as wasps, are also sold commercially as eggs. They kill insects by eating them from the inside.

## Microbials

Microbials are microscopic organisms that make the pests sick when ingested. Many microbial control agents are commercially available in powder form, and they are selective and harmless to good insects. *Do not use them on edible plants.*

- *Bacillus popillae* (milky spore disease) kills the grubs of Japanese beetles, so the grubs never become adults.
- *Bacillus thuringiensis* (BT) controls caterpillars.
- Nuclear polyhedrons virus (NPV) kills gypsy moth caterpillars.

## Insecticidal Soaps

Insecticidal soaps are widely used to control soft-bodied pests, such as aphids, spider mites, and whiteflies. A ground or powdered limestone and soap mixture is effective for leaf miners and Japanese beetles, among other insects—but use only in cases of severe infestation.

## Common Pests

Here are some of the most troublesome garden pests you may encounter.

### Aphids

Aphids are small, soft-bodied, pear-shaped bugs with or without wings, black, green, or gold in color. They suck the juices from stems, leaves, and flower buds and tend to go after new growth. The result is wilted or malformed leaves. They reproduce often, so early detection can be critical in controlling them.

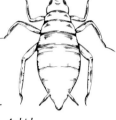

A strong spray of water from a hose is usually the best way to get rid of aphids. You can also control infestations by picking them off or removing and destroying the leaves with aphids. Ladybug beetles and their larvae, lacewings and their larvae, and syrphid flies all eat aphids. As a last resort, spray them with a mixture of dishwashing soap and water.

*Aphid*

### Caterpillars

Caterpillars can devastate foliage, and some caterpillars, known as corn and stalk borers, tunnel into the stems of many annuals and do a great deal of damage.

It's best to remove caterpillars on annuals by hand picking as soon as they appear. You can also use the microbial insecticide called BT to get rid of them.

### Cutworms

Cutworms attack young plants, chewing their stems at the base and causing them to fall over. If you have a cutworm problem, affix a plastic or cardboard collar around the base of your plants to protect them.

*Cutworm*

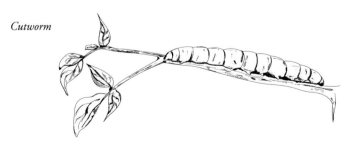

## Fire Ants

Fire ants are common in many parts of the United States, from North Carolina to California and throughout the Southwest. They are approximately $1/4$ inch in length and are yellow, reddish brown, or black. Queens (which live five to seven years!) and reproductive males have wings and are larger than the wingless worker ants. They chew on seeds.

Pour hot water on the mound to kill the ants inside. It's best to pour the water in the morning when the ants are near the top of the mound, but use extreme caution—some fire ants sting, and some people and animals can have mild to fatal allergic reactions. Avoid stepping on the mound, and wear protective clothing and boots. If that doesn't work, use a very weak solution of boric acid on cotton balls: Mix 1 teaspoon boric acid, 4 tablespoons sugar, and 2 cups water; then soak cotton balls. Place the cotton balls in an open jar; place the jar close to the mound and lay it on its side.

## Japanese Beetles

Adult beetles are about $1/4$ inch long and have metallic blue or green bodies and copper-colored wings. The young larvae, or white grubs, feed off grass and the roots of plants in your lawn; they hibernate through the winter and awaken as adults in the spring to eat your entire garden.

The first step in controlling Japanese beetles is to get rid of the white grubs by applying milky spore disease to lawns and grassy areas. Hand pick the adults. In severe cases, make a mix of equal parts water and dishwashing liquid and spray on the plants.

*Japanese beetle*

## Leaf Miners

Leaf miners are green or black insects that grow to $1/8$ inch. They tunnel between the upper and lower leaf surface, leaving a white trail behind them.

The best way to get rid of leaf miners is with biological controls, such as ladybugs and lacewings, which eat the eggs of leaf miners. Remove and destroy the infested leaves.

## Nematodes

Nematodes are microscopic, wormlike insects (not related to worms) that can be friend or foe in the garden. Beneficial nematodes are useful against a range of pests, including Japanese beetles and cutworms. The harmful nematodes can cause a variety of major problems, including burrowing into and destroying plant tissue. Nematode damage is evident by unsightly lesions and swollen roots and in yellow or wilted foliage.

The best way to prevent nematodes is by planting nematode-resistant varieties and keeping the garden bed clean. Some marigolds, specifically French and African, are inhospitable to nematodes; but you have to plant a lot of marigolds for them to be effective. If you do get nematodes, get rid of the plants. Don't plant in the same spot the following year.

## Spider Mites

Spider mites are tiny, orange, brown, or green arachnids that suck the juices out of plants, turning the leaves yellow, silver, or speckled. Regular hosing can help deter a spider mite infestation, as will importing the adults and larvae of ladybug beetles and lacewing larvae. As a last resort, spray the plant with insecticidal soap, lime spray, or a combination of both.

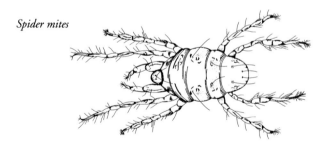

*Spider mites*

## Thrips

Thrips are a family of tiny yellow or black flies. The telltale sign that a plant has been attacked by thrips is a silvery area on the damaged leaves and wilting. Thrips thrive on plants that are under stress, sucking fluids from leaves.

The remedies for thrips are similar to those for spider mites. Hosing with water will help, as will releasing the adults and larvae of ladybug beetles and/or lacewing larvae. As a last resort, spray the plants with insecticidal soap in the early morning when thrips are least active.

## Small and Large Animals

Small animal, small problem; big animal, big problem, right? Unfortunately, this isn't true. Two of the biggest problems in the garden are two of the smallest members of the animal kingdom: slugs and snails, which are part of the mollusk family. But then birds eat seeds, deer eat tulips, and moles dig holes. While all of these creatures can act destructively at times, in the end they are no more than unwanted animals in your garden. Remember that the garden is your ecosystem, and you need to keep the system balanced. Don't be quick to use any harmful or cruel methods of eliminating unwanted animals from your garden.

Here is a list of the most common unwanted animals and some humane ways to deal with them.

### Birds

Birds can be a problem, especially when they eat the sunflower seeds right out of the seeded flower heads. Try a scarecrow or a wind chime, or drape netting over your crop until the seeds have begun to sprout.

### Deer

Deer are most effectively kept from gardens with electronic fencing; but they may be deterred by hanging Irish Spring brand soap from the plants. You can also try Milorganite, which is sewage sludge; reapply it to the soil after each rain, as it will wash away. This can be effective when properly used, but if you have a lot of deer you're going to have a lot of deer problems.

### Moles and Voles

If moles and voles are your marauders, try to get rid of the destructive tunnels they create throughout your lawn and garden by putting moth balls in the tunnels—they hate the smell. Or soak the soil around mole tunnels and

A few annuals the deer don't like:

Begonia
(*Begonia* × *semperflorens-cultorum*)
Moonflower (*Ipomoea alba*)
Morning glory (*Ipomoea purpurea*)
Pot marigold (*Calendula officinalis*)
Stock (*Matthiola incana*)

Marigold (*Tagetes patula*)
Mealy-cup sage (*Salvia farinacea*)
Mexican sunflower
(*Tithonia rotundifolia*)
Nasturtium (*Tropaeolum majus*)

mounds with castor oil, which they also dislike. Mix it with water in a 50:50 ratio and use it year round directly on the mole holes and tunnels or to create a barrier around your garden. It stays effective for about two months.

## Rabbits

If rabbits are feasting on your favorite plants, try planting them among the foods they hate, such as plants in the onion family. This will keep the rabbits away from the plants they like. Fox oil, also known as stink oil and bone oil, is an organic product that is said to deter rabbits with its pungent odor. You can pick it up in the pharmacy. Mix the oil with water and sprinkle it on the soil.

## Snails and Slugs

The most effective solution for getting rid of snails and slugs is diatomaceous earth (DE) This is an abrasive powder made from the finely ground remains of single-celled aquatic plants. Dust it on the edges of your garden bed to keep the mollusks away. DE kills the snails and slugs by dehydrating them when they crawl over it. Or try burying a dish (a empty cat food or tuna can also works well) of beer in the garden, buried up to soil level. They are attracted to the fermented smell, fall in, and drown.

The best way to keep your garden free of slugs and snails is to keep your garden free of debris. You can also search for slugs and snails at night and remove them by hand when you find them.

# the burpee basics'

# guide to

# annuals

## The Essentials

- Choosing the Right Annuals
- Plant Portraits

*Here you'll find a list of seventy-five great annuals. All the plants on this list are chosen for their easy maintenance, availability, and wide selection of sizes, shapes, and colors.*

# Choosing the Right Annuals

Choose your plants carefully! Although all annuals have the same basic needs—sunlight, soil or another medium to grow in, water, and fertilizer—plants' individual needs will differ. For instance, moss rose (*Portulaca grandiflora*) is a tough desert plant that thrives in sunny, dry, even poor conditions. A gardener in an arid part of the country would probably be able to provide these conditions easily, but a gardener in a cooler climate would have to create them by giving moss rose a sunny site, gravely soil, and little or no water.

Each plant presented here is listed with information about its cultivation and care. You should also make a habit of reading all instructions that come with the seeds or seedlings for pertinent data about each plant's requirements.

## Rating the Plants

Each annual has a "trowel" rating, which tells you how much work that plant requires so that you can choose the annuals that fit your needs. The lowest maintenance plants are designated "one trowel." These annuals, like ageratum, nasturtium, and moss rose, practically thrive on neglect. "Two trowels" go to plants that call for low maintenance, about ten to twenty minutes a week. "Three towels" designate annuals that need routine maintenance, such as petunia, snapdragon, and geranium. These plants may need pinching to promote a nice bushy shape, deadheading to remove spent flowers, or cutting back to promote new growth.

## Finding the Plants

Annuals are listed by their scientific names with their common names below them. It's a good idea to learn a plant's binomial name, because common names are not always reliable and may differ from one region to another or be shared by different plants. For instance, at least four plants (*Myosotis scorpioides, Brunnera macrophylla, Anchusa capensis,* and *Cynoglossum amabile*) are called forget-me-not. Some plant listings include suggestions for specific cultivars, which are noted in single quotation marks, as in *Ipomoea purpurea* 'Heavenly Blue'.

## A Regular Water and Feeding Program

How much water and how much fertilizer you give your annuals depends on many factors, not least of which is the plant itself. As you'll learn, some annuals can make do with less water than others but, in general, if your soil is well draining, you should give your annuals at least 1 inch of water a week. Unless it is very hot or windy, a once-a-week watering that moistens the soil to a depth of 6 inches is sufficient. During droughts, you should water your plants as they need it.

Most annuals benefit from a feeding of a balanced (20–20–20) liquid or granular fertilizer at the start of the season. Annuals that require little or no fertilizer—such as nasturtium (*Tropaeolum majus*), love-lies-bleeding (*Amaranthus caudatus*), and treasure flower (*Gazania rigens*)—are the exception, not the rule. These plants will create foliage at the expense of flowers when fed fertilizer.

> **GARDEN SMARTS**
>
> Some plants included in this list are perennial in warm climates (zones 9 to 10) but grown as annuals in cooler climates.

# Plant Portraits

## *Ageratum houstonianum*

Ageratum, flossflower
Height: 4–30 inches
Sun: Full sun

**What:** Ageratum's puffy clusters of lavender-blue, white, or pink flowers cover the plant from summer to frost and last a long time. The crinkled dark green leaves are round and soft.

**Where:** Use the dwarf forms of ageratum ('Blue Danube' is a good choice) for lining a path, in the front of a border, and in containers. The

*Ageratum houstonianum*
'Blue Danube'

taller forms of ageratum will grow to 30 inches and are good in the cutting garden or in the middle of a border. Ageratum also makes an excellent, long-lasting dried flower.

**How:** Ageratum prefers full sun. The tiny seeds can be difficult to work with, so you may want to start with nursery transplants. If you want to try the seeds, mix a handful of fine sand with them and then spread on the soil. The sand helps evenly distribute the seeds. Ageratum needs average, well-drained soil and steady moisture—don't let them dry out, particularly where temperatures are hot. Water regularly and feed monthly; no need to deadhead or pinch, but gardeners in cooler climates may want to deadhead to keep the plants blooming until the first frost. Ageratum will self-sow.

**Trowels:** ✔

## *Alcea rosea*

Hollyhock
Height: 3–9 feet
Sun: Full sun

**What:** The tall spikes of single or double flowers come in soft colors, such as white, pink, salmon, yellow, apricot, and rose, as well as in bold colors, like red, gold, maroon, and purple. The leaves are gray-green.

**Where:** Hollyhocks are great for the English cottage garden look. They make a nice vertical accent in the back of a border or against walls and fences. You can plant a stand of hollyhocks beside an entry or door for a quick, shrublike effect.

*Alcea Rosea*
'Fordhook Giants'

**How:** Sow seeds each year in a sunny place with average soil. Hollyhocks are not actually annuals (in fact, they are biennials and perennials); but because they are prone to fungal diseases, many gardeners use them as annuals, and then cut the stalks to the ground, discarding the plants after they flower. The taller hollyhocks may need staking.

**Trowels:** ✐ ✐ ✐

## Amaranthus caudatus

Love-lies-bleeding
Height: 3–8 feet
Sun: Full sun or partial shade

*Amaranthus caudatus*

**What:** Love-lies-bleeding is a wonderfully unusual-looking plant with long, richly textured tassels that are dusky red or bright green. The tassels can last for 6–8 weeks, making this one of the most useful plants for adding fall color to the garden.

**Where:** These plants look great with other tropical-looking plants, like cannas, celosia, and angel's trumpet. Use them in the back of the border, as an interesting accent plant for the garden, or even grouped together as a quick-growing, temporary hedge. The red tassels make particularly nice dried flowers, as the color deepens to a rich maroon and lasts through the winter.

**How:** Wait until the soil is warm and direct sow seeds in average garden soil in full sun or part shade. Germination takes about 14–21 days. They like it hot and dry; water sparingly, if at all.

**Trowels:** ✐

## *Antirrhinum majus*

Snapdragon
Height: 6–48 inches
Sun: Full sun

*Antirrhinum majus*
'Double Supreme' mix

**What:** Snapdragons' tall spires of tubular-shaped flowers are available in a wide assortment of colors: reddish purple, crimson, orange, pink, white, yellow, lavender, and bicolors. They get their common name from the shape of the "dragon-mouth" flowers that open and close when you pinch them with your fingers.

**Where:** Snapdragons are available in three heights: tall, medium, and dwarf. The taller varieties are spires that grow up to 4 feet tall; shorter varieties are similarly shaped, growing from 2–4 feet. Dwarf varieties are perfect for massing in low beds, edgings, and in window boxes. The taller forms provide interesting vertical accents to the garden. Grow them in a cutting garden, because they make excellent cut flowers.

**How:** Nurseries often have good selections of seedling plants, but you will find the widest selection of snapdragons with seeds. They will need to be started indoors up to 8 weeks before setting outside. Pinch seedlings to promote branching. Set them out in sun to partial shade in well-drained soil. They should be deadheaded, to encourage additional stems, and watered and fed regularly. If you want to use your snapdragons as cut flowers, cut the flower stalks when half of the flowers have opened. You will need to stake the taller varieties; so if that doesn't appeal to you, use one of the medium-sized varieties, such as 'Rocket'. These self-sow and sometimes winter-over in the south and protected sites in the north.

**Trowels:** 🌱 🌱 🌱

# Begonia × semperflorens-cultorum

Wax begonia
Height: 6–12 inches
Sun: Sun to shade

*Begonia × semperflorens-cultorum*
'Wings'

**What:** Wax begonias need very little care and are one of the easiest annuals to grow. The multiplication sign (×) in the scientific name tells you that these plants are hybrids, and in this case, hybridizing has improved the plant so much that they thrive in both sun and shade and bloom for a long period of time. Plants produce a profusion of pretty 1-inch flowers in white, red, pink, rose, and bicolors. The leaves are a glossy green to bronze-red.

**Where:** Use wax begonias wherever there is shade, in containers, window boxes, or massed in the front of a border.

**How:** Wax begonias take a long time to germinate, so it's best to start with seedlings that are easily available at nurseries and garden centers. They will need a cool, light, well-drained soil. Water regularly and keep the soil moist between waterings. Try not to let any water get on the leaves, as it may create the disease leaf spot. In the fall, lift the plants and bring indoors to be used as houseplants for the winter months.

**Trowels:** ✐

## Borago officinalis

Borage
Height: 12–18 inches
Sun: Full sun

**What:** Herbalists have cultivated borage for hundreds of years for its reputed properties of emotional strength and courage. If you have room to grow borage—it spreads as wide as 4 feet—do so for its brilliant blue, star-shaped flowers and fuzzy gray-green leaves.

**Where:** Borage droops and flops over other plants and is very pretty in an informal border with cosmos (*Cosmos bipinnatus*) and dusty miller (*Senecio cineraria*). It also works well in containers—anywhere there's enough room and sun.

*Borago officinalis*

**How:** Sow seeds indoors early or wait until after the first frost and sow outdoors in early spring. It self-sows easily, so be prepared for lots of borage in your garden. Give this sun-loving plant an average to rich soil. Mulch around plants to hold in moisture.

**Trowels:** 🌱 🌱

## Brassica oleracea

Ornamental cabbage
Height: 10–15 inches
Sun: Full sun

**What:** Ornamental cabbage and ornamental kale look a bit like their edible cousins, but with more interesting foliage and texture. The centers of ornamental cabbage are white rosettes tinged with pink, red, or purple, and the outer leaves of ornamental kale are fringed.

**Where:** These plants are wonderful for late-season foliage, and look pretty with the deep autumn golds and russets of mums. In the fall, replace the annuals in your window boxes, tubs, and large planters with mums (*Dendranthema* × *grandiflora*) and ornamental cabbage and kale for a great fall look. They may last through the holidays where winters are mild.

**How:** Give ornamental cabbage full sun and a rich, moist, well-drained soil. Very easy to grow.

**Trowels:** ✐

*Brassica oleracea*

## *Browallia speciosa*

Browallia, bush violet
Height: 12–18 inches
Sun: Full sun or partial shade

**What:** Browallia has velvety-textured, star-shaped flowers in deep blue, white, or violet and bright green leaves. It is invaluable as a shade-loving plant and is a great alternative to impatiens (*Impatiens wallerana*), which tends to be overused in shady gardens.

*Browallia speciosa*
'Blue Bells Improved'

**Where:** They look great massed in large planters and urns as well as in hanging baskets and window boxes.

**How:** Start with seeds 6–8 weeks indoors before the last frost, sow directly in the garden, or use nursery transplants—whatever is easiest. These plants are best in partial shade to shade; don't let them sit in full sun. Browallia does best with a rich soil that has good drainage.

**Trowels:** 🌱 🌱

## *Caladium* × *hortulanum*

Fancy-leaved caladium
Height: 2–3 feet
Sun: Partial shade

**What:** Caladium is a perennial grown as an annual and has long leaf stalks and pointed, veined leaves in pink and white, or scarlet. It makes a striking display in the shade.

*Caladium* × *hortulanum*

**Where:** Use caladium for its pretty foliage in a shaded corner as a backdrop to white impatiens. The large leaves with mottled pink and white veins also look good with other large-leaved plants, such as hostas (*Hosta* sp.).

**How:** Caladium is best started from nursery transplants. Plant in a moist, humus-rich soil; remove the flowers as they appear so that the plant keeps producing colorful leaves. After the leaves die down, store the tubers and replant them again in the spring.

**Trowels:** 🌱 🌱 🌱

## Calendula officinalis

Pot marigold
Height: 12–30 inches
Sun: Full sun

*Calendula officinalis* 'Gem'

**What:** Pot marigold flowers are pale yellow, apricot, deep orange, or white in single or double forms; the light green leaves have a spicy scent. Dwarfs grow just 12 inches high and the taller kinds grow 2–2$^1/_2$ feet tall.

**Where:** Calendula will work anywhere there is sun. Use the dwarf forms in containers and window boxes with pansies (*Viola × wittrockiana*) and the taller forms in the middle of a border or in cutting gardens with stock (*Matthiola incana*) and snapdragons (*Antirrhinum majus*).

**How:** Sow seeds outdoors in full sun in spring. Calendula likes a rich soil and cool weather. If the plants start to decline in the heat of the summer, cut them back to about 6 inches from the soil to stimulate growth.

**Trowels:** ✐

## Callistephus chinensis

China aster
Height: 6–36 inches
Sun: Full sun

**What:** China asters are available in many cultivars, varying in height, shape, and even bloom time. The large flowers come in a wide range of colors, including red, pink, rose, violet, lavender, and white, as well as pleasant mixes of these colors. The taller varieties have long stems and make excellent cut flowers.

**Where:** Because there are so many shapes and sizes, China asters can be used in a variety of ways. The dwarf forms are good for containers, edging a bed or border, or lining a walkway. The taller forms are great additions to the cutting garden.

*Callistephus chinensis*
'Dwarf Queen'

**How:** Seedlings are easily available, or you can start seeds indoors about 6 weeks before the last frost date. Keep the soil evenly moist, and when seedlings emerge don't allow the soil to dry out. Plant out China asters in a rich, deep soil in a sunny place. Like other plants in the aster family, China asters are susceptible to diseases in the soil. The best way to avoid soil-borne diseases is to set new plants in different locations each year, avoiding the same spot. The taller forms may need staking.

**Trowels:** ✴ ✴ ✴

## *Catharanthus roseus*

Madagascar periwinkle
Height: 4–18 inches
Sun: Full sun

**What:** If there were an award for "hero" plants, the Madagascar periwinkle would win it hands down. First, it has an extraordinary ability to withstand poor soil and air conditions. Second, it was instrumental in developing a cure for childhood leukemia. Grow it for these reasons or for the pretty star-shaped flowers in pink, rose, or purple.

*Catharanthus roseus*
'Pretty in Rose'

**Where:** You can grow Madagascar periwinkle just about anywhere; it's great where summers are hot and humid, hot and dry, even on a high-rise terrace where pollution and sun scorch would destroy another plant. It looks best in containers, because in a bed in can tend to sprawl and look messy.

**How:** Madagascar periwinkle is best started with seedlings from a local nursery. Plant in full sun in a soil that is warm and well drained. Pinch before planting to encourage a bushy plant.

**Trowels:** ✎

## *Celosia argentea* var. *cristata*

Cockscomb
Height: 6–36 inches
Sun: Full sun

**What:** Cockscomb has rich, textured flower heads in shades of pink, crimson, scarlet, yellow, and cream. The flowers keep their color a long time, making them perfect for dried arrangements.

**Where:** Plant the dwarf forms in containers, tubs, and in the front of the border for bright displays of color; the taller kinds are perfect for the cutting garden. For a stunning combination, try

*Celosia argentea* var. *cristata* 'Floradale'

pink celosia with scarlet gomphrena, gold rudbeckia, and a red salvia in a container or bed.

**How:** Cockscomb thrives in hot, dry conditions and is not fussy about anything. Sow directly after spring frost; seeds will sprout within a week. Deadhead to get bushy plants and more blooms.

**Trowels:** ✎ ✎

# Centaurea cyanus

Bachelor's button, cornflower
Height: 12–30 inches
Sun: Full sun

*Centaurea cyanus*
'Jubilee Gem'

**What:** Bachelor's button's round, buttonlike flowers are about 2 inches wide and come in a selection of pretty colors: bright blue, rose, pink, pale yellow, and white. It gets its common name cornflower because it's often found in cornfields. Plants usually grow about 30 inches high, but some dwarf forms (12–18 inches) are available.

**Where:** Bachelor's button self-sows easily and is ideal as a wildflower in an open meadow. Sow it in a large area or mass it with other wildflowers, such as calliopsis (*Coreopsis tinctoria*) and Shirley poppy (*Papaver rhoeas*). It looks nice in the middle of a border; use the smaller forms to brighten up the front. The pretty flowers are edible and make great additions to summer salads.

**How:** Direct sow in early spring in cooler climates and in late fall where winters are mild. Bachelor's button isn't fussy—just don't give it too rich or too moist a soil, as it flowers best in a poor, dry soil. It will self-sow and is a drought-tolerant plant. This plant's only downfall is that it is not a long-blooming annual, so sow it successively throughout the season for continuous bloom.

**Trowels:** 🖌

## Cleome hasslerana

Cleome, spider flower
Height: 3–5 feet
Sun: Full sun

*Cleome hasslerana*
'Queen' mix

**What:** Cleome is extremely quick growing and can reach up to 5 feet in one season. Its elegant clusters of single flowers in white, pink, purple, or burgundy sit atop tall, somewhat hairy, spiny stems. Long, narrow, pointed seedpods hang from the flowers, giving the plant its "spider leg" appearance. Spider flower has a peculiar odor: To some it's a fragrant lemony scent, to others it smells as bad as skunk spray! Keep this in mind if you want to use it as a cut flower—in a closed room the scent is quite pungent.

**Where:** Cleome's height and large flowers make it a real showstopper when used at the back of the border. Or let a row of cleome work as a temporary hedge or shrub.

**How:** Start seeds indoors 8 weeks before the last frost date in your area, or sow seeds directly in the soil after the last frost. Give it a hot, dry site in full sun. Deadhead if you don't want the plant to self-sow, but you may prefer to let it sow itself into the ground. The seedlings will be an entirely different or washed-out color, and cleome can be troublesome as a weed; but if you like this plant you won't mind a bit. Don't bother to remove the seedpods because it will continue to produce flowers even while the seeds are forming.

**Trowels:** ✎

## *Coleus* × *hybridus*

Coleus
Height: 6–36 inches
Sun: Partial to full sun

*Coleus* × *hybridus*
'Wizard' mix

**What:** Coleus is used for its exotic, multicolored leaves, which are chartreuse, red, bronze, cream, pink, gold, copper, and purple or combinations of those colors. The foliage is either lacy or lobed. White or lavender flower spikes appear in late summer but are not significant.

**Where:** The colorful leaves, especially the lighter colored leaves, look pretty with impatiens (*Impatiens wallerana*) and wax begonias (*Begonia* × *semperflorens-cultorum*) in a bed or container that gets light shade.

**How:** Grow coleus in filtered or light shade and give it a fertile soil with constant moisture. It's best to start with seedlings from a local nursery. To encourage a bushy plant, pinch the tips to remove flower buds as they form.

**Trowels:** 🌱 🌱

## *Convolvulus tricolor*

Dwarf morning glory
Height: 8–12 inches
Sun: Full sun

**What:** Dwarf morning glory's blue, rose, or white 2-inch flowers are saucer-shaped with yellowish centers. The plants are low growing and bushy with heart-shaped leaves.

**Where:** Use dwarf morning glories by themselves in containers or in the front of the border.

**How:** Sow seeds directly in the fall where winters are mild, or sow in the spring after danger of frost in cooler climates. They like full sun and a sandy, poor soil with low fertility. Fast-growing, easy, and tolerant of heat, dwarf morning glories require only occasional deadheading.

**Trowels:**

*Convolvulus tricolor*
'Blue Enchantment'

## Consolida ambigua

Rocket larkspur
Height: 3–4 inches
Sun: Full sun

**What:** Larkspur is a cool-season annual that blooms early and dwindles in the summer as the heat rises. The tall, stately spikes of blue, pink, white, or violet flowers add an informal cottage garden accent to the garden. You can get a pretty mix of all the colors in 'Giant Imperial' mix.

**Where:** These plants are great in cutting gardens and toward the middle or back of a mixed border. They are also excellent cut flowers.

*Consolida ambigua*
'Giant Imperial' mix

**How:** Sow larkspur outdoors in early spring (even as the snow is melting) for spring-to-summer blooms and then sow again in late summer for fall-to-frost blooms. Larkspur are best grown in cooler climates, as they don't take well to heat and humidity. They need full sun and a soil that is rich, light, and well drained. The taller varieties may have to be staked.

**Trowels:** 🌱 🌱

## Coreopsis tinctoria

Annual coreopsis, calliopsis
Height: 1¹/₂–3 feet
Sun: Full sun

*Coreopsis tinctoria*

**What:** These are fast-growing, bushy annuals in the sunflower family, with daisylike yellow or orange flowers, bands of contrasting colors, and purplish brown centers. Calliopsis flowers from summer through early autumn.

**Where:** These are cheerful plants for containers, borders, or anywhere there is sun. They are best in a big, open meadow where they will self-sow.

**How:** Sow seeds directly in place in full sun. Give them a dryish, gravely soil—they are tolerant of drought. Remove old flowers to prolong bloom. If plants fall over and need support, use stakes and string to tie them up. Place a few stakes around the group of calliopsis plants and encircle the group with string. Very easy to grow.

**Trowels:** 🌱 🌱

# Cosmos

Cosmos
Height: 1–7 feet
Sun: Full sun

**What:** Cosmos is a daisylike plant with delicate, lacy, light green foliage. It is available in a wide range of colors, such as white, pink, and red flowers. 'Sonata' mix includes these three colors. 'Candy Stripe' is a very popular hybrid with crimson-striped white petals.

*Cosmos bipinnatus*
'Sonata' mix

**Where:** These elegant plants are great in a wild-flower garden, toward the back or middle of an informal border, or in the cutting garden. White cosmos looks particularly pretty next to a blue mealy-cup sage (*Salvia farinacea*). Yellow cosmos (*C. sulphureus*) is brightly colored with yellow, red, and orange blooms.

**How:** Sow seeds outdoors after danger of frost in a sunny site in average to sandy soil. Cosmos is very easy; it isn't bothered by heat and blooms from summer to first frost. Some of the taller hybrids may need staking, and all plants need to be pinched early in the season for fuller growth.

**Trowels:** ✒

# Cynoglossum amabile

Chinese forget-me-not
Height: 18–24 inches
Sun: Full sun or partial shade

**What:** Similar to another forget-me-not, *Myosotis sylvatica*, Chinese forget-me-not has some of the prettiest blue flowers you'll find. The plants have soft, gray-green foliage to complement the tiny, sky blue flowers. Some of the best known cultivars are 'Blue Shower' and 'Firmament'. White-flowering Chinese forget-me-not is also available—'Snow Bird' is a good choice.

**Where:** The height of Chinese forget-me-not—about 2 feet—makes it perfect for the middle of a bed or border. Plants will self-sow, which make them useful additions to a cottage or rock garden.

**How:** It's easiest to start with nursery transplants. Chinese forget-me-nots are technically biennials and will flower from seed the first year only if the seed is sown sufficiently early, about 6–8 weeks before the last frost. Give them a soil that is fertile and well drained, in full sun, and water deeply when the plants are flowering.

**Trowels:** 🌱 🌱

*Cynoglossum amabile* 'Mystery Rose'

## *Dahlia* hybrids

Dahlia
Height: 1–7 feet
Sun: Full sun

**What:** Dahlias, which are grown from roots called tubers, come in many colors (every color in every shade except blue), bicolors, shapes (single, anemone, and pompon ball, for example), and sizes (some plants grow up to 7 feet with 6-inch flowers. They are invaluable in cooler parts of the country, performing brilliantly from spring to frost, but don't hold up very well where summers are hot and humid.

**Where:** Site dahlias in plenty of sun where their colors will show to their best advantage. The tall dahlias in vivid colors add brightness to a perennial border in warm colors or in a formal bed. The shorter varieties look nice edging a border or in large containers.

*Dahlia* 'Rigoletto'

**How:** Although dahlia tubers are easy to work with once you are familiar with them, it's easiest to start with seedling transplants. Plant in full sun in a fertile soil, water during dry spells, and feed dahlias regularly. Spider mites can be a problem where summers are hot and dry. Spray the leaves with water to get them off. Taller dahlias can produce spectacular blooms if you "disbud" the flowers. This sounds more complicated than it really is. Disbudding is simply removing (pinching off) the two tiny flower heads you see on either side of a dahlia flower. This forces the plant to devote its energies to producing a bigger flower. It's easy and worth it for pretty flowering plants.

If you want to go to the trouble, you can save the tubers, store over winter, and plant the next spring. Lift tubers after the tips of the foliage have blackened (after a frost), shake off any soil, bury them in dry peat moss or vermiculite and put them a cool, dry place.

**Trowels:** 🌱 🌱 🌱

## *Datura meteloides*

Thorn apple, angel's trumpet
Height: 3–5 feet
Sun: Full sun to partial shade

**What:** Angel's trumpet is a wonderfully fragrant, tropical plant with large, trumpet-shaped flowers. The creamy white or yellowish rose flowers have a tinge of purple in their centers.

**Where:** Angel's trumpet grows tall and is very useful as a dramatic plant in large containers on the patio or terrace, or as an accent plant in gardens. The white flowers are very showy and look beautiful by moonlight.

**How:** These are actually evergreen shrubs in warm climates (zones 9–10) but are used as annuals elsewhere. Start with nursery transplants and give them a rich soil, full sun or partial shade, and a sheltered location. They will need ample water while flowering. Bring potted plants indoors to winter-over; give them bright light and water sparingly.

*Datura meteloides*
'Fragrant Double Purple'

**Trowels:** 🌱 🌱 🌱

## *Dianthus chinensis*

China pinks
Height: 6–12 inches
Sun: Full sun

**What:** China pinks have flat clusters of small single or double flowers in red, pink, white, and bicolors. The low-growing plants' stiff, upright stems are blue-gray.

**Where:** These are wonderful plants for the front of any border or in a rock garden. Use them in an informal cottage garden with blue larkspur (*Consolida ambigua*).

**How:** Sow seeds in early spring directly in ordinary soil. Plants begin to produce flowers in

*Dianthus chinensis*
'Spring Beauty'

about 10 weeks from sowing. They require very little maintenance; you'll just need to deadhead if you want to keep getting flowers. Be sure to take off the base (the long stem) of the flower when deadheading.

**Trowels:** 🌱 🌱

## *Dolichos lablab*

Hyacinth bean
Height: 20 inches to 6 feet
Sun: Full sun

*Dolichos lablab*

**What:** Hyacinth bean is a very ornamental vine with pealike purple or white flowers, dense, dark, almost purple foliage, and shiny maroon bean pods. A green-leaved variety is also available, but it is less ornamental.

**Where:** Hyacinth bean makes a wonderful, fast-growing screen when planted with a trellis. Use it with yellow-flowering plants, such as creeping zinnia (*Sanvitalia procumbens*) or dwarf yellow marigold (*Tagetes patula*), to bring out the rich red-maroon color.

**How:** Direct sow in full sun when all danger of frost is gone. Be sure to provide a structure for it to grow on. Performs best where summers are long and hot.

**Trowels:** 🌱 🌱

## Dyssodia tenuiloba

Dahlberg daisy
Height: 6 inches
Sun: Full sun

**What:** Dahlberg daisies are wonderful where water is scarce, as they thrive in desert conditions. The plants have small gold flowers with yellow centers, pretty fernlike foliage, and bloom for a long time.

**Where:** Use Dahlberg daisies in containers, window boxes, hanging baskets, and as an informal edging for a garden or path.

*Dyssodia tenuiloba*

**How:** Sow seeds in early spring outdoors where winters are mild and indoors 6–8 weeks before the last frost. Or start with nursery transplants. Plants may begin to look raggedy by midsummer and will need to be cut back at this time to rejuvenate them. No need to deadhead.

**Trowels:** 🌱 🌱


## Eschscholzia californica

California poppy
Height: 8–12 inches
Sun: Full sun

**What:** California poppies are a glorious sight on the West coast, and fortunately these native plants can be grown all over the country. Poppies are papery flowers on tall, hairy stems and come in a wide range of colors including pinks, oranges, and golds. Look for 'Thai Silk' mix, which is a beautiful melange of these colors.

*Eschscholzia californica*
'Ballerina' mix

**Where:** Plant California poppies in a sunny place—they look best in a big open meadow, in informal gardens, or lining a path.

**How:** California poppies are actually a short-lived perennial in warmer areas and are grown as an annual elsewhere. They need to be sown directly in place because they do not transplant well. Thin seedlings to 10 inches apart when plants are 1–2 inches tall and deadhead to encourage continuous bloom.

**Trowels:** ✐

## Euphorbia marginata

Snow-on-the-mountain
Height: 18–24 inches
Sun: Full sun or partial shade

**What:** Snow-on-the-mountain is grown not for its flowers, but for its pretty, white-edged leaves that are attractive from early summer to frost.

**Where:** Use snow-on-the-mountain toward the middle of beds and borders to fill gaps between flowering plants. The white-edged leaves look quite dramatic when contrasted with purple basil (*Ocimum basilicum* 'Dark Opal').

**How:** Sow seeds in place or start them earlier indoors 6 weeks before the last frost. Give them an average soil; plants will self-sow.

**Trowels:** ✐ ✐

*Euphorbia marginata*

## Felicia amelloides

Blue marguerite, kingfisher daisy
Height: 12–18 inches
Sun: Full sun

*Felicia amelloides*

**What:** Blue marguerite is a daisy-like plant with cheerful blue rays, yellow centers, and thick, dark green leaves. It's a low-growing plant that flops, tumbles, and cascades but keeps a compact shape so that it never looks messy.

**Where:** Use blue marguerite in window boxes with purple and white lobelia and blue heliotrope, in large planters by itself, or in a mixed border with perennials.

**How:** Sow indoors 8 weeks before the last frost or sow outdoors in early spring. Pinch back plants when they get a few inches tall. Blue marguerite requires full sun and well-drained dryish, gravely soil. Let the plants dry slightly between waterings. Continue to pinch throughout the growing season to keep them bushy. Lift plants and bring indoors before frost in the fall.

**Trowels:** 🌱 🌱 🌱

## Gazania rigens

Treasure flower
Height: 6–15 inches
Sun: Full sun

**What:** The centers of treasure flower are usually dark with ray-like petals of yellow, gold, cream, orange, pink, red, or bicolors. The foliage is a silvery gray or bright green. 'Pinata' is a nice mix of warm yellows, oranges, and reds.

**Where:** Gazanias are a valuable ground cover because they spread rapidly and are perfect for difficult places, such as dry, sunny banks. They are also nice trailing from containers.

**How:** Sow outdoors after danger of frost. Treasure flowers need a light, sandy soil and full sun. They tolerate drought and do best in high temperatures. Lift plants before frost in the fall and use as a houseplant in a sunny window until the following spring.

*Gazania rigens*
'Pinata' hybrid mix

**Trowels:** 🌱

## *Gomphrena globosa*

Globe amaranth
Height: 9–30 inches
Sun: Full sun

**What:** Cloverlike solitary heads on tall plants in colors of purple, white, orange, pink, yellow, and lavender. Useful as a dried flower and in cut flower arrangements.

**Where:** This brightly colored flower does well in beds, borders and containers. By themselves in containers, *gomphrena* make a striking display with their brilliant, almost electric colors.

*Gomphrena globosa*

**How:** Give the globe amaranth full sun for best results and a rich, organic, well-drained soil. While it won't tolerate even the slightest frost, it will put up with wind, heat, and drought. Globe amaranth makes a great dried flower: Cut the bloom just before it opens and hang to dry in a dark, airy location.

**Trowels:** 🌱 🌱

## Gypsophila elegans

Annual baby's breath
Height: 18 inches
Sun: Full sun

**What:** Annual baby's breath is an airy-looking plant with a profusion of tiny flowers about $^1/_2$-inch across. The plants don't bloom for long, so it's best to make a succession of sowings.

**Where:** Baby's breath is perfect for the cutting garden or as a filler between other plants in a mixed border. Try them next to vividly colored annuals like moss rose and mealy-cup sage (*Salvia farinacea*).

*Gypsophila elegans*
'Snow Fountain'

**How:** Sow outdoors in spring in an average to sandy soil. Just scatter seeds and tamp them down firmly in the soil. Seeds germinate in about 10 days. They like it dry so allow the soil to dry between waterings. For use as a dried flower, hang plants upside down to dry.

**Trowels:** 🌱

## Helianthus annuus

Common sunflower
Height: 1–12 feet
Sun: Full sun

**What:** You might be surprised to know how many different kinds of sunflower plants there are: sunflowers with huge flower heads 1 foot in diameter; sunflowers in creamy yellow, bright yellow, orange, white, or gold; sunflowers that are 12 feet tall and plants that are only 1 foot tall. 'Sunrise' is a good choice for cheerful, lemony-colored 6-inch-wide flowers that grow on 5-foot stems.

**Where:** Sunflowers add a playful element to any garden. The taller varieties are very useful as a quick-growing screen or hedge, in the vegetable garden (along with a scarecrow to chase the birds away), in the back of a border, or in the cutting garden. Dwarf cultivars can be used in containers and planters. Perfect in a children's garden. Pick the cultivar that fits the spot.

**How:** Sow the seeds directly in ordinary garden soil in a sunny place after the last frost date. Sunflowers do not transplant well. Very easy to grow!

**Trowels:** ✔

*Helianthus annuus*
'Parasol' mix

## *Helichrysum bracteatum*

Everlasting flower, strawflower
Height: 2–3 feet
Sun: Full sun

**What:** Strawflowers have lots of long-lasting, sunny daisy-shaped flowers with papery textures. The color range is wide: yellow, gold, white, red, orange, pink, and every color in between. For a very attractive giant strawflower, get the 'Monstrosum' series.

**Where:** Plants are fast-growing and very useful where conditions are difficult, such as on hillsides and dry areas. Great also in cutting

*Helichrysum bracteatum*
'Bright Bikini' mix

gardens, and the smaller forms (such as 'Dwarf Yellow') work well in containers and hanging baskets.

**How:** Sow seeds in place in full sun. Give them a well-drained, average soil; they will self-sow. Strawflowers are not of much interest to insects and not bothered by much, which are just two good reasons to grow them. They tend to do best where summers are long and hot.

**Trowels:** 🌱

## *Heliotropium arborescens*

Common heliotrope
Height: 18–30 inches
Sun: Full sun

**What:** Heliotrope is an old-fashioned cottage plant with wonderful, vanilla-scented flowers in deep blues, violets, and white. Flowers grow in large, dense clusters; and the leaves have a dark, almost purple cast.

*Heliotropium arborescens* 'Marine'

**Where:** This plant belongs in containers near a door or under a window, massed near an outdoor bench, or planted wherever the sweet scent is best enjoyed. The darker heliotropes look best with light-colored flowers, such as stock, sweet alyssum, and globe candytuft.

**How:** Purchase nursery-grown transplants to set out in spring and plant in a rich, well-drained organic soil in full sun. They will not tolerate even a slight frost, so plant them later rather than earlier in spring. If the seedling has flowers, pinch the plants before planting to remove the flowers, which will create a bushier plant. Keep the soil on the dry side, as it will intensi-fy the fragrance. In very hot areas, containers with heliotrope should have afternoon shade.

**Trowels:** 🌱 🌱

## *Iberis umbellata*

Globe candytuft
Height: 6–12 inches
Sun: Full sun

**What:** Globe candytuft grows quickly from seed, developing a spreading mat of foliage and 2-inch clusters of white, pink, lilac, and violet flowers. 'Fairy Mix' has all these hues. These cheerful flowers last well as cut flowers and can be used in dried-flower arrangements.

*Iberis umbellata*
'Snowflake'

**Where:** Low-growing globe candytuft is perfect for edging a border or a walkway.

**How:** Where winters are mild, sow seeds in late summer directly in ordinary garden soil in full sun; in cooler climates, sow seeds in spring by scattering where you want the plants to grow. Thin seedlings to 6 inches apart. For blooms through to the fall, make another sowing in midsummer. To get a second flush of flowers, shear back after the first bloom.

**Trowels:** 🌱 🌱

## Impatiens wallerana

Busy lizzie, garden impatiens
Height: 6–18 inches
Sun: Partial shade

*Impatiens wallerana*
'Peaches'

**What:** Impatiens are probably the most popular flower for shady spots and one of the easiest plants to grow. Flowers are about 2 inches wide and come in shades of pink, red, white, salmon, burgundy, lavender, orange, and even striped and two-toned. Some flower forms are double and look like tiny roses. New Guinea hybrids are a group of impatiens that can tolerate direct sun. Their two-toned foliage looks a little more exotic, and the flowers are bigger (3 inches) and bolder than other impatiens varieties.

**Where:** Mass impatiens under deciduous trees, use them in the shade garden with caladium, begonia, and hosta, or plant them in containers and window boxes. Use all white impatiens around a shrub border to brighten it up and give it a neat, unified look. Use New Guinea hybrids on south-facing terraces in hanging baskets and window boxes.

**How:** Start with nursery transplants. Plants don't need to be pruned, pinched, or deadheaded, but they do need an average to fertile soil. Use a mulch of shredded bark around the plants to keep the soil cool.

**Trowels:** 🌱

## Ipomoea purpurea

Morning glory
Height: To 10 feet
Sun: Full sun

*Ipomoea purpurea*
'Heavenly Blue'

**What:** This is a quick-growing vine with pretty, funnel-shaped flowers. 'Heavenly Blue' is the most popular morning glory, with large, bright, sky blue flowers. Other morning glory flower colors are white, pink, lavender, and red, often with contrasting markings like five-pointed stars. Cardinal climber (*I. quamoclit*) has bright red flowers and moon flower (*I. alba*) has big, white, scented flowers that open at dusk.

**Where:** Morning glories are ideal for clothing fences, banks, and walls with flowers until the first frost. Blue morning glories always look pretty twining their way up a mailbox or lamppost. Use moon flower where you can best enjoy it by moonlight.

**How:** Morning glories climb by twining and need a structure to climb on. Seeds should be soaked overnight before planting to loosen up the hard seed coating and aid germination. Plant in ordinary soil; water sparingly and don't fertilize.

**Trowels:** ✔ ✔

## Lantana camara

Yellow sage
Height: 2–4 feet
Sun: Full sun

**What:** Yellow sage is a spreading shrub that is used as an annual in cold climates and as a hardy shrub in mild climates (zones 7–10). It flowers from late spring to frost with dense clusters of papery flowers in shades of pink, gold, yellow, orange, red, or creamy white.

*Lantana camara*
'New Gold'

**Where:** This is an excellent plant for large containers on the patio. There is a trailing form, *L. montevidensis,* which also works well as a ground cover and as a trailing plant from hanging baskets, window boxes, and planters.

**How:** Purchase seedlings from a nursery and plant in full sun and average soil. Yellow sage is not in the least fussy and tolerates drought and heat well. If aphids are a problem, simply spray them off with a strong spray of water from the hose. Plants may be pruned occasionally to keep their shape.

**Trowels:** 🌱 🌱

## Lathyrus odoratus

Sweet pea
Height: To 6 feet
Sun: Full sun to partial shade

**What:** Sweet pea is an old-fashioned annual with pretty, sweet-smelling flowers in clear shades of pink, white, purple, and rosy red. The vines grow quickly by tendrils and need a trellis, fence, or even a stick or string to climb on.

**Where:** Give sweet peas something to scale and use them as a decorative element in a vegetable garden (although they are not edible) or cutting garden, or just let them clamber over shrubs.

**How:** Sow seeds in the early spring in cooler climates and in fall where winters are mild. Immerse seeds in warm water and soak for 24 hours before sowing to aid germination; seeds will germinate in 14–21 days. Sweet peas do best in cool weather with a soil that is fertile and full of organic matter. Give them good air circulation (by allowing adequate spacing between plants), water during the growing season, and mulch to retain moisture. Deadhead regularly to prolong bloom.

*Lathyrus odoratus*
'Patio' mix

**Trowels:** ✓ ✓ ✓

## *Lavatera trimestris*

Bush mallow
Height: 3–5 feet
Sun: Full sun

**What:** Bush mallow is a Mediterranean native with dark green foliage covered by pretty, cup-shaped, red, white, or pink flowers, which bloom from summer to frost and reach up to 3 inches across. Plants will grow as big as a shrub in a single season. 'Mont Blanc' is a beautiful cultivar with pure white flowers.

*Lavatera trimestris*
'Ruby Regis'

**Where:** They make a quick-growing summer hedge or screen. Perfect for the small garden or border with hollyhocks (*Alcea rosea*) or in large half-whiskey-barrel containers and planters. Try to place the containers near a wall to give the plants some shelter.

**How:** Sow seeds directly in the garden in the fall or as early as the soil can be worked in the spring. Bush mallow loves the sun and takes just about any well-drained soil. It doesn't need deadheading or staking and will tolerate prolonged heat and cool coastal summers.

**Trowels:** 🌱 🌱

## *Limonium sinuatum*

Statice
Height: 1–2 feet
Sun: Full sun

**What:** Statice is commonly grown by commercial growers and sold as dried flowers. The delicate, papery flowers are often three colors: blue, lavender, or rose with white on the inside. The foliage has very few leaves.

**Where:** This is a great plant to grow in the cutting garden and use as a fresh or dried cut flower.

**How:** Statice is easy to grow. Sow seeds outdoors in early spring. Give plants a soil with good drainage. Statice tolerates heat, strong sun, and drought and does well along the coasts. Plants will often self-sow. No need to deadhead.

*Limonium sinuatum*

**Trowels:** 🌱

## *Eustoma grandiflora*
## (Old name: *Lisianthus russellianus*)

Prairie gentian
Height: 12–24 inches
Sun: Full sun to partial shade

*Eustoma grandiflora*
'Prairie' mix

**What:** Prairie gentians are native to the grasslands and prairies of Texas and New Mexico, with beautiful purple-blue flowers and soft, gray-green leaves. Prairie gentian flowers are also available in pink, white, lavender, and rose; mixed strains can also be found. These plants make excellent cut flowers, lasting a long time in water.

**Where:** Prairie gentian's soft colors are easy to use in any color combination, and the smaller sizes are perfect for window boxes and containers.

**How:** These plants grow slowly, so it's best to start with nursery transplants. Give them a moisture-retentive, fertile soil and full sun. Plants are tolerant of summer heat and, once established, even tolerate drought well.

**Trowels:** 🌱 🌱 🌱

## *Lobelia erinus*

Edging lobelia
Height: 4–8 inches
Sun: Full sun to partial shade

**What:** Lobelia is a compact plant with tiny, delicate-looking flowers that grow in clusters and are available in red, blue, violet, or white. Popular cultivars include 'Rosamund', with carmine red blooms and white centers, and 'Crystal Palace', with dark blue flowers.

**Where:** Lobelia plants cascade beautifully, making them ideal for use in hanging baskets and window boxes. Or use lobelia as an edging for walkways, gardens and in rock greens.

*Lobelia erinus*
'Crystal Palace'

**How:** Lobelia grows slowly so it's best to start with seedlings purchased from a nursery. Plant lobelia in ordinary soil then pinch off the growth on the tips to ensure that the plant develops a nice bushiness. After the first blooms fade, cut the plant back by half to keep it producing flowers. In mild climates, lobelia sometimes last through winter. Give them plenty of water during dry periods. In hot areas, give them partial shade.

**Trowels:** 🌱 🌱

## Lobularia maritima

Sweet alyssum
Height: 4–8 inches
Sun: Full sun

**What:** Sweet alyssum has tiny, scented flowers in white, pink, or lavender, and grayish leaves.

**Where:** This is a good plant for the front of the border, containers, or edging a path.

*Lobularia maritima*
'Easter Basket' mix

**How:** Sow seeds directly in the spring in cool climates and in midsummer to fall in the south. Scatter seeds liberally in the front of beds or in gaps in paving. Seed germinates in a week at 80°F; plants bloom 45–60 days later. In midsummer, cut back and fertilize the plants to get blooms until the first frost. Plants self-sow and are easy to grow. Give plants full sun or light shade and a well-drained soil of average fertility (even poor soil is fine for these easy plants).

Trowels: ✎

## *Matthiola incana*

Stock
Height: 12–30 inches
Sun: Full sun to partial shade

*Matthiola incana*
'Giant Imperial' mix

**What:** Stock has been around a long time. In fact, by the year 1629, it was already regarded as old-fashioned by gardeners! The single- or double-form flowers have a heady bouquet, which intensifies in the evening, and range in color from red, apricot, white, and blue to pink, lavender, and rose.

**Where:** Use these plants where you can best enjoy the sweet scent: in containers near windows and doors, in the cutting garden, in the front of a border.

**How:** Stock is easy to grow—seeds can be sown in fall where winters are mild or early in spring in cooler climates. Sow seeds in place, as stock does not transplant well. They like cool weather, full sun, and a rich, well-drained soil. Don't let seedlings dry out, and water plants regularly throughout the growing period.

Trowels: ✎ ✎

## Melampodium paludosum

Blackfoot daisy
Height: 1–2 feet
Sun: Full sun

**What:** Blackfoot daisy is a tough plant that withstands drought, heat, and humidity, needs very little attention, and produces cheerful yellow daisy-like flowers all summer What could be better?

**Where:** Use blackfoot daisy in any sunny garden, especially with other sunny flowers like calliopsis (*Coreopsis tinctoria*) and bright orange dahlias. The smaller forms look nice in containers.

*Melampodium paludosum*
'Derby'

**How:** Plants are easy to start outdoors when the soil has warmed up or indoors 8 weeks before planting to get an early start on blooms. Give them an ordinary soil and full sun. No need to deadhead, no need to stake: These are no fuss plants. Just enjoy.

**Trowels:** ✎

## Mirabilis jalapa

Four o'clock
Height: 2–3 feet
Sun: Full sun

**What:** Four o'clocks have round flowers that open in the late afternoon and stay open until the early morning. Colors are red, yellow, pink, or white.

**Where:** These tolerant plants grow even in the most difficult places—on south-facing terraces, banks,

*Mirabilis jalapa*
'Jingles' mix

and along driveways. They also work well in containers and in the middle of the border.

**How:** Direct sow in early spring for flowers by midsummer. Four o'clocks are easy to grow in average, well-drained soil.

**Trowels:** 🌱

## *Moluccella laevis*

Bells of Ireland
Height: 15–36 inches
Sun: Full sun

**What:** Bells of Ireland have very pretty calyces (the outer parts of a flower) that are apple green and shaped like little bells. The flowers themselves are white, small, and unimportant. This is a very useful plant for dried flower arrangements, as the green color eventually turns into a lovely creamy wheat color.

*Moluccella laevis*

**Where:** Plant bells of Ireland toward the middle or back of a border or bed, with shrubs, perennials, and other annuals, such as red-flowering nicotiana and purple petunias.

**How:** Sow seeds directly in ordinary soil after danger of frost, but first refrigerate the seeds for a week to help them germinate more easily. Water and fertilize regularly. These plants are not very heat tolerant and tend to do better in cooler climates. To use as a dried flower, cut the stems before the seeds ripen, then hang upside down in cool, dark place.

**Trowels:** 🌱 🌱 🌱

## *Myosotis sylvatica*

Forget-me-not
Height: 9–12 inches
Sun: Full sun to partial shade

**What:** These clear blue flowers with white centers bloom from late winter through to spring, self-sowing and spreading a beautiful mat of blue flowers. Plants have soft, hairy leaves. You can also get forget-me-nots in white or pale pink.

*Myosotis sylvatica* 'Blue Bird'

**Where:** Mass forget-me-nots for the best effect. The blue is the prettiest color and brings a cool touch to woodland and shady rock gardens, especially when planted with spring-blooming daffodils.

**How:** Sow seeds in ordinary soil in the fall where winters are mild, and in the spring in cooler regions. Give it full sun or partial shade. These plants are easy to grow and will self-sow.

**Trowels:** ✐

## *Nemophila maculata*

Five-spot
Height: 6 inches
Sun: Full sun to shade

**What:** Five-spot is a great plant for the shade—grow it instead of impatiens. The pretty, bell-shaped white flowers have five petals, each with a purple dot on the tip.

**Where:** They look pretty hanging from baskets and window boxes, or as an edging around walkways and garden beds.

**How:** Seeds can be sown directly in place as soon as the ground can be worked and will flower in early spring. Give five-spots shade, average to fertile soil, and deadhead to keep neat.

**Trowels:** 🌱 🌱

*Nemophila maculata*

## *Nicotiana alata*

Nicotiana, flowering tobacco
Height: 12–36 inches
Sun: Full sun to partial shade

**What:** Nicotiana is actually a tender perennial grown as an annual and loved for its wonderful fragrance. The star-shaped flowers come in shades of red, pink, lime green, yellow, purple, and white and are most fragrant at night. Woodland nicotiana (*N. sylvestris*) has loose, drooping clusters of white flowers and grows 3–6 inches tall.

*Nicotiana alata*

**Where:** Use nicotiana wherever you'll enjoy the scent, in beds, window boxes, or by a bench outdoors where you can sit and enjoy the sweet scent at night. These plants can take some shade (particularly woodland nicotiana) and make a dramatic accent in a shady garden.

**How:** It's best to start with seedlings. Flowering tobacco prefers a fertile soil that is well drained in partial shade to full sun. Some kinds will self-sow. Aphids can be a problem, but it's easy to simply spray them off with water from a hose. Deadhead to keep flowering.

**Trowels:** 🌱 🌱 🌱

## Nierembergia hippomanica var. violacea

Cupflower
Height: 4–15 inches
Sun: Full sun

**What:** Cupflower has blue or violet bell-shaped flowers that literally cover the plants all summer. Its foliage is bright green and fernlike. Plants have a compact, neat shape.

**Where:** Cupflower is very pretty in containers, hanging baskets, and window boxes. You can also use it as an edging plant for a bed or border.

**How:** Start with nursery-grown transplants in average soil with full sun or light shade. Remove any flowers on the plant (either just before or just after you plant), and pinch plants while young to get a full, bushy shape. Cupflowers are fairly heavy feeders, so use a balanced fertilizer and water regularly. Deadhead to get more flowers.

*Nierembergia hippomanica* var. *violacea* 'Purple Robe'

**Trowels:** 🛠 🛠 🛠

## Nigella damascena

Love-in-a-mist
Height: 18–24 inches
Sun: Full sun

**What:** Love-in-a-mist has beautiful starry blue, white, or rose flowers and foliage that is fine and lacy. They are fast-growing plants that form interesting seedpods and are great for dried arrangements.

*Nigella damascena*

**Where:** This is an old-fashioned flower that looks perfect in large, sunny cottage gardens. Mass love-in-a-mist or plant in wide drifts; use it in any open, sunny place. Or plant them in your cutting garden, as they make excellent cut flowers.

**How:** Love-in-a-mist is easy to start from seed; sow outdoors as soon as the ground is workable. In mild climates, sow seeds in October. Give these plants a fertile, well-drained soil, and thin seedlings when they have one set of true leaves to 6 inches apart. Feed regularly with a balanced fertilizer for best growth. Plants will self-sow. Deadhead to prolong flowering.

**Trowels:** ✔ ✔

## *Ocimum basilicum* 'Dark Opal'

Purple basil
Height: 12–18 inches
Sun: Full sun

*Ocimum basilicum*
'Dark Opal'

**What:** Purple basil is a beautiful plant in the flower garden. Its dark purple foliage and spikes of lavender-pink flowers are quite showy and last from spring to first frost.

**Where:** Use purple basil in containers or mass plant it with white flowering alyssum (*Lobularia maritima*) and plants with pale lavender flowers like stock (*Matthiola incana*) and blue-flowering love-in-a-mist (*Nigella damascena*).

**How:** Direct sow seeds in full sun in early spring when the soil warms up. Pinch plants to get a nice, bushy shape. Fertilize once during the growing season with a balanced fertilizer (10–10–10) and water regularly. Although you can enjoy purple basil as an edible herb, it has a slightly milder flavor than other basils.

**Trowels:** ✔ ✔

## *Papaver rhoeas*

Flander's field poppy, corn poppy
Height: 12–24 inches
Sun: Full sun

*Papaver rhoeas*
'Shirley' mixed

**What:** Poppies, long associated with sleep and death, have a fascinating history. Opium poppies (*P. somniferum*) are the source of opium and codeine and are illegal to grow in most of the United States. Corn poppy and Shirley poppy, a hybrid of *P. rhoeas*, are grown for their ruffled, papery-textured flowers that grow on wiry stems. The colors are white, pink, orange, yellow, rose, salmon, deep crimson, and bicolors in single and double flowers.

**Where:** Poppies look great in meadows and massed on hillsides and do wonders for a poor, dry site. If you haven't got a meadow or a hillside, use them in any sunny site with a mix of wildflowers or by themselves.

**How:** Poppies are very easy to grow: Select a sunny site where the soil is light to average, even sandy, and well drained. For even distribution, mix the tiny seeds with some fine gravel and sow directly in place in the early spring or fall where winters are mild. Seeds will germinate in only 8–10 days. When seedlings have developed one set of true leaves, thin plants to 6–8 inches apart. Cold weather won't bother poppies but heat and humidity will. Poppies often self-sow, coming up the following year where the wind and birds have carried the seed. For blooms all summer long, make successive sowings, every 2 weeks or so.

If you want to use poppies as a cut flower, cut off a stem and sear the base of it with a lighted match or plunge the end of the stem in hot water to seal in the milky sap.

**Trowels:** ✎ ✎

# Pelargonium × hortorum

Zonal geranium
Height: 12–24 inches
Sun: Full sun

*Pelargonium × hortorum*
'Earliana' series

**What:** Zonal geraniums were introduced during the reign of Queen Anne of England, and by the early nineteenth century, they were cultivated on an astonishing scale. Today they are still cultivated in great abundance and are available in red, pink, white, rose, lavender, salmon, and variegated. Try the ivy-leaved geranium (*P. peltatum*), which has a trailing or weeping form and comes in rose, red, pink, or white. Zonal geraniums are actually perennials (hardy only in zone 10) and grow elsewhere as annuals.

**Where:** One of the most popular of all plants, zonal geraniums are best when used in containers, as they tend to get rangy when left to sprawl in beds and borders. Use ivy-leaved geraniums in baskets, planters, and urns.

**How:** It's easiest to start these plants with seedlings. Geraniums prefer a rich, organic, well-drained soil in full sun and regular feedings with a balanced fertilizer. They grow best when they are almost potbound; repot to the next larger size container only during warm weather. Pinch young plants in the early stages of growth to get a bushy plant. Regularly remove faded flowers, along with their entire stems. Plants can be brought indoors in the fall and enjoyed through the winter as houseplants. Geraniums may seem to require more chores than other plants, but are really easy, forgiving, and long-lasting.

**Trowels:** 🌱 🌱 🌱

# Pennisetum setaceum

Annual fountain grass
Height: 2–4 feet
Sun: Full sun to partial shade

*Pennisetum setaceum*

**What:** While you won't necessarily grow fountain grass for its flowers, these fine accent plants do carry handsome spikes of pink, copper, or purple colors. The plant itself, on the whole, is quite dramatic and striking. The part of the inflorescense that is colorful is a bract that subtends each flower that makes up the spike. *P. setaceum* 'Rubrum' has purple leaves and flowers and is one of the prettiest.

**Where:** Fountain grass is ideal in container plantings and in the back of a bed or border; it makes a stunning display with tall cleome (*Cleome hasslerana*). Try fountain grass with black-eyed Susans (*Rudbeckia hirta*) and purple petunias (*Petunia* × *hybrida*); they also complement autumn mums (*Dendranthema* × *grandiflora*) and last through the fall.

**How:** Nursery-grown transplants are often available and are easier than starting by seed. They prefer a slightly dry location and are drought resistant.

**Trowels:** ✎

# Petunia × hybrida

Common garden petunia
Height: 10–18 inches
Sun: Full sun to partial shade

**What:** Petunias! There's no more popular annual for beds and borders, pots, and window boxes than the petunia, available in just about every color and shape. They come in single, double, ruffled, fringed, cascading, trailing, and dwarf forms, as well as in tall 24-inch plants.

**Where:** The trailing forms are great in planters and window boxes. Petunias are ideal plants for cities, as they withstand poor air quality.

*Petunia* × *hybrida*
'Surfina Blue Vein'

**How:** Start with transplants—you'll find a wide selection—and give petunias a well-drained, light, or sandy soil in full sun (partial shade will discourage blooms). Water regularly and feed the plants every month throughout the growing season with a balanced (10–10–10) fertilizer. Deadhead to encourage blooms and cut plants back by half in the heat of summer to rejuvenate plants.

**Trowels:** 🌱 🌱 🌱

## *Phlox drummondii*

Annual phlox, Texas pride
Height: 6–18 inches
Sun: Full sun to partial shade

**What:** Pink, lavender, red, purple, rose, scarlet, yellow, or white flowers grow in clusters on the top halves of the stems. This hardy Texas wildflower provides flowers from summer to frost, and is easy to grow.

**Where:** Annual phlox is perfect for containers and window boxes or as a low edging with sweet alyssum (*Lobularia maritima*) and ageratum (*Ageratum houstoniamum*).

*Phlox drummondii*
'Beauty Blue'

**How:** Sow seeds outdoors in full sun when the ground becomes workable or indoors about 8 weeks before the last frost where the growing season is short. Annual phlox tolerates poor, dry soil and hot weather.

**Trowels:** 🌱

## *Portulaca grandiflora*

Portulaca, moss rose
Height: 4–8 inches
Sun: Full sun

**What:** Moss rose is one of the very best low-growing annuals, providing flowers in colors such as cream, yellow, fuchsia, rose, pink, red, and white and growing where other plants will not. They love hot, dry, poor, even gravely soil. The single or double flowers are about 1 inch wide; and the foliage is spiky, silvery green, and succulent. The flowers are sensitive to light and won't open on overcast and rainy days.

*Portulaca grandiflora*
'Sundial' hybrid mix

**Where:** Use moss rose's brilliant colors in patio containers and in places where you need a sturdy plant: along the hot dry strip by the driveway, on exposed south-facing slopes and banks, and in the rock garden.

**How:** These plants prefer a hot, dry, well-drained, sandy soil in full sun. The key to success with moss rose is neglect: Never feed them, and water only in severe drought. While you can get seedlings at nurseries, seeds are easy to direct sow when the soil warms up. Mix the tiny seeds with dry sand and broadcast or scatter seed where the plants are to grow. Plants begin to bloom about 40–50 days from seeding and continue blooming to the first frost. No need to deadhead.

**Trowels:** 🌱

# Rudbeckia hirta

Gloriosa daisy, black-eyed Susan
Height: 12–30 inches
Sun: Full sun

*Rudbeckia hirta*
'Sondra'

**What:** These brilliant, golden-orange rays of flowers with chocolate brown centers are our native black-eyed Susans. Once confined to the prairie states, gloriosa daisies are now a familiar sight along highways everywhere. The flowers are bronze, mahogany, or golden, and the hairy foliage is medium green. The 1995 All-American Selection 'Indian Summer' is a great cultivar. It is very adaptable and tends to flower more than other cultivars. 'Irish Eyes' has pretty, lime green disks, or eyes.

**Where:** Gloriosa daisies are ideal plants for a meadow garden where they will self-sow and also look nice toward the middle or rear of an informal garden. Use them in the cutting garden—the taller varieties make excellent cut flowers.

**How:** Sow the seeds outdoors in early spring in full sun in a well-drained soil. Where summers are short, start plants indoors 8–10 weeks before the last frost. They will tolerate dry, poor soil but suffer from poor circulation and drought. Water during dry weather. Deadhead to keep the plant neat.

**Trowels:** 🌱 🌱

## Salvia farinacea

Mealy-cup sage, Texan mealy-cup sage
Height: 1–3 feet
Sun: Full sun

*Salvia farinacea*
'Victoria' and 'Porcelain White'

**What:** Mealy-cup sage has violet-blue or white spikes of flowers and foliage that is a soft gray-green. A native to New Mexico and Texas, this sage is actually a perennial but is grown as a half-hardy annual where winters are cold. Another salvia, Mexican sagebrush (*S. leucantha*), grows 3–4 feet tall and wide and is also a perennial grown as an annual in cooler climates. Yet another salvia, scarlet sage (*S. splendens*) is a true annual that grows to 3 feet tall with vibrant red flowers.

**Where:** Use these plants in containers, beds, cutting gardens, and borders. Scarlet sage is quite an intense red and looks best if planted next to something that will tone it down, such as white alyssum (*Lobularia maritima*) or dusty miller (*Senecio cineraria*).

**How:** It's best to start with salvia seedlings. They like an average soil and plenty of sun. Pinch the seedlings before planting to get a bushy plant.

**Trowels:** 🌱 🌱

## Sanvitalia procumbens

Creeping zinnia
Height: 4–8 inches
Sun: Full sun

**What:** Contrary to its common name, creeping zinnia is not really a zinnia, but it does look like one—its flowers have bright yellow rays with dark

centers. This is a very sturdy plant that's tolerant of heat, drought, and humidity and is
remarkably easy to grow. Blooms last from
summer to first frost.

**Where:** Use creeping zinnia in containers, as a
quick-growing cover for a bank, or as an edging
for a bed.

*Sanvitalia procumbens*

**How:** Direct sow seeds outdoors from early
spring where winters are mild to late spring in
cooler climates. All they need is sun and a place to grow.

**Trowels:** ✓

## Scaevola aemula

Fan flower
Height: 6 inches–1 foot
Sun: Full sun

**What:** This is actually a perennial, hardy in frost-
free, warm climates but grown as an annual
elsewhere. Flowers are about 1 inch across, fanning out in the shape of an open hand and
blooming from late spring to first frost. The
hybrid 'Mauve Clusters' has mauve pink flowers; 'Blue Wonder' has bright blue flowers.

**Where:** These plants trail over the sides of containers, making them excellent for hanging pots
and baskets. Use them in beds and borders,
where they will form a dense mat of flowers.

*Scaevola aemula*

**How:** Fan flowers are best begun with nursery transplants. Plant them in a well-drained, fertile soil and provide water throughout the summer. Pinching plants will ensure a bushy shape. In colder regions, take plants indoors before the first frost in the fall. Cut plants back to half and place in a sunny location. In the spring, plants can be taken back outdoors and hardened off.

**Trowels:** ✎ ✎

## *Senecio cineraria*

Dusty miller
Height: 8–30 inches
Sun: Full sun

*Senecio cineraria*
'Silverdust'

**What:** The soft-looking, woolly white leaves have a slightly greenish cast. Although yellow- or cream-colored flowers appear above the foliage, they are not nearly as attractive as the beetlike leaves.

**Where:** These lacy plants are invaluable in a white or moon garden and can help tone down brightly colored annuals. Try it with dahlias, globe amaranth, zinnias, verbena, and salvia. Use it as an edging in any garden or window box.

**How:** Dusty miller is easy to grow from seeds or seedlings. Give it a light, well-drained soil (it also does well in sandy soil) and light waterings. The only maintenance chores are pinching the yellow flowers as they appear and pruning the foliage to keep the shape neat.

**Trowels:** ✎ ✎

## Tagetes patula

French marigold
Height: 10–24 inches
Sun: Full sun

*Tagetes patula*
'Queen Sophia'

**What:** The popularity of marigolds is under-standable: They come in cheerful colors such as yellows, oranges, golds, and reds; the foliage has a pretty lemony fragrance; and they are one of the easiest annuals you'll ever grow. Try 'Naughty Marietta' with pretty yellow and maroon flowers.

**Where:** French marigolds are great in containers, window boxes, wooden tubs, and anywhere there is sun. In the garden, the dwarf forms work best in the front of the border; taller forms work well toward the middle. Plant drifts of tall French marigolds in the middle to back of the border to complement blues and grays in the garden.

**How:** Marigolds are very easy to grow. Direct sow seeds outdoors after dan-ger of frost, or sow inside for an earlier bloom. They prefer well-drained soil in full sun. Deadhead for more blooms—no pinching required.

**Trowels:** ✔

## Thunbergia alata

Clockvine, black-eyed Susan vine
Height: To 6 feet
Sun: Full sun to partial shade

**What:** This is a vine that grows by twining, with flowers like black-eyed Susans. The dark purple centers and white to orange-yellow rays literally cover the plant from summer to the first frost.

**Where:** Clockvine is perfect for hanging baskets and window boxes, or climbing up trellises and posts.

**How:** Give clockvine a rich and well-drained soil, full sun or partial shade, and a trellis or another structure on which it can climb.

**Trowels:** 🌱 🌱

*Thunbergia alata*
'Susie' mix

## *Tithonia rotundifolia*

Mexican sunflower
Height: 4–6 feet
Sun: Full sun

**What:** Mexican sunflower is a tall, quick-growing annual with big, bright orange rays and yellow centers. The flowers are 3–4 inches wide, and bloom from July to frost. The foliage is somewhat coarse.

**Where:** Use this plant toward the back of the border with other warm colors.

**How:** Sow seeds in place in early spring. These plants are very easy to grow and resist drought and heat, making them ideal where summers are hot.

*Tithonia rotundifolia*
'Sundance'

**Trowels:** 🌱

## Torenia fournieri

Wishbone flower
Height: 6–12 inches
Sun: Full sun to partial shade

*Torenia fournieri*
'Happy Faces' hybrid mix

**What:** Torenia are bushy plants with delightful flowers whose petals are blue, pink, or plum with tinges of white and a bright yellow dot on one petal. Plants bloom from summer through fall. The stamens are arranged in a wishbone shape, hence its common name of wishbone flower. Try 'Happy Faces' hybrid mix, which has a cheerful blend of colors.

**Where:** Torenia is a great alternative to impatiens and works well in pots, window boxes, and the front of the border.

**How:** Torenia is best started with seedlings. Plant in a fertile, well-drained soil, and keep them well watered. Plants can take full sun where summers are cool but otherwise need partial shade. Deadheading is not necessary.

**Trowels:** ✔ ✔

## Tropaeolum majus

Garden nasturtium
Height: Trailing to 6 feet or compact to 15 inches
Sun: Full sun

**What:** Nasturtiums are available in two types: those that climb and trail and those that develop a compact shape. Both have pretty, rounded leaves (edible, with a peppery flavor like arugula) and flowers that come in glorious colors, such as yellows, reds, oranges, solids, and stripes.

**Where:** Use the trailing ones for window boxes and other planters and the compact ones as edgings.

**How:** Sow seeds directly in the ground and give nasturtiums a light, sandy soil with good drainage. In hot climates, plant them in light shade. These are plants you definitely won't want to fuss over, as they prefer no watering and no feeding. In fact, feeding nasturtium will result in beautiful foliage and no flowers. Both the flowers and leaves are edible and are great in summer salads.

**Trowels:** 🌱

*Tropaeolum majus*
'Jewel' mix

## *Verbena* × *hybrida*

Garden verbena
Height: 6–10 inches
Sun: Full sun

**What:** Garden verbena is actually a short-lived perennial that is usually grown as an annual. The flowers are clusters about 2–3 inches wide and the foliage is bright green. Plants grow vigorously from spring until frost. Colors are white, pink, bright red, purple, blue, and combinations.

*Verbena* × *hybrida*
'Vivacious'

**Where:** It's low growing, so use it as ground cover, as an edging plant in your garden, in a hanging basket, or in a planter. Rose verbena (*V. canadensis* 'Homestead Purple') is a particularly nice choice for use as an edging plant.

**How:** Start with seedlings—seeds can be difficult. Verbena likes a rich soil and can take some light shade in the heat of the south. Pinch just before planting to encourage basal growth; no need to deadhead. Verbena will self-sow easily. Water deeply but not too often and give it good air circulation. Verbena can, unfortunately, attract whiteflies, but *V. bonariensis*, a perennial that can be grown as an annual, tends to be more resistant to whiteflies than other species.

**Trowels:** 🌱🌱

## *Vinca major*

Greater periwinkle
Height: Trailing to 15 inches
Sun: Full sun to partial shade

**What:** Periwinkle is actually a perennial but is grown as an annual in most climates, where it won't survive the winter. Plants grow quickly, developing long, trailing stems with oval-shaped, glossy green leaves and small, sparse blue or violet flowers. Stems will trail several feet in a year.

*Vinca major*
'Variegata'

**Where:** Vinca vine is an excellent plant for window boxes, planters, and anywhere it can trail. Try it in the window box between geraniums (*Pelargonium × hortorum*) and dwarf zinnias (*Zinnia elegans*).

**How:** Start with transplants. Plant in full sun in cooler climates and partial shade in warmer climates. Vinca is easy to grow and can be invasive in warm areas. It prefers a rich, well-drained soil. Give it plenty of water and feed it several times in the growing season. Bring plants indoors before the first hard frost to winter-over.

**Trowels:** 🌱

# Viola × wittrockiana

Pansy, violet
Height: 4–8 inches
Sun: Full sun to shade

*Viola × wittrockiana* 'Blues Jam'

**What:** Pansies come in a wide assortment of beautiful colors, such as blue, white, purple, orange, yellow, red, and bicolors and tricolors. Shakespeare called pansies love-in-idleness, which is just one of the more than sixty names this well-loved plant has been given in the English language alone. Pansies are perennials but are treated as annuals, even where winters are mild. Try Johnny-jump-up (*V. tricolor*), which has small flowers in purple, yellow, and white and self-sows readily.

**Where:** Pansies are invaluable as bedding plants and in window boxes and any container. In warm regions, they flower through the winter to spring; in cooler regions, they flower in spring and again in fall.

**How:** Where winters are mild, sow seeds from mid-July to August; in cool areas, sow indoors in January or February and plant outdoors in spring. To aid in germination, refrigerate the seeds for several days before sowing. Pansies like a rich, organic, well-drained soil in full sun to partial shade. Feed in the early spring for the best show of flowers. Plants can begin to look ragged as the summer heat rises and should be removed in mild winter areas. Keep pinching back plants to promote flowers and bushiness, and deadhead for more bloom (use the flowers for small vases indoors). Plants will self-sow.

**Trowels:** 🌱 🌱

## Zinnia angustifolia

Zinnia
Height: 1–3 feet
Sun: Full sun

*Zinnia angustifolia*
'Star White'

**What:** Zinnias come in bright bold colors (reds, oranges, yellows), sweet pastel colors (pink, white), and bicolors, solids, and stripes. The sizes of the flower heads vary.

**Where:** Use zinnias everywhere: The dwarf forms are great for edgings and containers; the taller ones work well toward the back of the border. They love the heat and are great everywhere except in cool coastal climates.

**How:** Sow zinnias directly in the ground after frost; average garden soil is fine. Cut as many flowers as you can for flower arrangements, because the more flowers you cut, the more flowers the plants produce. Zinnias are great as cut flowers, because they last a long time in water.

**Trowels:** 🌱

# USDA Plant Hardiness Zone Map

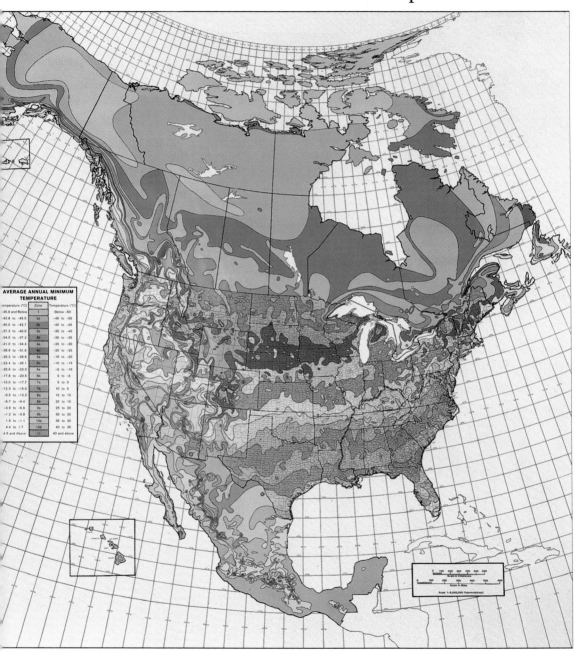

**AVERAGE ANNUAL MINIMUM TEMPERATURE**

| Temperature (°C) | Zone | Temperature (°C) |
|---|---|---|
| -45.6 and Below | 1 | Below -50 |
| -42.8 to -45.5 | 2a | -45 to -50 |
| -40.0 to -42.7 | 2b | -40 to -45 |
| -37.3 to -40.0 | 3a | -35 to -40 |
| -34.5 to -37.2 | 3b | -30 to -35 |
| -31.0 to -34.4 | 4a | -25 to -30 |
| -28.9 to -31.6 | 4b | -20 to -25 |
| -26.2 to -28.8 | 5a | -15 to -20 |
| -23.4 to -26.1 | 5b | -10 to -15 |
| -20.6 to -23.3 | 6a | -5 to -10 |
| -17.8 to -20.5 | 6b | 0 to -5 |
| -15.0 to -17.7 | 7a | 5 to 0 |
| -12.3 to -15.0 | 7b | 10 to 5 |
| -9.5 to -12.2 | 8a | 15 to 10 |
| -6.7 to -9.4 | 8b | 20 to 15 |
| -3.9 to -6.6 | 9a | 25 to 20 |
| -1.2 to -3.8 | 9b | 30 to 25 |
| 1.6 to -1.1 | 10a | 35 to 30 |
| 4.4 to 1.7 | 10b | 40 to 35 |
| 4.5 and Above | 11 | 40 and above |

# The Gardener's Calendar

Use the plant hardiness zone map on the facing page to find where you are, then use the following calendar of chores to schedule your maintenance tasks throughout the year.

## Zones 2–4

### Early Spring
- Order seeds from mail-order nurseries.
- Remove mulch to warm up soil where early seeds will be planted.
- Sow seeds indoors 6–8 weeks before last frost date.

## Late Spring

- Clean up beds and borders.
- Plant hardy annuals, such as pansies, calendulas, and bachelor's buttons.
- Watch for pests—it's easier to control them if caught early.
- Pot up containers, adding trellises for vines.
- Begin weeding on a regular basis.

## Summer

- Watch for last frost date; direct sow annuals accordingly.
- Put mulches in place in garden beds.
- Pot up containers with annuals.
- Perform basic garden tasks: weed, water, feed, mulch, deadhead.
- Continue pinching the annuals that need it for bushy growth.
- Cut flowers all summer to enjoy indoors.
- Water and feed plants in containers regularly.
- Stake plants as they need it.
- Shear annuals that have stopped blooming to encourage new growth.

## Early Autumn

- After first hard frost, cut annuals to ground level and add to compost heap.
- Plant mums and flowering kale and cabbage.
- Dig up dahlia tubers and caladium bulbs and store in cool, dry place.
- Begin to take annuals indoors to winter-over. Cut plants back by half and place them in a sunny window.
- Empty plants and soil from pots. Clean out terra-cotta containers and store in cool place.

## Late Autumn

- Rake the last of the leaves; shred and add to leaf mold pile to use the following spring as a mulch.

- Clean and store garden tools.
- Take down and store stakes for use next year.
- Cover heavy containers that are to stay outdoors with a board and a tarp.

## Winter

- Check stored dahlia tubers. Remove any that have rotted.
- Peruse garden catalogs.
- Walk around property and plan new garden beds.

# Zones 5–7

## Early Spring

- Order seeds from mail-order nurseries.
- Remove mulch to warm up soil where early seeds will be planted.
- Sow seeds indoors 6–8 weeks before last frost date.
- Plant, feed, and deadhead pansies.

## Late Spring

- Clean up beds. When temperatures begin to stay above 65°F, add soil amendments.
- Plant hardy annuals such as pansies, calendulas, and bachelor's buttons.
- Watch for pests—it's easier to control them if caught early.
- Pot up containers, adding trellises for vines.
- Weed on a regular basis.
- Sow poppy seeds every 2 weeks for a succession of bloom.
- Watch for last frost date; direct sow annuals accordingly.
- Begin to harden off plants that were wintered-over.

## Summer

- Plant annuals.
- Deadhead annuals weekly.
- Put mulches in place in garden beds.
- Perform basic garden tasks: weed, water, feed, mulch, deadhead.
- Continue pinching the annuals that need it for bushy growth.
- Cut flowers to enjoy indoors.
- Water and feed plants in containers regularly.
- Stake plants as they need it.
- Shear annuals that have stopped blooming to encourage new growth.
- Keep plants mulched and watered all summer.

## Early Autumn

- Plant mums and flowering kale and cabbage.
- Dig up dahlia tubers after the first frost and store in cool, dry place.
- Empty plants and soil from pots. Clean out terra-cotta containers and store in cool place.
- Fertilize pansies.

## Late Autumn

- After first hard frost, cut annuals to ground level and add to compost heap.
- Begin to take annuals indoors to winter-over. Cut plants back by half and place them in a sunny window.

## Winter

- Check stored dahlia tubers. Remove any that have rotted.
- Peruse garden catalogs. Order seeds.
- Plan new gardens.

# Zones 8–10

## Early Spring

- Deadhead faded flowers to keep them blooming.
- Spread mulch in garden beds.
- Thin seedlings.
- Watch for insect and disease problems.
- Turn compost pile as needed.
- Plant caladium bulbs.

## Late Spring

- Fertilize annuals and summer bulbs.
- Plant portulaca, marigolds, salvias, zinnias, and ageratum.
- Feed and water plants in containers.
- Put stakes in place.
- Begin looking for aphids.

## Summer

- Continue maintenance: deadhead flowers and control insects and weeds.
- Plant hardy annuals.
- Cut back annuals to rejuvenate and promote rebloom.
- Water when necessary—watch for plant stress from heat.
- Watch for spider mites.
- Order seeds for fall planting.

## Early Autumn

- Water and feed annuals.
- Deadhead frequently.
- Check containers often to see if soil is dry.
- Weed regularly.

- Dig and store caladium bulbs.
- Plant transplants of pansies, pentunias, verbena, alyssum, and flowering cabbage and kale for fall color.

## Late Autumn

- Deadhead and fertilize hardy annuals.
- Harvest flowers for drying.
- Continue monitoring garden for pests and diseases.
- Water as necessary.
- Stake plants as necessary.
- Control winter weeds and grasses.
- Plant bedding plants of pansies, calendula, petunias, candytuft, snapdragons.
- Cover marginally hardy annuals if freeze is predicted.

## Winter

- Sow directly nasturtiums and sweet peas.
- Water as needed when temperatures are above freezing.
- Protect half-hardy plants when frosts are predicted.
- Add leaf rakings to compost pile.
- Till soil deeply, incorporating organic matter.
- Remove fall garden debris, till soil deeply, incorporate organic matter.
- Renew mulches.
- Comb seed catalogs for new plants.
- Clean and sharpen garden tools.

# AVERAGE DATES OF FIRST AND LAST FROSTS IN THE UNITED STATES

| State and City | Mean Date Last 32°F in Spring | Mean Date Last 32°F in Fall | Mean Freeze-Free Days |
|---|---|---|---|
| **ALABAMA** | | | |
| Birmingham | Mar. 19 | Nov. 14 | 241 |
| Mobile | Feb. 17 | Dec. 12 | 298 |
| Montgomery | Feb. 27 | Dec. 3 | 279 |
| **ALASKA** | | | |
| Anchorage | May 18 | Sept. 13 | 118 |
| Barrow | June 27 | July 5 | 8 |
| Cordova | May 10 | Oct. 2 | 145 |
| Fairbanks | May 24 | Aug. 29 | 97 |
| Juneau | Apr. 27 | Oct. 19 | 176 |
| Nome | June 12 | Aug. 24 | 73 |
| **ARIZONA** | | | |
| Flagstaff | June 8 | Oct. 2 | 116 |
| Phoenix | Jan. 27 | Dec. 11 | 317 |
| Tuscan | Mar. 6 | Nov. 23 | 261 |
| Winslow | Apr. 28 | Oct. 21 | 176 |
| Yuma | Jan. 11 | Dec. 27 | 350 |
| **ARKANSAS** | | | |
| Fort Smith | Mar. 23 | Nov. 9 | 231 |
| Little Rock | Mar. 16 | Nov. 15 | 244 |
| **CALIFORNIA** | | | |
| Bakersfield | Feb. 14 | Nov. 28 | 287 |

*Frost not likely in these locations*
**Source:** *United States Department of Agriculture*

| State and City | Mean Date Last 32°F in Spring | Mean Date Last 32°F in Fall | Mean Freeze-Free Days |
|---|---|---|---|
| **CALIFORNIA** (*continued*) | | | |
| Eureka | Jan. 24 | Dec. 25 | 335 |
| Fresno | Feb. 3 | Dec. 3 | 303 |
| Los Angeles | * | * | * |
| Red Bluff | Feb. 25 | Nov. 29 | 277 |
| Sacramento | Jan. 24 | Dec. 11 | 321 |
| San Diego | * | * | * |
| San Francisco | * | * | * |
| **COLORADO** | | | |
| Denver | May 2 | Oct. 14 | 165 |
| Palisades | Apr. 22 | Oct. 17 | 178 |
| Pueblo | Apr. 28 | Oct. 12 | 167 |
| **CONNECTICUT** | | | |
| Hartford | Apr. 22 | Oct. 19 | 180 |
| New Haven | Apr. 15 | Oct. 27 | 195 |
| **DISTRICT OF COLUMBIA** | | | |
| Washington | Apr. 10 | Oct. 28 | 200 |
| **FLORIDA** | | | |
| Apalachicola | Feb. 2 | Dec. 21 | 322 |
| Fort Myers | * | * | * |
| Jacksonville | Feb. 6 | Dec. 16 | 313 |
| Key West | * | * | * |
| Lakeland | Jan. 10 | Dec. 25 | 349 |

*Frost not likely in these locations*

| State and City | Mean Date Last 32°F in Spring | Mean Date Last 32°F in Fall | Mean Freeze- Free Days |
|---|---|---|---|
| **FLORIDA** (*continued*) | | | |
| Miami | * | * | * |
| Orlando | Jan. 31 | Dec. 17 | 319 |
| Pensacola | Feb. 18 | Dec. 15 | 300 |
| Tallahassee | Feb. 26 | Dec. 3 | 280 |
| Tampa | Jan. 10 | Dec. 26 | 349 |
| **GEORGIA** | | | |
| Atlanta | Mar. 20 | Nov. 19 | 244 |
| Augusta | Mar. 7 | Nov. 22 | 260 |
| Macon | Mar. 12 | Nov. 19 | 252 |
| Savannah | Feb. 21 | Dec. 9 | 291 |
| **IDAHO** | | | |
| Boise | Apr. 29 | Oct. 16 | 171 |
| Pocatello | May 8 | Sept. 30 | 145 |
| Salmon | June 4 | Sept. 6 | 94 |
| **ILLINOIS** | | | |
| Cairo | Mar. 23 | Nov. 11 | 233 |
| Chicago | Apr. 19 | Oct. 28 | 192 |
| Freeport | May 8 | Oct. 4 | 149 |
| Peoria | Apr. 22 | Oct. 16 | 177 |
| Springfield | Apr. 8 | Oct. 30 | 206 |
| **INDIANA** | | | |
| Evansville | Apr. 2 | Nov. 4 | 216 |

*Frost not likely in these locations*

| State and City | Mean Date Last 32°F in Spring | Mean Date Last 32°F in Fall | Mean Freeze-Free Days |
|---|---|---|---|
| **INDIANA** *(continued)* | | | |
| Fort Wayne | Apr. 24 | Oct. 20 | 179 |
| Indianapolis | Apr. 17 | Oct. 27 | 193 |
| South Bend | May 3 | Oct. 16 | 165 |
| **IOWA** | | | |
| Des Moines | Apr. 20 | Oct. 19 | 183 |
| Dubuque | Apr. 19 | Oct. 19 | 184 |
| Koekuk | Apr. 12 | Oct. 26 | 197 |
| Sioux City | Apr. 28 | Oct. 12 | 167 |
| **KANSAS** | | | |
| Concordia | Apr. 16 | Oct. 24 | 191 |
| Dodge City | Apr. 22 | Oct. 24 | 184 |
| Goodland | May 5 | Oct. 9 | 157 |
| Topeka | Apr. 9 | Oct. 26 | 200 |
| Wichita | Apr. 5 | Nov. 1 | 210 |
| **KENTUCKY** | | | |
| Lexington | Apr. 13 | Oct. 28 | 198 |
| Louisville | Apr. 1 | Nov. 7 | 220 |
| **LOUISIANA** | | | |
| Lake Charles | Feb. 18 | Dec. 6 | 291 |
| New Orleans | Feb. 13 | Dec. 12 | 302 |
| Shreveport | Mar. 1 | Nov. 27 | 272 |

*Frost not likely in these locations

| State and City | Mean Date Last 32°F in Spring | Mean Date Last 32°F in Fall | Mean Freeze-Free Days |
| --- | --- | --- | --- |
| **MAINE** | | | |
| Greenville | May 27 | Sept. 20 | 116 |
| Portland | Apr. 29 | Oct. 15 | 169 |
| **MARYLAND** | | | |
| Annapolis | Mar. 4 | Nov. 15 | 225 |
| Baltimore | Mar. 28 | Nov. 17 | 234 |
| Frederick | Mar. 24 | Oct. 17 | 176 |
| **MASSACHUSETTS** | | | |
| Boston | Apr. 16 | Oct. 25 | 192 |
| Nantucket | Apr. 12 | Nov. 16 | 219 |
| **MICHIGAN** | | | |
| Alpena | May 6 | Oct. 9 | 156 |
| Detroit | Apr. 25 | Oct. 23 | 181 |
| Escanaba | May 14 | Oct. 6 | 145 |
| Grand Rapids | Apr. 25 | Oct. 27 | 185 |
| Marquette | May 14 | Oct. 17 | 156 |
| S. Ste. Marie | May 18 | Oct. 3 | 138 |
| **MINNESOTA** | | | |
| Albert Lee | May 3 | Oct. 6 | 156 |
| Big Falls | June 4 | Sept. 7 | 95 |
| Brainerd | May 16 | Sept. 24 | 131 |
| Duluth | May 22 | Sept. 24 | 125 |

*Frost not likely in these locations*

| State and City | Mean Date Last 32°F in Spring | Mean Date Last 32°F in Fall | Mean Freeze-Free Days |
|---|---|---|---|
| **MINNESOTA** *(continued)* | | | |
| Minneapolis | Apr. 30 | Oct. 13 | 166 |
| St. Cloud | May 9 | Sept. 29 | 144 |
| **MISSISSIPPI** | | | |
| Jackson | Mar. 10 | Nov. 13 | 248 |
| Meridian | Mar. 13 | Nov. 14 | 246 |
| Vicksburg | Mar. 8 | Nov. 15 | 252 |
| **MISSOURI** | | | |
| Columbia | Apr. 9 | Oct. 24 | 198 |
| Kansas City | Apr. 5 | Oct. 31 | 210 |
| St. Louis | Apr. 2 | Nov. 8 | 220 |
| Springfield | Apr. 10 | Oct. 31 | 203 |
| **MONTANA** | | | |
| Billings | May 15 | Sept. 24 | 132 |
| Glasgow | May 19 | Sept. 20 | 124 |
| Great Falls | May 14 | Sept. 26 | 135 |
| Havre | May 9 | Sept. 23 | 138 |
| Helena | May 12 | Sept. 23 | 134 |
| Kalispell | May 12 | Sept. 23 | 134 |
| Miles City | May 5 | Oct. 3 | 150 |
| Superior | June 5 | Aug. 30 | 85 |
| **NEBRASKA** | | | |
| Grand Island | Apr. 29 | Oct. 6 | 160 |

*Frost not likely in these locations

| State and City | Mean Date Last 32°F in Spring | Mean Date Last 32°F in Fall | Mean Freeze-Free Days |
|---|---|---|---|
| **NEBRASKA** (*continued*) | | | |
| Lincoln | Apr. 20 | Oct. 17 | 180 |
| Norfolk | May 4 | Oct. 3 | 152 |
| North Platte | Apr. 30 | Oct. 7 | 160 |
| Omaha | Apr. 14 | Oct. 20 | 189 |
| Valentine Lakes | May 7 | Sept. 30 | 146 |
| **NEVADA** | | | |
| Elko | June 6 | Sept. 3 | 89 |
| Las Vegas | Mar. 13 | Nov. 13 | 245 |
| Reno | May 14 | Oct. 2 | 141 |
| Winnemucca | May 18 | Sept. 21 | 125 |
| **NEW HAMPSHIRE** | | | |
| Concord | May 11 | Sept. 30 | 142 |
| **NEW JERSEY** | | | |
| Cape May | Apr. 4 | Nov. 15 | 225 |
| Trenton | Apr. 8 | Nov. 5 | 211 |
| **NEW MEXICO** | | | |
| Albuquerque | Apr. 16 | Oct. 29 | 196 |
| Rosewell | Apr. 9 | Nov. 2 | 208 |
| **NEW YORK** | | | |
| Albany | Apr. 27 | Oct. 13 | 169 |
| Binghamton | May 4 | Oct. 6 | 154 |

*Frost not likely in these locations

| State and City | Mean Date Last 32°F in Spring | Mean Date Last 32°F in Fall | Mean Freeze-Free Days |
|---|---|---|---|
| **NEW YORK** (*continued*) | | | |
| Buffalo | Apr. 30 | Oct. 25 | 179 |
| New York | Apr. 7 | Nov. 12 | 219 |
| Rochester | Apr. 28 | Oct. 21 | 176 |
| Syracuse | Apr. 30 | Oct. 15 | 168 |
| **NORTH CAROLINA** | | | |
| Asheville | Apr. 12 | Oct. 24 | 195 |
| Charlotte | Mar. 21 | Nov. 15 | 239 |
| Greenville | Mar. 28 | Nov. 5 | 222 |
| Hatteras | Feb. 25 | Dec. 18 | 296 |
| Raleigh | Feb. 25 | Nov. 16 | 237 |
| Wilmington | Mar. 8 | Nov. 24 | 262 |
| **NORTH DAKOTA** | | | |
| Bismarck | May 11 | Sept. 24 | 136 |
| Devils Lake | May 18 | Sept. 22 | 127 |
| Fargo | May 13 | Sept. 27 | 137 |
| Williston | May 14 | Sept. 23 | 132 |
| **OHIO** | | | |
| Akron-Canton | Apr. 29 | Oct. 20 | 173 |
| Cincinnati | Apr. 15 | Oct. 25 | 192 |
| Cleveland | Apr. 21 | Nov. 2 | 195 |
| Columbus | Apr. 17 | Oct. 30 | 196 |
| Dayton | Apr. 20 | Oct. 21 | 184 |
| Toledo | Apr. 24 | Oct. 25 | 184 |

*Frost not likely in these locations

| State and City | Mean Date Last 32°F in Spring | Mean Date Last 32°F in Fall | Mean Freeze-Free Days |
|---|---|---|---|
| **OKLAHOMA** | | | |
| Okla. City | Mar. 28 | Nov. 7 | 223 |
| Tulsa | Mar. 31 | Nov. 2 | 216 |
| **OREGON** | | | |
| Astoria | Mar. 18 | Nov. 24 | 251 |
| Bend | June 17 | Aug. 17 | 62 |
| Medford | Apr. 25 | Oct. 20 | 178 |
| Pendleton | Apr. 27 | Oct. 8 | 163 |
| Portland | Feb. 25 | Dec. 1 | 279 |
| Salem | Apr. 14 | Oct. 27 | 197 |
| **PENNSYLVANIA** | | | |
| Allentown | Apr. 20 | Oct. 16 | 180 |
| Harrisburg | Apr. 10 | Oct. 28 | 201 |
| Philadelphia | Mar. 30 | Nov. 17 | 232 |
| Pittsburgh | Apr. 20 | Oct. 23 | 187 |
| Scranton | Apr. 24 | Oct. 14 | 174 |
| **RHODE ISLAND** | | | |
| Providence | Apr. 13 | Oct. 27 | 197 |
| **SOUTH CAROLINA** | | | |
| Charleston | Feb. 19 | Dec. 10 | 294 |
| Columbia | Mar. 14 | Nov. 21 | 252 |
| Greenville | Mar. 23 | Nov. 17 | 239 |

*Frost not likely in these locations*

| State and City | Mean Date Last 32°F in Spring | Mean Date Last 32°F in Fall | Mean Freeze-Free Days |
|---|---|---|---|
| **SOUTH DAKOTA** | | | |
| Huron | May 4 | Sept. 30 | 149 |
| Rapid City | May 7 | Oct. 4 | 150 |
| Sioux Falls | May 5 | Oct. 3 | 152 |
| **TENNESSEE** | | | |
| Chattanooga | Mar. 26 | Nov. 10 | 229 |
| Knoxville | Mar. 31 | Nov. 6 | 220 |
| Memphis | Mar. 20 | Nov. 12 | 237 |
| Nashville | Mar. 28 | Nov. 7 | 224 |
| **TEXAS** | | | |
| Albany | Mar. 30 | Nov. 9 | 224 |
| Balmorhea | Apr. 1 | Nov. 12 | 226 |
| Beeville | Feb. 21 | Dec. 6 | 288 |
| College Station | Mar. 1 | Dec. 1 | 275 |
| Corsicana | Mar. 13 | Nov. 27 | 259 |
| Dallas | Mar. 18 | Nov. 22 | 249 |
| Del Rio | Feb. 12 | Dec. 9 | 300 |
| Encinal | Feb. 15 | Dec. 12 | 301 |
| Houston | Feb. 5 | Dec. 11 | 309 |
| Lampasas | Apr. 1 | Nov. 10 | 223 |
| Matagorda | Feb. 12 | Dec. 17 | 308 |
| Midland | Apr. 3 | Nov. 6 | 218 |
| Mission | Jan. 30 | Dec. 21 | 325 |
| Mount Pleasant | Mar. 23 | Nov. 12 | 233 |

*Frost not likely in these locations*

| State and City | Mean Date Last 32°F in Spring | Mean Date Last 32°F in Fall | Mean Freeze-Free Days |
|---|---|---|---|
| **TEXAS** (*continued*) | | | |
| Nacogdoches | Mar. 15 | Nov. 13 | 243 |
| Plainview | Apr. 10 | Nov. 6 | 211 |
| Presidio | Mar. 20 | Nov. 13 | 238 |
| Quanah | Mar. 31 | Nov. 7 | 221 |
| San Angelo | Mar. 25 | Nov. 15 | 235 |
| Ysleta | Apr. 6 | Oct. 30 | 207 |
| **UTAH** | | | |
| Blanding | May 18 | Oct. 14 | 148 |
| Salt Lake City | Apr. 12 | Nov. 1 | 202 |
| **VERMONT** | | | |
| Burlington | May 8 | Oct. 3 | 148 |
| **VIRGINIA** | | | |
| Lynchburg | Apr. 6 | Oct. 27 | 205 |
| Norfolk | Mar. 18 | Nov. 27 | 254 |
| Richmond | Apr. 2 | Nov. 8 | 220 |
| Roanoke | Apr. 20 | Oct. 24 | 187 |
| **WASHINGTON** | | | |
| Bumping Lake | June 17 | Aug. 16 | 60 |
| Seattle | Feb. 23 | Dec. 1 | 281 |
| Spokane | Apr. 20 | Oct. 12 | 175 |
| Tatoosh Island | Jan. 25 | Dec. 20 | 329 |
| Walla Walla | Mar. 28 | Nov. 1 | 218 |

*Frost not likely in these locations

| State and City | Mean Date Last 32°F in Spring | Mean Date Last 32°F in Fall | Mean Freeze-Free Days |
|---|---|---|---|
| **WASHINGTON** (*continued*) | | | |
| Yakima | Apr. 19 | Oct. 15 | 179 |
| **WEST VIRGINIA** | | | |
| Charleston | Apr. 18 | Oct. 28 | 193 |
| Parkersburg | Apr. 16 | Oct. 21 | 189 |
| **WISCONSIN** | | | |
| Green Bay | May 6 | Oct. 13 | 161 |
| La Crosse | May 1 | Oct. 8 | 161 |
| Madison | Apr. 26 | Oct. 19 | 177 |
| Milwaukee | Apr. 20 | Oct. 25 | 188 |
| **WYOMING** | | | |
| Casper | May 18 | Sept. 25 | 130 |
| Cheyenne | May 20 | Sept. 27 | 130 |
| Lander | May 15 | Sept. 20 | 128 |
| Sheridan | May 21 | Sept. 21 | 123 |

*Frost not likely in these locations

# The Gardener's Language

**Accents**   Single plants used in a garden design. Accent plants draw attention to themselves with their dramatic or interesting foliage or flower color.

**Acidic soil**   Soil with a pH value of less than 7.0.

**Alkaline soil**   Soil with a pH value of more than 7.0.

**Annuals**   Plants that live for 1 year or growing season.

**Beneficial insects**   Insects, such as ladybugs, lacewings, dragonflies, and certain wasps and flies, that eat or parasitize the insects that damage plants.

**Biennials**   Plants that complete their life cycles within 2 years.

**Broadcast**   To scatter seeds or fertilizer onto the soil by hand.

**Bud**   A flower bud develops into a flower; a growth bud on the tip of a stem or along the side of a stem will produce new leafy growth.

**Clay soil**   A type of soil with small, almost microscopic soil particles.

**Complete fertilizer**   A plant food, either organic or synthetic, with all three of the essential nutrient elements: nitrogen, phosphorus, and potassium.

**Compost**   Decomposed organic matter that is added to the soil to improve its composition and fertility.

**Cotyledon**   Seed leaves that are apparent upon germination of the seed. These first leaves are not "true" leaves and contain stored nutrients that aid the growth of the new plant.

**Cultivar**   A plant variety that is selected from cultivation, not from the wild. When propagated, it retains its distinct identity.

**Cultivate**   The act of tilling or stirring the soil surface to eliminate weeds and aerate the soil.

**Cultivation**   Any habitat inhabited by humans—areas that are not wild.

**Cutting**   The piece of a plant, usually a stem, cut off from the plant and rooted to make a new plant.

**Deadhead**   The act of removing faded flowers to promote further flowering, prevent seeding, or improve the appearance of a plant.

**Direct sow**   The act of planting seeds directly in the soil where they are to grow.

**Diseases**   Organisms (fungal, viral, or bacterial) that attack plants, hindering their development and producing mildews, rots, rusts, and wilts on stems, leaves, and flowers.

**Family**   A biological division within the plant or animal kingdom that comprises genera. *See also* **Genus**.

**Fertilizer**   Any material, synthetic or organic, that supplies nutrients to a plant.

**Foliage plants**   Plants used in gardens primarily for their attractive foliage rather than for flowers.

**Formal**   A garden laid out in a geometric pattern, usually filled with plants with neat habits of growth.

**Genus**   A group of plant species with similarities. A genus may contain one or more species. The common names for many groups of plants, such as cosmos, cleome, and begonia, are also scientific names for those genera. *See also* **Species**.

**Germination**   The beginning of plant growth from a seed.

**Harden off**   The process of introducing a plant to outdoor temperatures by gradually acclimating it to colder weather, minimizing the shock of the transition.

**Hardy**   Describes a plant's resistance to or tolerance of freezing temperatures. Hardy plants are those that survive cold winter temperatures.

**Heavy soil**   Used interchangeably with *clay soil* to describe a soil made up of minutely fine particles packed closely together.

**Humus**   Organic matter in its last stage of decay, usually brown or black.

**Hybrid**   A plant that has been produced by cross-pollinating different plants, to create a new plant that is distinct from or superior to its parents.

**Inflorescence**   The flower-supporting structure of plants: umbels, corymbs, spikes, and racemes.

**Informal**   A free-form garden design that incorporates plants that often drift and sprawl into each other and spill over the sides of the garden.

**Invasive**   A plant that spreads quickly and, if not checked, can take over a garden.

**Island bed**   A garden bed that is set within a lawn. Its shape may be geometric or free-form.

**Light soil**   Used interchangeably with *sandy soil* to describe a large-particled, loosely packed, free-draining soil.

**Loam**   A balance of sand and clay; the best type of soil.

**Manure**   Livestock dung, usually high in nutrients, used as an organic fertilizer and soil conditioner.

**Mulch**   Materials, synthetic or organic, spread on the soil surface to protect plants from excessive weather, stifle the growth of weeds, conserve moisture, or enhance the look of a garden.

**Native plant**   A plant that is naturally found in a particular region. Plants are easiest to grow in their native habitat, because they are adapted to that particular environment.

**Naturalize**   To plant out randomly in a way that imitates nature and makes it appear as though the plants grew there naturally. Some plants will naturalize once planted, meaning they will continue to spread or reseed themselves.

**Neutral soil**   Soil that is neither too alkaline nor too acid, it has a pH value of 7.0. The broadest spectrum of nutrients reach plants in soils with a neutral pH.

**Nitrogen**   One of the three most important nutrients for a plant. Nitrogen helps plants produce stems and leaves.

**Organic matter**   Any material that was once alive or that came from a living creature: compost, sawdust, and fish emulsion are examples.

**Perennials**   Plants whose life cycles take more than 2 years to complete.

**Pests**   The range of insects and animals that attack and damage plants, including aphids, mites, slugs, birds, rabbits, and deer.

**pH**   A measure of acidity or alkalinity in a soil on a scale of 0 to 14. The lowest end of the scale is the most acidic; the highest is most alkaline; and the middle (7.0) is neutral.

**Phosphorus**   One of the three most important nutrients for a plant. It helps plants develop flowers, seeds, and roots.

**Pinching**   A process of pruning (with forefingers or scissors) to keep plants growing compactly and encourage bushiness.

**Potassium**   One of the three most important nutrients for a plant. Potassium helps the plant grow and develop strong stems.

**Potbound**   The condition of a container-grown plant whose root ball is thickly matted.

**Root ball**   The entire root system of a plant in soil.

**Sandy soil**   A type of soil that has large soil particles.

**Seedling**   A young plant grown from seed (not cuttings).

**Self-sowing**   Plants that sow their own seeds into the ground.

**Slug**   An invertebrate mammal in the mollusk family that often hides under stones and boards, feeding on leaves in the night. Slug damage is apparent by the chewed leaves.

**Soil test**   An analysis of the soil to determine its pH level and the nutrients available.

**Species**   A group of plants within a genus that share many characteristics.

**Stake**   A structure to support plants that may otherwise flop over.

**Stolon** (runner)   A stem that spreads horizontally along the soil that can root along its length. Many weeds grow by runners.

**Succulent**   A plant with juicy, water-storing stems or leaves.

**Taproot**   The main root of a plant that grows directly downward.

**Tender**   Describes a plant's resistance to or tolerance of freezing temperatures. Tender plants are those that are sensitive to freezing temperatures and have a low tolerance for cold.

**Thinning out**   The act of pulling up plants so remaining plants have enough room to grow.

**Till**   To cultivate the soil.

**Transplant**   A newly moved plant; the act of moving a plant from one location to another.

**True leaves**   The leaves that emerge from a seedling after the cotyledon leaves. The first leaves that are true to type.

**Variegated foliage**   Foliage that has more than one color, usually white or yellow in spots, ribbons, or other identifiable pattern.

**Vermiculite**   A mica-type rock expanded by heat that is lightweight and absorbent; is used in seed-starting and growing media.

**Volunteer**   Seedling from a plant that sowed its own seeds into the garden.

**Weed**   An unwanted plant in the garden. Eliminating weeds improves the appearance of a garden and provides growing space for plants that are wanted.

**Wilt**   A disease that causes leaves to turn brown and often causes the plant to die.

# Index

Page numbers in *italics* indicate photographs or illustrations.

*Nierembergia hippomanica* var.
  *violacea*, 142, *142*
  'Purple Robe', *142*
*Nigella damascena*, 3, 16, 52, 142,
  *142*, 143
Nitrogen, 8, 9, 10–15
Nuclear polyhedrons virus (NPV),
  92
Nutrients, 8, 65, 76, 77

## O

*Ocimum basilicum* 'Dark Opal', 38,
  123, 143, *143*
Opium poppy (*P. somniferum*), 144
Organic matter, 6–7, 8–15, 65, 76, 84
Ornamental cabbage (*Brassica oleracea*),
  18, 106–7, *107*
Outdoors, starting seeds, 73–74
Overwatering, 85, 86, 87

## P

Panicle, 38, *39*
Pansy (*Viola* × *wittrockiana*), 2, 4, 16,
  18, 81, 82, 108, 158, *158*
*Papaver rhoeas*, 3, 30, 50, 52, 73, 75,
  81, 82, 112, 144, *144*
  'Shirley' mixed, *144*
Parasitic wasps, 90–91
Peat moss, 8, 12–13, 14–15, 65,
  78–79, 84
Peat pots, 70, *71*
*Pelargonium* × *hortorum*, 16, 46, 56,
  83, 87, 145, *145*, 157
  'Earliana' series, *145*
*Pennisetum setaceum*, 56, 146, *146*
Perennials, 2, 3, 4, 17, 32, 77, 101
Periwinkle (*Vinca major*), 157, *157*
Perlite, 14–15, 75, 84
Pesticides, 85, 86
Petunia (*Petunia* × *hybrida*), 3, 56, 87,
  146–47, *147*

*Petunia* × *hybrida*, 3, 56, 87,
  146–47, *147*
  'Surfina Blue Vein', *147*
pH, of soil, 7–8, 10–15
*Phlox drummondii*, 147, *147*, 148
  'Beauty Blue', *147*
Phosphorus, 8, 10–15
Photographs of garden, 43
Pinching, 80, *80*, 81
Pine needles, 78–79
Planning and mapping the garden,
  41–59
  container garden, 56, *57*
  garden for cutting, 54, *55*
  made for shade, 48, *49*
  moon garden, 50, *51*
  self-sowing annuals, 52, *53*
  sunny summer border, 58, *59*
  ten-minutes-a-week gardener's
    garden, 46, *47*
Planting annuals, 66–75
  from seed, 66, 70, *71*, 72–75
  seedlings and transplants, 66–67,
    *67*, 68–69, *69*, 73, 74, 75
Plastic containers, 25
Poison ivy, 62
Pollution, 19
Poppy (*Papaver rhoeas*), 3, 30, 50, 52,
  73, 75, 81, 82, 112, 144, *144*
Portraits, plant, 101–59
*Portulaca grandiflora*, 2, 18, 30, 58, 74,
  76, 81, 100, 126, 148, *148*
  'Sundial' hybrid mix, *148*
Potassium, 8, 10–15
Pot marigold (*Calendula officinalis*), 30,
  54, 56, 70, 73, 97, 109, *109*
Pots. *See* Containers, plants in
Potting soil, 14–15, 84
Powdery mildew, 87, *88*
Prairie gentian (*Eustoma grandiflora*),
  135, *135*